THE
Medicine Line

THE
Medicine Line

LIFE AND DEATH ON A NORTH AMERICAN BORDERLAND

Beth LaDow

Routledge
New York & London

Published in 2001 by
Routledge
29 West 35th Street
New York, NY 10001

Published in Great Britain by
Routledge
11 New Fetter Lane
London EC4P 4EE

Routledge is an imprint of the Taylor & Francis Group.

10 9 8 7 6 5 4 3 2 1

Library of Congress Cataloging-in-Publication Data
LaDow, Beth.
  The medicine line : life and death on a North American borderland / by Beth LaDow.
    p. cm.
Includes bibliographical references a(p.) and index.
  ISBN 0-415-92764-1
  1. Blaine County (Mont.)—History—19th century. 2. Cypress Hills (Alta. and Sask.)—History—19th century. 3. Fort Belknap Indian Reservation (Mont.)—History—19th century. 4. Frontier and pioneer life—Montana—Blaine County. 5. Frontier and pioneer life—Cypress Hills (Alta. and Sask.) 6. Northern boundary of the United States—History—19th century. 7. Indians of North America—Montana—Blaine County—History—19th century. 8. Indians of North America—Cypress Hills (Alta. and Sask.)—History—19th century. 9. Pioneers—Montana—Blaine County—History—19th century. 10. Pioneers—Cypress Hills (Alta. and Sask.)—History—19th century. I. Title.
  F737.B63 L34 2001
  978.6'1502—dc21

                          00-042496

For my parents, Jess and Jean,
who took me there

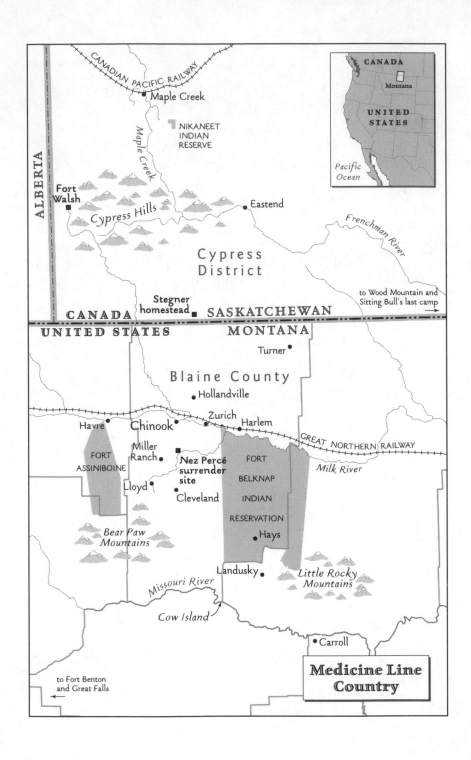

CANADIAN PACIFIC RAILWAY

Maple Creek

NIKANEET
INDIAN
RESERVE

ALBERTA

Maple Creek

Fort
Walsh

Cypress Hills

Eastend

Frenchman River

CANADA

Cypress
District

Stegner
homestead

SASKATCHEWAN

to Wood Mountain and
Sitting Bull's last camp

UNITED STATES

MONTANA

Turner

Blaine County

Hollandville

Zurich

Havre

Chinook

Harlem

GREAT NORTHERN RAILWAY

FORT
ASSINIBOINE

Miller
Ranch

Nez Percé
surrender
site

FORT

BELKNAP

Milk River

Lloyd

Cleveland

INDIAN

RESERVATION

Bear Paw
Mountains

Hays

Landusky

Little Rocky
Mountains

Missouri River

Cow Island

Carroll

to Fort Benton
and Great Falls

**Medicine Line
Country**

CANADA
Montana
UNITED
STATES
Pacific
Ocean

Contents

Acknowledgments IX
Prologue: Through the Looking Glass XI

1. Drawing the Line 1
2. The "Melting Pot of Hell" 23
3. Sanctuary 43
4. If You Build It, Will They Come? 73
5. Which Side Are You On? 89
6. A Living or a Way of Life? 103
7. What Are We Fighting For? 123
8. The Cosmopolitan Throng 149
9. "We Can Play Baseball on the Other Side" 173
10. Nature's "Incivilities" 193

Epilogue: Wallace Stegner and the North
          American West 213
Notes 219
Index 265

"No *frontier is marked between the Western landscape
and a country of fable.*"

—Bernard DeVoto, white historian

"*The great spirit makes no lines.*"

—The Hero, Oglala Sioux

To those whose generosity, knowledge, help, and encouragement made this parcel of vain strivings into a book, all of whom I cannot possibly name, my deepest gratitude: Dave Walter and the staff at the Montana Historical Society; Donny White and the Medicine Hat Museum and Archive; Malinda Drury and others at the Southwest Saskatchewan Old Timers' Museum; Jude Sheppard at the Blaine County Museum and Blaine County Library; Preston Stiff Arm and the Fort Belknap Tribal Archives, Fort Belknap College; Don Richan and the Saskatchewan Archives Board in Regina; and the staffs of the James J. Hill Reference Library, Eastend Museum, Manitoba Provincial Archives, Brandeis University and Harvard University libraries, University of Oklahoma Libraries Western History Collections, Glenbow Museum, American Museum of Natural History, Public Archives of Canada, U.S. National Archives and Records Administration, and Denver Public Library. Also, Robert Utley, Gerald Davidson, Michael Doxtater, Bill Asikinack, and others on-line on H-West and H-Amindian; John Bennett; Mary Stegner and JoAnn Rogers; Joyce King, Scott Armstrong, and Jennifer Long at Sherin and Lodgen in Boston; Lee Harrison and Irene Ford Grande in Helena; Michael Ober and Flathead Valley Community College; Waldine Miller Lindquist; George VandeVen, Anne Schroeder, Linda Haugen, Alice O'Hanlon, Olive Sattleen, and others in Chinook, including Richard Ford and his grouse; my students at Brandeis and Harvard Universities; participants in the University of Kansas Hall Center nature and culture colloquium, and the Western History Association and American Studies Association conferences at which I presented papers; and the Western History Association committee who gave this project the Rundell Award. I thank Ivan Doig for his early encouragement; Janet LaDow Payne and Christopher Payne for research and support; Neil Leifer, for advice on Indian law; the late John Conway, for teaching me about Canada; John Mack Faragher, for commenting on an early paper from which this project grew and William Lang and Montana, the Magazine of Western History for publishing it; David LaDow, for teaching me that writing is a craft; my extraordinary collection of neighbors in Winchester, Massachusetts, who understand community; and Andrew Caffrey and Lindsay Miller at WBUR, Boston, for discovering my radio voice.

I am especially indebted to Micha Grudin and Christine Heyrman, for inspiring me early on; Patricia Limerick for teaching me about the West and quoting from Lewis Carroll once in an airport, "we shall all be queens together;" Morton Keller, who reminded me during years of patient teaching just how far from the East the West really is; Peter Mancall, ace scholar, publishing advisor, and uplifting friend; the late Randy Swartz, kindred spirit and co-deviser of the diversity index, and the late Mark Alper—their spirits endure; Sarah Flynn, wise counselor and superb editor who never let me give up; and Deirdre Mullane, Publishing Director and editor at Routledge who understood this hybrid book better than I, and the Routledge staff for their outstanding work.

Finally, for striking me with the lightning of their intelligence and spirit, I thank the late Wallace Stegner, who dwelled in and reimagined this borderland; Donald Worster, best of all possible mentors and Kansans whose brilliant and lyrical understanding of nature, ideas, and people changed my life; my parents, Jess and Jean LaDow, whose joke "write that down, Flavus" I may have finally taken too far; my daughter Kate, twice my companion to the borderland who grew up with this book, lovelier than it by far; my son Sam, who increasingly seems to know more history than I do; and my husband Josh Alper, editor, supporter, and life companion nonpareil with whom I'll cross the border.

THROUGH THE LOOKING GLASS

W e do not know precisely when Sitting Bull abandoned hope, but he had certainly given up by July 12, 1881, and perhaps on that very day. In the dust of trader Jean-Louis Légaré's thirty-seven wagons and screeching Red River carts, he rode his pony through the fly-thick Canadian prairie heat, south across the Canada-Montana border, preparing to submit to the United States Army he and his Sioux followers had eluded in 1877, evading capture after their victory at the Battle of the Little Big Horn the year before. In eight days he would become the last Northern Plains Indian to surrender his rifle to a United States soldier. The surrender, like most moments of defeat, was a physical and mental journey.

Sitting Bull had been resisting surrender for years. Even though he had thought about giving up at least since November 1880, he had stayed the impulse repeatedly during the spring and early summer of 1881. Rain-in-the-Face, another Sioux leader, had surrendered the summer before, followed by Gall, who took 110 households from Sitting Bull's camp along with him, and then Crow King and others. Hundreds of Sioux were abandoning the uneasy refuge of Canada for the dull security of Standing Rock Agency, a reservation in Dakota Territory maintained courtesy of the U.S. government, one of several outposts on the Missouri River. Sitting Bull was the last holdout—the most stubborn, the most committed to his land and former way of life. By spring his remaining bedraggled band of followers was starving. Their clothes were rags, some of them rotting off their bodies. The Canadian Mounties were less openly hostile than American soldiers, but during the Sioux's four-year stay in the land of the "White Mother" it had become clear that food and aid were not amenities the refugees could count on. Cadging supplies from Mounties and traders, they wandered the rapidly diminished buffalo grounds between Eastend and Wood Mountain—from a Mounted Police post near the international border to a timbered trough in the prairie thirty-five miles east of Wood Mountain called Willow

Bunch, and then to the Qu'Appelle River a hundred miles north, an area that a *New York Herald* reporter described as a "beautiful" semicircular plain. To the south lay the border, and danger. By now they were living largely on mice, an occasional duck or fish, Légaré's largesse, or nothing at all.[1]

On May 26 Sitting Bull wavered. He told Canadian Indian commissioner Edward Dewdney that he would return to the country of the Big Knives, as the Sioux called the Americans. Then he retracted the offer. He was worth his weight in gold, he said. Why should he go? Your carcass is not worth ten cents, the commissioner scoffed. On June 14 Sitting Bull told the Canadian Mounted Police he would not surrender, that first he needed to see the familiar Mountie James Walsh, the only white man he completely trusted and who was now unfortunately exiled to eastern Canada for becoming too friendly with the Indians. And again in early July the Sioux chief told the *Herald* reporter he would not go south, saying, "I am not ready. I want to stay here to have a rest."

Sitting Bull had been brought to this point largely by Légaré's efforts. A jovial French-Canadian trader, Légaré, along with Walsh, was one of Sitting Bull's few non-Indian contacts. Légaré knew and liked these Sioux. He had been feeding them occasionally since April, more out of compassion than on the casual promise that the U.S. government would repay him for his efforts and supplies. He would invite them to his store at Willow Bunch for a feast, or they would just show up there or at his train of wagons, where he would cajole, plead, reassure, and entice them toward surrendering at Fort Buford, just south of the line, where an officer named Major David Brotherton, whom they feared might scalp or shackle them, waited. At a cost of $32 per Indian, Légaré estimated that beginning on July 11 he spent $6,400 getting Sitting Bull's camp of two hundred across the border. The grand total included a revolver for Sitting Bull valued at $15 and "one looking glass" worth $25.[2]

It is hard to say how effective these gifts were as incentives for surrender. Sitting Bull was having trouble seeing. He had a bad eye infection, which he shaded from the sun with a strip of dirty calico tied like a turban around his head and pulled down to shield his eyes. The mirror would have reflected the image of a thick-necked man, slightly stooped, about fifty years old, wearing a dirty, threadbare calico shirt and black leggings, gazing out onto one of the worst days of his life. "His appearance disappoints one," wrote the *Herald* reporter after catching sight of him, as if expecting a romantic-looking savage from a James Fenimore Cooper novel. "The Indian dash and vim are wanting."

In the lore of colonial North America, native peoples sometimes traded land for goods such as mirrors and other trinkets: Manhattan island, for example, sold in 1626 for a handful of beads or $24 worth of cloth and brass buttons, depending on the version of the story you choose to believe.

Winchester, Massachusetts, was supposedly traded to whites in 1639 by a gentle woman known as Squaw Sachem for twenty-one winter coats, nineteen strings of wampum, and three bushels of corn. Such stories abound. On the sun-scorched U. S.–Canada border in July 1881, however, these strategies were useless. For one thing, Indians no longer controlled these lands. For another, even if threatened with death, the *Herald* reporter wrote, "Sitting Bull refuses to relinquish poverty and circumscribed power." Only starving women and children finally compelled him to leave his hunting grounds. At best, the looking glass was for Sitting Bull the token of a passing era—of trade, abundance, and loyalty before diminishing resources and conquest took their toll. Coming from Jean-Louis Légaré, a friend, the looking glass may have been a reminder of all that: something less than a bribe, something more than a gift, rendered useless by his blurred vision and crusted eyes.

On July 2, Sitting Bull had brought his remnant band to Willow Bunch, offering Légaré cooperation in return for a meal. According to depositions taken of Légaré and his employee André Gandre in 1889, in a claim against the United States government for expenses accrued while luring Indians to the border, Légaré fed the ravenous Indians. He asked that in return they accompany him to Fort Buford in about a week when he went down to restock his supplies. On July 11, readying to go, Légaré handed out food and presents to the Sioux. On the twelfth, he assembled his wagons and a long string of Red River carts, small boxes attached to two giant wheels and a poplar axle notorious for squealing horribly, like fingernails scraping across a blackboard. Several Indians piled in. With his train of wagons and carts loaded with flour, pemmican, and Indians, Légaré headed south toward the border.

Légaré left seventeen carts behind, hoping the Indians would change their minds. Sitting Bull sat with a remaining contingent, refusing to move, then ordered his remaining followers into the carts and announced that they were headed back west, not south to Buford. That night, though, Sitting Bull's men found Légaré's camp. They demanded food, shot up a flour sack, and when Légaré refused them, they sat in a silent huff for two hours. The game was up. Sitting Bull said some brave words about finding rich hunting grounds to the west, but they all knew otherwise. Sometime on July 12, Sitting Bull understood that they would cross the border, as if passing through the looking glass into a world they dreaded, to a place that was no longer home.

Légaré sent an edgy message to Major Brotherton saying that Sitting Bull had finally agreed to surrender and wished "to have some half-breeds come out with provisions," full rations. "Send in a hurry," he wrote, "or they may make trouble or turn back." The note arrived at Fort Buford on Thursday night, July 14, and the next day six wagons and a U.S. army captain named Walter Clifford set out for Légaré's wagon train. The *St. Paul*

Sitting Bull's encampment at Fort Yates, Standing Rock Reservation, 1883, before his band had begun living in log cabins and after they had begun to plant crops.
Photo by David Barry, the Denver Public Library, Western History Collection.

Pioneer Press published Légaré's letter under the confident headline "Sitting Bull Bagged."[3] Clifford's troops arrived on Sunday, the seventeenth.

Clifford was supposed to be an Indian charmer. According to the Pioneer Press reporter, he could "talk an Indian blind, or swallow a jack knife for his edification if necessary." In this case, Clifford allegedly lived up to his reputation. Sitting Bull greeted him laconically, but by Monday they had "a long rambling talk" in which Sitting Bull expressed his fears and Clifford reassured him that the Americans were welcoming him "in a spirit of mercy." Clifford then handed Sitting Bull a knife. "If I am lying to you," he said, "you may kill me." The party arrived intact at Fort Buford on Tuesday afternoon, July 19, at 2:15.

Sitting Bull's surrender at Fort Buford was unremarkable. The fort was the northernmost of several U.S. outposts along the Missouri River, the superhighway of the prerailroad West that extended through Dakota and Montana Territories. Fort Yates, named for one of Custer's officers killed at Little Big Horn, and the Standing Rock Agency, where Sitting Bull and his compatriots were taken by steamboat on August 2, were to the south, below Bismarck. At the height of the afternoon, Légaré's motley caravan of ponies, vehicles, eleven employees, and forty Indian families rode through the fort parade grounds and on to a campsite between the fort and the Missouri River. The men, forty-three in all, shook hands with Major Brotherton and gave themselves up. They relinquished their few ponies and rifles. Sitting Bull's mother, sister, two wives, and five children, including two sets of twins, looked on as Sitting Bull said he would surrender his rifle the next day. Captain Clifford described him as "sullen and insolent." His family's thoughts went unrecorded.

The *St. Paul Pioneer Press* headlines milked drama from Sitting Bull's solitary surrender: "Captured at Last, He Is None the Less Haughty, Exacting and Greedy," "Clad in Dirty Calico, He Maintains a Mighty Monarch's Main and Manner," "Dramatic Presentation of the Redskin's Rifle by His Hopeful Scion." The "hopeful scion" was Sitting Bull's eight-year-old son, Crowfoot, to whom he gave his rifle to present to Major Brotherton. Through an interpreter, Sitting Bull spoke briefly. His son surrendered the rifle, he said, to teach the boy that "he has become a friend of the Americans" and must learn their ways. Sitting Bull wanted to be remembered as the "last man of my tribe to surrender my rifle." He mentioned Légaré favorably twice, including his wish that the trader "be rewarded for his services in bringing me and my people here." Then, as if in a time warp, he said he wished to live without a U.S.–Canada border. The "medicine line," as the Indians called it, had for some five years had the power to transform his people's social and political status. But now that its medicine was spent, he wanted to turn back the clock. "I now wish to be allowed to live this side of the line or the other," he said, "as I see fit. I wish to continue my old life of hunting, but would like to be allowed to trade on both sides of the line." Clearly, though, he understood his captivity. "The boy has given it to you," he said of his rifle, "and he now wants to know how he is going to make a living." This, as it turned out, was to become the $64,000 question of life on the prairie for everyone for the next fifty years.[3]

In an honest world, Sitting Bull's speech should have become one of the most familiar in American history. Yet no one remembers it. Instead, we repeat with sentimental fervor Chief Joseph's words upon the surrender of the Nez Percé in 1877, "From where the sun now stands, I will fight no more forever," written after the fact by an army lieutenant who garnered Joseph a position as one of America's great orators. The imperatives of violence and valor, not economic necessity, became the measure of the Native American story that white Americans have chosen to tell. As it was, the most dramatic moment of the surrender may have been the five-minute-long silence while everyone sat staring, waiting for Sitting Bull to speak.[4]

A carnival atmosphere erupted downriver the next week on a hot Sunday morning in Bismarck. Hundreds of people crowded the landing where the General Sherman, the steamboat carrying the captive Sioux down the Missouri, drew up to dock and temporarily disgorged its Indian celebrities. As Sitting Bull's biographer Robert Utley describes it, whites received him with the "strange blend of condescension and acclaim" that would characterize their treatment of him for the rest of his life. Sitting Bull spent much of his time on display, an object of fascination. He spoke with long pauses during questioning, silent sometimes as long as five to ten minutes. "It takes longer to get one good, satisfactory interview with an

Sitting Bull, his wife, and twins, one year after surrender, with a white woman, girl, and soldier, 1882. Denver Public Library, Western History Collection.

Indian chief" wrote the *Pioneer Press* reporter who interviewed him on August 2, "than it does to pump a column each from fifty white men."

By this time, Sitting Bull had acquired a pair of goggles to shield his sore eyes, which the *Pioneer Press* reporter described as "purging thick amber and plum-tree gum," and had changed into blue pantaloons and a dirty white shirt. He had painted red stripes down his sleeves. on his face and neck, and along the part in his hair. He was "the least adorned of his companions" and in a line of Sioux men was "the last selected as the notorious one by those unacquainted with him."[5] With a small group of Indians he first attended a formal reception, where he sat in a carpeted, cushioned Bismarck parlor signing autographs, puffing on his pipe, and fanning himself with a hawk's wing, and then a fine dinner at the Merchants Hotel, where spectators pressed against the windows as Sitting Bull conducted himself with some refinement, laughed at jokes, and was amazed by ice cream. Yet he told a reporter, "I have seen nothing that a white man has, houses or railways or clothing or food that is as good as the right to move in the open country, and live in our own fashion."[6]

Jean-Louis Légaré was never paid for his services. His lawsuit, filed in 1889 to reclaim assets spent ferrying and enticing Sioux across the border in 1881, presented an itemized list totaling $13,000 in supplies. The U.S. court of claims dismissed it on the grounds that the statute of limitations barred most of the claim, and that besides, Major Brotherton, who had given Légaré an informal promise to pay on behalf of the United States, "had no authority to contract . . . for services rendered or supplies furnished the Indians, during their return, but that he thought the Government, would pay a reasonable compensation," a statement "received by claimant," the court asserted, "without dissent or objection." There was no percentage in being nice.

As for Sitting Bull, he was killed nine years later by his own people. He had made something of a new life on and off the agency at Standing Rock. Buffalo Bill Cody asked him to join his Wild West Show to sign autographs and ride in parades and tour the East, which he did for a time, though he declined to go with the show to London. He gave whatever money he earned to beggars and children or spent it on friends, and developed a great fondness for Annie Oakley, whom he dubbed "Little Sure Shot." "The white man knows how to make everything," he once told her, "but he does not know how to distribute it."[7] At Standing Rock he lived a quiet life as a modestly successful farmer, doted on his seven children, two of whom were born on the agency, and still attracted hopeful nonconformists. Then in 1889 and 1890 the Ghost Dance religion, a messianic, semi-Christian faith invented by a Paiute named Wovoka during an eclipse of the sun, swept western reservations. Wovoka claimed that God had revealed to him a special dance, and that if the Indians danced and sang it long enough and hard enough, they would raise a paradise on earth, where all the white people would be buried beneath knee-high grass and new soil, horses and buffalo would return in abundance, and dead ancestors would be brought back to life. For Indians now ten years or more confined to reservations, this was an attractive vision.

Among the Sioux, the dancing became incessant. People stopped working. They danced until they fainted or were past exhaustion. They danced in the snow. Schoolhouses shut down. Trading posts were empty. And while Sitting Bull himself was a skeptic, he assented to the dancing and found himself on the government's list of "fomenters" slated for arrest. When the Standing Rock reservation agent cut short a plan to have Buffalo Bill quietly whisk Sitting Bull away to Chicago, a group of forty-four Indian police led by a lieutenant named Bull Head surrounded the chief's log cabin one early morning, awoke him from his pallet on the floor, and tried to force him onto his horse. Within moments, among a gathering crowd of angry supporters of both the chief and this trigger-happy group, Sitting Bull was shot dead through the head and chest. Four army officers and the four prisoners shoveling dirt onto his grave attended his burial.[8]

In the end, Sitting Bull's death was less remarkable than the moment lost to history in 1881, sometime between July 12 and July 19, when he crossed the medicine line for the last time. This stretch of border was the last quiet eye in a storm of exploration and settlement, conquest and convergence. It was neatly circumscribed by the waterway explorations of British adventurer David Thompson in 1786 and later, more famously, by Lewis and Clark in 1805.[9] But from the 1870s, when Sitting Bull and the Plains Indians crossed the line to take up their uncertain future, to 1920, when settlers such as the future novelist Wallace Stegner and his parents abandoned it, the line formed the center of a particular kind of experiment, a cross-boundary frontier. It saw the typical Western succession of weary surveyors, visionary railroad men, hard-bitten ranchers, and beleaguered homesteaders. William Faulkner once described his troubled South as a place "primed for fatality." This, too, was such a place. For some fifty years, medicine line country was to the West what Faulkner's imaginary Yoknapatawpha county was to the South—the hopes and limitations, complements and contradictions of people adapting to each other in a remote and difficult geography.

Had Sitting Bull been a European general or explorer, his surrender might have been recorded on canvas in the grand nineteenth-century tradition. But such a monument does not exist. This volume may serve as that portrait, tracing what happened along the medicine line before and after Sitting Bull crossed it—how the line itself came into being and then quickly faded from memory, in a story that turned out to be less about borders and nations than about the land itself. In Sitting Bull's odyssey is an opportunity for allegory, for hope and the death of hope, the great theme of the West.

DRAWING THE LINE

George VandeVen nodded toward the broad seascape of Montana prairie and gave his voice the inflection of someone dismissing a terrible rumor. "We didn't even know a line was there," he said. He was referring to the U.S.-Canada border, our destination that day driving north from the town of Chinook, and as we stepped from his Dodge Sierra pickup truck onto the homestead site where he was born in 1913, eighty-five years earlier, it was hard not to believe him.

North Americans tend to divide the American story from the Canadian along this boundary, as if it split the past as neatly as a meat cleaver. How many Americans know that in the summer of 1793 the British North American explorer Alexander Mackenzie made his own trip to the Pacific Ocean through present-day Canada, twelve years before Lewis and Clark famously paddled up the Missouri not fifty miles south of Chinook, carrying a copy of Mackenzie's *Voyages* in their boat, as well as copies of British explorer David Thompson's charts and British-made maps? How many Americans or Canadians know the saga of the building of parallel railroads, one American, one Canadian, some eighty years later less than a hundred miles apart across George VandeVen's childhood home? The West, we have come to believe, is an "American" story.

It was midmorning, soon after we had begun our four hours of jolting over dirt roads under an already furnace-hot sky, when VandeVen, a second Chinook octogenarian named Anne Schroeder, and my eleven-year-old daughter, Kate, and I made our first stop. We all clambered out of the truck except for Kate, who remained in the covered truck bed reading, patiently suffering her mother's historical field research. I could hardly blame her. The ground was a sparse mix of brown and green grasses a few inches high, clumps of silvery sage, and little prickly pears, connected by a dry and cracked tissue of gray earth. Cowless, telephone-pole-less, practically fence-less, to my eye it was an arbitrary port of call in a vast, undifferentiated ocean of space and distance. A place of forgetting, haunted by disappointment. But VandeVen was brimming with life. As we walked over the ground he gave shape to the place with memories. He introduced a human scale. Here, he said, was the site of the garbage dump, still riddled with shards of pottery and metal. Over there was the coulee where his pregnant mother had trekked down to get water, in what year? 1916? She had had to stop and rest on her way back up, burdened with the heavy bucket and with child. Here was the house. I followed George to a shallow pit about thirty feet by twenty feet where the sagebrush cropped up vigorously like the waves of a rough sea. He bent over into it and, like Crusoe finding his shipwreck, lifted one end of a slim twenty-five-foot pole, the roof beam to the underground house, called a dugout, where he was born and raised—the VandeVen place. "This will always be home," George said. It was, he insisted, a home indifferent to the international border twenty miles to the north.

The border, after all, had emerged more as a political construct than as a natural feature of the landscape. In April 1803, the United States purchased the Louisiana Territory from France without knowing much about its northern edge. Thomas Jefferson, then president, pulled from memory or from somewhere in his Monticello study an unratified article, buried in the 1713 Treaty of Utrecht between France and Britain, that proposed dividing New France from British North America. It specified a boundary at 49 degrees north latitude. On January 15, 1804, Jefferson wrote a memo to his diplomats in France and Spain suggesting this line as the northern boundary of the Louisiana Purchase, and the world's longest continuous straight international border was created.

To Meriwether Lewis and William Clark, whom Jefferson sent west to explore the Purchase in 1804, the Monticello memorandum was of little interest. Like Jefferson, they hoped to cross the 49th parallel along a Missouri River tributary, an American river extending north that might give the United States an excuse to claim more land. In May 1805, following the Missouri through a country they described as "desert and barren" and "astonishingly dry," the explorers would come close to Jefferson's boundary—just below its exact midpoint, in fact, between Minnesota and the Pacific Ocean, on the high plains of present-day Montana. Here they might have followed a smaller river north beyond the 49th parallel. Yet they did not. They had trouble finding firewood. They judged the soil "poor." While Jefferson believed it would take a thousand generations to settle the West, Clark judged as nil the prospects for populating this area along the Missouri. "I do not think it can ever be settled," he declared. As it turned out, both Clark and Jefferson were wrong. It took only five generations to settle the West, and the last generation came here, to one of the toughest arid prairie environments in the world, on a short stretch of the 49th parallel boundary between the United States and Canada that the last of the roaming Plains Indians would come to call "the medicine line."[1]

Today, history divides on either side of the border, into the distant camps of the American Wild West and the orderly Canadian hinterland, peacefully separate national stories. Since 1867, we believe, when Britain withdrew its military outposts and Canada became a nation, the U.S.-Canada border has lapsed into an agreeable somnolence. Yet what is now the world's most peaceful border, its largest commercial sieve, was for more than a century the battleground of empires. The United States and British Canada, after all, were continental rivals. By the late nineteenth century, in the wake of the American Civil War, escalating native-white conflict, and the making of an independent Canada, the struggle for empire aroused familiar and often nationalistic visions. The forces of nature, however, were so strong, and the populations so mixed, that telling an American citizen from a Canadian became increasingly difficult. All were driven or drawn to this place, their last, best hope—the Indians for escape and refuge, the settlers for the open western lands that seemed nearly gone—and lived a common story of hardship, disappointment, failure and, in fewer cases than not, persistence.

The medicine line forms a small part of the U.S.-Canada boundary, scarcely more than a hundred miles long—a place that most people have never heard of. Stand today on the border, at the center of the 49th parallel boundary curve, facing the Rocky Mountains 200 miles to the west, and you will see why. To the left, the American half of medicine line country, lies Blaine County, Montana, and near its center, just south of the old VandeVen place, is the small town of Chinook, thirty miles south of the border on dirt and gravel roads. Beyond that lie the Bears Paw Mountains, known locally as the Bear Paws, and the Missouri River at the county's southern border. To the right is the Cypress District of Saskatchewan, including the Cypress Hills and the towns of Eastend and Maple Creek, thirty and sixty miles north of the border. Together, the two sides cover an area about the size of Vermont. Natural boundaries are absent. There is no river here, no precipice, no mountain divide, no indentation or canyon. The prairie stretches seamlessly outward, as if the wind were blowing it toward the Rockies. Straddling the border, feet between cacti and clumps of gray-green sage, one conjures other borders with imposing names—iron curtains, great walls, grand rivers, Pyrenees. Those are borders where history has physical shape, borders that define peoples and their enemies.

Not so here. No guard keeps watch, no narcotics agent stands at the ready. There is only a fence with four strands of barbed wire, and sometimes not even that. This boundary seems the creation of a minimalist. Traveling the long stretches of the Trans-Canada Highway, or along U.S. Highway 2 to Chinook, it is easy to see why so many visitors compare this country to the ocean. The Rocky Mountains are a tidal wave to a vast, tawny sea. A mailbox, a gravel driveway, and trees clumped around buildings or in the long row of a shelterbelt indicate a ranch. Occasional fences cast a wide berth, nets of barbed wire cordoning off crops and ungulates that show from the roadside like bright algae or schools of fish. The small towns are strung out in lonely archipelagos, each island posted with signs, like pier posts along a quay: motels, cafes, chambers of commerce. "Rudyard: Home of 596 nice people and one old sorehead!" A country of reluctant charm, it is seldom crossed, less often visited. Walking along what seems scarcely more than a home for prairie dogs, we can hardly imagine a place more uneventful. Its history, however, holds another prospect.

My first introduction to this borderland came through reading *Wolf Willow*, Wallace Stegner's memoir of growing up in medicine line country. Stegner, who went on to win the Pulitzer prize for literature, spent his boyhood here, from 1914 to 1920, in the town of Eastend in winter and on a homestead on the boundary line during the summers. A brilliant, powerful writer and an even more charismatic and influential human being, Stegner framed the questions of this borderland frontier throughout his life. Yet he did not answer them. What was Canadian—the line, limits, the law? What was American—the frontier, the limitless, the lawless? The border, he wrote, "ran directly through my childhood . . . disturbing as a hair in butter"—somehow a divide in affiliations and loyalties, yet artificial, ignored, undistinguished. I was intrigued, charmed, and unsatisfied. Shouldn't the line by which we measure American and Canadian distinctiveness have stronger medicine than that?[2]

My interest in medicine line country is also rooted in a childhood conundrum of what it means to be an American. My first awareness of the U.S.-Canada border as something significant came at an early age. It wasn't so much that we crossed it every July or August on forays from my family's summer home in Montana, when I would press my nose against the car window to see the treeless swath through the forest that some mysterious boundary keeper had made with herbicide to make the border visible. It was to be found in the expression of an uncle of mine, a worried man with a mole in the exact center of his forehead, who used to sit at the kitchen table in our cabin in Glacier Park, not forty miles from the Canadian border, declaring that the condition of the United States had at last sunk so low that he was pulling up stakes. "By God," he would say in his customary tone of world-weary resignation, "I'm goin' to Canada."

Like most Americans, I wasn't sure what the border, or the borderland, meant. I knew the fame of the 100th meridian, the line where the arid plains so dramatically begin that has determined so much of the story of

America and the West. Only after I began to study history did I discover the medicine line. Here, I realized, was another line worth examining—one that could explain some deep part of the Canadian and American experience that our separate nationalistic television documentaries leave out. Following a long tradition that includes Stegner, I am a westerner come East, then returned West, in order that I might explain the West to myself.

When W. J. Twining brought his tired body and weather-beaten chronometer across the 49th parallel, he saw little sign of civilization. As chief astronomer for the United States surveying party in 1874, Twining was spending his third and last summer locating the U.S.-Canada boundary, and he had traveled much of the way on the upper Missouri River, through the Dakota and Montana Territories, in a boat that did not inspire confidence. "No one in search of the amenities need look on the deck of an up-river boat," Twining complained of his party's rig, the rattle-trap *Fontenelle*, whose rough machinery and primitive design he found "constantly suggestive of unpleasant accidents." Its condition was so bad that Twining attributed the absence of boiler fires or explosions on the upper Missouri to the "special providences" rather than to "any skill on the part of the builders or owners." "Certainly no thought of anything so worthless as human life entered into their calculation," he concluded.[3]

The scene awaiting the *Fontenelle* on July 24 as it pulled into Fort Benton in Montana Territory, the backwater burg where an upriver boat ended its journey, was no more an advertisement for civilized life than the boat itself. The eye could take it in "at one glance," as fur trader James Willard Schultz described it—the rectangular adobe fort with cannons mounted at the corners, a few log cabins and adobe huts, the scattered camps of traders and trappers, strings of canvas-covered freighter wagons, clustered Indian tepees, and the Overland Hotel, a log structure likely offering a dinner of "boiled buffalo boss ribs, bacon and beans, 'yeast powder' biscuit, coffee with sugar, molasses, and stewed dried apples."[4]

On the banks of the river waited a motley collection of Creoles, whites, and Indians, what Schultz described as "the entire population," turned out in the full regalia of a fading fur-trade economy: trader elites in long-tailed blue broadcloth coats with brass buttons and black cravats, their long hair neatly combed; trade company clerks and carpenters in black fustian suits and beaded moccasins; French-speaking Creoles in hooded coats and sash-tied buckskin trousers; bull whackers, mule skinners, and independent traders and trappers, festooned with knives and six-shooters and wearing buckskin suits and kit fox hats; Indians in leather leggings and calico shirts carrying bows and arrows or rifles; women in calico dresses and fringed shawls. Desperate for tobacco and liquor, they thronged the banks of the upper Missouri, the center of a thriving north-south trade zone, waving flags and firing cannons to greet the latest steamboat to arrive in Montana Territory. It was a greeting of exuberant, risk-taking hope reminiscent of the *Fontenelle* itself, the kind of hope a man of precision and science could not be expected to warm to—the kind of hope that, over the next fifty years, Twining's survey would unleash upon this borderland to a degree that he could not possibly have imagined.[5]

Twining himself was among the crowd that day. The boat's progress had been so slow he had unloaded the survey party's livestock somewhere past Bismarck, Dakota, and made his way upriver on land. He arrived at Fort Benton on July 12, twelve days ahead of the *Fontenelle*, only to discover that the overburdened steamer had off-loaded a good part of his provisions when it hit shallow waters at Cow Island, 120 miles downriver.[6]

In 1874, the calculations of engineers or astronomers like Twining had created few amenities on the Northern Plains. The fur trade, which had brought with it the presence of steamboats, distilleries, and the occasional cannon, had long since waned from its height in the 1830s. The cosmopolitan if crude Montana gold rush of the 1860s was over. The infant whiskey trade into Canada and the imminent arrival of railroads had yet to boost the economy. As Twining and his colleagues set out to meet their Canadian counterparts along the border, there was no promise of civilization in the air, only flies and dust.[7]

Outside Fort Benton, the land was still home to Sitting Bull and his counterparts, Crowfoot, Piapot, and Poundmaker. On the prairie, the surveyors crossed the paths of other groups. Sioux, Assiniboine, Blackfeet, and Piegan Indians "hovered about our trail," noted the American first lieutenant Greene—curious, doing the visitors no harm, keeping their distance. At closer range, the newcomers also found nature's tracings, the cautionary signs of drought in the parched earth. The weather was "intensely hot," reported Twining's colleague Captain Gregory; water was "very scarce," and what they found was scarcely potable. The ground was "dry, hard, and fissured," as if from a very dry season, according to the Canadian Boundary Commission geologist. It was a world of cracks and trails, wind and grass. The only plumb line these men could see was the enduring straight edge of the horizon, where the enormous sky met the land. They had come to remedy that situation, to visibly divide and subdivide the land, to realize what the confident U.S. commissioner called "the final fixing" of the boundary.[8]

By North American standards, they were a long time coming. The U.S.-Canada boundary had been uncertain since the Louisiana Purchase of 1803, when Thomas Jefferson had seized on the 49th parallel as its fixed edge. After the War of 1812, a complicated conflict fought between

Britain and America on the seas and along the western frontier that ended in 1814 with no clear victor, Jefferson's boundary was finally ratified in the Treaty of 1818. It designated the 49th parallel as the international boundary running from the northwesternmost point of the Lake of the Woods (which sits nearly centered along Minnesota's northern border), above the headwaters of the Mississippi and on west to the Rocky Mountains.[9] Two parallel and rival ways west—American and British—established in 1783 when the newly independent United States made an uneasy peace with Britain and British Canada in the Treaty of Paris, were now demarcated across the plains.

In 1823, five years after the border was established in theory, a United States surveying expedition under Major Stephen H. Long pounded an oak post on the west bank of the Red River bearing the letters G.B. on its north side and U.S. on the south. The first of several efforts to mark the boundary, Major Long's oak post had all the authority of a loosely anchored buoy at sea. Some jokester twisted it halfway around to put G.B. on the south side and U.S. on the north, a mocking testimony to the confusion over the border's exact location and its significance.

West of the Rockies in Oregon Territory, where border passions ran high by the 1840s, the slogan "Fifty-four-forty or fight!" made every schoolchild sound like an expansionist eager to extend U.S. territory north to the 54th parallel. This lasted until the Treaty of 1846 extended the boundary between the United States and Britain westward from the Rocky Mountains along not the 54th but the 49th parallel to the Strait of Georgia, between Vancouver Island and the mainland, stretching it to 1,300 miles of continuous curve. Settler agitation eventually prompted a joint British and American commission to survey the Oregon boundary, which took from 1857 to 1861. Except for a bitter dispute over who owned the San Juan Islands, which Kaiser Wilhelm I of Germany finally arbitrated in favor of the United States in 1872, the countries agreed on the survey in 1869.[10]

Over half of the 49th parallel boundary remained to be explored, 737 miles of it across the northern prairie. Here the border was determined with all the drama of setting up a tennis net. No slogans. Only petty disputes. Explorers and engineers visited only intermittently, disagreeing about where to fix its points. Major Long's oak post rotted before anyone bothered to turn it back around. The demarcating of the line from Ontario's Lake of the Woods to the Rockies could wait.[11]

That no one was in a hurry was understandable. Early reports from the borderland were less than enthusiastic. "It appears to be irremediably sterile and useless," wrote one skeptic. He, like others, was unfavorably impressed. "I sometimes wonder if the original geographer who left an immense blank in the middle of the map of America and labeled it 'Great

American Desert' was so far wrong," wrote one observer. Indeed the entire area was notably lacking in an essential resource. "Water was scarce, and usually unpleasantly alkaline. . . . Sometimes . . . so impregnated with buffalo-urine as to partake of its color, and to be altogether disgusting to the stomach." "The [boundary] line actually cuts no growth of trees, or even bushes of any size, for a distance of six hundred miles," observed W. J. Twining. Everything west of 102 degrees longitude through the Dakotas and present-day eastern Saskatchewan he judged "unreclaimable." Another lamented the "terrible country," so poor "nobody would want it." All disparaged the prospects of ever settling this prairie. It was deemed "permanently sterile and unfit for the abode of civilized men."[12]

They knew, above all else, that it was a dry country. They also knew what that might mean for anyone trying to live here. Aridity and drought, the most important ecological factors in the West's history, are, short of a dust bowl, subtle phenomena. But even an urban dweller cannot miss the sensation for long. The wind whacks at the backs of his eyeballs, and the extremes of heat, cold, and broad open space reduce him to an isolated speck of boiled or frozen flesh until he begins to notice that the place, where people inexplicably expect to grow things, is dry. Standing near the border, it is hard to believe that one-sixth of all the fresh water on earth is in Canadian lakes, ponds, rivers, and streams. The central North American plains have been in a rain shadow ever since the Rocky Mountains thrust up to the west about sixty million years ago. Mean annual precipitation in medicine line country is thirteen inches, and as low as nine to eleven inches in the driest section, a veritable desert near the international boundary. The rainfall that comes is fickle. About half the time, six to seven inches fall in May, June, and July. Other years, these months average about one inch less, except during drought years, which come unpredictably.

Many early travelers avoided the area altogether. Lewis and Clark hung close to the Missouri River where it now borders Blaine County and burned two dead cottonwoods for their campfires, the only wood they could find.[13] Adventurer William Butler and Canadian expedition geologist H. Y. Hind in the mid-nineteenth century veered north of the district. Captain Sullivan of John Palliser's British expedition traversed the area's western edge in 1859. He left from the Cypress Hills near present-day Eastend, where Palliser himself remained reading prayers and making pemmican with the main party, and traveled south to the boundary, but left no record of the journey. Nevertheless, Palliser apparently felt no compunction about giving his name to Palliser's Triangle, the name by which millions came to identify southwestern Saskatchewan as an extension of the Great American Desert.[14] In the middle of the nineteenth century, Palliser's Triangle had all the allure the Bermuda Triangle would exert a hundred years later. Even explorers avoided it.

And so it went until the 1870s, when John Macoun came along. An imaginative Irish botanist who became something of a Canadian Audubon and whose name still appears in the titles of Ottawa nature clubs, he turned the reputation of the Great American Desert on its ear. Passing through the country in what was probably an unusually wet year, Macoun gave an exaggerated description of its fertility. Palliser's Triangle suddenly became the prairie booster's agricultural Eden. Macoun hailed the region's agricultural promise with such fervor and conviction that his employer, the Canadian Pacific Railway (CPR), found in his report one more rationalization for moving its route from more settled country to the international borderland farther south, where the CPR could more easily compete with future American railroad lines.[15] Americans, too, turned optimistic, pushing relentlessly into the last remaining uncultivated ground in the United States, glorifying every alkali flat as potential farmland.[16]

Behind this change in view, of course, was political change. In 1865, the United States ended the Civil War, which had interrupted the nation's furious migration westward. In 1867, Canada became a dominion, gaining in a bloodless transfer of power from Great Britain significant political autonomy and the burden of defending itself from attack. And in March 1870, the two-hundred-year reign of the fur trade over the Canadian West ended when the Hudson's Bay Company ceded to the new Dominion of Canada, in an exchange of territory equivalent to the Louisiana Purchase, its lease on holdings called Rupert's Land. Rupert's Land was an enormous territory: virtually two-thirds of present-day Canada, including all or parts of western Quebec, Ontario, Manitoba, Saskatchewan, southern Alberta, and the eastern Northwest Territories. Anticipating settlement, both Canada and the United States were eager to survey their dormant border.

It took two and a half years for the United States and Canada to agree on the terms of a boundary survey. But in September 1872, gear in hand, the Canadian and American survey teams met at last at Pembina, Dakota. The Canadians, familiar with the tools of empire building, brought along a field library of several hundred volumes, including two volumes on Waterloo, *Fifteen Decisive Battles of the World*, the potentially useful *The Art of Travel* and *At Home in the Wilderness*, and a raft of novels, plays, and poetry. The Americans, who admitted "limited means," brought themselves and their "old and somewhat dilapidated" equipment.[17]

After waiting out a severe snowstorm lasting nearly four days, the surveyors hit their first snag. The Treaty of 1818 had specified that the boundary line should pick up from where it left off, at the "most northwestern point of the Lake [of the Woods]," to intersect the 49th parallel "due north or south as the case may be." The trouble was, nobody knew where the northwesternmost point of Lake of the Woods was. After some searching,

The International Boundary Commission Staff, 1872, including Maj. W. J. Twining (top row, second from left), Lieutenant F. V. Green to his right, Captain James Gregory, astronomer (bottom row, far left), Col. F. M. Farqueher, chief astronomer (bottom row, second from left), and Archibald Campbell, Commissioner (bottom row center). Photo courtesy Glenbow Archives, Calgary, Alberta.

the surveyors finally found a marker—inaccurate, they agreed—under several feet of swamp water. They began hewing their way south, hip deep through cold, boggy flats and then across the ice of the lake, until they located the 49th parallel. The American party, plagued by inadequate funds, soon retired for the winter, relieved that "no animals were lost, and none of the men seriously frozen." The Canadian party, meanwhile, in the true style of empire, grittily fought its way through Siberian conditions from the lake to the Red River, through ninety miles of swamps and timber to the plains. By spring, eight hundred miles of prairie stretched before them, across which they were to trace the curving, abstract line of the parallel. The Americans rejoined the Canadians in June, along with two companies of the U.S. Seventh Cavalry and five companies of the Sixth Infantry under the somber Major Marcus Reno, who had not yet made his name ignominious at the Battle of the Little Bighorn. The heavy escort, it turned out, saw no combat. It was assigned to protect both Canadian and American parties impartially, but there was no need: the Blackfoot and Sioux were neutral.[18]

For two summers the surveyors labored in shadeless, fly-filled camps, drinking fetid water, measuring their way West like a crawling inchworm chain by chain, cairn by cairn, mound by mound, over cactuses and coulees and buffalo wallows, across the Coteau du Missouri, past the half-Cree, half-white Métis hunting buffalo and the occasional band of Sioux or Assiniboine or Blackfeet, past the Sweetgrass Hills, south of the Cypress Hills, and on to the Rockies. They worked efficiently, each commission divided into several parties surveying alternate stations, averaging three and a half days at each. The astronomical parties measured their angles sixty times from the stars Cephei, Polaris, and Ursae Minoris at each of forty-one stations, hoping their errors averaged about seven feet. Building crews followed, planting eight-foot-high pyramidical iron pillars made in Detroit each mile to the western border of Manitoba, sixty of them in all, and thereafter building five- to eight-foot-high stone cairns or earth mounds every three miles across the plains, 388 markers all told. By August 1874 they were finished. They had marked the border, and in doing so, they had passed through a stew of races and cultures that would soon feel the significance of their work.[19]

Work crew building a mound marking the United States–Canada boundary, c. 1873.
Photo courtesy Glenbow Archives, Calgary, Alberta.

An Ojibwa standing north of the 49th parallel on the bank of the North Saskatchewan River with a land speculator in 1875 sensed trouble. "Do you see the Great White-man coming?" he asked his acquaintance. "No," replied the disingenuous speculator. "I do," said the Ojibwa, pointing east. "And I hear the tramp of the multitude behind him. When he comes you can drop in behind him and take up all the land claims you want, but until then I caution you to put up no stakes in our country."[20]

The Ojibwa man clearly understood something of how the white man advanced. Providing the inspiration were the visionaries, the eastern planners, politicians, and investors who rarely came west themselves: Thomas Jefferson and his contemporaries, whose century-old agrarian ideals still shaped American aspirations; Canadian statesman John A. Macdonald, who applied those same agrarian ideals to the Canadian prairies; Canadian-born American railroad magnate James J. Hill; and Scots-Canadian businessman and financier George Stephen, to name a few. They sent out a host of field specialists and laborers to divide up the land—astronomers, engineers, geologists, tracklayers—who came and went after a few seasons' work, spending not so much as a week in one spot. After these men who planted stakes and made lines came the multitudes. First and foremost, the Ojibwa intuitively understood, the makers of the lines were in the real estate business.

The United States got into real estate early. Strapped by national debt at the end of the Revolutionary War, the new nation sought solvency through the sale of its western lands. To that end, Congress devised an impressively simple and coherent scheme for turning public lands into private ones. Made into law as the Land Ordinance of 1785, the system closely followed the New England model of land distribution, with some concessions to the more free-form system of the South. The process went like this: After Indians and states ceded their lands to the federal government, surveyors from each state were to divide it into giant squares six by six miles called townships. Townships were then divided into thirty-six sections of one square mile or 640 acres each, numbered from one to thirty-six. The first axes of this grid to be established were a true north-south meridian drawn from a point on the Ohio River due north of the southern boundary of Pennsylvania, and an east-west baseline beginning from the same point. The government sold the surveyed land by township or section at public auction, and after the auction at land offices for a set minimum price, earmarking sales from section 16 and later also section 36 of each township to provide an interest-bearing fund for public schools. The government could also grant land for various purposes—to fund canals, roads, and eventually railroads. A few provisions were notably absent: land set aside for religious worship (customary in New England), limits on the amount of land that could be purchased, and something called preemption, a southern practice that gave preferential rights to squatters.[21]

This grid survey was the elegant brainchild of Thomas Jefferson. In the ongoing debate over Jefferson's brand of republicanism, we might expect to find in the survey, as we do, elements of both a republic of virtuous small landowners and a capitalist system of self-interested land use. From the beginning, of course, the scheme did not meet Jefferson's highest standard, which was to distribute public lands free of charge to the unemployed poor, in keeping with his notion that "small land holders are the most precious part of a state."[22] Even he recognized that sale was necessary and speculators inevitable. Nevertheless, the system did seem to promise a prosperous republican society of democratic freeholders, firmly grounded in liberty because firmly grounded in land. Jefferson may have rephrased John Locke's dictum, "life, liberty, and the pursuit of property" to "life, liberty, and the pursuit of happiness" when he borrowed it for the Declaration of Independence, but for the West, he rested his hopes squarely on property.

Aesthetically, Jefferson's system is elegant. Across more than two centuries and two million square miles of federal territory, its checkerboard pattern, still strikingly visible from the air today, has remained the framework for the sale and management of U.S. federal lands. In practice, the system proved difficult, an early prototype of the kind of mess often associated with a large federal program. Federal lands distribution became a taffy pull of political compromise and local illegal and extralegal modification. Between 1789 and 1834, Congress passed 375 land laws. Preemption, for example, a perennial point of contention between southerners and northerners, made its way back into law in a series of acts in the 1830s. In the 1860s, southern secession encouraged further complications. The North's extensive railroad grants and the Homestead and Agricultural College Acts produced years of debate between pro-business and pro-small-farmer factions, both of whom claimed to represent the interests of "the people." As for farmers, far from Jefferson's contented yeomen, they themselves proved to be speculators looking to profit from land sales.

The truth was, Jefferson's ideal remained just that. Railroad grants, large holdings, and alien ownership continued to concentrate land in the hands of developers and speculators as they always had, with the 1.4 million small farmers who received final patents on homesteads torturously bringing up the rear guard.[23] Even after disagreement over western lands erupted into civil war, the basic framework for their distribution remained intact. In the manner of a leaky upriver boat filled not just with surveyors but with cutthroat competitors, the system lurched along in serviceable, if precarious, fashion and, like Mr. Twining's *Fontenelle*, seemed spared from disaster, if not by acts of providence then through the exercise of power and fraud.

In theory, Canadians are the last people who would want to emulate such a system. They have earned their reputation of caution, moderation, and polite good sense partly by eschewing brash and grandiose American schemes and ambitions. Americans' rainbow-chasing individualism, irreverence for tradition, and bumptious pride in throwing over the old country for a new, mythically significant nation have never struck Canadians as admirable qualities. With a kind of quiet modesty, Canada has viewed itself as a mosaic rather than a melting pot, a composed salad rather than a fermenting stew, long before the emotional racial and ethnic claims of identity politics became fashionable. A Canadian says "about" with its rounded "o" as if the Scots heritage of skepticism and practicality were part of his mother tongue.

Nonetheless, the rationality of the grid—the seeming freedom-within-limits of a checkerboard plan that might have sprung straight from the mind of Edmund Burke, an esteemed figure in Canadian political thought—may have appealed to the cautious Canadian sensibility. Early on, Canadians admired this grand design for settlement. "The [public lands] system of the United States appears to combine all the chief requisites of the greatest efficiency," gushed Lord Durham, high commissioner and governor-general of British North America. In 1838, Durham went on to list eight virtues of the U.S.-model land survey, including equal terms of distribution "amongst all classes and persons," a misconception that betrayed his ignorance of the matter. He concluded that the system was the best device for promoting immigration in the "history of the world."[24]

By the 1860s, Lord Durham's admiration for the system belied an increasing feeling of national inferiority. "The non-occupation of the North West Territory is a blot upon our character for enterprise," lamented the editor of the Toronto *Globe* in 1862. "We settle down quietly within the petty limits of a province while a great empire is offered to our ambition." Compared to the American West, wrote a prominent Nova Scotian in 1866, the undeveloped state of the Northwest Territories was "a standing reproach to the British Government and a blot upon our civilization."[25] It was as if British North Americans after midcentury were engaged in a kind of Rorschach test of their economic mettle. While Americans basked in the diffuse glow of Manifest Destiny, filling in their grid block by block, the western prairie remained a disconcerting black mark on Canada's account book, a symbol of failure. It was an old Canadian soliloquy. "On the American side, all is activity and bustle," wrote Lord Durham in 1839. "On the British side of the line . . . all seems waste and desolate."[26]

Durham's words proved provident. Some thirty years later, with the newfound bounty of Rupert's Land, Canada suddenly found itself in the real estate business, too. For the Canadian provinces reluctantly bound into a loose federation, this vast acreage provided the impetus to a new way of thinking about their country. Canadian nationalists, led by Conservative prime minister John A. Macdonald, argued for federal control over western lands, and envisioned in a transcontinental railroad and prairie settlement the very *raison d'être* for Canadian federation. A populated midland, they argued, would unify their newly transcontinental country. The Conservative political victory in 1867, and the party's dominance of Canadian politics until 1896, radically altered the nature of the federation itself, temporarily transforming the compact of equal provinces, each with control over its own lands, into a centrally controlled empire. The 1870 Manitoba Act declared that "all ungranted or waste lands" in Manitoba and the North-West Territories were to be "administered by the Government of Canada for the purposes of the Dominion."[27] Suddenly the Dominion had to have "purpose" to give it legitimacy.

For the next sixty years, the Dominion had two mandates: build railroads and settle the land. Both out of admiration for and in defense against the United States, Canada succumbed to a fever for lines—surveys, railroads, telegraphs—that reached across the prairie and touched the Pacific. "Seldom has such a wealth of experience been appropriated with such abounding good will and admiration," wrote Chester Martin, a Nova Scotian who became Canada's foremost scholar on Dominion lands. "The sectional survey and the railway land grant system; the free-homestead system, school lands, 'swamp lands,' and pre-emption; above all the insistence upon federal control 'for the purposes of the Dominion,'" he marveled, "all these attest the American prototype."[28]

In 1869, a surveyor named John Stoughton Dennis, with his reputation at stake, launched the Canadian grid westward. In the summer of that year, Dennis proposed a plan to survey the Dominion lands before they were even finalized into law. In July, he received an order from William McDougall, the Dominion's first minister of public works and soon to be lieutenant governor of the new territories, to employ the "American system" to "survey townships for immediate settlement." A lieutenant colonel in the Canadian army, Dennis was anxious to transcend his military career, where he had been recently found reckless and inefficient in a military court for allegedly deserting his men under fire. That, too, had been in a nationalist cause, defending Fort Erie against a raid of Fenians, Irish Americans bent on harassing anyone remotely British to gain an independent Ireland. Now, as a surveyor, Dennis was defending Canada again, this time from encroaching Americans who might attempt to take over the West if the Canadians didn't get there first. Following McDougall's order to devise a survey system to parcel out the vast territory into small farms, he was prudent, efficient, and almost entirely unoriginal. In August, he recommended the United States system practically to the letter, expanding the dimensions of its townships to slightly under nine miles square (increased from the United States' six), containing sixty-four eight-hundred-acre sections. Dennis also allowed 5 percent of the area for public highways, and planned for a principal meridian drawn due north from the 49th parallel at a point just west of Pembina, Manitoba.[29]

With Dennis's proposal, the customary British North American styles of land survey—divided into rectangles in the Canadian West and into long, narrow holdings with river frontage along the St. Lawrence—were abandoned. On October 4, 1869, Ottawa authorities approved Dennis's scheme. It became law in the Dominion Lands Act of 1872, where it was shrunk down to United States proportions. "The Dominion lands shall be laid off in quadrilateral Townships," the act read, "containing thirty-six sections of one mile square in each"—the dimensions familiar in the United States—"together with road allowances of one chain and fifty links in width, between all townships and sections." Two sections were reserved for "purposes of education."

There were significant differences from the U.S. system nevertheless. The Hudson's Bay Company retained one-twentieth of surveyed lands—ultimately 6.5 million acres—apportioned by township. And unlike the U.S. Land Ordinance, the Dominion Lands Act limited land purchases to one 640–acre section (the standard limit in the United States was 160 acres), excepting special sales "deemed . . . expedient" by the secretary of state, though it also included a provision for homestead rights on one quarter section or less. It was an apparently tidy plan. As it happened, Lieutenant Colonel Dennis launched his Dominion lands scheme in the single worst possible place—the Red River settlements of the Métis.[30]

By this time, the Métis had become to the Canadian fur trade what slaves and indentured servants were to the southern tobacco economy: the essential link between resources—in this case furs and Indian labor—and white developers' profit. An ethnic group named for the French word for "mixed race," fathered by French or English fur traders and borne by the mostly Cree Indian women whose labor virtually enabled early-day traders to survive, the Métis were so indispensable that even the stiffly Protestant British, who initially resisted the French approval of intimacy with native women, eventually recognized their worth. "It would be most useful," wrote a colonial officer to the Hudson's Bay Company (HBC) London Committee, "to cultivate a small colony of very Useful Hands who would ultimately replace European-born servants."[31]

These "very Useful Hands" passed between Indian and white worlds with ease, creating their own social and economic niches. Based along the

Red River, between Winnipeg, Manitoba (then Fort Garry), and St. Paul, Minnesota, in the eighteenth century they occupied the cultural middle ground of the fur trade. In 1821, the Hudson's Bay Company gained a nearly fifty-year-long monopoly over Rupert's Land by absorbing the rival North-West Company, causing many Métis to lose their jobs as fur trade voyageurs. In response, they became indispensable as buffalo hunters and traders of pemmican, a kind of dried mash of meat, suet, and berries that was a fur trader's staple, and made forays onto the western plains. By 1869, reeling from a decade of bad crops and declining buffalo herds, and anxious over American and Canadian plans to survey and resettle their Red River lands, it was time, once again, to adapt. McDougall, whom Prime Minister John Macdonald described as a man of great ambition and almost no political sense, had sent the unlucky surveyor Dennis into a social powder keg.[32]

The Red River Métis welcomed Dennis as they might have greeted a tailor taking measurements for burial shrouds, and indeed, his new system spelled death for their livelihood. The Métis were accustomed to the European system of deep, narrow riverfront lots, like those of the French habitants along the St. Lawrence, where each settler had a small river frontage and water rights, and grazing or "hay" privileges in a common area behind it. He measured the two miles from the river to his lot boundary by sighting along a horizontal line underneath the belly of his horse. Despised by native tribes with no such notions of ownership, the Métis landowner was a hybrid. During the 1880s, the Métis finally yielded to the hundreds of young men of the Dominion Lands Survey and the United States Geological Survey, who came toting sixty–foot measuring chains, though remaining skeptical of this American-style surveyor talking of a ridiculous-sounding grid that took no account of water rights. Dennis announced to the Métis that he had no intention of interfering with their lands, assuring them in the local newspaper that whatever system he proposed, it would apply only to "lands not heretofore granted or to those unsettled at the present time." The Métis, however, viewed this as the sop that it eventually proved to be.[33]

Not surprisingly, young Louis Riel, son of the deceased Métis resistance leader Jean-Louis Riel and a man who had vowed to "try to walk in my father's footsteps," soon found himself walking on surveyors' chains. On October 11, 1869, a surveyor named A. C. Webb and his party reached the Red River lots near St. Vital and trespassed across the land of André Nault, Louis Riel's cousin. Though the surveyors were careful to build no mounds or markers on Métis land, the Métis nevertheless considered their very presence an intrusion. When the crew ignored Nault's protests against them, Nault sent his son for help.

Riel appeared at Nault's late in the afternoon backed by a group of Métis neighbors and asked the surveyors to leave. A young man just shy of his twenty-fifth birthday, Riel, who had fair skin, a stocky build, and a large, imposing head under a mass of curly hair, was not yet the great eccentric Métis hero he would become. But when Webb refused to leave, Riel planted his moccasined foot on the stretched-out survey chain and, so the story goes, the neighbors lined up silently behind him. "You go no farther," he said calmly in English. The surveyors packed up and left. By spring 1870, their retreat was total. Dennis, for his own protection, had returned to Ottawa disguised as an Indian woman, presumably the least threatening, most easily overlooked social type he could think of.[34] His system of dominion lands was baptized in racial strife that had no precise American equivalent.

The Métis, for their part, resisted Canadian annexation briefly, then gained a legislated peace in the Manitoba Act of May 1870. They received a grant of 1.4 million acres in Manitoba selected by the lieutenant governor for "the children of the half-breed heads of families," and in 1874 an addition of a half a million dollars in scrip to heads of families. It was a "lavish" gift to an "improvident" people, grumbled Dominion lands historian Chester Martin. In practice, however, as one member of parliament noted, it was a relatively cheap means of conquering and pacifying the natives, to be honored in the breach. Riel and his followers ultimately failed to gain the secure and influential community they desired. The territory they gained was a mere two thousand square miles of the present-day province, an area the size of Prince Edward Island that would fit like a postage stamp in the corner of the enormous public domain. Mapped against the vast Canadian territories, it had, in the words of one legislator, a "ludicrous look" that "put one in mind of some of the incidents in Gulliver's Travels." "These impulsiv [Métis] have got spoilt" by their uprising, cautioned Prime Minister Macdonald, "and must be kept down by a strong hand until they are swamped by the influx of settlers." Evidence remains spotty about the degree to which wily land speculators and unsympathetic officials swindled, manipulated, and forced the Métis out of their land, and to what degree the Métis voluntarily sold it, typically at reduced value. By whatever means, the Manitoba Métis community of about 10,000 people would be dissolved by the 1880s. Like the Sioux in their struggle against the U.S. military, the Métis had provided only a temporary setback to the western survey.[35]

After the Manitoba Act neutralized the Métis, Dennis and his fellow surveyors returned to their task with renewed vigor. In the summer of 1871, carrying their new U.S.-style survey manual and sixty-foot-long Gunter's chains onto the plains, the surveyors began once again to divide 200 million acres of land into 1.25 million homestead-sized quarter sections. By 1877 the so-called Special Survey, whose task was to lay out the base lines and meridians, had reached the fourth meridian, now the Alberta-Saskatchewan boundary. By 1881, the year of Sitting Bull's surrender, the framework for the grid was completed, and by 1883, surveyors were subdividing the townships in medicine line country, near present-day Maple Creek, burning in their campfires old buffalo bones drenched in coal oil and wood carted from the nearby Cypress Hills.[36]

Meanwhile, United States surveyors moved slowly and haphazardly toward the Northern Plains. They, too, had a vast territory—over three million square miles—to divide into small squares. To accomplish this, several surveyors general, who numbered sixteen in 1877, contracted out to private individuals the tasks of running lines, establishing corners, and preparing maps and plats. The result was widespread fraud and wretched inadequacy in the work actually accomplished. In addition, several federally sponsored surveys exploring the geography, geology, and commercial potential of western lands competed for funds and status. In 1879, Congress in frustration finally united the various state and federal surveys under one bureaucratic agency, the United States Geological Survey (USGS). Under the leadership of Clarence King, for whom staking out homestead plots was of little interest, the USGS concentrated its efforts on developing the mining industry. When John Wesley Powell, a Civil War veteran and visionary scientist, became the director of the USGS in 1881, the survey pressed to map the nation's topography. Not only were small farms low on Powell's list of priorities, but he argued against them, saying they were economically unsuitable for arid lands. Powell, in fact, proposed a more communally owned and run system of settlement, but found little audience for it. Congress extended the Homestead Act to the unsurveyed public domain in 1880, as if finally apologizing for the survey's perennial lagging behind advancing settlers. While Canadian surveyors raced ahead to beat settlers to western lands, the United States government pronounced the race moot. That the two sides of the border mirrored each other during their rapid transformation was neither a fluke nor the inevitable working of physical geography. Canadian developers seemed determined to do for their prairie whatever the United States could do for its own, only better. [37]

The one thing Canada lacked was a national myth, a story of its underlying purpose, an enterprise that for nineteenth-century Americans was something of a public pastime. The person who described that American narrative best was Wisconsin-born historian Frederick Jackson Turner. In 1893, at the celebrated Columbian Exposition in Chicago, Turner read to a group of historians a quiet address called "The Significance of the Frontier in American History" whose ideas and phrases about the West were to become so influential and familiar that they would become hackneyed. As Americans moved westward, wrote Turner, "the frontier [was] the outer edge of the wave—the meeting point between savagery and civilization," and the "line of most effective and rapid Americanization." Wilderness not only "fused" Europeans "into a mixed race" of Americans, the very act of entering the wilderness and then, in stages, progressing out of it, forged American character. Turner placed the frontier at the heart of America's essential story, at once grandly progressive and poignantly sad: a nation born on a frontier it was destined to overcome, finding its greatness in a wilderness it was destined to destroy.[38] As an explanation of United States history, Turner's frontier thesis has been a favorite dead horse to beat on since the 1950s. Whatever its merits, American historians have convincingly repudiated Turner's frontier as ethnocentric, misguidedly rural, naively cheerful, and hopelessly imprecise. If for a time it was a good parable about holy civic nationalism, it is deeply flawed as an explanation for it.[39]

Turner is also responsible for the fact that in the American West, the word "frontier" does not mean "border," its traditional European meaning. There, by the fourteenth century, "frontier" had evolved from a front line of troops facing an enemy to a zone of military defense. By the seventeenth century, it meant the external territorial outlines of a self-conscious nation.[40] By the nineteenth century, the old Europe of dynastic wars and interests had become a continental contest of newly aggressive, antagonistic nationalisms. After the French Revolution, European statesmen tried to associate a "natural" territorial boundary with national identity. Girondins and Robespierre alike invoked natural frontiers as symbols of a French people bound by the invisible principle of liberty, the source of a national myth.

Turner went them one better. "Frontier" in the United States would become a term to describe the westward-moving, national conquest of the continent. "The American frontier is sharply distinguished from the European frontier," he explained, "a fortified boundary line running through dense populations. The most significant thing about the American frontier is, that it lies at the hither edge of free land."[41] In the expansionist United States, "frontier" would signify the advancement of civilization into a wilderness, the New World environmental condition for American egalitarian democracy and individualism.

It was an ingenious substitution. Old World terms yielded to words reflecting New World conditions. Fixed zones became moving zones; borders became "zones of settlement"; places became a process; republican patriotism became Manifest Destiny. The New World frontier became the prop of American nationalism, a component of the civil religion. Borders fled to the margins of the national narrative.[42]

By contrast, Canadians have tended to identify with Europe, mainly with the British Empire. They have explained their westward movement as a herioc story of development, a story shared with the United States, but they have a more cautious nationalist imagination. Expansion and development has not meant liberation from Old World laws and flaws. Their ideological inheritance, as historian John Conway has pointed out, is rooted in the English conservatism of Edmund Burke, who wrote that "the restraints on men's liberties are to be counted among their rights."[43]

Despite themselves, westering Canadians did, to some degree, act like Canadians. They may have adopted the U.S. survey system wholesale, but in a more sparsely populated country with a westward movement that was positively arthritic by comparison, its operation took on the more orderly, authoritarian character on which Canadians prided themselves. The free-for-all style of the American system stiffened under Canadian application. Preemption, for example, the long-favored American practice of recognizing the rights of squatters even after the government survey had arrived, had no Canadian equivalent. In 1908, Canadians applied the term preemption to an entirely different law—the right of the homesteader with a quarter section to buy an adjoining quarter section at a fixed price of three dollars per acre. Canadian land historian Chester Martin likes to makes much of such differences, in order to set off Canadian westward expansion as the more precisely orchestrated affair that it was. Here was a kind of "preemption," he noted with delight, that "would scarcely have been recognizable" to its American champions in the 1830s.[44]

In the 1880s, however, such differences were subtle. On both sides of the boundary, the "multitudes" had begun to arrive, while Canadian Métis and natives were ultimately no better off than American native peoples. Even the surveyors, complain as they might, noted signs of a rapid shift in local life. By 1879 the Canadian Chippewa were no longer warning settlers off their land. They were plowing the earth with skill so impressive that one surveyor judged them "equal to what I have seen at some of the ploughing matches in Ontario." Another surveyor was shocked to find himself walking across a peneplain of bones, all that remained of a band of three hundred Assiniboine destroyed by the Old World scourge of smallpox a few years earlier. Still another penned a tellingly clinical description of the land's resources: "There were a great many fine springs. One in Township 21, Range 12 would fill a 12-inch pipe."[45] Here was not so much a natural site as a commodity to be measured for a new set of industrial fixtures. Landmarks situated previously only in human memory now became official locations, a matter of coordinates plotted against the stars.

The rapid and radical change that would characterize the Northern Plains for the next four decades had begun. Only the "half-breed road" of the Métis heading west from the Red River country seemed a "connecting-link with civilized life," wrote the incommoded Twining from the border-land in 1874. Twining endured the irregularities of the belching *Fontenelle* because he believed that surveyors ran ahead of civilization. Otto Klotz, a Dominion lands surveyor, put a finer point on it. "Oh—the handwriting is on the wall," he exclaimed in anticipation. "Where there is a railroad our work is done." Steamboats were the preamble, surveys were the dotted line, and the signature of civilization was the railroad. Klotz knew it would come soon. But, charting the uncharted, he was also drawn to the surveyor's oddly ambiguous relationship to the settled life. "We are like the Indian," he wrote in 1883, after heading out one morning onto the drainboard flat prairie west of Winnipeg to impose order on an unbounded land. "We ever flee from civilization."[46]

THE "MELTING POT OF HELL"

R obert Higheagle remembered it in a word. When he was a child, he said, the people in his Sioux village thought of the U.S.-Canada boundary as "holy. . . . They believe things are different when you cross from one side to the other."[1]

The need for a place where "things are different" is the constant theme of the West, Canadian and American. Opening the frontier has been a geographical quest marked by spiritual hunger, one we normally associate with white Europeans moving westward. But in the 1870s, when a dormant political boundary half a century old suddenly became an object of hope and nationalist divisions in the West, it appealed most to those who needed a refuge—to Robert Higheagle and other Northern Plains natives who found themselves in increasingly difficult circumstances with rapidly diminishing choices. The hundred-odd years before W. J. Twining's arrival in 1874 had not been easy. The threat of white settlement was only the latest misfortune in a world already made unstable by migration, warfare, disease, scarcity, and alcohol.

The way Andrew Garcia saw it, by the 1870s medicine line country was a "melting pot of hell." A wandering, tough-talking Rio Grande–born fur trader, Garcia arrived in Montana in 1876. "I was of the age," he recalled in his memoir, "when a fellow thinks that he knows it all, and in reality he doesn't. This is the one time in life when a fellow ought to have a guardian—one of the good old-fashioned, short-arm kind that will kick or pound the conceit out of him." Instead, Garcia took up with an unsavory hunter and trapper named Beaver Tom, and witnessed a world in which people truly pounded the conceit out of each other. As Garcia described it, a Blackfoot warrior might knock a Nez Percé woman's eyeball onto her cheek with one blow of a coup stick, Indian women fought each other with knives, and rough characters of every race and ethnicity lied, cheated, and stole indiscriminately from whites and Indians, women and men.[2] The stakes were high: food, territory, survival. The supply of game was shrinking. Between the Missouri and the South Saskatchewan Rivers, at the heart of medicine line country, tensions were growing. "During the months of June and July 1877," said a mounted police inspector, "Ft. Walsh was visited by large bands of Indians—Crees, Assiniboin, Sioux and North Piegans in fact the country surrounding us was covered with people each hostile to the other." Such were the native relationships when W. J. Twining steamed up the Missouri, and they were a long time forming.[3]

Whites coming to medicine line country liked to refer offhandedly to "the Indian," as if the native peoples had all been forged in a single mold of timeless, unchanging savagery. Yet the Northern Plains world that Twining, Garcia, and others entered in the mid-nineteenth century was not only complex, but of recent origin. Along with whites, the Plains Cree and Western Sioux were relative newcomers to the more established communities of Crow, Assiniboine, Gros Ventre, and Blackfeet.

The Cree and Sioux were migrating branches of Eastern Woodland tribes that became powerful on the northern plains during the eighteenth and early nineteenth centuries. Shrewd and adaptable traders, the Cree became middlemen in the English fur trade by the 1690s and began to spread north and west of Lake Superior. About this time they formed alliances with the Assiniboine, a recently split-off Siouan tribe living to their west near the Saskatchewan and Assiniboine Rivers in what is now Saskatchewan. Economic and cultural exchange cemented the Cree-Assiniboine relationship. The horse, which the Spanish brought to mainland America in 1519, diffused northward up the plains during the eighteenth century, drawing the Assiniboine westward from the Great Lakes woodland-plains borderland by 1750. The Cree gave the Assiniboine guns, the Assiniboine gave the Cree horses and introduced them to plains life; the result was considerable intermarriage and a powerful alliance. The Cree then pushed farther west and south in search of furs for their profitable trade, driving the Gros Ventre and Blackfoot (both Algonkian-speaking, like the Cree) and even the Assiniboine against their advance, although the game-rich plains were a magnet as well and may have attracted these tribes there as much or more than the Cree pushed them.[4]

These realignments were often horrible and bloody. During the 1840s and '50s, Edwin Thompson Denig, the fur trader with the most prolific pen on the subject of upper Missouri natives, self-described as the rare voice of informed and balanced judgment after twenty-two years among these peoples, provides ghastly details. In his lengthy 1850s treatise on five tribes, which in the twentieth century helped earn him the highest standing among scholars, Denig wrote that sometime before 1838, under a ruthless and thoroughly unpleasant Assiniboine leader called the Gauche, who allegedly rose to power by poisoning people, a combined force of Cree and Assiniboine massacred thirty lodges of the Gros Ventre while all but a few of the men were gone hunting. They killed about 130 women and children, including roasting some of the children alive by driving sharp sticks through their bodies and planting them before a hot fire. Denig's source is not known, but he did not shrink from the macabre. When John James Audubon visited him at Fort Union (on the present-day Montana–North Dakota line) in the summer of 1843, he not only collected bird and mammal specimens, but procured for Audubon the head of an Indian chief from a treetop grave. [5]

Like the Cree, the Sioux acted as middlemen in the fur trade farther south on the Minnesota and Missouri Rivers, first trading beaver pelts to English Canadians to their north and then buffalo robes and pemmican to French and Spanish traders to the south and west. The Sioux, in many small bands, also pushed west and south, seeking beaver and ultimately buffalo for the fur trade, overwhelming their once formidable agricultural foes. Denig judged the Sioux as generally quarrelsome and "expert in waylaying their enemies around their homes."[6] By 1800 the Arikara, Hidatsa, and Mandan along the upper Missouri had yielded to the Sioux advance, and within a few years the Omaha and Ponca on the lower Missouri followed suit. The Oglala Sioux, meanwhile, were contesting the Kiowa, Arapaho, Crow, and Cheyenne for the Plains country farther west. With the passing of a few decades, the old borders and balance of power along the Missouri were in shambles.[7] Sioux and Cree conquests had redistributed power and territory among native peoples. Between 1780 and 1820, a new order on the Northern Plains emerged.

Indian warriors, however, could not take all the credit. If any one thing shaped the new Indian geography, it was disease. It was a sadly familiar story, repeated countless times since the Arawak greeted Columbus in 1492. Smallpox, a European-introduced scourge against which the natives had no immunity, devastated entire villages, and while no tribe escaped its mortal touch, the more sedentary, concentrated, and smaller horticultural populations suffered most. The widespread epidemic of 1780–81 ravaged the Assiniboine, for example, who lived in larger, less scattered groups than did the Cree. They were hit again in the epidemic of 1837–38, when a steamboat carried the germ along with annual supplies to Fort Union in June. According to Denig, who himself caught the epidemic and survived, by autumn a thousand Assiniboine were reduced to about 150 survivors. A man he knew named Little Dog was so distraught after losing his favorite child that his wife agreed he should kill the entire family rather than have them face disfigurement and death, as long as he killed her first, "as she did not wish to witness their death." Little Dog carried out the plan and then killed himself.[8]

Assiniboine Council near Fort Walsh, North-West Territories, c. 1878.
Photo courtesy Glenbow Archives, Calgary, Alberta.

Smallpox and cholera similarly crushed the Omaha in advance of Sioux aggression. The epidemic of 1800–01 killed two-thirds of the Omaha, including their celebrated chief Washinga Sakba, a ruthless leader known for poisoning rivals. He was entombed in a bluff overlooking the Missouri astride his favorite war horse, buried alive beneath him. The Arikara, Mandan, and Gros Ventre were similarly devastated.[9] By comparison, the dispersed and nomadic Cree and Sioux may have suffered a relatively low mortality rate of 50 percent. Smallpox wrested once powerful nations from their positions; it "left them," as explorer William Clark wrote of the Omaha in 1804, "to the insults of their weaker neighbors, who had previously been glad to be on friendly terms with them."[10] The fur trade provided a motive for conquest. Smallpox cleared its path.

By the time Lewis and Clark pushed up the Missouri in 1804, the new territorial arrangement was largely in place—a brief constellation of cultures that hunted buffalo from horseback that lasted through most of the nineteenth century. Their geography resembled a moving jigsaw puzzle. The Blackfoot or Blackfoot Confederacy, comprising the Blood, Blackfeet, and Piegan groups, settled at the base of the Rocky Mountains, southwest of their traditional hunting grounds in the North Saskatchewan River valley. (Those in the United States were called Blackfeet, and were actually the South Piegan). They pushed out the Shoshone, who though probably the first on the Northern Plains to acquire horses and rise to their zenith as feared mounted warriors, were the last to acquire guns and just as swiftly fell to the status of "miserable old women" whom the Blackfoot boasted they could defeat with sticks and stones.[11] The Gros Ventre, whose legends suggest that they were once southern-roaming Arapaho, landed south of their former territory, at the center of medicine line country between the South Saskatchewan and Missouri Rivers. Their sometime Blackfoot allies lived to the west, the Cree to the north, and the enemy Crow to the south. The Assiniboine, whose numbers and territory shrank as the Cree's increased, also moved southwest and settled along the upper Missouri east of the Milk River. Their initially powerful alliance with the Cree disintegrated, perhaps because the Shoshone decline eliminated their common enemy, or because disease devastated the Assiniboine.[12] The Plains Cree and western Sioux, winners in the territorial sweepstakes, roamed large portions of the Northern Plains.

Then there were the Métis. They also began to hunt on the Northern Plains in the late eighteenth and early nineteenth centuries. As the buffalo emerged as the staple of the Métis trade-based economy, it drew them west from their Red River settlement and threw yet another wrench into Northern Plains politics. Unlike the Anglican, English-speaking mixed bloods of the Hudson's Bay Company, often called the "country-born," who became integrated into white society, the Catholic, French-speaking Métis of the rival North-West Company nourished their own culture. Much like the Apache after the acquisition of the horse, they adapted to the land's aridity with a half-horticultural, half-nomadic hunting economy. These, Louis Riel's people, were the group that went west. [13]

The Métis are renowned in Canadian history for being twice oppressed, mounting rebellions against government abuses in 1869 and again in 1885. Yet they, too, were invaders of a sort. More resistant to European diseases

Métis Red River cart convoy, commonly seen hunting buffalo across the western prairie in the 1860s and '70s.
Photo courtesy Montana Historical Society, Helena, Montana.

than their rapidly thinning full-blooded cousins, they were biological opportunists filling a widening niche. They assaulted the dune-colored prairie monotony with their unforgettable screeching caravans of huge-wheeled Red River carts, whose ungreased poplar or cottonwood axles could set a coyote's teeth on edge. "The Red River cart brigades never sneaked up on anybody," recalled Joseph Kinsey Howard, Montana journalist and writer, who spent much of his childhood in Canada and pretended to drive them in his boyhood war games.[14] These upgraded travois wheeled off from strip farms along the Red and Assiniboine Rivers two hundred or more at a time, cacophonous, dust-clouded cavalcades swarming with mosquitoes, children, extra horses and oxen, and dozens, sometimes hundreds, of dogs. The prairie fur trade's answer to the canoe, these efficient cart brigades freighted pemmican and buffalo robes, and every June or so, like some strangely exuberant and exotic military operation, set out on the annual buffalo hunt.

Those Métis less bound to agriculture eventually wintered on the western hunting grounds, amidst the newly aligned Indian groups. They built stone and wood cabins at the east edge of the Cypress Hills, where the town of Eastend now stands, and there endured the long cold months in an unventilated squalor unknown to Indian tepees. They stayed—the

Frenchman River is named for them—but they were not always well liked. "Louis Riel's French-Crees," remembered Montana trader James Willard Schultz, who was eventually adopted by the southern Pikuni (Piegan Blackfoot),

> with their high, one-horse, two-wheel homemade squeaking carts, roamed the plains close about, some of them, and others built and lived in cabins in the river bottoms below us. The men were good hunters and trappers, their women fine tanners of buffalo robes. We liked their trade but did not like them. They were, in fact, more than disliked by all Indian tribes, save the Crees, and by the whites of their country and ours, too. I myself could hardly bear to stand behind the counter and trade with them, for in their bastard French, they were always reviling us, all the *sacre Americaines*.[15]

Such hatreds were not unusual. The character of this native-dominated political world, as Schultz suggests, was no pastoral idyll. Ecological balance toppled under the fur trade, if it ever existed at all, and social harmony was an impossibility. War, the enthusiast's game that some writers portray as the means to individual glory, was also a serious contest for power, territory and resources. Moreover, things were only getting worse, and between 1869 and 1877, the Northern Plains world began to realign a second time.

First, there was scarcity building toward famine. The fur trade, though initially a boon, ultimately took its toll on the Northern Plains economy. Under its aegis, native peoples transformed the buffalo hunt from a means of subsistence and small-scale trade into a system of resource extraction for a large trade economy. White hide hunters, despite earning their dark reputation by individually killing twenty-five bufffalo a day, did not destroy the buffalo by themselves in their fifteen post–Civil War years of profligate slaughter. At three dollars apiece, buffalo robes were a natives' gold mine.[16] By trading pemmican—the fur trader's staple—and buffalo robes to European and North American markets for horses, guns, ammunition, blankets, tools, goodwill, and whiskey, native peoples were creating a Malthusian squeeze before the 1870s, despite declining native populations.

As on the Southern Plains, there were signs of food scarcity by the mid-nineteenth century, though the evidence is sketchy. As late as 1877, the Sioux recalled "plenty" of game in their Canadian refuge between Wood Mountain and the Cypress Hills—the last pocket of plenitude for buffalo hunters. Nevertheless, between 1830 and 1843 the American Fur Company and the Hudson's Bay Company together moved eighty thousand buffalo robes a year, many of those hides from Métis and Indians eager for trade. The boundary surveyors witnessed Métis hunting camps in which each hunter would kill six or eight buffalo a day, taking along with the hides only the tongues and hump ribs and leaving the rest to rot. In 1846, Denig witnessed a local famine among the Assiniboine so dire, he claimed, "they ate up their dogs and horses, and in some instances devoured their own children."[17]

By the 1860s, the anxious Cree were blaming the Métis and whites for the scarcity of game. In 1879 Edward Dewdney, lieutenant governor of the North-West Territories, besieged by starving Blackfoot and Cree, admitted to a "crisis." In the spring of 1880 the buffalo had "entirely disappeared from the Milk River country," noted one observer, and though they returned briefly in October, it was for the last time; by 1881, the year of Sitting Bull's surrender, the Indians were destitute, selling their horses, eating mice, and begging. The whites, making their move onto the northern plains, could press their advantage.[18]

For a population weakened by famine, alcohol was a second fatal blow. Whiskey is the tried-and-true tool of empire building—the "deadly medicine," as one writer has described it, of North American colonization. Whiskey traders, like native peoples on the margins of civilized life, were the first to exploit the international border. Even more than disease and the demise of the buffalo, liquor is totemic in the literature of the medicine line in the 1870s—"The Americans sold it, the Mounties controlled it, and the Indians couldn't hold it" one might have quipped—the powerful fuel of both hope and despair.[19]

Canadian novelist Bertrand W. Sinclair captured the border tensions in his popular novel *Raw Gold.* In a typical scenario, the trim-looking Mountie, his boot on the whiskey keg, its contents trickling into the prairie grass, demands an answer of his detainee. "'Where is your authority to have this stuff?'" Old Piegan Smith, a hot-tempered American whiskey trader, flies off the handle despite his ordinarily good judgment (which, Sinclair reminds us, "a man surely needed if he wanted to live out his allotted span in the vicinity of the forty-ninth parallel those troubled days"). Naturally, Old Piegan, unsteeled against temptation, had been sampling his own goods and "put enough of the fiery stuff under his belt to make him touchy as a parlor-match." "'Here's my authority, yuh blasted runt,'" the American reprobate yells, drawing his six-shooter, forgetting "he was in an alien land where the law is upheld to the last, least letter." The unarmed Mountie, his back "eloquent of determination," symbolic of the "peace and dignity of the Crown," reminds Old Piegan that there are more Mounties where he comes from, and calmly turns his back to walk over to his horse. Astonished at this display of "cold-blooded courage," the outlaw is overcome with admiration. He invites the Mountie to dinner. The Mountie accepts, and the reader chalks up another improbable triumph for Canadian peace, order, and good government.[20] While Sinclair's Mountie endured as a stereotype, the reality was a good bit messier.

The Mounties were the brainchild of John A. Macdonald's government, a force patterned after the classic British constabulary but designed to control natives. Macdonald originally conceived the North-West Mounted Police in the 1860s as a kind of Royal Irish Constabulary for hinterland Canada, to fend off the Americans in the West much as Britain had fended off the French in Ireland during the Napoleonic Wars. In 1873, in an incident that became known as the Cypress Hills Massacre, he found reason to use it.

By that year, one of the most active whiskey trades in Canada's North-West Territories was thriving among natives and Americans along the border, a trade increasingly unpopular among the more defensive Canadian nationalists. In May 1873, a skirmish began over some horses that a band of northern Assiniboine had stolen from a small party of white hunters and traders in Fort Benton, Montana Territory. The whites got mad and pursued the thieves north to the Cypress Hills just north of the line, where, at Abe Farwell's whiskey trading post on Battle Creek, they met up with another angry victim of Assiniboine horse snatching named George Hammond. At this point the various accounts blur into a welter of contradictory interests and hearsay, while exactly what happened remains unclear. Perhaps the whole incident would have ended there had George Hammond, who had just bought his horse back from these same Assiniboine, not discovered it stolen a second time shortly after the Fort Benton party arrived. The whites rode out to the Indian camp and spoke fighting words. The Indians were insolent. The whites took cover in a coulee. Somebody fired first, and the resulting encounter left scores of Indians and one white man named Ed Grace dead. On Grace's behalf, the whites indecorously burned to the ground (as a funeral pyre) the trading post of Moses Solomon, Farwell's rival trader.

The Cypress Hill incident seemed to confirm Canadians' worst fears about American lawlessness, and the press had a field day. Nasty American "scum" and "gangsters" were arousing Canadian Indians, growled Canadian news reporters. "Thirteen Kit Carsons" were defending their property, the "advance guards of civilization," trumpeted their Montana counterparts. Most of the participants on both sides had been drinking, and although at least half and perhaps two-thirds of the thirteen (in some accounts fifteen) whites involved in the attack were Canadian, this all-important detail was left out. A story about Canadians killing Canadian Indians would not make very good Canadian propaganda. And so it went. The incident did not form public opinion so much as measure it, and like a flare, it ignited incipient hostilities that had grown up around the liquor trade to the Indians. The Cypress Hills Massacre, as it came to be known, marked the beginning of national stereotypes across the medicine line.[21]

As it happened, by the 1860s and '70s most of the independent borderland traders were Americans. The Canadian journalists were right about that. Initially, however, this was not the case. The rival Hudson's Bay and American Fur Companies penetrated the Northern Plains in the 1830s, staying until they wearied of low profits and the inhospitable Blackfoot, who enlivened relations by occasionally burning down a trading post. The proximity of the Missouri River, however, kept some Americans in the game after the Hudson's Bay Company withdrew. Enterprising independent American traders and merchants were eventually able to fill the niche the larger companies left empty. The reasons for their success are unclear. It did not hurt that by the mid-nineteenth century, the large companies and their profits were fading and Blackfeet power was continually eroding under the ill effects of disease and alcohol.

Even so, the Americans-as-ruffians view dear to Canadian nationalists grievously distorted the history of alcohol in the North American West. Liquor was a time-honored and popular trade item on every European frontier, and British North America was no exception. "We all traded whisky," recalled a former Hudson's Bay Company employee; "the Hudson's Bay Company traded rum up to the year 1860. I have seen as maney indans Drunk at Edmonton and Rocky Mountain House as ever i seen aney where else." Competing French and English traders had wooed northwestern Plains Indians with alcohol since the eighteenth century.[22] To the mythologizers of the Cypress Hills Massacre, the notion of evil American riffraff corrupting western Canada with whiskey and violence was potent justification for the Macdonald government's plans to develop the West. But it was as much nationalist propaganda as it was truth. Not Canadian virtue and defense against American brutishness, but the effective and rapid advance of American business enterprises into former fur company territory were responsible for the American liquor trade with Northern Plains Indians in the 1860s and '70s.

Nor was the American borderland as lawless (nor Canada as lawful) as popular writers have made out. The United States government attempted to control the whiskey trade in the 1870s by imposing a penalty of not less than one year imprisonment and a fine of not less than $100 for introducing liquor to Indian country. It raised the penalty to a minimum of two years and $300 in the early 1880s, punishments comparable to those in Canada.

Nevertheless, the Cypress Hills Massacre was enough to speed Prime Minister Macdonald's orders to dispatch the Mounted Police sooner rather than later. The hastily assembled troops left Ottawa for the west in October

1873, just one month before Macdonald's Conservative government fell. Given the new economizing administration of Alexander Mackenzie, without the massacre, the Mounties might never have been established at all. From that point on, law enforcement did distinguish the two sides of the border. Local American juries tended to refuse to convict their enterprising liquor-trading neighbors, whereas the Mounted Police commissioner and superintendents were "*ex officio* . . . justice[s] of the peace" with the authority to try most of the suspects they apprehended. This was authority that the broader array of local sheriffs, federal marshals, and the U.S Army on the other side of the border lacked.

The Mounted Police in fact exercised greater power than the 1867 British North American Act allowed. Under the act, law enforcement and the administration of justice were made a provincial responsibility, following a precedent deeply rooted in British law. But in a place nearly empty of white provincials, suspending this requirement seemed prudent.[23]

True to their calling, as *Raw Gold* so earnestly dramatizes, early Mounties indeed spent much of their time trying to keep liquor at bay. The North-West Territories Act of 1875, superseding similar acts dating from 1867, prohibited the importation, sale, exchange, barter, and manufacture of liquor in the territories except by special permission of the lieutenant governor. In theory, this would protect the Indians and, more to the point, preserve social order while allowing white settlers controlled tippling. In practice the law was ludicrous. The permit system proved to be a hornet's nest of fraud and political bickering. The overwhelmed lieutenant governor pressed his governing body, the North-West Council, into permit-granting service to relieve the pressure. Like the attempts to contain the landscape in a well-organized grid, the liquor law was neat in conception, messy in execution.

Enforcement was impossible. Until the newly elected Territorial Assembly repealed the law as an admitted disaster in 1891, violations of the liquor law were the largest single category of criminal offenses—more than 25 percent—listed in North-West Mounted Police reports of the 1880s.[24] The police made a respectable enough effort to shut down most of the trade to the Indians. The notorious Montana whiskey forts closed without a whimper. Nonetheless, the illegal liquor seized was by all accounts a drop in the bucket. A few hundred Mounted Police patrolling a vast chunk of continent and tens of thousands of people might have been likened to a few flies buzzing a scattered herd of livestock. To energetic whiskey smugglers, the police were a nuisance but not a deterrent.

American soldiers in the West were themselves known for their fondness for drink. One traveler to Fort Assiniboine, just west of Chinook, in 1894 found his way there easily by following "the empty beer and whiskey

North-West Mounted Police at Fort Walsh, North-West Territories, 1879. First row, E.D. Clark; second row (l. to r.), A. G. Irvine, James F. Macleod, Doctor John Kittson; third row (l. to r.), Percy R. Neale, Francis J. Dickens, W. D. Antrobus, J. H. McIlree, E. Frechette, Cecil Denny. Photograph by W. E. Hook, Wisconsin.
Courtesy Glenbow Archives, Calgary, Alberta.

bottles from the edge of town." But the Mounties enjoyed their liquor, too. Punishment for drunkenness among members of the force grew more severe as the problem failed to abate. A $3 to $6 fine in 1874 was in 1881 increased to one month's pay (about $23 for a subconstable) and reduction to the ranks. The alcoholism of Frank Dickens, wayward son of novelist Charles Dickens, during his time on the force contributed to his eventually being denied further employment in public service. One constable recorded an instance of several of his fellow policemen—his entire patrol, in fact—going horizontal from drink during their encounter with liquor smugglers at the international boundary. "The night was bitterly cold and we had no blankets but those under our saddles," the policeman wrote in his diary.

> The two prisoners and Jerry [Potts, the Mounties' skilled Métis guide] were soon howling drunk and the rest of us managed to keep from freezing by taking frequent doses of alcohol diluted in water which Jerry called "mix." About midnight a priest who was camped not far from us came over and was persuaded to take a drink for his stomach's sake, it was not too long before he and Tom La Nauze became very jolly and were toasting each other drinking out of two old fruit cans and touching them together at every sip. Callaghan had long retired, crawling in between David and Cochrane who were to drunk to prevent him and before morning I had the honour of being the only sober man in camp although I must admit that I took quite enough to keep the cold out.[25]

Never mind the ill-advised effort to ward off cold, these men were violating the Mountie code. The Mounted Police were sent west to keep down alcohol, one observer quipped, and that was exactly what they were doing.

Confiscated liquor, however, proved a difficult thing to waste. Spoils from a captured smuggler's wagon undoubtedly motivated the police in their vigorous patrol of American liquor traffic, and antismuggling patrols were known to cache captured liquor for their own use. Sometimes they buried it. Offenders occupied all ranks. "Captain Crozer wants three gals your best whisky," wrote an agent from Fort Macleod to a Montana trader. "Send it to him with bill, packed securely and marked. He is all right on the pay."[26] James Willard Schultz recalled smuggling kegs of whiskey to two Mounted Police officers in the mail sacks (off-limits to Mounted Police searches) that traveled every two weeks from Fort Benton to Fort Macleod in the days before the Canadian Pacific Railway brought mail across Canada. One of the officers, Commissioner James Macleod, held the force's highest rank. So much for the "last, least letter of the law."

A policeman such as Macleod, however, could use drink to tender social advantage. Contemporaries portrayed Macleod as a rugged, graceful, intelligent Scot, curious and well read, likable to Indians and whites alike. He was a "broad-minded [man] of culture" and a "pleasure to talk with," recalled Schultz, with whom Macleod often stayed overnight on frequent trips south to Fort Benton. Macleod, who mingled freely on both sides of the border, was a respected and effective leader who seemed to better administer the spirit of the law by occasionally violating the letter of it. The Mounties controlled the liquor supply, but they manipulated it as well, and Canadian law was not always the straight-laced authority in the borderland that Sinclair and other writers have made it out to be.[27]

The international whiskey trade was also more socially complex than legend suggests. Traders were a mixed lot—a social spectrum ranging from wealthy Helena merchants to scrappy, striving trading-post middlemen to ragged and peripatetic trappers, hunters, and "wolfers" (professional wolf hunters). Some, such as Montana merchants T. C. Power and Colonel C. A. Broadwater, ran extensive regional businesses that included illicit liquor trade with the Indians, probably on both sides of the border. The eastern business register Dun and Bradstreet, Inc., in their abbreviated style of notation, recorded under the listing "T. C. Powers" (misspelled) in 1870: "consid an honest man," worth "50m or more." But there was a caveat: he was "engd in illicit trade with the indians & . . . engd in manufac of whiskey contray to law," and consequently "in dngr. of being broken up by Govmt. if such is the Case." Power and Broadwater escaped U.S. prosecution, probably because of widespread social approval of such trade, bribes to officials, and the insulation their middlemen provided, and because they folded their Canadian operations as soon as the Mounted Police arrived.[28]

Alcohol brought out distinctions of class and race among the region's people that in truth overshadowed the competing national distinctions reported in the eastern press. Louis Riel, no longer the rising Métis youth of his surveyor-chasing days but an exiled eccentric living on the Missouri River in Montana right in the middle of the liquor trade, called for action. From his place just southeast of present-day Chinook in 1882, he wrote a series of letters pleading for the prosecution of Broadwater and his traders. Riel demonstrated native peoples' awareness that along the new white man's borderland, alcohol was having a pernicious effect. "Why is it," he pleaded in awkward English in an unpublished letter to the Helena *Independent*, "that he who would denounce any one as having traded illegally on indian reservations, as having sold liquor to indians, is generally looked upon as a man of small character? Is it not that too many people in our community have traded more or less unlawfully in that manner," he continued, "and that they are yet liable to take . . . chances on the same grounds?"

Remaining polite but clearly outraged at the miscarriage of justice, Riel went on to denounce the social and economic class system that perpetuated continued white exploitation of other races, and even other whites. Broadwater and Company's influence was so great as to be "obnoxious in proportion"; the U.S. marshal, whom Riel had notified of the illegal liquor trade, he suspected of having taken bribes from the company; traders, out of Broadwater's control, dealt dishonestly in "intoxicating liquor and trickery . . . throw[ing] [the Métis] into demoralization and poverty;" and, finally, the "big merchants" such as Broadwater himself were robber barons who kept "the poor citizen, who tries to start in business . . . under [their] thumb," and the laborer "under the mastership of all those influences mixed up together." Such, he wrote, was the sorry "mercantile atmosphere . . . from the Snowy Mountains to the international line."[29]

Riel was in this instance at least partly right. Many independent traders, like Sinclair's Old Piegan in *Raw Gold*, were tough, not very bright drunkards who lived from hand to mouth between traps and trades, whores and drinking sprees. They had colorful names like Slippery Kanouse and Liver-Eating Johnson, and were and are the kind of characters people love to invent stories about. "Dear Friend," began a probably apocryphal letter from a callous trader called Snookum Jim: "My partner Will Geary got to putting on airs and I shot him and he is dead—the potatoes are looking well."[30]

Andrew Garcia, floating through his "melting pot of hell," tells more credible tales. Garcia described life with his partner, Beaver Tom, with a mixture of revulsion and sympathy. Partner and camp both smelled "like a slaughterhouse," noted Garcia, who, from the looks of his own sartorial state, must have been pretty hard to disgust. If the smell failed to dull the appetite, there was always the food. Beaver Tom's "ideas of cooking were simple; he put large chunks of buffalo meat or venison on sharp sticks around close to the coals and fire. After they cooked a while, he would cut off a place which was half raw and eat it like a hungry dog." Beaver Tom's code of ethics was a lot like his cooking. It was a hard, risky, isolating way to make a living, a life in which "a man soon forgot his father and mother, and even his God." Upon returning to the trading post, where he was at the complete mercy of the trader and his unfair prices, he understandably, or so thought Garcia, spent everything "for the vilest kind of whiskey." Small-time operators such as these had little power against the big traders. At the same time, many borderland traders belied the stereotype. James Willard Schultz, for example, who derided the Métis, was an intellectual who sympathized with the Indians and married into the Blackfoot tribe. One Mounted Police officer, Sir Cecil Denny, attested that the police found American traders to be "a very decent lot of men in spite of all we had heard against them."[31]

Even so, the strains in the whiskey trade in medicine line country were felt not just along the fault line of class, dividing whites and natives, but in the stresses of nationalist allegiance that erupted in the Cypress Hills Massacre. The Cypress Hills propaganda had a long precedent. Since the first loyalists fled to Canada to escape the American revolutionaries, Canadians have by turns been critical of the United States' form of government. The Civil War illustrated for many late-nineteenth-century Canadians the dangers of American popular sovereignty—in their view a credo of excessive individualism that ultimately endangered liberty through sectional strife and a weak central government. The threat of American encroachment and ultimately of Canadian annexation was a recurring concern. The Fenian Brotherhood, the organization of displaced Irishmen, used the United States as a friendly base for violent raids on Canada. And Britain, after all, had granted Canada dominion status in 1867 largely because it believed annexation to the United States was highly likely, and regarded British military support against such an invasion a poor trade for Canada's small market for British goods. During the 1870s, the government of John A. Macdonald was protectionist and defensive toward the United States, led by a vision that "Canada is for Canadians," by which Macdonald meant workers in an industrialized Canada with factories and an international railroad, not perpetual colonials doomed to remain "hewers of wood and drawers of water."[32] Canadian journalists at the time, as well as later popularizers such as Sinclair, liked to suggest that the borderland's whiskey traders were all American low-lifes. Canada Firsters, supporters of Canada's fledgling nationalist movement of the 1870s, fed in part on anti-American sentiment.

By the early 1870s, however, it also became apparent that Canadians had more to worry about than pesky Americans on the outer frontier. Explosive tensions within Canada required a strong hand as well. The transition to Canadian nationhood was far from tranquil. Political and religious violence were common occurrences even in the East and would undoubtedly increase, thought Macdonald's advisors, as settlement encroached onto native lands farther west. Local police and militia had performed miserably in Manitoba, where ethnic tensions between Métis and whites remained unresolved, and the earlier failures of Hudson's Bay Company courts and police in Rupert's Land further encouraged reversion to the British colonial model successful in India, Ireland, Australia and elsewhere. The Mounted Police, then, were progenitors, not products, of "peace, order, and good government," the motto enshrined in the British North America Act.[33]

In the midst of these national antagonisms, what was the role of native peoples in the liquor trade? In Sinclair's sketch, and in the entire 311 pages of *Raw Gold*, they are conspicuously absent. One hesitates to dignify the liquor sold to Indians with the word *whiskey*, a mixture called "the Paralyser" that would gag a hyena: one quart of alcohol, one pound of over-ripe black chewing tobacco, one large handful of red peppers, one bottle of Jamaica ginger (or, failing that, a bottle of mare's sweat), one quart of black molasses or red ink, poured slowly, and water (to taste). Some Indians and Métis, such as Louis Riel, opposed the liquor trade as a scourge, and there is evidence that a number of Indian leaders concurred. "[A]t times, ignoring the commands of their chiefs," recalled trader Schultz, Crees and "Riel's Red River mixed bloods" would "come in to camp close to us, trade their robes for *uskiti waubu*, 'fire water,' and have a grand spree."[34] Most sources suggest that those on the spree outnumbered those opposed. During bad times, people would find their deadly medicine.

Old Piegan and his kind may even have had a place in Indian hagiography. Anthropologist John G. Carter saw as much in a mural he found on the ceiling of St. Paul's mission at the Fort Belknap reservation, Montana, a few miles from Chinook, in 1909. An Indian Michelangelo had left a florid testament: "Heaven is near the altar," Carter wrote, "and consists of God sitting on some very pink clouds, and looking like the old family Doctor of years gone by. Surrounding God are a number of bearded white men wearing black stetson hats, who look like whiskey traders. These are the elect. Toward the door of the church is hell. It is full to running over with Indians, who all look very uncomfortable, and gaze upward with envy in their glances to the happy booze runners sitting on the pink clouds and enjoying the society of the Creator of the Universe."[35]

The painting may have been an outburst of sardonic humor on the part of the artists, but there was some truth to this painter's universe. Sources from the period suggest that many Indians, like many whites, drank heavily. "An Injun will go to hell twice every day and three times in the night, for or to get whiskey," declared Andrew Garcia. His description of a band of drunk Piegan (eagerly joined by the non-Indians of his own camp) pursuing libations after a visit from six white whiskey traders has Garcia's signature wit: "Never was a healthful and life-giving rainstorm in the deserts received with greater joy and acclaim, or licked up quicker by the parched burning sands of Arabia than when that bunch of Injun found out they could get all the whiskey they wanted." Health and life, Garcia knew, were precisely what whiskey took away. His friend Mexican Pete reported that the Piegan had virtually cleaned themselves out of worldly goods in exchange for the traders' liquor. At least one of them, however, did not approve. In-who-lise, Garcia's Nez Percé wife-to-be, did not imbibe, and was both disgusted by and jealous of Garcia's affections when two Piegan women who had been traveling with their camp returned from the party and collapsed in a drunken stupor on Garcia's buffalo robes. When Garcia asked her to move them, she snapped at him, he recalled, "snorting like a mad buffalo": "'Does An-ta-lee think I would put my hands on his drunken hussies? No, I would rather stick my knife in them.'"[36]

Often in such accounts, drinking fostered acts of violence, to no surprise. Schultz recalled an Indian who killed a Métis in a "drunken row," and a drunken Cree who abducted an Indian woman. How often, one wonders, did such outbursts occur? One reads of drunken Indian orgies that erupted in violence—eighty-eight northern Blackfeet killed in drunken brawls in 1871, thirty-two Piegan in 1873, likewise seventy Blood killed in drunken fights by their own relatives. The Blackfeet agent in Montana estimated that six hundred barrels of liquor were traded to the Blackfoot in 1873, and that in the six previous years 25 percent of the members of these tribes died from the effects of liquor, some by violence, others frozen to death travel-ing between the whiskey fort and home. This is not to say Northern Plains Indians were incapable of peaceful imbibing. Schultz described a scene among Cree and Métis that the participants at a college fraternity party might envy: how "strange it was," he wrote, "a thousand Indians, men and women, drinking, chatting, singing, dancing around their evening fires, and quarreling not at all. All winter long we had no trouble," save the above-mentioned abduction.[37]

With such spotty and varied evidence, the effects of alcohol on the Northern Plains tribes are difficult to measure. Alcohol was in part a refuge from physical and cultural assault. Like disease, intertribal enmity, and the scarcity of game, liquor played an important role in creating the medicine line. Alcohol weakened Indian independence and resistance to the white onslaught, and turned natives toward whichever side of the boundary offered them protection. Just as Canada became a refuge from American captivity for the Sioux, for the Blackfoot and others it became a refuge from American whiskey. When the Methodist missionary John McDougall brought the news of a new mounted police force to Canadian Blackfoot chief Crowfoot in 1874, he related the chief's grateful response to a friend: "If left to ourselves we are gone," Crowfoot said. Whiskey "is fast killing us off" and "[we are] totally unable to resist the temptation to drink. . . . Our horses, Buffalo robes, and other articles of trade go for whiskey," he lament-ed, and "a large number of our people have killed one another and perished in various ways under the influence, and now that we hear of our Great Mother sending her soldiers into our country for our good we are glad." As the Mounted Police reduced the liquor traffic, Blackfoot society improved. Not until 1879, desperate for food and pursuing buffalo south across the boundary into Montana between the Bear Paws and the Little Rocky Mountains, did Crowfoot's band return to the bad old days of the liquor trade with their drunken orgies and violence. Frustrated and ignored by his own warrior elite, Crowfoot could not wait to recross the medicine line to the Queen's land.[38] No surprise, then, that soon after the surveyors came, the natives of the northern plains began to regard the boundary as the "medicine line," a thing with magical political power.

They first named it the "medicine road." Captain William F. Butler, an Irishman in the British military with a passion for the land and an astute and vivid writer of the time, commented on the beauty of such native terms. "To tell the Indian title of such things is generally to tell the nature of them also," he wrote of his travels through western Canada in 1869. Butler's book, *The Great Lone Land*, is a classic of the western prairies, and his is an apt description of the term "medicine road," or in Sioux, *"pejuta canku."* It is a poetic phrase. The word *medicine* among Northern Plains tribes applied to objects supposed to have magical influence or mysterious power. Not far south of the line the "Medicine River" (probably the Marias) entered the Missouri River just above its great waterfall near present-day Great Falls, Montana—so named, speculated Lewis and Clark in 1805, "from this unaccountable rumbling sound, which like all unaccountable things with the Indians of the Missouri is called *Medicine*." Nearby was the "medicine stone," a "large, naked, insulating rock," noted the James expedition in 1823, that aided the Gros Ventre in "propitiating their Man-ho-pa or Great Spirit." The border was medicine; it had power. It was also a "road" or "way." While a line is a mapmaker's abstraction, an inert barrier, a road is the path of something living. For whites, the line was a frontier in the European sense, a way of establishing the law, where one declared and fortified one's political identity. For natives, by contrast, the line was an instrument of camouflage, a stay against the erosion of life that had begun decades earlier.[39]

It is unclear, and probably unrecorded, when the terms "medicine road" and "medicine line" first appeared or came to mean the same thing or who coined them. In 1880, the Mountie L. N. F. Crozier wrote, "Now [the Indians] call the boundary the 'Medicine Line,' because no matter what they have done upon one side they feel perfectly secure after having arrived upon the other." Mounted Policeman James Walsh, who figures prominently in this early borderland story, recalled it occurring frequently in conversations with the Sioux in the late 1870s. The term "medicine line" probably originated in the East. The Iroquois of Ontario and upstate New York have used it, perhaps for centuries. According to one Mohawk scholar, "the term is used colloquially by the Old Ones." He has heard the elders of the Iroquois Confederacy "talk about the 'medicine line'" created during the Seven Years' War in the 1760s, when one group of Mohawk tried to persuade another group of Mohawk to rejoin the confederacy. They promised to police this line in order to prevent the whites from warring with each other, and represented the medicine line on their wampum belts as a white line between two black lines. Another Indian scholar and Ashinabe Indian of southern Ontario (a group including Ojibwa, Potawatomi, and Ottawa peoples) has heard old stories passed down describing the boundary that divided the United States from Canada along the Great Lakes after American independence "as an 'invisible or medicine' line that artificially divided their territories." In his view, as "the boundary stretched westward the concept traveled with it." Although the Ashinabe speak an Algonkian language, unlike the Sioux, the western Sioux and Iroquois both speak Macro-Siouan languages, making such a connection even more likely.[40]

Though many plains tribes found refuge and power in the medicine line, others were nostalgic for the pre-medicine-line prairie. Iron Horn, a man older than Robert Higheagle, fondly remembered a different world. As a northern Assiniboine born about 1840, Iron Horn recalled an itinerant childhood unmindful of the international border: "We wintered on the other side of the Little Rocky Mountains and in the spring moved up to Maple Creek," a habit that in the 1880s almost left the northern Assiniboine, as it did the Montana Cree, a tribe without a country. Indians crossed and recrossed the international boundary, often without giving it a thought. "The great spirit makes no lines," an Oglala called The Hero once said. "The meat of the buffalo tastes the same on both sides of the border."[41] To the Métis, too, as Joseph Kinsey Howard noted, Mr. Twining's boundary was absurd. Their buffalo hunt ignored the line. So did their Catholic missionaries. Trails, rivers, and trade ran efficiently north-south—in the east from Winnipeg down to Pembina (near the border) and St. Paul, and in the west between Fort Benton and Fort Walsh (in southwestern Saskatchewan's Cypress Hills) and Macleod (in present-day Alberta.) Métis citizenship was dual, uncertain, or disregarded entirely, a state of affairs that led one Indian agent in frustration to denounce the Métis as those "Mississippi demi-civilized Canadian mongrel English-American citizens." They seemed to know exactly who they were without benefit of the 49th parallel. Others looked to the future, imagining that one day the thinning buffalo herds would reemerge in huge numbers from the Cypress Hills and the white people would vanish like a bad dream. No medicine line, no need for one.[42]

In the meantime, many natives recognized that the medicine line marked off new politics and that they must use it to what advantage they could. Cross this line, as Robert Higheagle remembered, and one's powers and status changed. One writer put it succinctly: "The Indians . . . called the International Boundary the 'Medicine Line,' assuming that in the absence of any agreement between the two Governments relative to crime, they were perfectly safe on one side of the line with regard to what had been done on the other." Whether the Indians were "very well pleased" with this condition of affairs, as another commentator glibly noted, depended of course, on what advantage they could gain. By the late 1870s, the American side meant exposure, pursuit, and captivity; the Canadian, sanctuary. Cross the line into the Great Mother's country, and there was still hope of living as hunters rather than the hunted. "You are altogether different," added Higheagle. "On one side you are perfectly free to do as you please. On the other you are in danger."[43] Sitting Bull, who led Robert Higheagle's people north across the medicine line in 1877, understood that better than anyone.

SANCTUARY

The women, it turned out, thought of seeking sanctuary first. By sundown on the first day of the attack they began taking down tepees and packing for flight. Their camp stretched along the west bank of Greasy Grass Creek in south-central Montana, probably the largest off-reservation gathering of Indians ever seen. It looked like "maggots on a carcass," said Kill Eagle, a Blackfeet Sioux. The Blackfeet, Hunkpapa, Oglala, Sans Arcs, Brulé, and Miniconjou—six groups of Sioux—and the Cheyenne were strung together like the segments of a caterpillar. At around noon on June 25, 1876, the advance of Lieutenant General George Armstrong Custer's Seventh Cavalry took them by surprise.

They all remembered what they were doing when the Battle of the Greasy Grass, known to whites as the Battle of Little Bighorn, began. Moving Robe, a twenty-three-year-old Hunkpapa, was digging for wild turnips with a group of women on a hill. They saw the soldiers first. (She grabbed a revolver and rode her horse into the battle, shooting one soldier and hacking another to death with her knife, later saying, "I was a woman, but I was not afraid.") The wife of Spotted Horn Bull, Sitting Bull's cousin, was preparing buffalo meat. Oglala holy man Black Elk, a slight boy of thirteen, was swimming and playing with friends in the Greasy Grass, feeling "queer," he remembered, "as if something terrible was going to happen." Wooden Leg, a Cheyenne warrior, napped beneath a willow tree. Suddenly, "the squaws were like flying birds," recalled Sitting Bull, "the bullets were like humming bees." By dusk the women and children were moving camp, and by morning they had crossed Greasy Grass Creek, beyond the sound of gunfire, where groups of warriors began to join them. Their annihilation of Custer's forces that day and the next is the most famous defeat of the U.S. Army in the history of the West. It is the most famous Indian military victory. It was also, for the last roaming tribes, the beginning of the end of freedom. "We kept moving all summer," a man named Red Horse recalled, "the troops being always after us."[1]

The Indians had seen this coming. The Sioux and the United States were both expanding their territories. The Sioux had been moving ever since many of them left the Great Lakes region for the plains in the late eighteenth century, and the United States had been pursuing the relentless westward migration that poured across the western plains beginning in the 1840s. They fought bloody battles throughout the 1850s and '60s and made treaties at Fort Laramie on the North Platte River—in 1851 to control intertribal warfare and protect westering whites, and in 1868 to create a "Great Sioux Reservation" out of what later became South Dakota, with additonal hunting grounds west in the Yellowstone and Powder River country of present-day Montana and Wyoming. At the same time, in 1869, the Grant administration formed an idealistic Indian Peace Commission just as determined to turn the Plains Indians into crop-growing Christians as the U.S. Army was to round them up or kill them. Even in the 1870s, many Indians disregarded the treaties entirely, especially the young hotheaded ones and those most resistant to change. The Sioux still pushed westward, gaining turf from the Crow. Faced with a choice of falling into the hands of earnest humanitarians or fighting and starving, many chose the latter.[2]

By the time Custer and the Seventh Cavalry arrived at the Greasy Grass, the Sioux were restive. In the summer of 1874, Custer himself had led an expedition of soldiers and miners into what the Indians called Paha Sapa, the Black Hills, which jut four thousand feet from the plains in what was then the western third of the Great Sioux Reservation, and they found there substantial gold deposits. "From the grass roots down it was 'pay dirt,'" announced the *Chicago Inter-Ocean*. White fortune seekers fueled by the depression of 1873 defied the treaty provisions, and the Sioux's young men, who regarded the hills as their reliable "food pack," or storehouse, "began to talk bad," as Sitting Bull put it, against the invaders.[3] Farther west, Sitting Bull was still preoccupied with fighting the Crow. The government had sent commissioners to purchase the Black Hills, and he refused even to meet with them and scorned other Sioux leaders who considered signing the agreement. Now the whites were infuriated. Fifteen thousand miners already in the Black Hills would not be denied. In December 1875, Grant's commissioner of Indian affairs sent the free-roaming bands an ultimatum: report to an agency by January 31, 1876, or face all-out war. "They wanted to give little and get much," noted Sitting Bull. [4]

The Battle of the Little Bighorn at the end of June was actually no contest. The Indians were still elated over a successful attack against General George Crook's forces on Rosebud Creek a week earlier, and although the cavalry held the element of surprise ("We thought we were whipped," Sitting Bull would later say), the Indian warriors outnumbered the soldiers three to one. The Indians fought "without discipline," said Kill Eagle, "like bees swarming out of a hive," and others recalled later that the dust and smoke reminded them of hell. They remembered that the soldiers fought like "a thousand devils" and were "brave and fearless," and that Sitting Bull never even saw Custer. In battle, they said, "Indians and whites were so mixed up that you could hardly tell anything," like "thousands of dogs might look if all of them were mixed together in a fight." Covered with white dust, in their confusion they killed and scalped one another by mistake. Nevertheless just as Sitting Bull had foreseen in a vision, the heedless "soldiers without ears" fell "upside-down into camp." None in Custer's immediate command survived. Black Elk, though sickened by the smell of blood, declared himself "a happy boy," but Chief Red Horse, who was digging turnips with the women when the attack began, said, "I don't like to talk about that fight. If I hear any of my people talking about it, I always move away."[5]

As shocked Americans absorbed the defeat that all but spoiled the nation's centennial, the veteran Civil War commanders Philip Sheridan and William Tecumseh Sherman, who now directed the war for the West, quickly reinforced General George Crook, General Alfred H. Terry, and Colonel John Gibbon, who had the Sioux at their backs. To salvage a mission that had quickly turned into a disaster, they sent Lieutenant Colonel Elwell S. Otis and the Twenty-second Infantry to the Dakota Territory, and Colonel Nelson Appleton Miles and the Fifth Infantry, celebrated Indian fighters in Texas, to the Yellowstone River.

Miles left Fort Leavenworth, Kansas, in July, exactly one week after news of Custer's death at the Little Bighorn, to supplement the nearly four thousand men under Generals Terry and Crook with four hundred more. In accordance with the Fort Laramie Treaty of 1868, Miles intended to move the free-roaming bands east to the Great Sioux Reservation, a condition Sitting Bull had never agreed to. Miles's unstated mission was to avenge Custer's death, to chase the Sioux into submission or sanctuary. Custer, the undisciplined and charismatic soldier who had always enjoyed himself too much the icon of the irrepressible, brazen American, remained so even now. He became the cause celebre that forced the Indians over the medicine line.[6]

Others, too, would seek sanctuary on the border. Like the Sioux, the Canadian Métis and the Nez Percé fled their homelands between 1877 and 1885. Usually these stories are told separately, tales from the disparate pasts of distinctive cultures. The Métis, particularly, are commonly presented as the peculiarly Canadian historical sore point of the prairie West. Yet these natives in varying degrees knew one other, conferred about their prospects as they crisscrossed the border, befriended and fought the same white traders and soldiers, and even sought refuge with one another. The medicine line was the thread that bound them together.[7]

After their victory at the Greasy Grass, the Sioux and Cheyenne spent a miserable fall and winter. Sitting Bull traveled the Sioux country, unwilling to join those Indians who had started to drift back to their agencies as soon as the wild plums began to ripen, intending instead to winter with his band in their hunting grounds along the Yellowstone and perhaps head north to Canada in the spring. Miles, Crook, and Terry chased them relentlessly. The Indians lived in constant fear of soldiers bursting in upon their villages. They lost food and supplies and people. At Slim Buttes, just north of the Black Hills, after General Crook's attack on scattered camps of Sioux on September 9, Sitting Bull had come upon the bodies of old women and children lying in the mud where they had been killed: a suckling child with its mother; a girl nine or ten years old, covered with hay; an old woman in a blue woolen dress; an infant, the child of Little Eagle's daughter, born and then dropped as the terrified mother fled. They had died inside the borders of the Great Sioux Reservation, on their way to surrender to U.S. agencies. Their mistake was to camp near soldiers short on rations. [8]

To compensate for this loss, some of Sitting Bull's young warriors stole forty-seven mules from an army wagon train. Some days later, they tried to seize supply wagons from Colonel Otis, who was on his way to meet Miles at Custer Creek, a Yellowstone tributary. Sitting Bull dictated a note to Otis that his interpreter, a mixed blood named John "Big Leggins" Bruguier, wrote in English. A courier left it on a stick within the colonel's sight. "I want to know what you are doing traveling on this road," it read. "You scare all the buffalo away. I want to hunt in this place. I want you to turn back from here. If you don't, I will fight you again." The message was partly a bluff. Unlike Crazy Horse, many Sioux were weary of fighting. Sitting Bull and several leaders of other bands met a few days later in his tepee and agreed to listen to what the soldiers had to say. On October 20, two emissaries met with Miles and arranged a conference for later that day. Sitting Bull and Nelson Miles would come together for the first time at Cedar Creek, near the Yellowstone River in east-central Montana Territory.[9]

The day was cold, the sky sullen. There was no snow. The men approached each other on foot. (Frederick Remington later painted them grandly on horses under a bright sun.) Sitting Bull and his retinue spread a buffalo robe on the flat plain and invited Miles to sit. Miles initially demurred, then sat or knelt opposite Sitting Bull. Big Leggins Brughiere sat between them, acting as interpreter. The wind was blowing. A handful of Indians sat around Sitting Bull, unarmed; both parties had agreed to leave weapons behind for the meeting. Sitting Bull was about five feet ten inches, in his mid-forties, shirtless, without feathers or ornaments, and wearing leggings, moccasins, a breechcloth, and a buffalo robe. He passed a peace pipe. Colonel Miles, a tall, mustached man in his late thirties with piercing blue eyes, wore a fur cap and a long coat trimmed with bear fur on the cuffs and collar. The Sioux dubbed him "Bearcoat."[10]

The atmosphere was tense. Two hundred mounted warriors stood on a hill a short distance behind the conferees. Miles's troops stood facing the warriors a short distance back, with cannon placed on another hilltop. Within the circle on the buffalo robe sat Sitting Bull's nephew White Bull, who suspected that Miles and his aides carried weapons. "I was looking for knives and pistols," he recalled. In fact, by Miles's own admission, the soldiers were indeed armed. Miles had had a foreboding dream the night before. ("I woke up with a shock as I seemed to have been struck directly in the forehead by a ball or some powerful instrument," he wrote his wife, Mary, "[and took] it as a warning from my guardian angel to avoid unnecessary danger.") Promises notwithstanding, he was taking no chances. The meeting soon resembled a game of chicken. The distant soldiers, whom a white observer described as "fidgety," were creeping outward, as if trying to surround the council. Sitting Bull ordered his warriors to do likewise. Miles asked Sitting Bull to order his men to group together. The chief said Miles should order his own men to bunch up first. Miles gave the order; Sitting Bull followed suit. After more volleying of challenges in this way, they seemed to agree to a stalemate. They resolved nothing but parted amicably.

When they met again the next day, however, like two gamecocks in a curious dance, their initial politeness had vanished. Tempers flared. In his autobiography, Miles claimed it was Sitting Bull who became enraged, revealing the Indian's uncivilized nature: "His whole manner appeared more like that of a wild beast than a human being . . . his jaws were closed tightly; his lips were compressed, and you could see his eyes glistening with the fire of savage hatred," Miles recalled. Indian sources claimed that it was Miles who had a belligerent attitude at the second meeting and lost his composure. "You are losing your temper," Sitting Bull said to the colonel. (He had just called Miles a liar for meeting him amicably one day and angrily the next.) "Let us dismiss the council."

When the meeting ended, the Indians set fire to the prairie, which they often did when annoyed. The soldiers, their "strong hearts [growing] weak as our thoughts flew back to the Custer massacre," as trumpeter Edwin M. Brown described it, retaliated with artillery. Despite their haunting thoughts, the soldiers seemed to have plenty of fighting spirit. In the confusion of the smoky air, a sergeant and his men came down a gully to scalp dead Indians they had fired on, only to find their own scouts, who had been returning from a reconnaissance mission. Such zeal, for which Miles was known, ultimately paid off. Casualties totaled two soldiers and perhaps five Sioux. But more important for the army's cause, some Sioux from the Miniconjou and Sans Arcs bands agreed to make peace with Miles. The Indians' motivations seemed clear. After signing the paper, a leader named Bull Ghost voiced what many of the Indians might have been thinking: "We have now agreed; when do we eat?"

Along with Crazy Horse and the Oglala farther south, Sitting Bull, Gall, and the other Hunkpapa continued to hunt for food. Temperatures plummeted. Miles found the cold "simply appalling." By November it was often ten degrees below zero, and by December thirty below, with a bitter wind. Miles, his men swaddled in heavy buffalo shoes and overcoats, continued to chase the Indians. After one attack, eleven Cheyenne babies froze in their mothers' arms.[11] At another point during the winter, Miles's lieutenant, Frank Baldwin, found a little howitzer tube and some solid shot at nearby Fort Peck. He used it to drive Sitting Bull's followers from their camp and managed to seize several hundred buffalo robes, tons of dried meat, and many of their animals. In mid-March, a sudden flood of the Missouri River washed away most of what Sitting Bull's camp had left. The time of reckoning had come. During the first week of May 1877, while Crazy Horse and 889 Sioux surrendered at Camp Robinson, Nebraska, Sitting Bull and about 1,000 destitute Sioux from some twenty different bands crossed the medicine line into present-day southern Saskatchewan, then part of the huge North-West Territories. "They are "hunting me," Sitting Bull lamented, "like wild animals seeking for my blood."[12]

That week, as spring began to tint the prairies green, Sitting Bull first met Inspector James "Bub" Walsh in the shallow valley of Frenchman's River (then called White Earth Creek or White Mud Creek), on the international border just east of the Cypress Hills. The Indians sometimes called it Shining River because its banks glistened with clay. Walsh was the official emissary for the Canadian government, sent to greet refugee bands as they crossed into Canadian territory. Anticipating refugees after Custer's defeat at the Little Bighorn, the Canadian Department of Justice had called Walsh back to duty from the spas of Hot Springs, Arkansas, where he had gone with his family to seek relief from a skin ailment. That May he found himself, in pleasant weather, setting out on horseback for the third time in six months from his post at Fort Walsh in the Cypress Hills, headed toward the "stone piles that mark the International line" to explain Canadian law to incoming Sioux.[13]

In contrast to Walsh's clear and straightforward task, Sitting Bull and his followers, like the other bands of refugee Sioux already arrived, were torn by mixed emotions as they entered Canada. They were more than a little reluctant to give up their old hunting grounds. They missed the many friends and relatives who had gone on to the U.S. reservations, some at Sitting Bull's suggestion. Hunting was becoming difficult as buffalo and ammunition grew scarce. They were exhausted from fighting, weary of being chased. They sought peace and rest, and were hopeful, as Sitting Bull said, of "gentle" treatment. "War," as one of them put it, "had made the children forget how to play."[14]

As was his custom, after his scouts and interpreters held some preliminary discussions with the Indians, Walsh rode nonchalantly into this emotionally unsettled Sioux camp at midday with just four constables and two scouts—one a man named Gabriel Solomon and the other the painstakingly loyal Louis Leveille, who considered himself Walsh's bodyguard. According to Walsh, Sitting Bull was astonished. "We were in the camp of Sitting Bull—the first time in his life that white men [much] less soldiers and Scouts, marched into his camp and settled themselves down as unconserned as if his camp were not present." "White men different from any I ever saw before," Walsh recalled the chief remarking the next morning; "bold and fearless . . . they plant their lodge by the side of mine and defy me—have I fallen, is my reign at an end[?]"[15]

With typical immodesty, Walsh suggested that he performed his duty with whirlwind efficiency. He laid down the law to the Indians in Old Testament fashion. There would be no killing, no stealing, no injury of any kind to any person or property. Women and girls would be strictly protected. Raids south of the border with the intention of committing depredations would be deemed just as serious. If the Indians had any qualms about following these laws, they should turn back now; if they obeyed them, they were welcome to sanctuary. Without these laws, Walsh cautioned, "you cannot live on British soil—no more than fish can live without water." Nonetheless, Walsh advised them that Americans were not as bad as they believed and that they should consider turning back.[16]

As a demonstration of his sincerity and the seriousness of Canadian law, Walsh publicly threatened to arrest White Dog, an American Assiniboine who had the misfortune of arriving in the middle of Walsh's visit leading three horses belonging to the local Catholic priest. In a circle of fifty or sixty warriors, Walsh, who spoke Assiniboine, rattled a pair of leg irons at White Dog, demanding that he explain the presence of the stolen horses or be shackled and taken to Fort Walsh. White Dog played innocent, saying that he had found the horses wandering on the prairie and had intended to keep them in camp until the owner called for them. Walsh, intending the incident as an object lesson, warned him to "never again . . . molest property . . . north of the line." Not wanting to appear submissive, White Dog threatened Walsh, but was immediately forced to back down. "In 24 hours after they had entered Canada," Walsh noted proudly, "they witnessed British law at work."

Miles had fought his way into the military elite in search of his own past. Page nineteen of his first memoir (he wrote two, a tribute to his talent for self-promotion) shows an engraving of Miles Standish, the first Indian fighter in the "advancing wave of civilization," who fought not for conquest but for the higher aim of finding haven from oppression. The verso page shows a similar engraving of the author's father, Daniel Miles, proud descendant of a leader of colonial forces against the Indians in King Philip's War and of two soldiers of the American Revolution. From these two pages shine the values and ambitions Nelson Miles was to pursue throughout his life. Fireside stories of the "lofty patriotism" of his ancestors inspired him. Vigorous outdoor activity sustained him. He would become an Indian fighter.

His timing was good. Miles was born in 1839, four months before his more famous friend, George Armstrong Custer. He was twenty-one when the Civil War began. Raised on a farm outside Westminster, Massachusetts, he was well versed in outdoor skills. Beyond this, however, Miles's résumé as an aspiring military commander became more unorthodox. Unlike Custer, he did not attend West Point, which his family could not afford. He spent five years in Boston as a clerk in Collomare's Crockery Store studying business and, when the political horizon grew stormy, absorbing military history and tactics. He frequented the city's lecture halls and learned drills and discipline in his free time from an old French colonel.

When the war began, Miles felt the shortcomings of his background. He recruited his own company using family and borrowed money, only to have the governor of Massachusetts deny him its captaincy in favor of a political friend. "I, therefore, began my military service as a captain reduced to a first lieutenant," Miles recalled with some bitterness. What others regarded as impertinence, egotism, bad grace, or even foolhardiness— "That officer will get promoted or get killed," commented one Civil War general after watching Miles climb a tree to view the defenses at Richmond—Miles considered his only means for advancement. He volunteered for dangerous tasks. He gave superior officers unsolicited advice. He hurried his recuperation from injuries. He exploited every chance to promote himself. And it worked. He achieved the rank of major general by the war's end, commander of twenty-six thousand officers and men at age twenty-six, a record of rapid promotion and youthful success that only the more politically advantaged Custer could equal.[17] In 1869, assigned to command the Fifth United States Infantry, stationed at Fort Hays, Kansas, he at last had a part in what he called "the battle of civilization." In that role Miles proved exceptionally able. "[His] spirit of adventure is very strong within him," the war correspondent for the *Chicago Times* wrote of Miles; he gave the impression of being "creditably ambitious and boiling with native courage."[18] The drive and self-confidence of the self-made soldier is evident in his photographs. His gaze is intense, magnetic, charismatic.

General Nelson Appleton Miles or "Bearcoat," age 37, in 1876.
Photo courtesy Montana Historical Society.

Biographers and historians universally acknowledge Miles as a brilliant field tactician, an inspiring leader, a keen judge of character, and an able negotiator with the enemy. But regarding his personality they disagree, not about the fact that there was something unorthodox about Miles, but about exactly what shape it took. President Harrison thought him a "troublesome man," "disobedient," who "made difficulties."[19] Theodore Roosevelt, who lost no love for the man, called him a "brave peacock." Others, such as Robert Utley, simply attribute Miles's controversial side to his "less attractive traits rooted in vanity and ambition," traits arguably in the psychological profile of most strong leaders.[20]

When Miles set out for medicine line country from Fort Leavenworth in 1876 with six companies of the Fifth U.S. Infantry Regiment, assigned to force the Sioux onto reservations and repair the moral and military rent that Custer's annihilation at Little Bighorn had caused, we might well wonder what aims and assumptions he carried with him. Both the southern and northern plains were powder kegs of Indian resistance. American officials acknowledged their peace policy to be a dangerous farce. Miles thus willingly entered a campaign conceived by Generals Sherman and Sheridan as "total war," reminiscent of their Civil War strategies against the South. As Sitting Bull knew, surprise attacks on villages that included sleeping women and children was its main tactic. When the men of the Fifth hoisted their haversacks onto the train for Montana that humid July day singing "Sherman's March to the Sea", Miles was to raise the fallen guidon in a ruthless war, a job in which any feeling for native peoples would have little place.[21]

Although he later professed sympathy toward the Indians that far exceeded Custer's, and was reluctant to initiate violence at Wounded Knee and in the Spanish-American War, Miles embraced the use of force against the Sioux with enthusiasm. His tendency toward a creative and headstrong style of command set a standard of aggression for the campaign. He was determined to "follow the Indians as long as possible," even to their retreats "where they think we can not go," he wrote his wife, Mary. "It is only in that way that we can convince them of our power to subjugate them finally." Miles was tempted to kill Sitting Bull on at least one occasion, writing his wife that he passed up the opportunity because "that would have been vio-

General Nelson A. Miles, center, and officers of the United States Fifth Infantry, prepared to chase the Sioux in twenty-below-zero weather on the plains of Montana, 1877. Photo courtesy U.S. National Archives and Records Administration.

THE MEDICINE LINE

lating a flag of truce and the whole civilized world would have denounced it." Miles gladly would have ignored the boundary on many occasions, calling it "one of the troubles of this business." He employed a stunningly successful network of Indian and white civilian scouts, whose spying outraged Sitting Bull. He designed special cold-weather gear, including buffalo robe coats, leggings, and mittens as well as face masks cut from woolen blankets, so his troops could withstand an active winter of Indian pursuit in subzero temperatures, an activity Miles likened to the "condition of a ship in northern latitudes" tracking icebergs in a dense fog.[22]

Yet Indians were once noble characters, according to Miles. Indeed, they were natural democrats who "respected" and "duly ascertained . . . the opinions, the wishes, the rights and interests of the majority and minority" of their race. American virtue, he believed, was not the innate quality of its white citizens. It was environmental or "atmospher[ic]," an intangible "something" in the physical place of the American continent itself that inspired a respect for natural rights. Sounding like a bad rendition of a James Fenimore Cooper novel, Miles would tell his readers that even the most "stoical savage . . . standing amid the primeval forest, or on the west of some butte towering above the prairie," inhaled democracy in a seemingly enchanted atmosphere. The Indians of Miles's memoir were intelligent and complex human beings governed by "the same motives and impulses that sway people everywhere"; they were victims of history, he warranted, provoked to violence by white invasion.[23]

Later in his career, after attaining his military ambitions, Miles became an outspoken critic of unnecessary aggression. During the Sioux conflict, Miles at least once gave his troops "explicit instructions to prevent firing upon women and children."[24] But in 1878 Miles's admiration for Indians was at odds with his ambitions and his vision of American expansion. Friendliness toward the Sioux was the road to neither personal advancement nor, in his view, national progress. In later years, never was Miles more proud than when referring to his conquest of the Sioux. Even in his second memoir, published in 1911, the glory had not faded enough to prevent his reprinting in their entirety the letters Generals Sheridan and Sherman wrote commending his actions.[25]

James Walsh of the Mounted Police was in many ways similar to Nelson Miles. Like Miles, he resisted bureaucracy and orthodoxy with creative panache. At times he held his superiors in disdain, and he had a zest for bravado and histrionics. Walsh was in his mid-thirties, four years Miles's junior, a lean man of medium height, driven, bold, extremely athletic, and capable of extreme temper or coolness. Walsh's unregimented Mountie was a match to Miles's unorthodox general. His sartorial flair rivaled Custer's. A fringed buckskin suit, a long sword (hence his Indian

North-West Mounted Police Inspector James Morrow Walsh or "Long Lance," Sitting Bull's Canadian confidant among officials, in non-regulation dress.
Photo courtesy Saskatchewan Archives Board, Regina, Saskatchewan.

name, Long Lance), and a rakishly cocked old army hat banded with a long cloth constituted his sometime field attire. He was a picture of individuality in a culture that revered authority. Yet, mysteriously to American observers, his authority was uncompromised.

Like Miles, as a young man Walsh had cast about for adventure. The eldest of nine children, son of a ship's carpenter from a town on the St. Lawrence River, he had a varied career as a machinist, railroad man, dry-goods clerk, stockbroker, hotel keeper, athlete, fire captain, and cavalry officer. Unlike Miles, he had formal military training at the Kingston Military School, where he garnered highest honors in gunnery and cavalry classes. Having tasted excitement in the militia against the Fenian raid by Irish Americans in 1866 (the same attack that tarnished surveyor John Dennis's careeer), impatient for a life of action, Walsh was among the first to enlist in the North-West Mounted Police upon its creation in 1873. He was given the dual rank of superintendent and subinspector (later changed to inspector) and sent out to recruit Ontarian "men of sound constitution." The 1873–74 recruits were overwhelmingly Canadian; out of nearly four hundred men, sixteen were from Ireland, eleven from England, a handful from Scotland, France, Italy, and Germany, and five from the United States. But in other respects the force displayed a strong British influence. Walsh's D troop of about fifty men, one of six such troops, was organized like British cavalry regiments.

Such was the mixture of Old and New Worlds that Walsh accompanied as adjutant and riding master on the force's march west in the fall of 1874. Called the Long March, it was a disastrous ordeal—not surprising, as one officer put it, for a group "with such complete faith in themselves and such utter ignorance of what they were undertaking." In a climate that could easily kill them all, their saving grace was adaptability. Only with the aid of the whiskey traders they had come to suppress did the Mounties manage to establish four posts by the summer of 1875, one of them, in the Cypress Hills, named for James M. Walsh himself.[26]

Like Miles, Walsh greatly admired Indians. He found them a "very intelligent people possessing a strong sence of justice and very capable of judging between right and wrong, truthful and honorable, faithful as a friend." His affinity, however, extended beyond admiration. Walsh believed that he was defending the Sioux against what he assumed was American hatred, misunderstanding, "tyranny and coersion." "On the U.S. side there were numbers[;] on [Sitting] Bull's side there were principles," Walsh stated bluntly. The Canadian police, he added, "were sent into the country to conquer it but not with bullets but with justice." The force, he argued, regarded Indians "as men with natural rights and not an article of game to shoot at for amusement." "I now have read Mr. Finertys' book," he later wrote of the *Chicago Times* reporter's *War-Path and Bivouac*, hot off the press in 1890, and "am now going to tell you what I know of the yet unwritten history of these people who I shall not call as Mr. Finnerty does infernal devils—it was this unkind feeling that so many American[s] entertained towards the Indians, that forced them in self defence to act like devils . . . feelings towards men, that only wished or asked to maintain the freedom that nature gives as a right—to every man."[27]

Walsh was smitten with a romantic vision of Native Americans. If Miles revealed his sense of American identity with windy passages about Puritan morals and Manifest Destiny, Walsh spoke lyrically in the romantic language of the British empire:

> [A]bout 10 a.m. the next day a most beautiful morning—nature appeared to be out in her best form—thousands of horses feeding on the green spring grass—Indian warriors sitting in groups on the little hill tops—hansomly and picturesque dressed maidens moveing about with all the grace of princesses. Women arranging their lodges—children amusing themselves with bow and arrow—old men lounging in the shade discussing the situation the whole a picture as beautiful as it is posible for words to paint—away down the Silent Valley we hear

the Indian war whoop coming you would think from a thousand voices . . . and a grand spectacle appears moving along the winding stream two hundred warriors in paint and feathers headed by the war chief 'Black Horse' accompanied by 'Medicine Bear' and the 4 Teton messengers—This increased the grandure of the picture. Marching along the green grassed valley hawks 300 feet high the stream tinged with rose blushes and willows hillocks ornamented by Indian maidens dressed in bright colours 300 braves with prancing studs, plumes flying high in the air marching like conquering heroes. It reminded us of the tales of atilla and his huns . . . we could not help recognizing the Romance and the strange beauty of the whole scene.[28]

Walsh was an eminently practical man, but his mental borderland was a place of fading grandeur. Canadians have never wholeheartedly taken the idea of a character-building frontier as their own. Their "metropolitan" thesis plants the significance of the frontier squarely in the cities and their economic domination of the countryside (an idea that American historians, grown skeptical of holy nationalism, have found an attractive alternative.) Thus Walsh lacked what Miles was raised on: an American literary and historical tradition devoted to revealing the myths and symbols of a prophetic American errand into the wilderness. Canadians, by contrast, have sought to present Canada as "a country without a mythology."[29]

The practice of Canadian Indian policy in the 1870s suited Walsh to a T. Under the Indian Act of 1876, a consolidation of laws that has no parallel in the United States, the Canadian government's goals were essentially the same as those of the United States: to protect and control Indian reserves and virtually all aspects of Indian life, and to advance Indian assimilation through the ownership of private property, the practice of agriculture, sobriety, and the franchise—in short, to "train them for a more civilized life," as a member of the House of Commons put it. The Canadian enforcement of this policy through the Mounted Police and the Department of Indian Affairs had its good and bad points. Its officials were less corrupt than those of the U.S. Bureau of Indian Affairs, more gradual in implementing their goals, clearer in their definition of who was Indian. They were also at times neglectful of their wards through inertia, conservatism, or deliberate action. For Walsh, the imperative to control and civilize Indians simply was not as urgent on the northern side of the boundary as it was to the south. The "tide of immigration in Canada has not been as great as along our frontier," Miles observed in his memoirs. As a result, the Canadians "have been able to allow the Indians to live as Indians, which we have not, and do not attempt to force upon them the customs which to them are distasteful." In 1877, Walsh received a letter directing him to "cooperate with [U.S.] Commissioners

Mounted Police officer visiting with a Sioux woman, scout in background, 1878.
Photo courtesy National Archives of Canada.

[seeking the Sioux's return]," but not to "unduly press the Indians. Our action should be persuasive, not compulsory."[30]

From the Long March of 1874 until his resignation in 1883, Walsh was afforded the luxury of time and space; Canadian settlement was years behind the westering American throng. The effect was a far less aggressive military policy on the Canadian side of the border. As Sitting Bull well knew, Miles alone commanded more than four hundred men, a contingent larger than the entire North-West Mounted Police force, which totaled 335 in 1876 (slightly fewer in 1881), spread over the entire North-West Territories. In dealing with western tribes, Canadians viewed their small numbers as an advantage. For one thing, it distinguished them from Americans, allowing Canadians, in the words of governor-general Lord Dufferin, to "appear on the scene, not as the

Americans have done for the purpose of restraining and controlling the Indian tribes, but with a view of ameliorating injuries inflicted on the Red man by the white." Americans, everyone knew, were "abhorred by the whole Indian people," so it was wise to set Canadians apart at every opportunity. Walsh, too, though he cooperated with the Americans, warned that the Indians must not even "imagine that we are forming an alliance with the Americans," as it would "completely destroy our influence."[31]

Thus while Miles and Walsh had similar sympathies toward native peoples, their different circumstances determined their behavior toward them. Canadian policy would not allow persecution or demand capture or extradition of refugee tribes: "We might as well try to check the flight of locusts from the south or the rush of buffalo from the north," wrote Prime Minister Macdonald, superintendent general of Indian affairs from 1878 to 1895. "Humanity, as well as Policy, demands that the Indians of the North West should be allowed to hunt on both sides of the line," the secretary to the North-West Territories' governor general wrote to the Privy Council. Once this became clear, Walsh seemed the perfect man for the job. His unorthodox streak and affinity for Indians made him the refugee Sioux's closest white contact. At the same time, he read them the law with great seriousness. He regularly informed Miles of their whereabouts. He claimed to have encouraged them to return to the United States.[32]

By 1879, however, there was growing suspicion that Walsh had taken the Indians' part. The difference between Walsh and Miles in their relationship with the Sioux was never plainer, the meaning of the medicine line never more vivid, than in a meeting between the two in July of 1879. Miles was camped on the boundary. Walsh was wearing his buckskins. He and Miles chatted amiably in the colonel's tent. They discussed their strategic situation. Miles was eager to fight and said so. Walsh, marveled reporter Finerty, "paint[ed] the Sioux character in such glowing colors that . . . he might be suspected of consanguinity with the aborigines." When Walsh angered his superiors with unauthorized excesses regarding the Indians, it was for his affections rather than his aggressions: "Walsh undoubtedly has influence with 'Bull,'" Macdonald wrote to the governor general, "which he tried to monopolize in order to make himself of importance and is I fear primarily responsible for the Indians' unwillingness to leave Canada." Louis Riel claimed in 1879 that it was "generally known in this territory" that "major Walsh . . . takes advantage of the presence of Titons [Sioux] around him, both to gratify his national pretension that the english are good to indians while the americans are not; and to exaggerate his personal usefulness in the Northwest."[33]

At the same time, the Canadians were far from benevolent conquerors, as the native peoples have attested.[34] Riel was certainly critical of Walsh's claim to moral superiority, commenting that circumstances, not a more tolerant system, afforded the police a gentler conquest along the medicine line. The governor general of the North-West Territories, noted his secretary, could observe early in 1881 "with much regret that the American troops have been set in motion against several of the Bands," since it "has the effect of preventing an insignificant number of them, amongst whom is Sitting Bull, from immediately surrendering." Then fell the velvet hammer: "his surrender may be secured without bloodshed," the secretary continued, if only the United States could "be moved to prevent further measures of intimidation, leaving hunger to do the work."[35] Hunger soon complied, driving the Blackfoot, Cree, and other tribes to reservations as swiftly as bullets drove the Sioux and Nez Percé. If Canadian order was maintained with less violence, it could be, just as brutal.

As the Sioux weakened, Miles's aggression became increasingly gratuitous. "I tell you honestly," Walsh said to Miles in 1879, "the Sioux don't want to fight the white people any more." East of the White Mud at Poplar River in January 1881, on the American side of the line, the scene became poignant. The only Indian to raise a hand against Miles's troops was an old woman, Whirling Bear's sister. In grief or outrage she began firing arrows at the American soldiers, whom she had just seen kill three of her people, including one woman. The Sioux themselves stayed her hand. Three-fourths of the group surrendered, yielding less to the force of arms than to hunger.[36]

By late 1880, Walsh and Miles were gone. Walsh had become so sympathetic toward the Sioux that he seemed to represent them rather than the Canadian government. When he began planning to negotiate on the Indians' behalf in Washington and Ottawa, Prime Minister Macdonald saw that his usefulness had come to an end. Walsh was given extended leave in 1880 and forced to resign from the force in 1883. He eventually became reinstated as police superintendent of the Yukon District during the gold rush of 1898. Miles finally received his promotion, not without Sherman's resistance. "I have told him plainly that I know of no way to satisfy his ambitions," complained Sherman to Sheridan, "but to surrender to him absolute power over the whole Army, with President & Congress thrown in." Perhaps Sherman finally decided that the only way to remove Miles from the border was to make him a brigadier general. Dispatched to a higher command, Miles left the medicine line in late 1880, a few months before Sitting Bull surrendered.[37]

The Battle of the Little Bighorn had given Sitting Bull great notoriety. Before the battle, he was influential in drawing together an unusual coalition of tribes (hoping, as Wooden Leg put it, "that the combined camps would frighten off the soldiers" and leave the Indians "freed from their annoyance"), and at a sun dance three weeks before, when Jumping

Bull gouged fifty bits of flesh the size of a match head from each of Sitting Bull's arms in the ritual dance, Sitting Bull saw a vision of the battle. He also had an impeccable war record that was revered by his contemporaries. But he saw little military action at the Greasy Grass. ("If someone would lend him a heart," grumbled Oglala chief Low Dog, "he would fight.") He gave directions and charged himself with protecting the women and children.[38]

Nevertheless, in 1877 Sitting Bull was the one the journalists wanted to see. Reporters came to the medicine line to meet the famous Sioux, Custer's nemesis, "the most mysterious Indian chieftain who ever flourished in North America," the one, they told their readers, who held "the magic sway of a Mohammed over the rude war tribes that engirdle him." They sat across from him, enchanted by his charisma, rapt with his expression of "exquisite irony," admiring of his small but powerful hands. Was he the belligerent, conceited, and narrow-minded enemy of white progress? Was he a flexible, politically savvy leader? Since Sitting Bull himself wrote only a hieroglyphic autobiography—a few dozen simple figure drawings recording his exploits as a warrior—his qualities as leader and borderland strategist take shape in a cloudy tableau of secondhand portraits. He was one among many Sioux headmen, not always the most powerful. Indians respected him—as a warrior, as a spiritual man of inspiring character and wisdom, and as a leader of several elite men's societies, including one he founded called the White Horse Riders. "He had a big brain and a good one," said Wooden Leg, "a strong heart and a generous one."[39]

Among white Americans, he first became known as a determined patriot, as uncompromising as the Oglala Sioux leader Red Cloud was willing to negotiate. During his lifetime, Jerome Stillson and Charles Diehl, reporters for the New York Herald and the Chicago Times, respectively, rendered a relatively intelligent and principled Sitting Bull to a broad readership. But many contemporary journalists and popular writers, including the New York World reporter who described Sitting Bull's "Mephistophelian mouth," thoughtlessly perpetrated the image of the canny savage. James McGlaughlin, the agent at Standing Rock reservation, where Sitting Bull lived out the end of his life, prolonged this view. He found the Sioux headman "pompous, vain, and boastful." McGlaughlin's early autobiography, My Friend the Indian, further reduced the World journalist's canny savage to a man uniformly obstinate and belligerent with whites. Not until the 1930s did historian and ethnographer Walter Stanley Campbell, under the pen name Stanley Vestal, correct McGlaughlin's portrait. A great admirer of Plains Indian culture, Campbell interviewed Sitting Bull's closest compatriots in the 1920s and offered valuable insight into the Indian point of view. He gave us the gilded heroism of great Sioux warriors—figures whom he, a World War I veteran, found immensely

Sitting Bull in 1882, one year after his surrender at Fort Buford, Dakota Territory.
Photo courtesy U.S. National Archives and Records Administration.

appealing—and a Sitting Bull to match. Other writers have since supplied their readers with saintly Indian victims of white genocide. Historian Robert Utley has restored the balance in his well-researched biography, emphasizing a wise if weary leader's growing depression and describing how he faced the end of native nomadic life.[40]

While such portraits have their merits, none fully conveys the give-and-take along the borderland. Power still hung in the balance. Before Sitting Bull became the clearly unhappy man of July 20, 1881, when he surrendered his pony and gun to U.S. agents at Fort Buford, he spent several years as a strategist and negotiator, trying to improve his people's position in the complex political landscape of the medicine line. Even in James Walsh's self-congratulatory memoirs can be found a depiction of Sitting Bull as an intelligent, independent tactician and negotiator, trying to take full advantage of his situation. First, Walsh described the powerful aura of the man, what Walsh called "the love of free life that exists around Bull," which the Sioux leader used to arouse his forces. Sitting Bull's "unsettled camps keep up a constant friction amongst the Indians on both sides of the line," Walsh reported. Moreover, Walsh acknowledged that Sitting Bull had thoughtful, well-developed attitudes and plans. If he eventually became tractable to the Americans, it was not without a long and deliberate process of negotiation. "Permit me to explain how the change in this man and his followers was brought about," explained Walsh in 1880, seven months before Sitting Bull's surrender. "Sitting Bull is the shrewdest and most intelligent Indian living," Walsh wrote. He "has the ambition of Napoleon and is brave to a fault; he is respected as well as feared by every Indian on the plains. In war he has no equal, in council he is superior to all. Every word said by him carries weight, is quoted and passed from camp to camp." In his own tale, Walsh was still the hero, but here also was Sitting Bull's painstaking diplomacy, hardly the kind of protracted debate a "Mephistophelian" savage would demand. "Neither hunger nor prospective starvation in his camp at any time tended to effect it, as many persons imagine, but it was done by patient, hard work, days and nights of steady persuasion, argument, and illustration." [41]

Walsh's superior officer, Mounted Police assistant commissioner Lieutenant Colonel Acheson G. Irvine, corroborated Walsh's view of Sitting Bull as a sophisticated leader. Irvine came away from his first meeting with the Sioux leader greatly impressed, noting that Sitting Bull's speeches "showed him to be a man of wonderful capability," one who "knew his subject well, and who had thoroughly weighed it over before speaking."[42]

A recent tale by Canadian humorist and playwright Eric Nicol, published in 1989 as *Dickens of the Mounted*, the "letters" of Mountie Frank Dickens, portrays Sitting Bull in all his brilliance. In his reimagined universe of the Northern Plains, Nicol embellishes the Mounted Police career of the real Frank Dickens, third son of Charles, who came to Canada in 1874, a stammering, small, humorless, fair-skinned, and gloomy man with a taste for alcohol, a talent for ordinary prose, and a lifelong string of failures. "His misadventures," caustically notes the entry on Frank Dickens in the *Dictionary of Canadian Biography*, perhaps Nicol's inspiration, "contributed to the strong prejudice against English officers [among] the mounted police in the late nineteenth century. . . . He was partly responsible for the serious deterioration in relations between the NWMP and the Blackfoot in the 1880s" and "made a definite, if negative, impact on the Canadian West." Nicol has the hapless Dickens pulling on his boots and riding frantically across the plains to meet with the great Sioux leader, hoping to shed his life of mediocrity by cutting a deal that could change the course of events in western Canada. He enters the chief's lodge with his Métis interpreter Louis Leveille (another historical figure), is seated before the great man, and tells him with regret that "the law is the law" and the United States has a reservation that he must go to. At this, gazing at Dickens "as though we both knew that the Queen's law was something to be got around," Sitting Bull produces a dog-eared book and hands it to the Englishman—a cheap, pirated American edition of *Oliver Twist*, which falls open to a page marker. Dismayed, the great man's son reads aloud to the great man: "'If the law supposed that,' said Mr. Bumble . . . 'the law is a ass, a idiot.'"[43]

Dickens of the Mounted is now acknowledged as paperback fiction, but with good reason it rode the Canadian nonfiction best-seller list. Nicol liked to tell jokes, and what one writer recently called the "ideological limbo" that is Canadian national identity makes Canadians particularly receptive to joking, even about the kinds of stories Americans elevate into national drama. Even so, Nicol has the essentials and the spirit of the historical situation right. The Sioux were in fact close to Dickens's post at Fort Walsh in the Cypress Hills in June 1878. Buffalo and food were scarce; the Canadian government gave the Sioux ammunition for hunting, but no food, and the credit and goodwill of traders had nearly reached its limit. The Indians had just broken their camp farther east at Wood Mountain and scattered west across the country north of Fort Walsh, determined to, as Sitting Bull had once vowed, "send children to hunt and live on prairie mice" rather than surrender to become wards of the United States government. They had frequent contact with whites, and although Sitting Bull did not speak English, a copy of a Dickens novel could have changed hands. And finally, Sitting Bull was a nimble negotiator with great political sagacity and a wry sense of humor that could strip empire builders of their smug superiority. If Americans revere Crazy Horse and Sitting Bull as free, unrestricted men, it is not surprising that at least one of them should appear in Canadian literature as the joking deflator of grandiose, nation-building dreams.[44]

The real Sitting Bull also liked to tell jokes. According to his nephew One Bull, who repeated several of his uncle's jokes to Walter Stanley Campbell in the early 1930s, one went like this: A bunch of Indians were gathering at the Indian agency for rations when some white people from the neighboring towns came through for curiosity's sake and to do a little business. One white man, evidently a newcomer, drove over to see the natives. He hitched his team near where many Indians had likewise tied theirs, caught the eye of a passing Sioux policeman, and asked, "Chief, do you think my team and wagon are safe here?" The policeman looked care-fully around the premises and replied, "Yes, perfectly safe. There are no white people nearby."[45]

In a native culture that celebrated humor, Sitting Bull could joke about how difficult it was to take white society's law seriously. In another of Sitting Bull's stories, which One Bull also told to Walter Stanley Campbell, an eld-erly bachelor named Blue Thunder spent many moons wooing Rocky Butte, age seventy and a strong Christian. She finally consented to marry him, pro-vided he became a·Christian and married "in the lawful way" in church. Agreed at last, they marched to the altar in front of a large crowd. "Blue Thunder," queried the minister, "will you take this woman for your lawful wife?" "That's what she said," Blue Thunder replied. "Rocky Butte," contin-ued the minister, "will you take this Blue Thunder for your lawful husband?" "He surely had the hardest time trying to win me," she shot back in turn. "He said he'll talk himself to death if I don't marry him." Blue Thunder, for his part in the joke, makes it clear that the woman, not the law, is the authority responsible for his presence in the church that day. Rocky Butte, too, despite her religious conversion, makes the same joke. In the mock adversity of Blue Thunder and Rocky Butte's wedding vows, the law is an ass, honored in form but mocked in substance. Sitting Bull's jokes reveal a man neither too noble nor too primal, with human character—a man able to regard himself and those around him with some measure of understanding. In the diplomatic triangle between the United States, Canada, and the Sioux, Sitting Bull did not hesitate to use his keen sense of theater on his people's behalf.[46]

A time line of Sitting Bull's four years in Canada reads like a diplomat's wartime date book: frequent councils with the Mounted Police, particular-ly Walsh, his favorite; ongoing negotiations with his own followers and hot-headed young warriors, who occasionally required discipline; a reluctant council in Canada with the diplomatic envoy of Americans headed by General Terry, where he refused to shake hands, and where, after a long pause and much pipe smoking, he delivered a stinging rebuke; and several encounters or attempted alliances with the half dozen or more groups who had previously found the Sioux less than friendly, including the Nez Percé and two long-standing Sioux enemies, the Crow and the Blackfoot. By 1881, when these native alliances had come to nothing, Inspector Lief Crozier (Walsh's successor) anticipated open warfare between the Sioux and the Canadian Indians. "[They] say they will kill Sitting Bull if they have a chance," he noted. It was a complex borderland, demanding skill in both diplomacy and warfare. Starvation was not the only reason Sitting Bull crossed the medicine line for the last time.[47]

Despite the Indians' long odds, the Sioux thought Sitting Bull was a crackerjack negotiator. A Miniconjou Sioux once dispatched a two-page pictograph to the Cheyenne River Agency in Dakota Territory to inform agency Indians of their kinfolk's situation in Canada. In reality a political cartoon, it shows the American general Alfred H. Terry, after negotiations with Sitting Bull and his Sioux delegation, about to shoot himself and fall into a newly dug grave.[48] White journalists, too, kept Sitting Bull's notoriety alive. One reporter asked the exiled Sitting Bull to compare the "White Mother," Canada, to the "White Father," the United States.

"Have you an implacable enmity with the Americans?" the reporter asked; "[D]o you think you can only obtain peace here?"

"The White Mother is good," the chief replied.

"Better than the Great Father?"

"Hough!" the chief scoffed.

"Don't you see that you will probably have the same difficulty in Canada that you have had in the United States?" the reporter suggested.

"The White Mother does not lie," Sitting Bull said.[49]

Sitting Bull's dichotomy made a lasting impression. The story of the Sioux's flight to the north is still used to illustrate the Canadian government's relatively amicable relationship with native groups, in contrast to the United States' "reservation or extermination" policy of the late-nineteenth-century Plains Indian wars. Sitting Bull's descriptions upheld the broader and commonly held stereotypes of the two societies: the welcoming Canadian mosaic, a loose and sparsely populated allegiance of groups that tolerated differences (a notion Quebec has recently stretched to the breaking point), versus the violent and rapidly expanding American melting pot, which demanded assimilation. The North-West Mounted Police have long been the symbol of the benevolent authority of the Canadian frontier, just as the United States Army and the Texas Rangers have more recently served as symbols for a brutal, racist white conquest of the American West.[50]

Describing Canada as the benevolent "White Mother" and the United States as the evil "Great Father" was a memorable scheme. Yet it did not actually portray the situation in which Sitting Bull found himself in the late

1870s. The early Northern Plains borderland defied simple categories, as all sides engaged in some degree of diplomatic posturing and triangulation. The Americans pretended to welcome the Sioux back (with the exception of Nelson Miles, practically foaming at the mouth to follow his quarry across the border) but were actually happy to unload them onto the Canadians. The Canadians gingerly urged the Sioux to return south while trying not to get them riled up or appear too sympathetic toward the Americans, and at the same time, the Sioux worked whatever advantage they could to enhance their negotiations and obtain food. Transborder Blackfoot, Crow, Métis, Sioux, Nez Percé, and others flirted with various hostilities and alliances, as national differences along the medicine line grew out of particular circumstances rather than the absolutes of political and cultural traditions.[51]

The Métis, as much as the Sioux, were the quintessential product of circumstances, a kind of cultural, economic, and geographical third rail in Canadian politics. From their native and white heritages they had distilled a distinct social and religious culture, both Catholic and mystical. From the fur trade and the buffalo hunt they formed a third economic niche, as interpreters, guides, and hide and pemmican traders. From their eastern and western ties they formed a geographical niche at the Manitoba Red River colony, and then, when that began to disintegrate in the 1870s, farther west in the valley of the South Saskatchewan River in the settlement of Batoche, now in central Saskatchewan. And finally, from their U.S. and Canadian connections they formed a border-straddling community, a constellation of settlements in Minnesota, Manitoba, and the Montana, Dakota, and North-West Territories.

Seven years before the Battle of the Greasy Grass, even before the surveyors had stretched their chains out onto the prairie, the Métis discovered the power of the border.

On a rainy August morning in 1870, a schoolteacher named James Stewart came galloping through the gates of the Red River settlement's Fort Garry (not yet Winnipeg), found the young Métis leader Louis Riel at his breakfast, and gasped, "For the love of God, save yourself." One year after he had run John Dennis and his surveyors off Métis land, the young and charismatic Riel found himself seeking exile as well. The newly formed Canada had just bought the vast western territory of Rupert's Land from the Hudson's Bay Company, including the (Catholic and francophone) Red River Métis colony. In the winter of 1869–70, some twelve thousand Métis resisted the sale, delaying the transfer of land with their demands: bilingual institutions, religious schools, local control of public lands, provincial status.

As leader of the Red River resistance, Riel allowed a firing squad to execute a white Ontarian named Thomas Scott who opposed him. He then won most of his demands in the Manitoba Act of 1870, securing the primacy of the Métis "language" (French), "religion" (Catholic), and "rights" (to use the land in keeping with their aboriginal title), and became the chief target of English Protestant wrath in Ontario against French Catholic Quebec. On that rainy August morning, some of them planned on killing him. For the Métis, as for Riel, the meaning of the border they had ignored for so long was about to become clear: the American side meant sanctuary in exile, the Canadian, persecution or difficulty.[52]

Riel fled across the border. The next fourteen years were spent among a wide network of Métis and Franco-Americans. He stayed with his former Latin teacher in Dakota Territory and briefly in St. Paul, both places he had lived in the 1860s while in his early twenties. (Born in 1844, Riel was about ten years younger than Sitting Bull.) Restless and largely unhappy, he spent brief periods in Manitoba and Quebec evading arrest, and floated among French Canadian homes in New England and New York State; he bargained with Prime Minister Macdonald, expecting an official pardon (which never came) for his role in the resistance; and he visited a Franco-American named Edmund Mallet in Washington, D.C.[53]

In December 1874, the Canadian House of Commons granted Riel amnesty if he agreed to two years' imprisonment or five years' exile from Canada. He chose exile. Within a few months, in an interview with President Grant arranged by Mallet, he presented a plan for a quasi-independent Manitoba, and then had a divine revelation in a Washington, D.C., church. "God," he later wrote, "anointed him with His divine gifts and the fruits of His Spirit, as Prophet of the New World." Frustrated in politics and harboring a case of messianic zeal that even his friends could not distinguish from madness, Riel spent 1876 and 1877 in two suburban Montreal insane asylums. The truth of his mental state has never been finally determined, but once released, he was, ironically, offered a job helping a Catholic missionary entice Sitting Bull's Sioux back across the border to the United States.[54]

Riel rejected the offer. He had his own divine plan to execute. In December 1878, he wrote a poem saying he would go to fetch the "nations sauvages" on the banks of the Missouri to help the Métis, and eight months later he was in an ox cart passing through medicine line country, joining the "Metis hunters of the Big Bend of Milk River" and eating buffalo meat. "I am glad to see the prairie," he wrote home to his mother. Like Sitting Bull and his followers, who sought a new life in Canada, Canadian native Riel also thought "it better to begin a career on the other side of the line." ("I Louis Riel," he vowed in the Third Judicial District of the

Territory of Montana in the spring of 1880, "do declare on oath that it is bona fide my intention to become A Citizen of the United States of America, and to renounce forever all allegiance and fidelity to all and any foreign Prince, Potentate, State and Sovereignty whatsoever, and particularly to *Victoria Queen, of Great Britain and Ireland and Empress of India of whom I am a subject.*") From 1878 to 1880, while Sitting Bull's Sioux lived just north of the line, crisscrossing it to hunt buffalo, Riel and Métis "in force" lived just south of the line on the Milk River doing the same. Riel's whole design, though, was to overcome the border. He believed that the Métis and Indians held aboriginal title, not of use but of ownership, to western lands. He dreamed of a great confederacy of native peoples, which, under the circumstances, was not so far-fetched. Others had already made overtures for tribal alliances: the Cree chief Big Bear to the Blackfeet and Sioux in the Cypress Hills area; Sitting Bull to the Cheyenne before the Battle of the Greasy Grass, and in Canada to the Blackfeet leader Crowfoot (for whom Sitting Bull named his son). Riel envisioned a pan-native alliance, using Montana as a base to invade Canada and create an independent native republic, setting himself up as a New World prophet.[55]

Riel became a trader, shepherd, ranch hand, and teacher. He spent time at Forts Assiniboine and Belknap; befriended Thomas O'Hanlon, the Fort Belknap trader who became a founding father of Chinook; married a Métis hunter's daughter named Marguerite Monet; and eventually moved to nearby Carroll on the Missouri River, a place the Helena (Montana) *Daily Herald* described as a small hamlet "in a barren, cheerless country" with a population of eighteen. Like a labor organizer, he worked to unite the many native factions, apparently without mentioning the religious significance of his mission. In the summer of 1879 he signed an agreement in blood (or red ink) with the Assiniboine declaring that the country belonged to "the Indians and their brothers the half-breeds." In December, Crowfoot and his Blackfeet went south of the line to join Riel's Métis for the winter, about when Riel also appealed to Chief Big Bear and the Cree. In January, Sitting Bull came south of the line to meet with the Métis leader. In August 1880, Riel made an offer to General Nelson Miles to use his influence among the Indians in exchange for a Métis reservation. Riel was a compelling figure and a great orator, but for reasons we shall never really know, the others rejected his appeals.[56]

The Métis, however, still looked to him for leadership. In the winter of 1885, the discontent in the central North-West Territories (now central Saskatchewan) was palpable. The Métis, nearly without buffalo as the last of the herds died out, and with their transportation services threatened by steamboats and railroads, had lost the basis of their economy. They wanted land, either grants for what they had already settled along the South

Saskatchewan River or scrip—a certificate for all Métis heads of family redeemable for Dominion lands—that they could sell to land speculators, as they had done after the Manitoba Act of 1870. The Indians, also without buffalo or a livelihood, had little recourse but to seek rations on reservations. The Canadian whites—both farmers and businessmen, led by a young man from the town of Prince Albert named William Henry Jackson—were infuriated by distant control over their services, transportation, taxes, tariffs, and their lives generally. They wanted provincial status and greater local control, and they even threatened secession.

Rebellion, at least according to many Métis, required Louis Riel. He was, in Machiavelli's phrase, their "prophet in arms." In June 1884, a contingent of four rode down across the border to Montana to get him. By then Riel had become a schoolteacher of Blackfeet children at St. Peter's mission in Carroll, and in the evenings he wrote passionate verse on religion and politics in a cabin whose poverty surprised his visitors. Here was their hero, humbly devoted to a calling, but required by a higher purpose. They could not have appealed more to Riel's messianic sense of mystical significance. "The whole race is calling for you," they wrote in a letter they presented to him in the mission yard, where they had called him out of mass. Making the most of the occasion, he wrote out his response, which he gave them the next day: "[Y]our personal visit does me honor and causes me great pleasure. . . . I record it as one of the gratifications of my life."[57]

When he passed through medicine line country into central Saskatchewan just north of the town of Battleford, Riel discovered that an alliance would require various forms of persuasion. With the Indians, he tried histrionics. Blackfoot leader Crowfoot recalled that Riel publicly trampled on a copy of Treaty No. 6 (one of several treaties the Canadian government made in the 1870s to place natives on reserves), in an effort to convince the Blackfoot "to join with all the Sioux, and Crees, and half-breeds . . . [to] capture the North-West, and hold it for the Indian race and the Métis." With whites, Riel met with William Henry Jackson and gave moderate, reasonable-sounding speeches, although they disagreed irreconcilably that the Métis had claim to aboriginal rights. Once again facing many irreconcilable groups, Riel failed to persuade. By March 1885, he had managed to assemble a paltry force of a few hundred men, mostly Métis and a few Salteaux, Cree, Sioux, and Canadian allies, into a last gasp of native armed resistance against the Canadian government. "We march, my braves!" Riel cried as he proclaimed the Provisional Government of Saskatchewan. At every halt in their progress, against better-armed Mounties and Canadian militia, Louis Riel made his motley rebels recite the rosary. The rebellion lasted eight weeks—from March 18 to May 12, 1885. The Canadian government fielded about eight thousand Mounties and volunteers, its first national army, which won by sheer force of

Métis Leader Louis Riel as a prisoner outside the guard tent during the 1885 Rebellion in Canada. He would be hanged for treason soon after.
Photo courtesy Glenbow Archives, Calgary, Alberta.

numbers. Even the Blackfeet, inspired by food and ammunition, fought on the government's side. By November 16, Riel had been captured, tried, convicted of treason, and hung.[58]

Years before, in 1879, a group of Métis arrested in Montana Territory had been asked their nationality. Ten said they were British, and were escorted to Canada; 140 said they were American, and were advised to settle on the high plains of central Montana. We do not know why they responded this way. But judging from native leaders, the medicine line was a temporary expedient. Sitting Bull remained emphatically Sioux. Riel, nominally a citizen of the United States, remained a Métis at heart. "It sored my heart to say that kind of adieu," Riel later mourned publicly of his new citizenship, "to my mother, to my brothers, to my sisters, to my friends, to my countrymen, my native land."[59]

When Riel crossed the border for the last time in mid-June of 1884, loaded, like the Sioux in 1881, in his Red River cart with his wife, two children, and few possessions, he marked the end of an era. With Riel died the natives' hope of crossing to safety or a better life—of returning to the native geography not just of one's homeland but of the heart. Except for the Ghost Dance religion of 1890, the desperate set of skirmishes known as the Riel Rebellion was the last great attempt at native unity along the medicine line in the nineteenth century.[60]

History loves a dramatic failure. On a frigid September 30, 1877, on the grassy plain halfway between the badland "breaks" of the Missouri River and the shallow trough of the Milk River just south of the U.S.-Canada border, the Nez Percé surrendered to U.S. soldiers at the Battle of the Bear Paws. They had fled for 115 days, traveling more than a thousand miles in a long, winding route through southern Montana from their eastern Oregon and Idaho homeland—their sad journey seeming like a northern version of the Cherokee Trail of Tears—to escape the gold seekers, settlers, and bad treaties forcing them out of their ancestral homeland, the Wallowa Valley, onto a smaller reservation. A refined, honest, friendly people whose livelihood depended on salmon, buffalo, and their Appaloosa herds, they endured many deaths and grim prospects, and when all that remained was one final dash across the border to sanctuary, General Nelson A. Miles took them by surprise. After all that, they were caught in a web laid for the Sioux.[61]

The Nez Percé were taken prisoner and sent to Fort Leavenworth, Kansas, where many died, and then on to Indian Territory. The skirmish between Miles and the Nez Percé is remembered in popular history by the words attributed to Chief Joseph at the formal surrender, when the sun, according to a newspaper correspondent named Sutherland, "was dropping to the level of the prairie and tinging the tawny and white land with waves of ruddy lights." "Hear me, my chiefs," said Joseph in the fading light; "I am tired; my heart is sick and sad. From where the sun now stands, I will fight no more forever." The popular legend was deflated, however, when the original draft of the report was revealed to show the handwriting of the poet, lawyer, and lieutenant C. E. S. Wood, who claimed to have taken down the great chief's words on the spot. In the margin it read, "Here insert Joseph's reply to the demand for surrender."[62]

The battlefield, ten miles south of Chinook, is little changed from the way it looked in 1877. The revisionist Park Service plaque describes "the usual forked tongue methods of the whites, which had deprived these Indians of their hereditary lands," and the trails through the prairie battlefield cast an eerie peacefulness over the scene. Tiny red, yellow, white, and blue medicine bundles, tied together like kite tails with white string, rest next to cylindrical silver markers about the size of automatic sprinkler heads imprinted with the names of famous Nez Percé. Looking Glass, the formidable military strategist of the Nez Percé's 115–day flight from Idaho, had the top of his head shot off on a little hillock. Too-hool-hool-zote, another leader remembered for his thick, powerful build and deep-voiced resistance, died nearby in a rifle pit. So did Chief Joseph's brother Ollicut. Even more than the Sioux or the Métis, the Nez Percé felt the limits of law along the medicine line.

After their surrender, a few hundred Nez Percé managed to slip into Canada and temporary asylum—"some riding double and crying," as one Sioux remembered, carrying wounded children into the Sioux's Canadian camps across the line. Though the Nez Percé were long-standing enemies in a harsh political climate, the outraged Sioux took them in as brothers, "all packed like sardines," the Sioux witness remembered, in too few tepees. The village of hope, they were all learning, was rapidly running out of room.[63]

CHAPTER FOUR

IF YOU BUILD IT, WILL THEY COME?

Nations, like men, are travelers." Many an optimist could have written that line, but the smart money would bet on a nineteenth-century American, and the smarter money on a railroad man like James J. Hill. By the mid-nineteenth century the United States was in the midst of a full-blown transportation revolution, and railroads were its shock troops. "To do things 'railroad fashion'," wrote Henry David Thoreau in 1854, "is now the byword." A nation that developed its railroads and natural resources was a nation on a mission, traveling toward prosperity on one of its "highways of progress."[1]

Highways of Progress was the title of Hill's 1910 discourse on the American economy and its prospects. Hill was a railroad man through and through. In medicine line country, he was *the* railroad man. "By Jesus H. Chee-rist and Jim Jam Hill" was a phrase heard falling from the lips of more than one vexed farmer along the vast northern stretches that became Hill's domain. If Hill's vision of endless progress eventually dissolved over the rough course of the twentieth century, he was at least right about the transforming power of the railroad. Along the medicine line of the 1880s and '90s, the greatest hopes of westward-looking capitalists rode the rails. Thanks to Hill, the Northern Plains, as if with a greediness unexpected from such a frugal landscape, got two of them.[2]

Like Sitting Bull, James J. Hill crossed the border to great effect. When the stocky, forceful, one-eyed, Scots-Irish Canadian American pounded the table, the vibrations shook from St. Paul to Ottawa. A well-read farmer's son raised in an Ontario backwoods log cabin, Hill made his way into business early, a fireball of energy and ambition with a brilliant, practical mind. As one biographer noted, Hill lived his own Horatio Alger rags-to-riches story before Alger had even dreamed it up. In his early thirties, Hill outdid the Hudson's Bay Company in the steamboat freight and passenger business on the Red River, hauling Icelanders and Mennonites to new settlements and Métis fur trade goods across the international border. In 1878, based in St. Paul, he entered the railroad business, extending the bankrupt St. Paul and Pacific line (soon renamed the St. Paul, Minneapolis, and Manitoba) to the U.S.-Canada boundary to meet the Winnipeg line running south along the Red River. Burning with purpose, Hill walked the grade to personally supervise construction. When snow drifts impeded progress, a railroad worker recalled watching his boss climb from his comfortable private car, as if driven by steam himself, to snatch a shovel and start pitching snow to clear the way. Though Hill's goals were economic gain rather than political survival, his was a dash for the border with hopes as high as the those of the Nez Percé and Sioux the year before.[3]

Once in the game, Hill's impact was enormous. Local histories of the Canadian borderland seldom mention Hill. But there he is, having his way, looming godlike, across every prairie anniversary jubilee, the patriarch of the entire course of a history that otherwise might never have been. In 1881 the forty-two-year-old Hill orchestrated the Canadian Pacific Railway's most momentous and controversial decision: an agreement to change the

James J. Hill exhorting a crowd on the Great Northern Railway line, 1913.
Courtesy the James J. Hill and Louis W. Hill manuscripts, James J. Hill Reference Library, Saint Paul, Minnesota.

railroad's planned transcontinental route from the so-called fertile belt of the prairie through Edmonton to the much less populous Palliser's Triangle area to the south, along the border. (Not Hill, however, but John Macoun, the overly enthusiastic Canadian naturalist, would later be blamed for the southerly route's shortcomings.)[4]

It still bothers historians, as it did Canadians at the time, that Hill suddenly decided to move the CPR route further south. The northern route had withstood ten years of careful government planning and had already been partly surveyed at considerable expense, and it was, after all, an American who found the southern pass through the Rocky and Selkirk Mountains. In May 1881, Hill had hired for the CPR a Yale-trained U.S. army engineer, an unlikely character named A. B. Rogers. One biographer describes Rogers as "a short, sharp, snappy man with long, wild-flying Dundreary whiskers," a "master of profanity" whose "scientific equipment consisted of a compass and an aneroid slung around his neck" and whose "idea of a day's substantial provisions for an engineer was a plug of chewing tobacco in one pocket and a couple of slabs of hardtack in the other." Unkempt and foul-mouthed enough to repulse the butler of one of Hill's partners when he appeared on his doorstep, Rogers announced to Canadians that he was there to investigate southerly passes through the Rocky Mountains. Of Rogers the *Toronto Globe* reported huffily, "We are not inclined to credit the Yankee employees of the [CPR] syndicate with all the prodigious engineering feats that they promised to perform."[5]

Rogers found the passes, the one through the Selkirks bearing his name. Against the odds, Hill had pulled it off, though why he did so is a matter of debate. Harold Innis, an economic historian, argues that the southerly route was a canny business decision for Canadians to "divert [western] trade from the United States to eastern Canada." Historian Doug Owram, who emphasizes the power of myth making in the Canadian push west, stresses naturalist John Macoun's role as propagandist in declaring the former "desert" a farmer's paradise. Writer Pierre Berton suggests that Hill and the syndicate wanted a route through "virgin territory" for maximum control over real estate and trade along the line itself. The usually vehement observer Chester Martin is strangely silent on the subject. In any case, the choice to go south was certainly more than a whim. That the southern route was shorter was in its favor. It was also far less settled, in fact almost entirely unpopulated, giving the CPR total control as the hinterland's creator. And from Hill's point of view, as his biographer Albro Martin points out, the route's closer proximity to the border gave Hill's Minneapolis, St. Paul, and Manitoba a more direct extension west, and a better foothold to compete with its old rival, the Northern Pacific, which was routed through central Montana.[6] At the time of the route change, one assumes, Hill could

Canadian Pacific Railway track to the West.
Photo courtesy Glenbow Archives, Calgary, Alberta.

not foresee that within a decade he would be just across the border building the Great Northern, not a hundred miles from the CPR, thumbing his
nose at his former project to build another railroad across the same godfor-
saken plain.

Fittingly, Hill was a hybrid. As with the prairie countryside, so it was
with him—impossible to tell where the Canadian stopped and the
American began. At age seventeen, fresh from his rural Canadian childhood, like his heroes in the wild and romantic pages of Lord Byron he set
out for the Orient. He got as far as St. Paul and never really left. He spent
his adult life in the United States, where he became a citizen at age forty-
two.[7] The twin railroads of the United States-Canada borderland—a grid
whose shape and location traced a record of his own will, alliances, and dis-
affections—belonged to Hill more than anyone.

The Canadian Pacific Railway, incorporated after years of delay by an
act of Parliament in 1881, pushed through the Great Plains in 1883 and
reached its first terminus at Port Moody, British Columbia, in November
1885. It was an enormous national project. The CPR contract granted a pri-

vate syndicate—Hill's—twenty-five million acres of dominion lands and a direct cash subsidy of $25 million, which eventually grew to more than $98 million of government capital in subsidies and loans. The land grant did not set a North American record; that honor belonged to the Northern Pacific Railroad, which in 1864 had been granted thirty-nine million acres by the U.S. government. But it did more than double the transcontinental Union Pacific's windfall of twelve million acres.[8]

The second of Hill's projects, the Great Northern Railway, was laid west from Dakota Territory in early 1886 as an extension of Hill's St. Paul, Minneapolis and Manitoba line. When in 1883 Hill's fellow CPR directors decided to extend a rail link from Lake Superior to Winnipeg without informing him—a move that would effectively cut Hill's Manitoba line (and his chief financial interest in the CPR) out of the picture—Hill resigned. Convinced that his St. Paul—based Manitoba line would be denied its fair share of east-west traffic from Winnipeg once the western route was completed through Canada, he made plans to push it west himself through the United States. Known colloquially as the Manitoba, Hill's second railroad across the northern plains reached Fort Assiniboine, Montana Territory, in 1887, just past the future site of Chinook, where it turned south to the city of Great Falls. In January 1893, now operating under the corporate name Great Northern, Hill completed a further extension from Fort Assiniboine to the Pacific Ocean at Everett, Washington.[9]

Unlike its Canadian counterpart, the Great Northern received no federal land grants. It appeared at the end of what one historian calls "the cycle from prodigality to revulsion," when the private control of railroads over vast tracts of the American public domain came to an end.[10] Undeterred, Hill carved out the 1,700-mile-long right-of-way for his transcontinental extension entirely on private financing. The United States government obliged by further shrinking Indian lands in 1888, eliminating the Blackfeet and Gros Ventre reservation that had been established in 1874, a vast area between the Missouri River and the Canadian border stretching from the Rocky Mountains to Dakota Territory.[11] The government moved the Blackfeet farther west and carved out the Fort Belknap Reservation for the Gros Ventre, a rough rectangle about twenty-six miles wide by forty miles long, extending south from the Milk River to the Little Rocky Mountains, taking up what would someday be the southeast quarter of Blaine County. Within two years of its establishment, the Gros Ventre and Assiniboine had removed to the reservation, just south of the Great Northern tracks. Like a medieval lord reviewing his battlements (an analogy reinforced by his Summit Avenue mansion in St. Paul, with its commanding view of the Mississippi), Hill wrote glowingly to a friend of "our own line in the North, which protects the International Boundary line for a distance of 1600 miles . . . built without any government aid, even the right of way, through hundreds of miles through public lands, being paid for in cash."[12]

The borderland was transformed. By early 1893, mirror-image transcontinental railways squeezed just one hundred arid prairie miles between them. The region and its people felt the push and pull of the railroads, with commerce in particular realigned along an east-west axis. Arrive in Northern Plains country in 1880 and you would find yourself on a riverboat, landing at the region's main terminus of Fort Benton, met by the same motley crowd that greeted W. J. Twining and the American surveying party in 1874. Arrive via rail in the 1890s and you would find a better-supplied assortment of ranchers, farmers, merchants, and real estate developers, dressed in fine cloth and felt hats, accustomed to the frequent stops of the train, and sending and receiving a predominantly cross-country trade.

The railroads did not create a capitalist or commercial culture on the Northern Plains; the arrival of the fur trade, horses, and steamboat had already done that. Nor did they introduce a cosmopolitan element; the vari-

The Great Northern Railway under construction across the Montana plains, 1887. Courtesy the James J. Hill and Louis W. Hill manuscripts, James J. Hill Reference Library, Saint Paul, Minnesota.

ety of peoples was impressive both before and after the railroads. What they accomplished instead was that peculiar feat of certain technologies that Karl Marx called "the annihilation of space by time." As Thoreau suggested at midcentury, "The startings and arrivings of the cars are now the epochs in the village day." The railroad changed what had once been a relatively isolated fur-trade and subsistence hunter-gatherer economy into a mining and agricultural hinterland. The word *hinterland*, which in German means "behind land," as early as the 1890s began to assume more importance than its English translation "back country" might suggest.[13] North America and its railroads stretched the notion like the parallel shafts of a rubber band. Reorganized once to respond to the demands of the fur trade, the Northern Plains borderland was again reshaped. The unified north-south commercial and cultural zone of trappers, traders, native peoples, and wagon-train merchants tucked between the great waterways of the Missouri and South Saskatchewan Rivers became the east-west hinterland of not one coastal metropolis but two, Canadian and American. How Hill orchestrated this improbable achievement is a classic borderland story in all its tangled glory.

When plans for the Canadian Pacific began anew in December 1880, the contract was made between the Canadian government and, in addition to Hill, a collection of regional capitalists: George Stephen (later Lord Mount Stephen), a tall, elegant, and reserved man risen from a Scottish herd boy to become president of the Bank of Montreal, the most powerful financier in the Dominion, and board member of James J. Hill's Manitoba line; Richard B. Angus, also a Scot and a born money manager, head of the Bank of Montreal and on the Manitoba line's board as well; John S. Kennedy, yet another flinty and laconic Scot, a New York financier also on the Manitoba's board; Hill's early-day mentor and business partner Norman W. Kittson, another Canadian-become-St. Paul-shipping-agent and former Hudson's Bay Company trader; Duncan McIntyre of Montreal, manager of the Canada Central Railway; and two interests represented by Londoner Pasco Du Pont Grenfell—a London company and its New York branch representing British capital, and a Paris and Frankfurt company whose interests lay in colonization and emigration. An eighth partner, Donald A. Smith, George Stephen's cousin and former chief commissioner of the Hudson's Bay Company, remained tactfully absent from the contract because of his enmity for Prime Minister Macdonald.[14]

In this entrepreneurial community American and Canadian partners were conspicuously intertwined. Hill and Kittson were old friends and associates, and Hill, Stephen, Kennedy, and Smith became fast friends. They would quarrel, make up, and tramp the Canadian countryside together on salmon-fishing treks. The affiliations carried over to Hill's Great Northern project, even after Hill regretfully abandoned the CPR in midstream. Canadians George Stephen and Donald Smith were on the Great Northern board of directors, if nothing else a testament to their affection for the "blessed old road," as Stephen once called the former Manitoba line, despite conflicts of interest that had become painfully apparent. Stephen resigned from the board in 1892 after moving to England, where the queen raised him to the peerage and he eased into life in a country manor. Then, hoping to "shake the dust of Canada off my feet . . . forever," Stephen resigned from the CPR as well in 1893. With Stephen gone and its British financial backing in bankruptcy, the Great Northern became a predominantly American-financed and -operated railroad. But Stephen was by no means finished with Hill. Several of the old core CPR syndicate members remained among each other's closest associates.[15]

Why did these men work for apparently competing railroads? There is limited credence to the notion that they perceived the twin lines as mutually beneficial, building a strong regional economy. Socially, however, the common interest is not hard to fathom. Both the CPR and the Great Northern were private enterprises drawing on a small and intimate pool of capital and entrepreneurial talent that traversed the United States-Canada frontier. The distinction between Canadian and American identities blurred as if the international border were itself fluid. The CPR's guiding hand after 1881 was an American named William C. Van Horne, James J. Hill's choice for the job, a native of Illinois, and former general superintendent of the Chicago, Milwaukee, and St. Paul line.[16] A big, autocratic man, Van Horne left any Yankee sentiment he may have had at the border. His was a total conversion to the Canadian cause. He became so passionately devoted to the CPR, serving as its general manager after 1881, on the executive committee of its board of directors after 1884, and as its president from 1888 to 1899 (holding it dearer, he said, than "anything else in the world aside from my wife and children"), that after just two years his partisanship helped drive an aggravated Hill out of the syndicate. In 1885, Van Horne arguably became the man most responsible for crushing Riel's rebellion when, like a mad field marshal, he moved five thousand troops into Saskatchewan in just nine days, laying unfinished rails on ice and snow in temperatures of fifty degrees below zero to transport them. Another American, Ross J. M. Egan, ran the CPR operating department in western Canada, and Van Horne's protégé and successor as president, Thomas G. Shaughnessey, came from the Irish ghetto of Milwaukee. Though he returned there to visit, Shaughnessey, too, became native to the CPR, a fish in a whorling stream. At the eye of the whirlpool was James J. Hill himself. [17]

Amidst these numerous alliances, what were the Canadians' interests and what the Americans'? In the mounted battles of the 1870s the partici-

pants felt sure that they knew. But with the advent of the capitalist con-
quistadors running out their long-distance lines in the 1880s and '90s, old
distinctions fell temporarily aside. The new developers seemed bound by a
predominantly Scots and Irish ancestry and culture that no international
border could readily sunder. For Hill's Great Northern, nationalism was
never an overriding issue. By 1890, the United States had several transcontinental railroads already, and the lavish days of public financing were gone.
Following the Union Pacific, Southern Pacific, and Northern Pacific, the
Great Northern was merely one of many conduits west.

Canada, on the other hand, a latecomer to the transcontinental race
and impressed by the apparent success of the Americans, entered the railroad land-grant business just as monopoly-fearing Americans were ending
theirs. Since the 1870s, Canadians had been intensely nationalistic about
their railroad. The first efforts to organize a transcontinental Canadian railway foundered in the early 1870s in a political imbroglio that brought down
the Macdonald government. The affair, known as the Pacific Scandal of
1873, was in historian Leonard Bertram Irwin's account a case of Canadian
"statesmen," buoyed by Canadian nationalism, crushing the attempts of
Canadian "capitalists" to build the Canadian transcontinental line with the
cooperation of the U.S. Northern Pacific.[18]

The distinction between statesmen and capitalists is somewhat disingenuous, since the leading statesman, Prime Minister John A. Macdonald,
was for all practical purposes also a capitalist who needed money for his
nation's railroad and turned to the Northern Pacific to get it. Nevertheless,
Irwin vividly describes the perennial Canadian problem of scarce Canadian
capital combined with resentment of foreign—especially American—
investment and control of Canadian enterprises. In this case, public sentiment, carefully manipulated by the opposition Liberal party, demanded an
entirely Canadian national railroad. Macdonald's unpublicized plan to
involve the American-owned railroad in the project was the target of a politically charged exposé, made worse by the revelation that Hugh Allan, president of the government railway company, had contributed heavily to
Macdonald's campaign for office. The scandal brought an unexpected five-
year hiatus to Macdonald's Conservative government (Alexander
Mackenzie led a Liberal government from 1873 to 1878) and delayed the
building of a Canadian transcontinental railroad ten years. Once back in
office, Macdonald was not to make the same mistake twice. In the wake of
the Pacific Scandal, attractive proposals from the Northern Pacific of shared
track crisscrossing the international boundary were nonetheless shunned.[19]

But the lavish investment of national resources was at stake, and
despite Macdonald's efforts, by the late 1880s nationalist Canadians again
found the Canadian Pacific syndicate offensively tainted by Yankees. "It is

rather curious that all my Minnesota associates are Canadians," noted an uneasy Stephen, reassuring Macdonald about the backgrounds of CPR directors on the eve of parliamentary debate over the contract; "Mr. Kittson is a native of Sorel . . . and Hill is from Guelph. Not a Yankee in the concern. Kennedy . . . is a Scotchman, President of the N.Y. St. Andrews Society. . . . I mention these things in case you may be exposed to attacks of selling the country to a lot of Yankees."[20]

Stephen was right to worry. The original CPR syndicate of Stephen, Hill, Angus, and Smith, co-owners of the St. Paul, Minneapolis, and Manitoba Railway between St. Paul and Winnipeg, had not been Macdonald's first choice. Haunted by the Pacific Scandal and generally uneasy about things American, he had twice tried and failed to entice British capital into heading the contract. The fury with which the Canadian parliament reacted to the U.S.-infected syndicate he had proposed made him even sorrier he had failed. The Liberal opposition, though fundamentally for the railway, seized the floor in a fit of rhetoric against Macdonald. Unfortunately for the Liberals, flowery debate proved less persuasive than the perceived imperative of transcontinental union, and at last, after two and a half months of haranguing, a weary parliament signed the bill into law in February 1881.[21]

The Canadian government had in this instance proven itself more attracted to American methods than it was repulsed by American control. Yet as it turned out, it was not land grants, much less Yankee influence, that could make or break a railway. American railroads discovered this soon enough. Both the Union Pacific and the Northern Pacific fell into receivership in the depression of 1893. Northern Pacific land sales eventually brought in nearly $136 million, well exceeding the $70 million cost of the road's construction, but too late to prevent the crisis. By 1894 proceeds from Northern Pacific land sales totaled only about $28 million. Like its grant-rich American cousins, the young Canadian Pacific approached financial crisis so many times during the 1880s that its president, George Stephen, neared despair. As a man with railroad interests on both sides of the 49th parallel, Stephen felt particularly disappointed in his Canadian project. By 1884 he felt "like a man walking on the edge of a precipice." While serving as a symbol of Canada's unity, the railroad managed to be a conduit for the nation's considerable disunity. Self-interested provinces, the Toronto *Globe*, and enemies of the Conservative party all worked feverishly toward sabotage. With their encouragement, the CPR was soon as well hated in Canada as were its counterparts in the United States. Comparing the CPR to his American line, Stephen lamented, "On one side it is all turmoil and agitation and politics, on the other every man is working and saying nothing." "How it will end God knows," Macdonald wrote to a confidant as the potential for failure loomed, "but I wish I were well out of it."[22]

Ultimately, nationalist ambitions and the Conservative government's will for self-preservation won out. In November of 1885, Donald A. Smith, a fur trader become railroad magnate, and Louis Riel's adversary in 1870, drove the CPR's last spike into a British Columbia mountainside. Nine days later, amidst a much larger crowd, Louis Riel hung dead from the end of a rope in the railroad town of Regina, enough of a coincidence to have assured the mystical Métis leader of his divine role in history. Not only was the CPR completed and basking in the nation's momentary good graces for having carried troops to defeat Riel's second Métis rebellion, but it was soon solvent. At Stephen's insistence, it repaid its $30 million in government loans on June 1, 1886, three days after the first train from Montreal left for the Pacific coast, ushering in a new era in Canadian history.[23]

By comparison, Hill's Great Northern was to be a model of quiet private enterprise. To considerably less public notice, the Great Northern drove its last spike into a mountainside in Washington State in January 1893. Far from creating a maelstrom, the Great Northern rose above one. Amidst widespread economic depression it treaded water, while financial crisis sucked under the heavily indebted Union Pacific, Northern Pacific, and others. "We have carried the load to the top of the hill," gloated one of Hill's financial advisors, "the reward is certain."

But the real problems for both the CPR and the Great Northern began after construction. The two railroads had seemingly willed an east-west reorientation of a north-south economy, a north-south business alliance, and a north-south natural environment.[24] But the load was not yet to the top of the hill. The railroads first had a prairie to sell.

Selling the North American wilderness is one of modern Europe's oldest professions. "The earth bringeth foorth all things in aboundance, as in the first creation, without toile or labour," wrote Walter Raleigh's publicity agent about the prospective site for Roanoke, Virginia, in 1584. The CPR and the Great Northern told it no differently. "Wonderfully fertile Montana valley," trumpeted the Great Northern. "Go to opportunity land," "room for thousands more today—millions." "Winters are pleasant and healthful," advertised an agent for the CPR in his promotional pamphlet, "conditions to make prosperity are there."[25] Familiar tunes for unfamiliar ears.

Despite the propaganda, the northern prairie was initially a hard sell. To the CPR's first appeals for emigrants, in the early 1880s, England yawned. In 1882, on an early promotional visit to London, George Stephen found the British press impenetrably preoccupied with Jumbo the elephant, whom P. T. Barnum, in his restless pursuit of suckers, had recently purchased from the London Zoo. Colonize Canada? What was that compared to a live elephant? Jumbo was "a matter of ten times more interest to London than twenty colonies," complained Stephen. Turning elsewhere, in 1884 Stephen floated a plan to subsidize the Irish, who he hoped might care to settle western Canada. Prime Minister Macdonald was less than thrilled. "*Entre nous*," he wrote Charles Tupper, the new Canadian high commissioner in London, "we don't want the Western Irish emigration. They are bad settlers and thoroughly disloyal."[26] The plan was quashed in any case by Prime Minister Gladstone and numerous members of parliament averse to state-aided emigration.

British Columbians, meanwhile, were alarmed that the Chinese railway laborers might decide to stay on as settlers. Worry not, Prime Minister Macdonald reassured them; the Chinese were "sojourner[s] in a strange land . . . the same as a threshing machine or any other agricultural implement which we may borrow from the United States or hire and return to its owner." So virulent was Canadian prejudice against the Chinese that a tax of $50 a person enacted in 1885 placed them among paupers, diseased persons, and criminals as the only immigrants screened from entering an otherwise "open door" country.[27] Japanese were later restricted, and blacks informally prohibited. Though not officially unwelcome, non-Anglo-Saxons of all types bore the brunt of the Anglo-Saxon majority's ethnocentrism, ironically even from those "progressive" reform movements promoting the social gospel, prohibition, and women's rights. All was not quite the amiable cultural mosaic for which Canada is often touted. Land agents made it no secret that they preferred eastern Canadians, Americans, and Britons, but when these groups showed a weak response, they branched out to expatriate French Canadians and assorted Europeans: Icelanders, Russian Mennonites, Russian Jews, Hungarians, and, most popular, Germans and Scandinavians.

To make matters worse, many Canadians themselves contradicted the glowing prairie propaganda. Explorer Henry Youle Hind offered the opinion that the overly optimistic explorer John Macoun had vaunted the North West Territories as a "fictitious Garden of Eden." The Canadian high commissioner in London declared the land bordering the CPR between Moose Jaw and Medicine Hat, including the Maple Creek district, worthless for agricultural purposes. The *Toronto Globe* mounted a virtual crusade to publicize that same section as unfit for settlement. By 1900, after thirty years of hard selling and just before the homestead boom to come, Canada had recorded only 20 percent of its eventual total net homestead entries.[28] If not worthless, especially to the ranchers already there, the whole of Assiniboia and Saskatchewan, the future province of Saskatchewan, remained virtually wheatless.

On the American side of the line, the Great Northern company weathered the depression of the early 1890s by tightening its belt. Hill declared gently in 1893 that the "general outlook for business is not in the direction of an increase." Hill and the man he had made into head of the CPR, the American William Cornelius Van Horne, sparred over traffic on the eastern and western ends of their railroads, while Hill and his old Canadian friend George Stephen wrestled with J. P. Morgan to work the Northern Pacific and the Great Northern into friendly alliance. Meanwhile, prairie settlement crawled forward. "You'll never bring anything out of that country but buffalo bones!" was the jibe that James J. Hill was said to have heard all too often.[29]

As outsiders, the Northern Plains Indians figured out early, and perhaps more clearly than many white settlers, that the two new nations along the border shared basic assumptions about suborning the land to commerce. At first, the Indians did not know quite what to expect. In the 1870s, on the eve of crisis, they garnered hints of what was to come from conversations with the Métis, who told them that the trains would burn up the grasses and drive the game away. After centuries of trading furs to distant urban markets, they well understood the effects, good and ill, of the European economic system. They were learning more about its negative aspects every day, witnessing the demise of the buffalo from overhunting. But they also valued the benefits of the white man's commerce. "I am glad the railway is coming," contended the Blackfoot leader Crowfoot. "It will cheapen our food." By and large, however, they could only imagine the coming agricultural empire and its peculiarly uninformed relationship with the land.[30]

Initially, the Indians regarded the rails and markers and wires themselves as curiosities. The new landscape, like the new agricultural society, was alien to them. "On my journey through the country of the white savages, I came to a big trail which was made of iron," recounted one young Indian traveler to his villagers upon returning from an escorted trip to eastern Canada in 1885. The speaker was either North Axe of the Piegan or One Spot of the Blood, two Blackfoot men who became a single composite speaker in the records of Reverend John Maclean. "[A]s I was curious to know what it was for," the young man continued, still standing over the rail, "I stooped down and felt it with my hands. The iron trail was so heavy that I could not lift it, and the savages had fastened it to the prairie, lest some thieves might come along and steal it." The train itself startled and amazed the youth, and the only way he could make sense of it at first was to describe it as a horse that "shouted and started to run on the iron trail."

The white man's lines would take some getting used to. In fact, cheaper food or no, most Indians hated them. They were a menace to Indian property and well-being. Assiniboine chief Little Mountain did not take lightly an accident in 1883 that broke one woman's leg when a train carrying Indians out of Maple Creek to the reservation at Qu'Appelle ran off the track; he demanded carts to transport the tribe the rest of the way. "The iron road has frightened the game away and the talking wire stretches from sunrise to sunset," lamented Foremost Man, a Cree who refused long after Indian removal to leave the Cypress Hills. "It is too late; it is too late."[31]

Nelson Miles called them "lines of civilization"—the stone cairn that reporter John Finerty hunted up along the international boundary in 1879, the gridlines that had so methodically delineated parcels of property, the iron tracks. Behind them stood an extraordinary and powerful set of assumptions, a world devoted to commodities and communications designed to organize the countryside, connect it to future land seekers from far-flung places, and connect those land seekers and their products to metropolitan markets. The empire was to be built on real estate, and the real estate cultivated to grow grain for export. The "lines of civilization" on the North American plains were the structural elements of a specific social and economic model: commodity-based agriculture and resource extraction, operating according to the ideals of agrarian democracy, harnessing the agricultural practices of Ontario and the eastern United States and supporting a hinterland population that in turn demanded eastern goods and services. To a nineteenth-century Irish adventurer, this model would only seem to bear out his hunch that "American and Canadian" where "only names that hide beneath them the greed of united Europe." Both Canadian and American democracies assumed that widespread land ownership was the key to the broad diffusion of property and power necessary to a democratic union, not to mention economic prosperity. Paradoxically, developing the prairies into fertile landed democracies drew—and most believed they required—the efforts of powerful organizations, concentrated wealth, and central governments.[32]

Historians debate when North Americans changed from a society dominated by small, subsistence farm households to one devoted to the production of commodities for profit. On the Northern Plains, however, there is no need for such debate. Beginning with the native peoples who migrated there during the eighteenth and nineteenth centuries in search of furs, people came to the Northern Plains to produce commodities. The first commodities did not need advanced technologies; trading posts, waterways, and the overland paths of the Red River carts proved adequate for the fur trade. But in late-nineteenth-century North America, commercial agriculture, the desire for private property, and the pressure for territorial expansion demanded them. So, too, did the more inchoate Victorian notion that civilized man had risen above dependence on his birthplace, locality, and even his God and was destined to control the natural world for his own purposes. When Nelson Miles wrote that the "lines of civilization" were a protection against "savage ferocity," he was only expressing the philosophy of his time.

Along with its utilitarian purposes, the push West held a mythical allure for whites. Every deluded western writer put more imagination into his glorifying vision of the West than did even that young Indian trying to describe a train to his friends. "Rain follows the plow," promoters claimed, in what was surely one of the most delusional pseudo-scientific promotional schemes in North American history. Nature would offer no restraint that could not be overcome. Many convinced themselves that the mythology was real, that the land policy of the Hudson's Bay Company was "not a real estate proposition at all," as a CPR official once averred, but "the building up for an empire in the West."[33]

Despite such boosterism, there was no guarantee that people would come. Nor did it mean that they, or the railroads who brought them, would succeed. The survey system, expanded onto the arid plains during and after the Civil War, had met its tragic flaw. In the 1862 Homestead Act and the 1872 Dominion Lands Act, Americans and Canadians, respectively, became newly committed to the western settlement of small farms. This system of small freeholdings, a vision from the humid East, assumed enough water for agriculture on each farm. But when settlers pushed west of the 98th meridian they found water harder to come by. In much of the West, annual precipitation was below 20 inches. Without irrigation, 160 acres proved to be a hard-scrabble sink hole where, in a just world, sweat and tears might have counted for something in the rain gauge. Beyond the iron rails was the hard reality of turning a real estate transaction into a community and a livelihood, the place where the capitalists' abstractions turned into the deeply human struggle with life. If you were the farmer standing somewhere in the dirt, whether Ojibwa or British, what, really, was the difference between real estate, home, and empire? The agricultural industry that the railroads were counting on demanded great numbers of settlers. "Highways of Progress," as Hill already knew, were fraught with risk. Failure and discontinuity pressed back the borders of hope even as Hill and the CPR and all their magnificent lines enlarged them. As they began to seek settlers, the builders of the Northern Plains railroads could only hope they had gambled wisely on a dry country.

CHAPTER FIVE

WHICH SIDE ARE YOU ON?

On a hot summer day in 1891, a rider from the TU cattle outfit on Cow Creek sets out on horseback north from the spot on the Missouri River where the *Fontenelle* once ran aground, beneath the vast northern Montana sky across eastern Chouteau County. It has been ten years since Sitting Bull crossed the medicine line. Steamships are becoming obsolete. Two railroads now run parallel on either side of the border. Benjamin Harrison, a rather colorless Republican, is president. John Macdonald, newly reelected champion of a dying Conservative Canadian nationalism, has himself just died. Chouteau County, named in 1864 for a prominent St. Louis fur trade family, is vast—as large as Ireland, two-thirds the size of Ohio, 27,280 square miles. It is also, even by American standards, relatively empty, with 8,500 people, less than one inhabitant for every three square miles. Thirty-six percent of them are concentrated in three places: Fort Benton, the county seat and old trading post to the southwest on the Missouri River; Fort Assiniboine, erected in 1879 near the Milk River, thirty miles west of where Chinook now stands; and the Fort Belknap Indian reservation, just east of Chinook.[1]

The rider, bound for Maple Creek, Saskatchewan, on ranch business, follows the Cow Creek trail up from the river bottom, where a well-worn landing near Cow Island still harbors keel-dragging upriver steamboats bound for Fort Benton during low water. The squared-off buttes of the Missouri's benchlands glisten with gypsum crystals, as in the old hobo anthem "The Big Rock Candy Mountain." For thirty miles he winds through the rocky buttes and eastern foothills of the Bear Paw Mountains, through the yellow loco weed, blue lupine, and wild roses of midsummer. After two dry years the growth seems lush. He fords Peoples Creek, leading east through the center of the Fort Belknap Indian reservation, and veers northwest toward Lloyd, a site on upper Snake Creek where the prospector and trapper William L. Wilson is out hammering together a store and post office.

Past Lloyd lies the ranch of Samuel and Clara Lamb, where Clara, the current Lloyd postmistress, holds a few letters for neighboring ranchers. To the west and north Clear Creek winds toward the Milk River through knee-high grasses, past Bear Paw Jack's, Milk River Bill's, justice of the peace Fred Scott's, and a dozen other places, but the rider bears northeast past a prairie dog town, through a stretch of sticky "gumbo" soil, to ford Bean Creek and eventually plunge downhill past a coal mine to the level sagebrush flat of Three Mile Coulee and the green-gray waters of the Milk River. Whitefish, pike, and catfish dart against the flow that carries them southeastward, into the Missouri and on to the Mississippi.

Across a wooden bridge, the tiny treeless settlement of Chinook crouches along the bank of the Milk River along the Great Northern line, a few hopeful buildings on a little hill, barely more than the dream of a few white men at the Fort Belknap Indian agency. "They could almost see that city sitting on the hill," recalls resident Ruth Reser Gill from a childhood memory, echoing the Puritan John Winthrop's description of the Massachusetts Bay Colony in her choice of phrase. Chinook is not even listed in the 1890 federal census. It amounts to a hotel, a livery service, a blacksmith shop, the O'Hanlon general store and warehouse, several open all-night saloons, and a rather prominent sprawling white frame whorehouse called the "White House," perched near the top of the hill as if to announce that the town's moral distance from the Puritans equals its geographical distance. Grass and weeds grow tall along Indiana Avenue, thick with heat and flies. A few out-of-work drifters stock the bars. The aroma of Arbuckle's coffee wafts from the coffee mill in O'Hanlon's store, where Irishman Tom O'Hanlon stands on the threshold with his moon face and warm manner, pressing candy into children's palms. Over at Lohman's, the competing store, plays young Lillian Miller, whose mother, fearing the street as hazardous territory full of snakes and stampeding horses, last year tethered her to a table. Across a shallow slough are the four-year-old Great Northern railway tracks, and past them an old Assiniboine travois trail northwest of Chinook where the children of newly settled rancher Ezra Reser are out looking for Indian beads. Past two gravestones—one of an infant, the other of a woman accidentally shot—stretch the sixty miles of sage-filled flatland known as the "Big Flat" or the "hard country," virtually unpopulated, disturbed mostly by wind and prairie fires, antelope and cattle, and an occasional shepherd with his flock driven north from the Bear Paws for summer forage.[2]

Soon after hitting the North Fork, a stream draining south from the Cypress Hills, the rider passes an obelisk that uneventfully marks the U.S.-Canada border. He picks up the Mounted Police patrol route and continues up the stream, known in Canada as Battle Creek. No telltale signs suggest that he has entered another country, a different place. On the Canadian side of the line lies the district of the North-West Territories called Assiniboia West. Jurisdiction resides in the A division of the North-West Mounted Police, some hundred men scattered at a dozen outposts headquartered at Maple Creek.

After traveling thirty miles or so over cactus-studded hard clay along southern Battle Creek, a trail swings eastward around the north side of grassy Old Man on His Back Plateau to the white clay foothills along the Frenchman River, named for the Métis buffalo hunters who built log cabins here. It is sometimes called the White Mud, as if Sitting Bull still camped here. Some thirty tumbling clay chimneys survive from a vanished Métis village, and a three-room log house serves as post for half a dozen Mounted Police stationed at what they call Eastend for the eastern edge of the hills, an abandoned Hudson's Bay Company post and Métis ruin thirty-five miles north of the border. The rider chooses instead the better-traveled route northwestward, following the looping curve of Battle Creek from the plateau, passing near Basque rancher Michael Oxarat's place, called The Pyrenees, at the west end of Davis Lake, to the Battle Creek post, where another handful of Mounties have recently built a kitchen behind their quarters. Twenty more miles of benchland rise above the heat-stunned plain, into the lush ecological island of the Cypress Hills, where cool pine and spruce forests open south toward the Bear Paws, a view unclouded this summer by the black smoke of prairie fires. Headstones in a clearing record the names of Mounted Police, store manager Frank Clarke, Chief Little Bird, Métis names in abundance—Dumonts, LeBarges, and Gardipees— and what seems like too many children and infants. Fort Walsh is a ruin, a measure of the speed of recent history in this place. Mounted Police headquarters from 1875 to 1883, it was abandoned in 1883, when Indian removal and the newly arrived Canadian Pacific Railway ended its geographical importance. All that remain are the outlines of buildings dismantled or burned by prairie fires, and the rock by the parade ground from which a goose used to scold approaching visitors.

Northwest toward the town of Medicine Hat, a name that Rudyard Kipling blessed as having the "red mystery and romance that once filled the prairies," lie the creek and coulee named for police constable Marmaduke Graburn, mysteriously murdered there, and the dozen howling hounds and collies on former policeman Scotty Gow's shorthorn cattle ranch.[3] Northeast lies the Gap. The rider descends the Gap past the Pollock and Cheeseman brothers' ranches, crossing through a few miles of short-grass prairie to the waters of Maple Creek. A weekly patrol from Mounted Police A division headquarters is leaving for Eastend, passing quickly beyond the sound of policemen's hammers building a paint shop.

Across a bridge is the well-established town of Maple Creek, popula-tion 687, which sprang up around the shed and cabin of a Canadian Pacific construction crew where cold weather stopped work on the tracks in the winter of 1883. Even compared to Chinook it is no landmark of refinement. The edifices of its main street in 1892 include a tent and a log house.[4] Up the dirt street past the shops is another set of railroad tracks across the Northern Plains, the Canadian Pacific Railway, now eight years old. A few Indians, mostly Cree, straggle around the depot, polishing buffalo horns to sell to the next trainload of whites—Indian Mike, perhaps, or Medicine Rabbit Woman, Turkey Legs, Old Teeth, Wolf Woman, Man-Who-Got-Lost, all arrested periodically for drunkenness or cattle killing, reduced and toughened into depot-sitters.[5]

Many made this trip, or some version of it, in the days before the rail-roads: foul-mouthed bullwhackers freighting goods by wagon from the Missouri River to Fort Benton, a hundred miles west of Cow Island, and on from Fort Benton to the Mounted Police at Fort Walsh; Mounties off to gather information or a few amenities at Fort Benton; scouts or supply wag-ons bearing horse thieves or dried goods back to the mansard-roofed brick buildings of Fort Assiniboine, rising west of Clear Creek; leather-skinned cowpunchers on the job from the Matador, a British and American opera-tion, or some other big cattle outfit; or, even after the railroads came, the occasional fugitive horse thief, deserting Mountie, or ill-prepared Fort Assiniboine deserter, hobbling, midwinter, on frozen feet across the line toward refuge in Maple Creek. Some autumn between 1883 and 1887, one might have come upon a spring wagon carrying Ed and Mamie Keaster and their two young sons, accompanying the Shonkin Association's cattle roundup from Chouteau County north to the depot at Maple Creek. But after the arrival of the Great Northern railroad in 1887, few had reason to make the trip. Bullwhackers and long-distance shippers were fading, their old paths carrying a new and different population.[6]

Even so, the old medicine line culturally dividing "Europe," as Nelson Miles's soldiers liked to say, from America had not entirely disappeared. With some effort, we might imagine it scratched with a stick in the prairie dirt somewhere across the North Fork/Battle Creek trail, a small redoubt of Mounties, marshals, and customs agents, a division across the center of a cactus-spined playing field. In the Canadian field we can make out the Mounted Police A division cricket team at practice, or perhaps a Mountie or two jostling a couple of drunks disturbing the peace on the streets of Maple Creek. Rancher Harry Bettington, an Englishman known as the Professor, sporting a thick mustache and a dry sense of humor, poses for a photograph with seven friends, his left eye opened extra wide as if holding the monocle he often wears.[7] In the American field we see the "half dozen

Englishmen posing as cowboys, Maple Creek rancher Harry Bettington (back row, second from left) and friends.
Courtesy Southwest Saskatchewan Old Timers' Museum, Maple Creek, Saskatchewan.

Assiniboine toughs," as the editor of the *Chinook Opinion* referred to six Fort Assiniboine soldiers alleged to have energetically smashed up the Chinook depot, and Mr. Freeland, the night depot operator with the quintessentially American name, reassuring our image of a rough-and-tumble American frontier. These are images Sitting Bull, or the Canadian cultural nationalists who have championed their differences from the United States ever since, would have expected.[8]

There was truth in these images. United States and Canadian census material (from 1890/91 to 1926) reveals that the border marked a real division—in birthplace, religion, and ethnic and racial origin. Throughout the settlement period, the area that became Blaine County in 1912 remained primarily American-born, and, as far as we can tell from an inadequate U.S.

record of religion, predominantly Catholic. Maple Creek and Eastend remained mostly Canadian and British, predominantly Anglican, Presbyterian, and Methodist.[9] Demographic differences between the two sides of the border were at their most striking during the 1890s. The U.S. manuscript census for 1890 burned, making Chouteau County more inscrutable. We do know that of the county's some 8,500 residents that year, a full 44 percent were Indian, a figure that would drop dramatically to 11 percent during the next decade. The Fort Belknap Reservation, although a segregated population, added significantly to the area's diversity. Of the roughly 4,700, non-Indian residents, 70 percent were U.S.-born.[10] The Maple Creek school district, by contrast, with 689 people, had a much larger white population and was full of Ontarians (its largest group by birthplace, which totaled 26 percent), Scots, and Anglicans. Not only was the majority population different from that on the U.S. side of the border, there was less overall diversity. The foreign born in the two populations were similar in number. In Chouteau County, 30 percent of non-Indians were foreign born—nearly 10 percent of them in Canada and Newfoundland, and nearly another 10 percent in Ireland, England, and Scotland. Maple Creek's foreign-born population totaled 35 percent, of whom three-fourths were from Ireland, England, and Scotland, and roughly one-eighth from the United States.

Still, the differences stand out: on the Canadian side, Métis freighters and their large families accounted for nearly 14 percent of the Maple Creek population, roughly the same as the number of Mounted Police, at 12 percent. And since most of the Maple Creek area's Indians were removed to reservations outside the area, there was no equivalent to Fort Belknap. The Department of the Interior's Indian Farm a few miles south of Maple Creek closed in 1883. The Assiniboine were sent to Qu'Appelle, an early-day fort 250 miles east, on the ill-fated train that Chief Little Mountain refused to ride after it ran off the track. Most of the Cree went to Qu'Appelle and other reserves in Saskatchewan and Alberta or migrated south to Montana, where along with many Métis they eventually collected on the Rocky Boy Reservation. A small number of Cree lingered to form the Nikaneet Reserve, south of Maple Creek, in 1913.[11] With such a demographic profile, clearly two new populations were emerging: one Canadian and one American.

Newcomers on the Canadian side, especially, brought Old World pretensions and expectations. Dan Tenaille (pronounced "ten-eye"), a French aristocrat on the plains, was a good example. He had refinement. He wanted the simpler pleasures of a frontier along with it. "What have you learned in Canada?" asked Madame Tenaille of her son, who at age twenty-three in 1903 had spent $60,000 of his family fortune to build a ranch near the Cypress Hills of Canada's North-West Territories. "I can blow my nose with my fingers and swear in English," he replied, or so went the story.[12] Such were the beginnings of a prairie education among few French and fewer aristocrats.

A visitor to Dan Tenaille's ranch could not easily tell whether he was in Canada or the United States, but he would quickly recognize the effects of imported money and grand aspirations. The site was just north of Eastend on Little Frenchman Creek, harboring amenities the French-speaking Métis buffalo hunters of decades past could scarcely have imagined. The Tenaille house sat, startlingly large, on the wooded creek bank.[13] In a country of dirt-floor shacks and two-room ranch houses, it was a marvel: two stories, French-style shingles, two double-decker porches, a glassed-in veranda, thirteen rooms, wooden ceilings, cedar paneling flawlessly matched by a carpenter brought over from France, imported French linen wallpaper, gaslights, indoor running water, a wine cellar. There was a darkroom for developing photographs, one of Tenaille's many hobbies, and an outdoor exhibit of wild animals in cages and hillside enclosures. Tenaille bought land from homesteaders—a modest 560 acres, according to family records—and named his New World playground Eastend Ranch. He stabled purebred horses—Percherons, Thoroughbreds, and polo ponies—and let the rest of his livestock roam south to the international border. He played polo, chased coyotes in an early Ford automobile, and tobogganed down the hills at breakneck speed, racing against a stopwatch.[14]

On any frontier, extended families, ethnic groups, and countrymen often settle together or seek each other out, and the small population of French-speaking people in medicine line country was no different. Dan Tenaille, his brother Jean, to whom Dan was "deeply attached," and Guy Armand Thomas De Cargouet, a man who claimed to be a French viscount, formed a small phalanx of French aristocracy across southwest Saskatchewan. Jean built a stone residence on Sixteen Mile Lake, just north of Maple Creek, that was even more elaborate and formidable than Dan's house. It had glassed-in shelves, a window where hired help received wages, a large dais on which the dining room table sat, and an observation deck on the roof for sighting and shooting ducks. "The two families met very often," Dan's daughter recalled, "alternating and joining with other ranchers of French and Belgian descent living in the same region." De Cargouet, the alleged nobleman, settled on the Frenchman River west of Eastend in 1902. People called him the French Count, and, until he disappeared in 1908, knew him mainly for "raising fine horses and consuming huge amounts of whiskey" with friends.[15]

"Quite a few French fellows," as the daughter of one put it, settled in the region, including Jacques Terraine Garissere (known as Jake), from the

Base-Pyrenees; his cousins Joe and Pete Chourrout from France; and Anton Lognos, a homesteader who arrived in 1909 and had studied pharmacy at the University of Marseilles. In Maple Creek, Jean Claustre, Frenchman and a former Mountie, ran the first general store, and Joseph Renaud, a Quebecer, carried the mail to Eastend from 1901 to 1910. Most were keenly interested in horses, beginning with Michael Oxarat, the Basque, who died in 1896, before most of the other French arrived. A Métis jockey and cowboy named Johnnie Leveille raced Oxarat's horses in St. Louis and elsewhere. Almost everything this network of Frenchmen did extended south into Montana. In 1894, at age sixteen, Jake Garissere had come to Harlem, Montana, just east of Chinook, to work for a French family of horse ranchers. Pete Chourrout had also arrived first in Montana, in 1896, where he met and married Edna Mae Anderson of Chinook before moving north.[16]

Among these men there was some French chauvinism. "Never saw a Canadian you didn't have to push," Joe Chourrout liked to say. On July 14, Bastille Day, Dan Tenaille flew a "huge French 'Fleur de Lis' flag," recalled Jake Garissere's daughter. When some wisecracker complained that there was no Union Jack above it, Tenaille raised "a tiny post-card sized Union Jack" above the French emblem.[17] The political climate was tolerant enough to absorb such humor, despite the presence of easterners. Canadians, still under a monarchy, did not object to the royal fleur-de-lis, more than a century out of favor in France.

Along with the French, patrician elegance and attitudes tended to concentrated on the Canadian side of the line, a peculiar feature of this area. On many of its earlier frontiers America had harbored an effete class. Other Montana valleys had their Oxford-educated polo-pony ranchers and upper-class lady photographers with brothers in Gladstone's British parliament. But they were not prominent here. One Chinook resident who admired Theodore Roosevelt liked to point out that in his acquaintance with Mr. Roosevelt while cattle ranching in western Dakota, the future president "put on no airs whatever."[18] In sports, customs, and connections, the Chinook–Bear Paws region did not rival its northern neighbors' pretensions.

In this, the English apparently outdid the French. The effects were sometimes hilarious. One Englishwoman, in a caustic description of a cousin's ranch fifty or so miles east of Maple Creek near Swift Current, Saskatchewan, delighted in the absurdity of her relatives' grand gestures of refinement. "Out there on the bald prairies, these two lived like they were in the heart of Dorset," she recalled. Teatime particularly amused her: "cousin Harry would come in" from "chasing those coyotes with his damned dogs all the time . . . 'By Georging' it and 'By Joving' it all over the place," while she and her cousin, dressed in formal tea gowns, would pour. "No mail to open, no newspapers to read. No gossip. Goodness, their nearest neighbor was six or seven miles away, across two creeks, a gully, a coulee, and a ravine," she lamented. "So there we were, two English creatures in a fine house with our eggs, our scones, our curled butter, and our India tea. My dear, it was ludicrous." It was not the landscape that bothered her (on the contrary, she soon married and moved to Alberta); it was her cousin's refusal to adapt. "[T]he next big decision would be where to walk," she added, skewering the charade of contrived elegance on the bald prairie. "Would we walk west or east? Or would it be north or south?"[19]

The Maple Creek–Cypress Hills region held a number of such cultured Englishmen. Like the French, they formed networks. Oxford-educated Myles Bolton arrived in the Cypress Hills with his valet in 1892. Another Englishman, Spencer Pearse, joined him before establishing his own ranch. In 1901, an eighteen-year-old Yorkshire schoolboy named Frank Barroby and another English lad arrived at the Boltons' as "remittance men," willing to pay Bolton four hundred dollars a month to "learn ranching." Donald Corry followed in 1907, fresh from the same school as Barroby, where Myles Bolton's brother-in-law was headmaster, to work for Barroby. His brother Barrett Corry came shortly thereafter. They were not all so priggish as the Swift Current cousins, but their affect was English and cultured. Harry Bettington, who ran horses and cattle with Spencer Pearse, wore his monocle. Bolton built a tennis court and a large stone house. Bolton, Pearse, and Corry by turns held Anglican church services at their ranches. Pearse considered himself a naturalist. He was an avid bird-watcher and introduced ruffed grouse to the Cypress Hills. Donald Corry, whose photo album is displayed in the Eastend Museum, returned to England for his wedding, which included guests from Eastend, and held large parties at his ranch on Boxing Day and picnics at which the main entertainments were cricket, "football," tennis, and table tennis.[20]

British sports were popular among a wide circle of former Britons. In 1897 the North-West Mounted Police A division cricket team, looking consummately British with white shirts, a terrier mascot, and a tobacco pipe, posed outside the Maple Creek barracks for a photograph. For three years beginning in 1909 Maple Creek won the provincial tennis cup. And in 1909 an English billiard tournament was held at the Jasper Hotel.[21]

The effete discovered that refinement did not always graft well to the prairie. One story describes the refined pair of Bolton and Pearse on a journey home from Maple Creek in their early days as ranchers. They stopped for lunch, and Bolton, a good musician, brought out his new cornet to try it out, the sound of which caused the horses to break loose and bolt for quieter parts. The spot was thereafter dubbed "Cornet Coulee." James Bolingbroke, an Eastend-area bachelor, cultivated a fabulous garden including "a special strain" of imported sweet peas, while his cattle, which "came second" to gardening, ran wild. The Masterses, a well-off family of Londoners who arrived in 1902, had a large pack of Russian wolfhounds that would "jam themselves under the table at supper time," one granddaughter recalled, and indiscreetly expel gas. As late as the 1910s in Eastend, a group of tea-drinking, tennis-playing English transplants in Eastend, the objects of a certain amount of derision, constructed a tennis court in the silty clay bottomland and "one morning sallied out in their flannels, ignoring the ill-bred snickering of the village," one observer recalled.[22]

It is tempting to imagine a cultural crevasse. We envision it, a perceptibly widening defile of differences opening outward. British-dominated Mounted Police outposts on one hand, and the itinerant American troops gradually replaced by Fort Assiniboine soldiers on the other, including the black Tenth Cavalry, headquartered there in 1894. These military organizations remained a study in contrasts. Yet in the 1890s, and into the twentieth century, there was no strong evidence in the Cypress Hills–Bear Paws region that the international boundary had become much of a social dividing line. In fact, the newcomers seemed instead to be slowly obliterating the old familiar counterpoint of Indians, merchants, outlaws, Mounties, and nationals, grading them over with a hodgepodge population connected by only loosely related pasts and, outside a few ethnic enclaves, largely circumstantial affiliations. For this particular borderland, initially marked by distinct national identities, the process of becoming a hinterland was an oddly homogenizing one, even in the midst of diversity.[23]

By 1896, the border itself had not fared well. The stone pile markers were becoming harder to find—five miles apart, scrambled by weather and animals—and people virtually ignored the boundary. They crisscrossed the cairn-dotted line as if it were no more substantial than a threshold. Within one three-week period in the spring of 1890, Chinookites Flynn and Gerts were "up into the Maple creek country" selling horses, while Riley Thompson from Maple Creek was meeting with the manager of the Conrad Cattle Company in Chinook. Only livestock and outlaws felt the sting of borderland pursuit. Northward-wandering American sheep and cattle, turned back from grazing in a Canadian pasture by a single vigilant Mountie, often felt the effects of the border more than did their untroubled owners.[24]

With proportionally fewer Indians and fugitives seeking the border's refuge, the markers seemed even less important. In the Canadian field one might see the Maple Creek baseball club, and the wiry, vigorous figure of young Horace Greeley, a leading Maple Creek merchant and the New Hampshire–born cousin of America's most famous journalist. The rancher Bettington and friends form a jaunty group in an assortment of cowboy

T. C. Power & Bro. general store, Maple Creek, North-West Territories, an American company based in Helena, Montana, managed by Horace Greeley (nephew of the American newspaperman) — typical of early cross-border commerce.
Photos courtesy Southwest Saskatchewan Old Timers' Museum, Maple Creek, Saskatchewan.

hats, smoking and passing around a bottle of "special," suggesting a milieu where the Montana cowboy might be indistinguishable from the outback English gentleman. On the American side, within sight might be a well-to-do Irish-born Catholic merchant with his own monocle and elegant suit, breaking the horizon on a bicycle specially fitted to ride on railroad tracks, off to visit an Ontario-born Presbyterian down the line to talk about irrigation, and perhaps discuss former Hudson's Bay Company fur trapper Jack "Bear Paw" Griffin's latest acquisition in fine horseflesh out along Clear Creek. Can we so easily distinguish what was north from what was south?

It is difficult to label either population as characteristically "Canadian" or "American." For one thing, a substantial flotsam of seemingly nationless peoples, holdovers from another era, floated among the newcomers and across the border: the Métis freighters and their families, with at best a troubled allegiance to Canada; itinerant Indians picking up odd jobs; and the so-called squaw men of the Bear Paws, who had squatted on U.S. reservation land with Indian wives before the reservation

shrank. Among whites, the T. C. Power and Co. mercantile operation of
Helena, Montana, had substantial dry-goods stores in both Chinook and
Maple Creek. There were leading citizens of shifting identities as well:
notable Chinook area settlers such as Bear Paw Jack and Murdock
Matheson were Canadians, and merchant Tom O'Hanlon and his brother
were Irish; Horace Greeley, despite his strong American associations,
ranched and managed the Power & Bro. Store in Maple Creek, and was
soon to become a conservative member of the North-West Territorial
Assembly. He was widely known, in an anonymous biographer's hyperbole,

*North-West Mounted Police near Eastend Post, North-West Territories, beneath a
native grave (possibly Sioux) with a horse skeleton in the foreground, suggesting a
passing era. c. 1878. Photograph by W. E. Hook.*
Photo courtesy Glenbow Museum, Calgary, Alberta.

as "the very hypothesis of rectitude and fair dealing," surely a Canadian compliment for a Yankee.[26]

Fair dealing did not describe the experience of the Indians at the Fort Belknap reservation. They eked out an existence in what seemed, even to reservation agents during the 1890s, an ill-starred vortex of economic and cultural confusion. They survived on government rations, an unsavory combination of bad flour and "ridiculously small" quantities of beef, coffee, and sugar (frequently raided by nearby white residents) that maintained 70 percent of the population. This they supplemented with sporadic herding, largely unsuccessful farming, and odd jobs on and off the reservation. As if fulfilling some storyteller's parable of desperation, they literally sold snake oil. Albert Sperry, traveling through the area by train in 1894, noted "a dead rattlesnake hung on almost every barb of the two-wire fence along the right of way with an old tin can under it to catch the grease and oil fried out by the sun." Someone explained to him that the Indians sold the oil as a "supposed cure for rheumatism." "They were always hungry," recalled a sheep rancher's son who watched visiting Indians eat at the ranch table after everyone else had been fed. Despite such conditions, they managed to maintain traditional habits, dances, and ceremonies. As late as 1909, the most visible of these jutted from the hilltops of southeastern Chouteau county—the dark silhouettes of Gros Ventre burial boxes and little board houses for the dead.[27]

As it turned out, the small French influence in Eastend did not last. Those who had come so eagerly to the prairie were to find that something more was required of them than their imported parcels, their hopes, and their pretension. By the time the Poulin family from Quebec arrived in 1913 and the Piquards from Belgium in 1919, most of the other French-speakers were dead, gone, or soon to be gone. Nor did English pretensions outlast the French. "The educated and the English, who were often but not invariably synonymous," noted one observer, "found that it was impossible to keep alive on the frontier the things that made life agreeable," or at least agreeable to them. Many died or sold out and moved away, and the impetus for high culture gradually lost momentum. The amused visitor to her hyperelegant relatives near Swift Current gave the fate of gentility an appropriately cartoonish send-off: "[T]hey went belly up the next year," she said. "Not even their toes wiggled."[28]

A LIVING OR A
WAY OF LIFE?

Charlie Russell was the most famous artist and perhaps the worst busi-nessman ever to live in Chinook. He arrived in Montana at age sixteen in 1880, worked as a cowhand in the region during the 1880s and '90s, and by the 1910s was one of the West's most renowned artists and cowboy sto-rytellers. And he was anything but genteel. He became the proprietor of one of Chinook's many saloons and gave away so many free drinks that the saloon's duration, he later wrote, was "like the life of a butterfly, short but verry merry." During his brief residency in Chinook, where a bronze statue of him now stands in the town center, he shoved stolen chickens, grease popping in their roasting pans, under the bunk when sheriff Frank O'Neal made an unexpected call. He stored potatoes in the back of A. S. Lohman's Chinook Mercantile. He and his cronies, whom the newspaper editor dubbed the "Hungry Seven," told off-color stories there, too, sometimes too loudly to suit the local women who gathered at the front of the store. Charlie Russell depicted his own view of the cowboy in his popular *Rawhide Rawlins Stories* and other accounts. When an "eastern girl" asks her moth-er if "cowboys eat grass," the old lady replies, "No dear, they're part human." "I don't know but the old gal had 'em sized up right," Russell added. These men understood cattle so well, Russell joked, that "you'd think they growed horns 'n was haired over."[1]

Like Russell, local cowboys and ranchers, who became established in medicine line country in the 1890s, portrayed themselves as bound to the land, rooted in a sense of place, particularly the ones who began to supplant the huge cattle operations that had started to fade all over the West. Many seemed to grow accustomed to the landscape more quickly than to their assorted new neighbors. In their isolating business, the more pressing covenant of adaptation was environmental, not social. And if their job was to produce commodities for the unlovely slaughterhouses of Chicago, they

An illustrated envelope from Charles M. Russell to friend Edward "Kid" Price of Chinook, Montana, June 10, 1902, showing Russell and his Chinook cowboy cronies, "The Hungry Seven," stealing chickens for dinner, the sheriff in pursuit.
Photo courtesy Montana Historical Society, Museum Collection, Helena, Montana.

felt great affection for and pride in their animals and their rangeland, and in their knowledge of them both.

They were unassuming men and women. They called the California vaquero "fancy" with his single-cinch high-horned saddle, long rope, and "hoss jewelry." The cow men among them were the east-of-the-Rockies type who weren't "so much for pretty," as Charlie Russell noted. They favored a low-horned double-cinch saddle, shorter rope, and plainer gear. Many may even have been consciously imitating the popular imagery they had absorbed from novels and Wild West shows. Some had names such as Shorty or Slippers or Fiddle Back, the kind of casual, semiderogatory epithets one finds in Western novels.[2]

Russell, for one, came to the Chinook area in the late 1880s in order to approximate the landscape and heroes of Ned Buntline's western dime novels, which filled his imagination during his Missouri boyhood in the 1870s. Even in 1908, his cowboying days over, Russell thrilled at intimate encounters with the powers of nature, and wrote with some nostalgia of a recent night spent in the wagon of a freighter friend, "the last jerk line man in this part of the country." "[T]here's no better snoozing place than a big Murphy wagon with the roar of the storm on the sheets," he wrote; "nature rocked my cradle an sung me to sleep."[3] One largely forgotten Eastend-area cowboy with a touch of lyricism recalled with relish the isolated outdoor living his job required. "I would rather hear a meadow lark sing, crickets chirp or frogs croak around a slough, than to hear Gilbert and Sullivan orchestras or Shuberts lofty music," he wrote. His, he declared, was a "happy and carefree life," in which he would "rather be bitten by a sage tick than any housefly."[4]

These men undoubtedly felt this way about "the great outdoors," but one cannot help but wonder in such cases if nature, for the cowboy and herder, was merely the last, best refuge from their subordinate position in the social order. One member of the Miller sheep ranching family remembered thinking of sheep herders as "riff raff," and a retired Canadian cowboy gave an unforgettable summation of the cowboy's lot that suggested the plantation slave. The "owner in the big house," he said, in what is probably the most succinct description of the cowboy's status ever written, "thought of cowboys as shit, just as low as you can get." Perhaps such a "simpleton," as this man deemed the abused cowboy, was equally simple-minded when he spoke about the idyll of pastoral life.[5] The cowboy's alienation from his boss may explain why his job—to grow a profitable commodity for sale in a distant land—was somewhat at odds with his spiritual connection with the natural world.

Ranchers, too, often claimed an emotional attachment and even restraint toward the natural environment. These qualities historians often find weak or lacking in capitalist cultures with an instrumentalist posture toward the land. Yet bonds to the land were idealized in local mythology. Some area rangemen "never got beyond being ordinary cowboys and didn't desire anything bigger," gushed one local chronicler, yet were the lone "giants" of the region.[6] There are indeed hints that some ranchers tried to develop sustainable land-use patterns. They studied the prairie grasses, according to one source, and recognized the need for winter hay for their livestock. And through trial and error they learned, for example, that upland "prairie wool" made more nutritious hay than the taller slough grasses.[7] In local reminiscences, however, the number of people who used these methods is uncertain—the practice is attributed to the universal pronoun *you*, as in "You did this, see?"

To find people who would wax eloquent about "balls of fire which glowed on the tips of the cattle's horns," a phenomenon that sometimes occurs during lightning storms, one can read the work of anthropologist John Bennnett, a ranch-loving anthropologist who studied the Maple Creek district's society extensively in the 1960s.[8] Bennett illustrates something of the early ranchers' attitudes toward the land. He discovered in local ranchers streaks of romanticism and nostalgia for the "wide open spaces." He found a "mystique" about human relationships with livestock and animals, as in "'He really knows his cow, that feller. He can tell what she's going to do every time before she does it." And he found a persistent resource-conserving ranching culture that valued moderation and isolation in its land-use practices. Although Bennett is at his best when making such incisive distinctions and categorizations among social groups, he is stingy with evidence. He assumes as a "basic fact" that the "natural resources of the region are ideally suited to livestock raising." Moreover, in a later cross-border study of the region, Bennett and his coauthor, Seena Kohl, emphasize ranchers' desire to thrive over sensitivity and appreciation of the landscape. They boil down residents' attitude to the borderland environment as that of soldiers in a battle to construct "viable human communities in a kind of Siberia." This "determination," they write, glossing over variations among groups as well as the affection for the land suggested in Bennett's previous studies, is "the cultural significance of the environment of the northern plains."[9] Ranching on the borderland, in other words, was something like war and something like romance.

The brief span of a century, the blink of an eye on a vast prairie that has seen eons of constant change and disruption, is hardly epic. Nevertheless, between Bennett and the local chroniclers, Northern Plains ranchers took on the aura of demigods or a natural aristocracy. Local sources spoke of "ranching in the blood," as if it were an inherited physical condition.[10] "Ranching, in the early days," as one Cypress Hills woman put it, "was a way of life rather than a way to make money though some managed to combine the two."[11] A way of life suggests commitment to a place and its resources uncharacteristic of land speculators or profit-driven capitalists. It suggests enduring human-ecological harmony. Yet whether or not these natural resources were ideally suited to livestock raising was not only unproven but often a matter of opinion. The wheat-raisers who skinned and hung out their neighbors' sheep did not think so, nor did the Fort Belknap Indians, who found time-consuming livestock a poor substitute for buffalo. And those ranchers defeated by harsh winters and prolonged drought (and there were many) might have agreed. Before one can understand how these settlers viewed their natural environment, one needs to understand whether or not their way of life was unique to the region.

By all accounts, ranching in medicine line country was at least distinctive. People in this area quickly mixed practices and invented new traditions. From the 1890s through the 1920s and beyond, these ranchers' ways of doing things were in a state of constant change. Sheep raisers, according to Peter Miller, "had to learn how to run sheep and what to expect of the country."[12] The same applied to cattle and horse ranchers. Experimentation and learning by trial and error were in this country tried-and-true agricultural methods. The weather alone created its own local folklore of prediction and expectation. Fog meant rain ninety days later. Coyotes howling before sunrise in cold weather forecast a change. The crescent moon "on its back" was a dry moon. And chinook winds, of course, were a regional phenomenon that yielded its own terminology: chinooks that failed to melt all the snow, for example, a stock-raiser's curse, were called "bob-tailed chinooks." Chinooks (which extended north and south beyond this borderland area) were such an important and distinctive regional characteristic that local ranchers identified themselves as residents of "the chinook belt."[13]

Just as significant, ever-changing market demand and local availability of resources created a kind of fluctuating round-robin of land use and livestock. Excluding the Denison Germans, a cluster of settlers who raised only sheep, many ranchers might raise horses, then cattle, then sheep, then cattle again over a period of years, depending on what was profitable and most easily possible. The *Ranching News* of Maple Creek in 1903 even suggested dairying, a "thing abhorred" by most local ranchers, as a response to the "fencing and the crowded state of the country." By all indications local ranchers tried to make a living however they could. When one operation floundered, they improvised, waited for conditions to change, or imitated a more successful neighbor. "In the early days there was a very limited market for horses," noted Maple Creek rancher George Stewart, describing the finer points of the local economy; "most horse ranchers shipped their surplus stock to Manitoba," he continued, and took as payment "stocker cattle which they shipped back home," fattened, and then shipped "to England which for many years was the only market for beef cattle. So most ranchers carried both cattle and horses."[14] While local ranch children had curlews and berry picking on their minds, their parents were trying to interpret a complex web of economic and ecological forces.

Of course, all were capitalists, in the sense that they tried to make a living in a system of free-market capitalist trade and agriculture. When and how people became capitalist agriculturalists has consumed the attention of many North American historians. But here, the settlers lived by the train lines they had arrived on. On such a market-soaked frontier, the presence of the international wheat, beef, and wool markets was assumed. It was the reason most of these people were here. A more interesting question is whether, as a consequence of their participation in capitalist markets, these borderland boosters were uniformly utilitarian in their attitudes toward the land, or whether some of them did indeed seem to have "growed horns 'n was haired over."

Contrary to local folklore, there were signs of a purely utilitarian attitude toward nature, even among the early ranchers. The newspapers blared it. They were development's cheerleaders, wearyingly so. Make Chinook the "metropolis of the Milk river valley," they crowed; bring your immigrant money to Maple Creek, they broadcast in twenty thousand pamphlets; irrigate with every cubic inch of water; put every acre of land into productive use; "laugh at pessimists." One historian has identified in such exhortations a booster "ethos," peculiar to newspapermen who prescribed an admirable communitarian morality for rural and small town life.[15] Whatever else it was, it expressed mammoth expectations and false optimism, if not arrogance toward nature, and the settlers operated in its wake. Some did dream of big profit, selling out for a small fortune, the mother's milk of every boomer, schemer, gambler, and rainbow chaser who ever went West. One can find the phrase "get rich quick" in local ranching documents, and land acquisition was part of the rancher's repertoire. Many would hire Scots or others to homestead, "prove up," and then sell the land to the ranch, "kind of a put-up deal" as one rancher described it with a chuckle. These hirelings "weren't really settlers," he added, "and I don't think they planned to stay there."[16]

The Miller family's large-scale ambitions literally shaped the map of the territory. Soon after entering the Blaine County Museum today a visitor comes upon a large, mostly green-colored map along the left-hand wall. A close reading shows it to be the Millers' 1952 holdings and leases, shown in green. Miller Bros., Inc., became the largest landed interest in Blaine County. They had grazing privileges on about 343,000 acres, about one-fourth of the land in the county, and were one of the biggest sheep operations in Montana.[17]

At the same time, ranchers could express an acceptance of limits, caution, even moderation that does not sound like mere local mythology. "Take care of the range; it's been taking care of us for generations," wrote two members of the Gilchrist clan about their family's seventy-five year tenure on the southwest Saskatchewan range. "My father, he was an old timer," recalled Chinook rancher James McCann; "he thought the grass was free and it ought to stay that way." The elder McCann would not buy up land even when everyone else was doing so, because "he just didn't believe in it." Whether it was because he had faith in abundant resources or in social restraint we can only guess.[18]

These settlers' sense of what life owed them was humbled by the sheer power and immediacy of the natural environment, by disease and illness and accidents, and by familial obligations. Ask ninety-two-year-old Olive Ramberg Satleen, who delayed marriage and gave up her hope of becoming a nurse because her parents needed her on their ranch west of Chinook, if she felt resentful growing up in two rooms with eleven siblings in such a climate. "Why, no!" she'd cry. Unchinked cracks in the house she moved into as a newlywed—now *that* was something to complain about, an unmet expectation, she recalled.[19]

Such steadfastness might be attributed merely to a strong work ethic. In every document promising the reader a chance to "get rich quick" comes the required sentiment that "struggle and hardship" were the accepted "routine" of life. These were not people who counted on winning any cosmological lottery. Yet an area biologist confidently asserted in 1986 that "much of our native range is in better shape after a hundred years of ranching than it was in the buffalo days." This may be a small compliment, but it surely reflects another kind of ethic at work—a common regional pride in stewardship of the land.[20] If the mythologizers exaggerated, they also captured a grain of truth. The rancher's relationship with nature was one of enduring intimacy and perhaps some restraint.

One would never guess this from the fantastical images in the region's promotional and agricultural books and pamphlets—showing the farmer behind a plow turning soil into rooster tails of gold coins, or posing as a muscle-bound Atlas holding up a cornucopia full of Canadian produce and tall buildings.[21] Local photographers, however, showed people not only as they wanted to be—the successful domesticators of a wild land—but as they were, a struggling, diverse collection of newcomers facing awesome natural forces they could not avoid and places to which they were developing emotional attachments. With their cameras and in their written words, borderland residents revealed the constant push and pull of nature on their lives.

The photographic record is extensive and vivid. Walk in the door of Chinook's Blaine County Museum or Eastend's town museum, or flip through the photo files at the Maple Creek Old Timers' Museum, and the long, straight lines of the prairie horizon and scruffy hardscrabble foregrounds grow quickly familiar, the settings of a working rural life. A photograph in the Maple Creek museum with the words "The Last Cattle Round Up on the Range, Montana," written across the bottom in white ink is typical. A wide-angle view, its cowpunchers trail their herd as a seamless, integrated aspect of the enormous, panoramic landscape. In other photographs we see ranches, houses, storefronts, machinery, livestock, threshing crews, ice cutters, picnickers, children at swimming holes, leading citizens, Métis families, and Indians all in the ungroomed nature they moved in.

Few, if any, of these photographs celebrate nature or the outdoors for its own sake. They are about people and their accomplishments. Yet even in photographs that consciously exclude it, the landscape often asserts itself. The surfaces of the cramped interior of every sod house or roughly hewn log structure are alive with the memory of raw elements. In the foreground of photographs of squat buildings are prairie grass and a strip of packed earth, unadorned or dotted with ranch detritus—a democratic expanse of dirt that fronts equally the twelve-foot-square homestead shack with a family seated before it and the English-style clapboard house with its

The Last Cattle Round Up On the Range, Montana, no date.
Photo courtesy Southwest Saskatcehwan Old Timers' Museum, Maple Creek, Saskatchewan.

wraparound porch. These pictures show people who, if not seduced by their landscape, are all intimately acquainted with it.

In the Eastend museum, a photograph labeled "Mrs. Daintry and infant" bears striking witness to this relationship. The wife of the First Anglican clergyman of Eastend, Mrs. Daintry is seated not in a chair with antimacassars or framed by the solid wooden rectangle of a porch, but embraced by what can only be described as thick brush, holding a baby in her arms. The Daintry portrait is tucked into the family photo album of Donald and Gladys Keddell Corry, whose emotional ties to their native England are abundantly evident, their album filled with images both of Saskatchewan and of England and English visitors and relatives. One comes upon a photo of a train breaking through a prairie snow drift or the diving board at the ranch swimming hole, and then one of Donald and Gladys in the spring of 1914, posing in their wedding clothes in a sunny Essex, England garden, surrounded by forty-one people in fine clothing. Just before the Daintry photograph is one of the Corrys' daughter Hazel on her fifth birthday, clutching her fur muff in front of the leaded stained-glass

Round Up on Range, Montana.

windows and elegantly carved arched doorway of her grandparents' house in
Essex, England. From little Hazel and her retrieval of English elegance to
the backwater priest's infant nestled in a desert bush, one travels the enormous distance from these people's pretensions and cultural memories to
their unbuffered presence in the West.

If newcomers viewed the plains as undiminished open space, the
natives observed with each successive treaty a landscape shrinking before
their eyes. They felt distant from a place they thought they had known.
Those who remained, as the scanty evidence suggests, were trying to imagine their way out of diminished circumstances. The Métis responded by
either fleeing to the bushlands at the northern edge of the Saskatchewan
and Alberta prairie, to various Montana Métis communities formed after
the failed rebellion of 1885, or to a Métis reserve established in Alberta in
1901, or by trying to live as best they could as outsiders on the social and
geographical margins of white and Indian society. Irene Grande, an elderly
Métis woman from Helena, Montana, recalled that until recently mixed
bloods lived as outcasts, accepted by neither Indians nor whites. For a group

of Gros Ventre to refuse a Métis traveling companion, saying "We do not wish to travel with half breeds," was not unusual. The Métis relied on their own strong social bonds. "Heck, I'm a halfbreed and proud of it," bragged Mrs. Grande. The hunting and trapping culture, and the position as economic intermediaries that characterized the zenith of Métis life in the mid- to late nineteenth century, had largely vanished. From her comfortable ranch house on the outskirts of Helena, Irene Grande told long stories of rural poverty, struggle, and disease.[22]

The Indians at Fort Belknap, an uneasy convergence of Gros Ventre and their former enemies the Assiniboine, clung tenuously to traditional spiritual views of the natural world. In this, they were not unlike the newcomers, who through a mix of religious and secular beliefs sought coherence in and control over their surroundings. But even more than non-Indians, native groups sought order through a process of religious or secular negotiation with nonhuman powers. Among the Gros Ventre, religious

Gros Ventre Indians at a dance, Fort Belknap, Montana, 1906. White reservation agents discouraged native dancing.
Photo courtesy the American Museum of Natural History (Neg. No. 338934).

fervor sometimes swelled in response to new adversities. The Ghost Dance movement that swept Plains Indian cultures in the 1890s, for example, came to Fort Belknap in 1890 with a mixed-blood Arapaho–Gros Ventre from Wyoming named Returns to War. The Ghost Dance was one of many practices and rituals by which the Indians tried to enlist supernatural aid— in this case, aid to literally transform the landscape by burying the white invaders under new soil and restoring the buffalo and their grazing grounds to the Indians.

For the Dakota Sioux, this strong antiwhite message caused tragic remonstrance at the massacre at Wounded Knee, South Dakota, in December of 1890. The Ghost Dance was a powerful spiritual movement, and U.S. government agents and soldiers were intent on crushing it.

It was late December, Sitting Bull had just been killed, and Big Foot's band of Minniconjou, demoralized and fearful, was on its way to visit Red Cloud in Pine Ridge. They camped beside the icy waters of Wounded Knee Creek, many of them veterans of the Battle of the Greasy Grass and wearing the white muslin Ghost Shirts they believe would protect them from bullets. When the Seventh Cavalry, sent to arrest Big Foot, searched them for weapons, a scuffle with a deaf man named Black Coyote began the attack in which the cavalry's Hotchkiss guns killed nearly 300 of the 350 men, women and children in the band. Fittingly, Nelson Miles arrived, now commander of the military Division of the Missouri, to finish the blow to the Ghost Dance movement, although to his credit he later attributed the massacre to "blind stupidity or criminal indifference."

The Gros Ventre experience was less dramatic but more clearly revealed the internal confusion that rattled many Plains cultures. The Ghost Dance religion's hopeful message was only briefly popular at Fort Belknap, and eventually it died as a result of corrupt leadership. For many reasons, the spiritual horizon seemed to be shrinking along with the landscape. The surviving remnant of the Ghost Dance among the Gros Ventre was a guessing game, played with sticks and a button, in which players would try to win by praying for supernatural aid, a hauntingly diminished manifestation of what had been a grand spiritual vision.[23]

By 1900, as the fate of the Ghost Dance suggests, Fort Belknap residents found themselves disoriented and sometimes desperate in a once-familiar landscape. They spent the winters not in their traditional lodges, made from thirty skins of July or August buffalo, but in poorly heated, poorly ventilated log cabins. The Indian agent in 1911 estimated that 90 percent of the reservation's Indians had tuberculosis. They no longer knew how to make a living: "They can take our [food] tickets up and starve us to death," complained The Male in 1901 of a government threat to reduce rations, "yet we cannot be self-supporting until we are furnished the means." If

Gros Ventre views of nature did not change, their expression of them did. Children observed but did not adopt the ceremonies their elders used to appease and negotiate with animals and the elements. As late as the 1930s, many Gros Ventre believed that their difficulties with nature were directly attributable to the loss of traditional cultural practices. "We have all kinds of bad luck," an elder observed. A flood, he noted, swept down from the Little Rockies because "somebody didn't do right with that Pipe." Like others, these Indians found themselves divided and uncertain about their relationship with the natural environment.[24]

During the thirty years between 1890 and 1920, the fragmented agricultural settlement of such a remote and inhospitable landscape might have understandably become an increasingly daunting task even to non-Indians, or at least to anyone who could see through the exaggerations of a promotional brochure. In the wider world, swelling hope in science and Progressive reform, a hope that inspired both Canadian and American agricultural promoters, encouraged optimism. This optimism competed, however, with widespread feeling that local control, even civilization itself, was rapidly falling into disarray. Some historians have argued that Progressive optimism, Theodore Roosevelt–style visions of the full and rational mastery and management of nature, filled the rural communities of the Great Plains, but there is little evidence that this is true.[25] Pioneer Cypress Hills rancher Rube Gilchrist expressed instead the wary detachment that grew out of the landscape: "Most of our problems stem from the everlasting fight of freedom versus authority," he noted with characteristic Canadian moderation that was in fact a borderland sentiment. "We always have too much of one or the other, and it keeps the world in a turmoil trying to find a balance."[26]

Indeed, modernity came rushing in like a chinook in January. By the mid-1890s, the railroad, federal surveyors, and land offices had created an urban-linked infrastructure. And even though trucks and tractors were rare until the 1920s, by 1915 automobiles, movie theaters, telephones, the Bureau of Reclamation, and World War I had closed the distances between the area's people.[27] As the twentieth century wore on, any degree of isolated intimacy with the land faced increasing challenges and made local assumptions about nature, it would seem, susceptible to change. The distant marketplaces, culture, and entertainments of Chicago, Toronto, California, and Europe all exerted their pull. These external forces, however—those that would abstract local residents from the land—were not the only catalysts for change. This was, after all, the kind of landscape that demanded one's attention.

The people in this corner of the West generally sought balance, not only Gilchrist's sort of political balance between what they wanted from other people and their own self-reliance, but one between being a part of nature and controlling it. The turmoil of personal adversity, a difficult climate, and an increasingly diverse, industrial, and media-stirred continent soon dampened any unbounded optimism or naive hopes of a controlled and secure world. Socially, the region's residents, even its natives, could not rely on an automatic community of religion, ethnicity, language, or even on the fledgling safety net of state aid.

The one constant on this late frontier were the unpredictable and often difficult forces of nature, which technology had not yet made remote. In the writings of two women on the Canadian side, the two most substantial diaries that survive from this period, entries were frequently little more than terse records of extreme weather and its consequences.[28] "1901, Feb. 17 Blizzard in afternoon," wrote Lorana Marshall, an American who settled with her husband, Henry, and children on Battle Creek south of the Cypress Hills in 1895. "Feb. 18 very hard wind all night till 3.30 am froze up everything in house. Henry stayed home." "Feb. 27," her litany continued, "big chinook lots of snow gone away Myron's calf died. Feb. 28 froze a little this morning. Mar. 1 thawed all night creek running high water broke in coulee by the barn. Mar. 2 began to snow at 9 am. Mar. 3 all froze up and a hard wind north . . . April 14 Sunday snowed during the night and a good deal all day April 15 froze up hard. Canada a steer." (The last, cryptic phrase is perhaps a disparaging comment.)

Summer, her diary attests, provided no respite from the harsh climate: "1905, July 25 two fires started on the hills west at noon . . . children came home from school and in a few minutes it began to rain & hail and lasted for 20 minutes broke all the windows in the west side of the house and destroyed all the rhubarb & potatoes and beat the hay all down." A photograph of the Marshall place taken from a high, distant vantage point shows a log house rising like a raft adrift on a vast, sloping, treeless plain, an experiment launched onto an unforgiving sea of weather.[29]

The other diarist, an Englishwoman with the grandiloquent name of Winnifred Perrin Hancock, who married a Mountie and also settled south of Maple Creek, recorded similar storms, winds, and cold temperatures in 1907–8, along with colds, sore throats, and seemingly endless games of solitaire. And though Hancock wrote of a pleasurable moment when she watched sixty antelope from the top of a hill, there were no hints that either she or Marshall identified wilderness with virtue or democracy, as American national mythology would have it. Here certainly was a place to engender the "garrison mentality" with which Canadian social critics have characterized their country's hostile relationship to nature.[30]

Canada generally calls to mind a harsher set of landscapes than does the United States. Environmental differences do in fact distinguish much of the Canadian from the American West—shorter growing season, colder climate, more abundant water. Yet this borderland environment, though full of local variety, contained the same elements on both sides of the line. These similarities went beyond shared crises of disease and drought. For every diarist's blizzard north of the boundary, there is a cowboy south of the line with a thorn in his knee who remembers dropping his pants at forty below zero to get it out. The blizzards, chinook winds, prairie fires, hailstorms, and varieties of terrain are no different in the records in Montana territory than they are on the Canadian side.[31]

The two diarists held neither typically Canadian nor typically American attitudes toward nature. They had instead what we might call a split personality of hostility and affection. For different reasons, many people were attracted to the place despite its difficulties. Though there was little hope for respite, many even grew to love it. Local literature is full of paeans to the area, lyrical nostalgia about the "home place." Those who stayed liked it for its remoteness, its stark beauty, its challenge, the high standards it imposed. Marshall and Hancock lived out their entire lives there.

These earliest settlers knew that the natural environment was stingy with its rewards and shared what little advice they could. Local folklore began early and persisted. Even by the early 1890s, when Ontarian John Matheson arrived in Chinook to try mixed farming and ranching, there was old-timers' lore that "if you didn't have water you were just out of luck," noted John's son Murdock Matheson. From Cow Creek to Maple Creek, the place quickly accumulated an agricultural past. The Indian's buffalo culture held little meaning for newcomers, but they listened carefully to the traders, Indian agents, and squaw men as they described the characteristics of the land. Some bought out squaw men, who had already discovered the best sources of water. Others arrived as Mounted Police and settled on the best sites of the vast territory they had patrolled. Together, as did Marshall and Hancock, they endured an onslaught of horrible winters, spring floods, and droughts, and responded by changing the way they did things. In their shared wisdom were the sure signs of community, a sense of place.[32]

By 1900 local folkways had created a remarkably consistent, remarkably transborder social ecology: a marginalized native and Métis population surviving on odd jobs, government assistance, and erratic agriculture; a few large ranching outfits; and a growing population of diverse creekbed ranchers, all hinterland capitalists, who counted on summer herd migration and supplements of natural or irrigated hay to sustain horses, cattle, and sheep through the winter. The ranches in the Chinook and Maple Creek area were a local and mixed variant of the major ranching frontiers. Blaine County and to some extent Cypress Hills cattle ranching was somewhat influenced by the Anglo-Texan system of north-central Texas, characterized by a distaste for sheep and the assumption of a self-sufficient or neglected herd in stationary free-range pastures. This essentially subtropical canebrake and salt marsh ranching system, common to coastal Louisiana and Texas, followed the Rocky Mountains north, where it ran straight into the brick wall of the Northern Plains' harsh winters in 1886 and 1906.[33] Sheep ranching, the other major early ranch culture in the area, began near Chinook under a group of German-Americans from Denison, Iowa. Some thirty of them, all greenhorns with names such as Ruhe, Lehfeldt, Hofeldt, Kuhr, LaFrantz, Martens, and Mundt, arrived in the early 1890s and followed what historical geographer Terry Jordan calls the British-derived midwestern herding system, known for its horizontal pasture shifting and hay production for winter feed.

Both of these Blaine county pastoral cultures moved north of the international boundary into the Cypress Hills–Maple Creek area, apparently to a greater degree than in any other part of the Canadian West, making it an exception to the distinctive regional cattle culture of the Canadian Rocky Mountains.[34] Still other, if sketchier, influences included Michael Oxarat, a Basque (from either Oregon or the Pyrenees, depending on the source) who had spent time in Texas, raised Thoroughbred horses and cattle, and ranched in the Cypress Hills from 1883 until his death in 1896; the huge Sir Lister-Kaye operation known as the 76, north of Maple Creek, a mostly British-staffed, wildly experimental, diversified, and short-lived ranching and farming operation run by an English gentleman; and what in the local histories is described as a large number of Scots who were "taken [with] the prairies."[35]

As in other parts of the West during this period, sheep successfully overtook the fading cattle dominion. They were fast becoming the people's choice. "John Cumberland from Maple Creek, Northwest Territory," reported an unremarkable notice in an 1890 issue of *Chinook Opinion*, "is here for the purpose of buying a band of sheep, which he intends to take to his ranch across the border." The Maple Creek district became a refuge for Canadian sheep ranchers who, in the words of one Maple Creek rancher, "had no friends in the cattle country to the west." By 1901 the sheep-to-cattle ratio in Assiniboia West, the large district including Maple Creek, was much higher than anywhere else in the North West Territories, largely due to the American influence from the Bear Paws, where in Chouteau County by 1900 sheep outnumbered cattle ten to one. "This country's built on sheep," an early Bear Paws rancher concluded, and he was right.[36] "[I]f he couldn't lick them, he'd have to join them," recalled another rancher's son of his father's conversion from cattle to sheep.[37] While trying to draw a winning hand, they all knew that some players won and some did not.

By November 1906, ranchers' confidence was high. Not boastful, brochure-language confidence. No one had an easy time of it. This was an

Ranch house of Lillian Miller and family, south of Chinook, with Lillian's brothers Chris and Henry in foreground. Five miles from the site of the Nez Percé surrender in 1877, it became the base for one of the largest sheep ranches in Montana.
Photo courtesy Linda Haugen, Chinook, Montana.

environment with no fat, a country that demanded both extremely hard work and good luck for those who would live by commercial agriculture. The people were quickly learning that there were no guarantees. But it appeared as though agricultural life had achieved some stability—that the local cowboy and sheepherder would last a good long time.

So it seemed in the memories of Lillian Miller, daughter of a sheep rancher south of Chinook, in the Bear Paw Mountains in the 1890s. We read memoirs with caution. In novelist Robertson Davies's words, they present the "classic problem of autobiography: it's inevitably life seen and understood backwards."[38] Even so, Miller's "I Remember Montana," is founded on galvanizing childhood experiences. Written in the 1960s and one of only two long childhood memoirs among settlement period documents (Wallace Stegner's is the other), it captures the intimacy of the early settlers' landscape. Miller arrived by train with her family in 1892. Her parents' sheep ranch about fifteen miles south of Chinook was in the foothills-prairie environment of early ranchers on both sides of the border. The log ranch house, four rooms and the only shingled roof in the region, was Lillian's base for roaming, and remembering. Miller's simple cataloguings of childhood memories are fresh, artless, and lengthy—insects, snakes, birds, flowers, rocks, wild fruits and berries, animals, gardens, grasses. She knows them intimately, as one knows one's children. In describing them, she conveys the sights and smells and textures of walking the countryside: raspberries grow on Berry Mountain, gooseberries along creeks, buffalo berries near Chinook; sarvis berries are bland, wild strawberries scarce; buffalo grass is five or six inches high, grama grass is slightly taller, blue joint grows in meadows and on hills, all are native and nutritious stock food. Loco weed makes an animal "utterly stupid [and] lifeless," and speargrass blinds a sheep by working through the wool around its eyes; bull snakes help the rancher by eating rodents; magpies "would peck at a sore on an animal's back until it died" or carry off chickens.[39]

Sometimes she traces the history of her landscape. Foxtail and cockle-burs she knows are non-native, and Canadian thistles are the product of dry-land farming. Ranching had displaced the bear, mountain lion, bobcat, deer, and buffalo, whose "trails were almost like paths around the hills." More often, though, Miller is entranced by beauty—a water snake that "swam with beautiful, graceful movements" with a striking "yellow line down its bright green back"; the "beautiful dragonflies with the sheerest of blue wings, whirring." She depicts a milieu in which the observation of nature was at times even a social event, though compared to Evelyn Cameron, the English country-gentlewoman photographer living then near the Yellowstone River to the south, whose effects included a leather-bound naturalists' library, Miller suggests more raw innate interest.[40] "We children, especially," she remembers, "tried to see how many different birds we could see," yellow canaries or gold finches, thrushes, black birds, field sparrows, juncos, chickadees, swallows, prairie chickens, sage grouse, ducks. Their observations are close field work: curlews came from a marshy area "near the north fence" with long legs, a long curved bill, their nests "built in the grass with very little feather padding and contain[ing] eight to ten blue eggs with large patches of brown scattered over them."[41]

Particularly in her portraits of flowers, Miller differentiates little between the human and natural orders of things. Wild and domestic flowers are catalogued in consecutive lists. In nature, Miller noted, "as in a well ordered garden there was a succession of bloom." She begins with shooting star, a "deep rose" color, also called "Adder's Tongue," "Johnny Jump Up," or "Star of Bethlehem," whose petals "curled back and at their base the black stamens with the pistil protruded," giving the meadows a rosy sheen. These and others, she continues, made a "veritable flower carpet"—buttercups, violets, primroses, wild iris, snapdragons, wild strawberry blossoms, Indian paintbrush, creeping phlox, low-growing lupine, many kinds of cacti, the occasional bitterroot with its "sheer, delicate pink blossoms," sagebrush, blue lupines, and finally the wild rose, whose blooms she put in a rose jar to open for the scent in midwinter. For her reader she then traverses the paths of her mother's garden, edged with candytuft and fragrant sweet mignonette reminiscent of the "old English gardens you read about in books," bordering "tall, fragile Iceland poppies native to the West," petunias, marigolds, nasturtiums, verbenas, yellow California poppies, and, along the house, sweet peas climbing six feet high with huge blooms.

The adult cares of making a living occasionally impinged on childhood idylls. Miller remembered her father's unbroken devotion to his work: "Other people take vacations, a sheepman, conscientiously, never." Why couldn't the Millers have ice cream like the Rosses? she would ask. "Mr. Ross [is] a cattle man," her father would say dryly; "we [run] sheep."

Still, in a lengthy psalmlike floral catalogue, nature and nurture, and West and East—perhaps even cattle and sheep men—are hardly separable. Whereas the English gentlewoman Cameron valued untouched wilderness, or, as she phrased it, "what may be accomplished where the peace of nature is never disturbed," Miller imagines herself easily in this intimately known landscape, part wild, part domestic. Like a backwater stand-up comic, she imitated "all animal calls, sheep, lambs, cattle, calves, dogs, cats, birds and even coyotes." Her recollections are not sentimental. These things, both wild and cultivated, not only made her parents' living, they shaped her identity, formed the architecture of her imagination.[42]

What, other than geography, could bind people here? More than gender, age, ethnicity, nationality, or even livestock, the environment dictated the bonds of the ranching community. As easily as a shopkeeper on Manhattan's Lower East Side might inventory the residents of a city block, Otto Moir ticked off by name his "neighbors," who inhabited an area thousands of square miles in size: they "consisted of the Boltons," he began, "Laurel Reid and family, the Freels, Spencer Pears, Oswalt Gibson, the Hermans, Joe and Harold Bull and a Mr. Hardy, Walter Humphrey, Beddington, and the Wylies."[43] Moir, like Miller, was the son of an early borderland rancher, and when he recalled what amounted to a "neighborhood" in around 1902, it was geographical rather than ethnic. "Our neighborhood," he wrote, "went from Maple Creek to Chinook, Montana, and east and north to East End." Community was a matter of geography, not nationality. For many of its inhabitants this was one land, a place within which one could move north or south, dig ditches, plow dirt, plant seeds, herd sheep, make love, raise children, and cheat at cards indiscriminately.

For a while, the ranchers thought they could keep it that way. "There was not a plowed field to be seen," wrote T-Down Bar ranch foreman Harry Otterson of the landscape near Eastend in 1906. "The day of the wheat king still to come." Otterson was an American working for the Bloom Cattle Company out of Malta, Montana, which assumed the name T-Down Bar to become a legal Canadian operation north of the line. It was with optimism that Otterson and his wife set out in their buckboard that November to cross the 125 miles from Malta to Eastend, their furniture and belongings rattling along a different route behind a cowboy on a heavy wagon, accompanied by their hired wolfer (a professional wolf hunter) and his two enormous deerhounds. The region still had few settlers. Like Muir, Otterson could list his neighbors, complete with vignettes, in a few pages: Howard Parker, the English pianist who felt the "call of the wild"; Major and Mrs. Moody, who had lived among Eskimos; Dan Tenaille, the Frenchman with $60,000 and little sense. Wolves, they must have thought, would be the worst of their problems that winter.[44]

But the coming storms set a new standard for catastrophe. There had been notable disasters before: there was the "Big Die-Up" of 1886–87—a devastating winter for stock; the drought of 1890–91; the April blizzard of 1892; the winter of 1902–03 and the May blizzard that followed it. But in the big snow of 1906–07, blizzard followed upon blizzard. Cattle, never the smartest of range animals and too stupid to paw up grasses on high ground, walled themselves into six-foot-high cells of snow in low-lying areas with the packing action of their hooves. They wallowed on their dead kindred, stacking themselves in grisly mounds of death. Haystacks were hidden beneath an ocean of snow, snow drifted over water holes, stunned cowboys straggled into camp snowblind and exhausted. Stock losses averaged around 50 percent. Seasoned cattlemen with experience on every range north of Texas shook their heads and retired. Large owners further reduced their herds or sold out for what they could get—$16 to $20 a head, with suckling calves thrown in. Open Canadian range that most certainly would have been leased in previous years went unclaimed.[45]

Despite the devastation, there was no mass exodus from the region. While many of the largest outfits left, the smaller, locally based ranches persisted, with cattle, sheep, or both. If the inhabitants were not yet eating grass themselves, as Charlie Russell's joke averred, they at least hoped to find some for their livestock. Russell himself gave up the prairie. He visited friends in Chinook and Fort Belknap for the Fourth of July in 1905. By now a successful artist, he lived in Great Falls, traveled to New York, and built a cabin in the forests of Glacier Park. Russell knew that in the long run the prairie could be a great leveler of social distinctions, which for him was part of its attraction. He also knew that along the way, the people on it could be as violent as the weather and as difficult as the terrain.[46]

CHAPTER SEVEN

WHAT ARE WE
FIGHTING FOR?

Landusky, a tiny gold and silver mining town still tucked next to the southwestern corner of Blaine County, established its reputation early. Landusky was the sixth white settlement in the area, following Maple Creek, Fort Walsh, and Old Fort Belknap (the site of present-day Chinook), and two ill-fated early trading posts—the Hudson's Bay Company post at Eastend, burned out after three seasons in 1872 by disapproving Blackfoot, and Fort Browning on the Missouri, successfully strangled off from general trade by the Sioux between 1868 and 1871. But when it came to saloon violence, Landusky came first. By the 1890s, medicine line country had developed its own folklore of violence, one that distinguished America from Canada, peaceful tendencies from violent ones. The Mounted Police north of the border figured large, as did the rowdy whiskey traders and horse thieves they suppressed. South of the border, Landusky became a symbol of the region's rough male-dominated past, a place where violent bickering was a way of life. "It's a sociable camp," Charlie Russell said of Landusky in his 1921 *Rawhide Rawlins* stories, "life there bein' far from monotonous."[1]

Russell's days as a Chinook saloon keeper were brief and inglorious. But while he may have been no businessman, he knew how to tell a Western yarn. "The leadin' industries," he wrote of Landusky,

> is saloons an' gamblin' houses, with a fair sprinklin' of dance halls. For noise an' smoke there wasn't nothin' ever seen like it before the big fight in Europe starts. Little lead's wasted, as the shootin's remarkably accurate an' almost anybody serves as a target . . . . Funerals in Landusky is held at night under a white flag, so that business ain't interrupted in the daytime.[2]

We have no way of knowing just how violent Landusky truly was, but beneath the coarse exaggeration of Russell's humor lies some truth. Landusky drew its population from the Missouri River badlands, home to

Illustrated letter from Charles M. Russell to Edward "Kid" Price of Chinook, Montana, June 19, 1902, depicting Russell with his customary Métis sash and a bottle of whiskey.

Photo courtesy the Montana Historical Society, Museum Collection, Helena, Montana.

a collection of hunters, traders, wolfers, and rustlers who, in the words of another, less ironic local historian, "could see no particular use for law and order." Neither, apparently, did Landusky's lawmen. In 1899, deputy U.S. marshal and stock inspector Horace Lamkin shot a man named Charles Perry twice in a saloon brawl over a card game. According to the *Chinook Opinion*, he "has not been arrested and the chances are, will not be."[3]

The most notorious of the badlands bad men was Kid Curry, real name Harvey Logan. Kid Curry robbed trains. He also murdered miner Pike Landusky, town father and sometime sheriff, in a Landusky saloon. The story of Sheriff Landusky's end is noteworthy, if only to corroborate Russell's view of Landusky as a common one among local residents. The sheriff, by reputation a kind-hearted man with a shot-up jaw and a taste for rotgut whiskey, had borrowed a plow from the Logan brothers and returned it late and the worse for wear. Worse, he had on another occasion publicly sullied the reputation of the Logan brothers' mother, apparently an insult the Kid would not tolerate for long. The Kid's retribution, pieced together from two sources, reads like a scene from a John Ford movie: a shot of whiskey, a look, harsh words, Kid Curry's fist drawing blood, Landusky reaching for his revolver, the two finding themselves in the kind of savage embrace reserved for boxers and mortal enemies, the Kid's gun suddenly in Landusky's chest, a shot, a getaway wagon rattling up the street, a crowd gathering in its dust.

Kid Curry was never caught to stand trial. A Fort Benton judge acquitted the Kid's brother Lonny, apparently on trial as an accessory, calling the shooting a case of self-defense. The Kid himself made his way to Knoxville, Tennessee, to a gambling house where he was arrested in 1903, but again he escaped.

Pariah though he might have seemed, the Kid was not viewed as such among ordinary Montana citizens. When he cared to, he had no trouble seeking refuge in Montana. Though he was no Robin Hood, Kid Curry was a lesser kind of "social bandit" who enjoyed some degree of goodwill among the people. He apparently had many friends in early Chinook, at least according to storekeeper Mrs. A. S. Lohman, who rather liked him. One member of a local posse sent out to capture the Kid avowed that it did not chase him very hard. Area resident Jim Moran fed Logan when, dressed in hobo's rags and blackened with coal dust, preparing to make a dash for the border, he paid Moran a surprise nighttime visit. Another contemporary suggested the less sanguine interpretation that these friends' affection might have been encouraged by the fear that "he might come back some time and place them in such a condition that they would cease to have an opinion."[4]

Because medicine line country lacked the political radicalism on whose crest the outlaw heroes of other Western regions rode, the Logan brothers remain in a position of relative obscurity in the pantheon of Western bandits. Nevertheless, they may be somewhat typical of their time and place. If the Logans were the most storied of the region's villains, their exploits are not the only evidence of violent disturbance to enliven the pages of local newspapers. To borrow a phrase from one writer, a visitor would not have easily mistaken any of these towns for a Quaker village.[5]

One afternoon in 1901, reported the *Chinook Opinion*, a man with the sweet-sounding name of Patsy Rowle began to scuffle with Leno Lopez on the streets of town. In the middle of the fight, something came over Rowle. He sheathed his knife, walked into Lehfeldt's general store and bought a .41 Colt revolver and shells. He came out shooting holes in nearby hotel windows, and finally found his mark, who for unknown reasons was still dawdling in the street in front of the bar. The bullet entered Lopez's shoulder and exited above his left nipple. Though Lopez, who survived, denied it, Rowle claimed that his victim owed him for "labor at the shearing pens and money loaned." Rowle went to jail, and when he escaped, it was apparently a relief to Chinook residents, not because they "condone[d] his crime," according to the *Opinion*, but because it saved "a considerable expense to the county."[6]

There were other sorts of violence as well. Someone, perhaps the Logans (though sources disagree), blew up an express car on the number three train near Chinook in the summer of 1901 and made off with several thousand dollars belonging to a Helena bank. The newspaper reported occasional shootings, and there seemed to be a most un-Quaker-like public indifference to the violence. To their credit, townspeople were apparently alarmed if they stumbled upon a dead body, as Charlie Baird thought he had one summer day on a Chinook back street. Baird rounded up the coroner and justice of the peace to investigate, and came trailing behind them with a group of concerned citizens, only to find the body risen up on one elbow, the better to address the coroner in his buggy, asking for a drink of ice water.[7]

The story of Patsy Rowle has the ironic elements of a Mark Twain story. It also suggests that the borderland was a rough-and-tumble frontier, at least on the U.S. side of the line. The truth was that in medicine line country, violence, like Rowe's gunfight, was more complicated than its folklore, or even such anecdotes, suggest. As on some biblical plain, conflict in the Maple Creek–Chinook borderland had a long history. Battles between Assiniboine, Blackfoot, Gros Ventre, Crow, and Sioux during the mid-nineteenth century had baptized it as bloody ground. Violent Indian-white conflict had characterized the 1870s. By the 1890s, whites were fighting whites along with everybody else. The amount of mayhem put the region in company with the rest of the American West, which was exceptionally violent between 1850 and 1920.[8]

Class warefare was a western pastime, and Montana was famous for it. The writer Dashiell Hammett saw Montana class warfare firsthand from his vantage point as a Pinkerton agent. Describing Pelsonville (his fictitious name for Butte, Montana) in 1902, he displayed the pithy use of metaphor that made him a great writer of detective stories: "When the last skull had been cracked, the last rib kicked in, organized labor in Pelsonville was a used firecracker."[9] He also displayed an essential grasp of Montana history. Much of the history of Western violence and its folklore involved local resistance to large companies. Montanans, particularly, had a long-standing sense of themselves as the uneasy fiefdom of the Anaconda Copper Company, whose laborer resistance brought Hammett to Butte in the first place.[10]

True to type, Montana-Saskatchewan borderlanders had had their struggle against large organized interests. In the spring of 1894, buckling under national economic depression, the Great Northern Railway cut wages by 15 percent. Just weeks before the landmark national strike against the Pullman Company in June, the winds of crisis swept northern Montana. Workers, following the lead of the American Railway Union under Eugene V. Debs, struck from St. Paul to the Pacific coast to protest the cut, stopping the trains on their tracks. As the jobless men from Ohio called Coxey's Army marched on Washington, drawing a nationwide gathering of the unemployed, striking local workers, stranded along the great Northern wherever the trains had stopped, rigged handcars with sheets and, like figureheads on tiny ships, sailed home across the prairie at sixteen miles an hour.

It looked as though Nelson Miles, still commander of the Division of the Missouri, might have the opportunity to return to his old Sioux-chasing grounds to quell another rebellion. Within months he would, after all, defend the Pullman company management against strikers in Chicago. But the Great Northern strike was no ideological catalyst, and Miles never came. It was a reminder to northern plains newcomers that they were indeed a railroad-dependent island, and a trans-border one at that. "It will not take many days," reflected worried *Chinook Opinion* editor Bill Kester, "to start a small size famine." After just two weeks, high-line towns (as settlements along the Great Northern were called) had already begun to suffer. Glasgow ran out of matches. Malta was out of sugar. Ranchers were short of seed grain for feed. Two Chinook freight wagons were readying to leave for Maple Creek to buy flour, supplied by the nonstriking Canadian Pacific Railway, when the strike ended after two and a half weeks in compromise. A resident north of the boundary may have best expressed the ambivalent relationship locals had with their railroads: "I realize that these railroad big shots were a bunch of pirates," he said. "[They] should have been sailing the Spanish Main. But remember this, they got the job done."[11]

As this resident's tempered criticism suggests, labor unrest and political radicalism was much cooler here than in many Western areas. On either side of the border, there was no great love lost for either the railroads or the government, the powers that had brought most of them here. "The gummint just bet me ten bucks against a half section that I can't stand this climate for three years," was the homesteader's standard wry lament.[12] Beneath the humor, though, the homesteader's joke acknowledges the speaker's own responsibility in the matter, his own willingness to gamble, an assumption widely expressed in local documents. Federal aid in the form of development capital, reservation rations and leases, water management, and cheap grazing lands gave these people that familiar western disease, dependency and loathing. A mass meeting of Chinook-area businessmen and ranchers might urge on the national government the necessity of proceeding with an irrigation project, and then request local control on small farms "by actual settlers and homemakers," who would "repay the government" for construction costs and maintenance: "We want no . . . encroachments on the rights of the people" by "a few large corporations," they declared. This notion of paying back the loan with no strings attached expressed a typical message: Don't interfere, just send money. The arid plains were a tough place to make a living, and Indians and whites alike were reluctant dependents on federal largesse.[13]

For a combination of reasons, including an economic base in ranching and mixed farming, the northern Montana-Saskatchewan plains were no hotbed of populism, as were the neighboring Montana mining towns and

Dakota farming communities. The Chinook vote in the 1900 elections was solidly Republican: 174 votes for McKinley and only 94 for Democrat-Populist William Jennings Bryan, who achieved a landslide victory in the state of Montana. "Naturally," wrote the *Chinook Opinion*'s correspondent on Lower Peoples Creek, "there are very few in this part of the country who advocate Bryan and Free Trade, and they are not only avowed enemies to themselves, but to the interests of their employers as well." In Saskatchewan's first provincial election in 1905, while northern Saskatchewan elected almost exclusively liberal candidates, southern Saskatchewan voted one-third for the Liberals, and two-thirds for the status-quo Provincial Rights party, a loosely defined collection of antifederalist and anti-Catholic conservatives.[14]

Like all people lacking a common and unequivocal enemy, the region's people fought mostly with each other. The border hardly mattered. The two territories, Canadian and American, faced one another with a kind of fraternal familiarity, and like the broad, seemingly undifferentiated prairie landscape from which they grew, conflicts among borderland residents were powerful and often subtle. They fought for legal and political control of institutions and resources, and they fought for social standing. They jockeyed for cultural dominance, for the authority of individual over individual, family over outsiders, or one ethnic, racial, or social group over another. There was a sort of underclass of losers. The area sporadically became a "starving land" for the snowbound or the dispossessed, conditions reserved for livestock, loners, Indians, Métis, and other marginal groups who arrived naïve or unprepared or who were unsuspecting victims of climate and location. Such people appear in local documents as nuisances or cautionary tales—ragged groups of homeless Indians and Métis who scrounged and stole livestock, and unfortunate whites such as the residents of Hungry Hollow, south of Chinook, who after the harsh winter of 1901–02 simply left—"starved out," as the locals said. They and others like them received the tailings from the local competition for resources and power.[15] The question of precisely who fought whom, and how violent they were, is tangled in local folklore.

Chinook's reputation was mild and genial compared to that of Havre, a town twenty miles west of Chinook along the Great Northern line. Havre-area residents reputedly witnessed lawlessness and violence in broad daylight well into the 1920s. What Dodge City and Deadwood were to their regions, Havre was for the Northern Plains; it became the local Sodom and Gomorrah, notorious for its lawlessness, gambling, hard drinking, and violent population. According to Gary A. Wilson's *Honky-Tonk Town*, a lively chronicle of iniquity, Havre was for decades the bootleg and contraband capital of the Northern Plains borderland, trafficking alcohol, opium, illegal aliens, and whatever else was profitable through a network of tunnels beneath the town's saloons. Havre's draw for local residents with appropriate talents, in fact, undoubtedly left Chinook a duller if more law-abiding place. Among Havre's toughest women were former denizens of Chinook—Emma "Dutch Em" Bronson, whom one frequenter of Havre recalled as "the first demimonde" in the district, and Carrie McLean, better known as "Cowboy Jack," who eventually established a prosperous brothel in Lethbridge, Alberta.[16]

Turning northward, one imagines that Canadians must have given up a few local bad guys in medicine line country, testing the Mounties' watchful eyes. During the early 1870s, the hard-living American whiskey traders, a group that disappeared from southern Canada as quickly as the Mounted Police could be dispatched to remove them, earned their notoriety in local folklore. During their residency "[a] man's life was worth a horse," noted an Edmonton newspaper editor, "and a horse was worth a pint of whiskey." This was an ethos that would have made Russell's Landusky residents feel right at home. In 1903 there were opium smugglers trafficking from Canada to Harlem, just east of Chinook. That same year a gang of petty thieves in Canada near the Dakota-Montana border kidnapped an American man for thirteen days, before he could testify against them in Canadian court.[17] Where was the local gang that rivaled the exploits of Kid Curry's band?

"Dale, Mrs. B.J.," begins an entry on page 276 of the 630-page Ravenscrag local history. (Ravenscrag, a village of less than a thousand a few miles up the Frenchman River from Eastend, demonstrates an interest in history that well exceeds its size.) Mrs. Dale, it tells us, was born in the United States to a saloon keeper father. She homesteaded in the Farwell (or Fairwell) Creek district in about 1914, taught school there, "ranched and farmed some," married a second time, did "tea cup readings" in British Columbia cafes in later years, was "a good artist," and "did very nice crochet work" until she died, in the 1960s. So Mrs. Belle Dale, aka Mrs. Willard, aka Mrs. Bill Kinnick, is recorded in the local history, a dull tale of accomplished ranch wife turned crochet hobbyist and tea leaf reader. As an afterthought, the author makes only the politest allusion to Mrs. Dale's role as the "brains" behind a gang of local horse and cattle thieves, plunging us into an extraordinary pastoral tale of deceit and detection.[18]

"Cattle Country at Last Rid of Gang of Thieves" headlined the Medicine Hat, Saskatchewan, Morning Leader on December 6, 1924. "Six of Band Who Operated for Years Are Jailed after Sensational Trial." For ten years, the story recounted, a group of "outwardly respectable" ranchers had plundered the livestock of southwest Saskatchewan by night. "Rogues of a picturesque kind," the gang included A. P. McDonald, a Canadian-born Scot with a correspondence-course law degree and a facility for public discourse, who often advised neighbors on legal matters; Buck Drury, a young and debonair cowboy who had displayed his extraordinary horsemanship in a show troupe to England; and Belle, a bright, attractive person as refined in the courtroom as she was tough at the ranch (where she allegedly "possessed a vocabulary of invective comparable with that of a captain on a pirate ship.") Belle's husband, Bill Kinnick, whose fear of retribution she said had caused him to flee to the United States in 1923, was believed to have acted as receiver for the stolen meat and livestock across the international boundary.

"By reason of the confidence and trust of neighbors," the reporter wrote, "they were enabled to secure easy access to information vital to the success of their schemes." Concealed by riding low among the deep coulees and dense scrub of the Cypress Hills uplands, "[t]hey moved in a Jeykil-Hyde [sic]atmosphere, lived double lives," employing "the cloak of honesty to rob friends and associates." An undercover agent, Mounted Police constable George Hillock, in the guise of a range rider at a nearby ranch, investigated the details of the gang's nighttime activities. He discovered the gruesome evidence of an immense rustling operation—animals with stitched-up eight-inch-square wounds where their brands had been removed, which healed into the "pine tree" mark common in the rustlers' herds; more than twenty branding irons in a Kinnick outhouse; and at the bottom of an old eighty-foot-deep masonry-lined well at the Kinnick ranch, covered with quicklime, a column of bones and entrails thirty feet thick.[19]

If the place of Kid Curry and his brothers was given short shrift in Chinook's historical narratives, Belle Kinnick was even more slighted. Years later her descendants all but denied her involvement in such gruesome activities. Indeed, if the mythical American West seems a tale of male hormones writ large, perhaps the mythical Canadian West presents a more feminine face, one of law and order, in which Belle Kinnick was an odd "man" out.[20] An unattributed poem in a local history book celebrates not the outlaw but the law. "So fair and charming was the lass," goes the "Ballad of Robber's Roost,"

> Her guilt was not suspected
> Many stockmen suffered loss
> Before she was detected.

> Then arrives the Mountie, in this version disguised as a hobo, to investigate.

> He asked no questions, told no tales
> Did chores to earn his keep
> Wrote secrets in a small black book
> While others were all asleep.

> And so, the poet concludes, justice was done.

The rustlers had to face the judge
For them he had no pity
To jail they went to pay for sin
And with them went the lady.

Until 1903, Mounted Police annual reports to Ottawa consistently comment on the absence of "serious" or violent borderland crime, and the Maple Creek newspaper's reports of violence are indeed few during the early 1910s.[21] A postmortem examination on the body of an American man found in a coulee in 1910 suggested murder with a blunt instrument. A girl named Nettie Livingston was abducted from the schoolhouse one day in April 1911 by her father, labeled a "worthless fellow" who had on one occasion "attempted improper relations with Nettie." They were, the paper noted, originally from Dakota. In these stories, the outlines of a new border distinction emerge, one that fits the classic mythologies of American lawlessness versus Canadian respect for the law. One visitor to Saskatchewan in the 1910s, Elizabeth B. Mitchell, an intelligent and articulate young Oxford graduate visiting Canada to observe its society and town planning, noted that "the administration of justice" in the Dominion "appears to inspire a confidence which has not always been given to that of the United States." Though the population was "gathered from the ends of the earth," she noted, "[a] vast British Peace broods over it all."[22]

It is difficult to completely gauge the southwest Saskatchewan attitude toward outlawry. Despite the "vast British peace," Elizabeth Mitchell admitted to finding in area residents' enthusiasm for "untrammelled individual action" increasingly little distinction between the Canadians of western Saskatchewan and the Americans. "The elements of the experiment are strangely the same on the two sides of the border," she noted, "and there are indications of a close repetition of history." "The speculative spirit," she lamented, a phenomenon she linked with unbridled self-interest, "has come in strong on the decent agricultural prairie." Economic inequities, she believed (to which she might have added ethnic divisions), and the resulting social tensions were a graver danger to the Canadian social order than outlawry.[23]

The region's aggressive characters held their place in the local imagination long after they were defunct. Even if the folklore the border divided rowdy America from re-spectable Canada, a distinction that has long persisted in the national mythologies, violence faded on this particular American ground. By 1890, the influence of the Mounted Police in Canada and the homestead-centered, transborder society of the incoming agricultural population had leavened the volatile mix of bachelor- and whiskey-loaded trading posts and mining camps. By 1909, when the next homestead rush began in the Chinook area, Kid Curry and his brothers were legends.

Havre had always been singular in its violent mien. Landusky fell quiet well before the 1910s. While elsewhere in the West whites rioted against the Chinese and engaged in open class warfare in mining and mill towns, the territory between the Missouri and the border seemed a haven. Refugees from Wyoming's famous Johnson County cattle war were known to seek out the peaceful conditions here in the 1890s.[24] Criminal records on both sides of the border east of Havre reveal little violent crime, or at least little prosecuted violent crime, in the 1890s and the first few years of the twentieth century. Despite the aptitude that drunk young men in mining and honky-tonk towns had for personal violence, one would not characterize the dark side of the regional temperament as one of routinely violent confrontation, collective or individual.

As the American side of the line cooled down, however, the Canadian side heated up. Cases of violent crime and the total number of criminal cases increased noticeably on the Canadian side of the line during two periods, beginning in 1903 (inexplicably) and again in 1911 during a second homestead rush. Violent crimes peaked in the Maple Creek district in 1913 and 1914, most of them assaults, and most of those accused were convicted (101 of 132 accused). In those years, Blaine County in Montana reported a mere three violent crimes. Yet these statistics provide an imperfect comparison. The Mounted Police were vigilant law enforcers, compared to more lax enforcement in the United States, where figures may significantly underrepresent actual crimes. Moreover, the Maple Creek district included the large railway towns of Swift Current and Medicine Hat, whereas Blaine County did not include Havre, the U.S. equivalent.[25] Even so, the statistics suggest that on both sides of the border, crime was on the wane.

By 1900, the borderland region had become a relatively peaceful corner of the West, a refuge, even, from more violent and crowded lands to the south. The big cattle operations, including Granville Stuart's Montana vigilantes of 1884, the most notorious citizens' band of cattle-and horse-thief killers in American history, had already concluded their violent wars against smaller interests to the south and east and were in decline by the time this region was settled. Land and water claims, although frequently a point of contention after Indian removal, did not pit any corporate interest against large numbers of individuals with a common grievance (as it did just north in central Saskatchewan during the 1885 Riel rebellion or south in Montana's copper mining towns). And the early presence of the Mounted Police in the Cypress Hills, with its reinforcing effect on Fort Assiniboine, just west of Chinook, was an influential force for order. With Indian removal and the influx of new settlers, new conflicts arose. But these conflicts changed a violent neighborhood into a land of ordinary vices, revealing people characterized not by unbridled greed, unusual violence, or even a desire to change history, but by more modestly hopeful intentions, prejudices, and cruelties.

Lillian Miller, one of the best witnesses we have to this era, was six years old when she arrived in Chinook, Montana, from Iowa on the Great Northern Railway in the early spring of 1892. She, her mother, and her twelve-year-old brother, Louie, joined her father and two older brothers on their year-old sheep ranch, established on a squaw man's camp in the Bear Paw Mountains five miles west of where Chief Joseph and the Nez Percé had surrendered only fifteen years earlier. From the outset, race and ethnicity were prominent features of Miller's new childhood landscape. Chinook area diversity between 1890 and 1900 was at its peak, higher than that of the United States generally. In a statistical analysis based on census material, the borderland held human variety comparable to New York City in 1910.[26]

Indians were immediately a curiosity to Miller, who caught roadside glimpses of braided hair, brown children, and scrawny, "spiritless" animals loitering around a cabin or crouching in a wagon. She assumed them to be lesser or pitiful beings. "We wondered what they were thinking," she recalled, "if they were admiring or envying us." She became no less mystified by close contact. Set-Em-High, an "old" Gros Ventre chief in a blue soldier's uniform with brass buttons who would frequently enter the Miller house without knocking, one day "galloped over the hills" with a jar of the Millers' pickles tucked under his arm for a sick "papoose," leaving the Millers "dumb founded." Other Indians visited, "two and three at a time," and "you learned the only way to get rid of them was to feed them" leftovers from the family dinner. Any further leavings the Indians scraped into a "dirty red bandana handkerchief" to tie to one of their saddles. Every morning on the way to school, Lillian and Louie uncomfortably passed an exposed "wooden box" they knew to be an Indian grave. Contact eventually turned Miller's fear or distaste into the desire for understanding and even cautious affection. Set-Em-High made her a pair of moccasins. "We picked up a few words here and there by pointing to objects," and Set-Em-High would "give us the Indian word but it never led to real conversation," she noted with regret. "How much we would have appreciated knowing what [his] deeds of bravery were" when the Indian "was master of the plains."[27]

As are most children, Lillian Miller was acutely attuned to signs of hierarchy or differentiation among the people around her. She noted her differences from the "half-breed" Adams children, who attended her country school. All the pupils drank from the same long-handled dipper, and the teacher treated them as equals, but Lillian found the Métis rather unclean and poorly dressed. She kept her distance from "poor Nancy," who "had a running sore on her neck and always wore a half soiled white rag around it, which usually slipped down to expose the ugly thing." Conversely, she felt self-conscious and awed by the fine walnut furniture of their nearest neighbors, the Rosses, family of her lifelong best friend Jessie, elegance that the "rich" Mrs. Ross referred to glibly as "second best." These observations sprang from her dawning awareness of social hierarchy, though she minimized it, declaring that "in pioneer country, backgrounds become unimportant." Pioneer equality was what Miller, the adult author of a memoir, wanted to believe in and found evidence for in her childhood affections. The "hard-working peasant woman" Greten Jess, a German whose husband worked for the Millers, was "loud and gruff, she walked like a man with long strides," Miller recalled, but had a "heart of gold." The women, particularly, seemed to overcome their differences in a network of mutual support and goodwill. Her mother nursed the sick "from near and far," and the female storekeepers, teachers, and "ladies of Lloyd" were bound in her memory as a strong, close-knit community.[28]

Miller's memories, however, often deny her pleasant generalizations. One of the Millers' best-loved women friends, Maggie LaFrantz, though "outwardly . . . always gay and cheerful," was troubled by a husband who drank and stayed away from home for days at a time. It is a rare hint of domestic abuse in a culture that rarely committed such matters to public discussion. Darker still were the ethnic tensions Miller learned about through her father, sheep rancher Peter Miller. As a newly arrived German immigrant hauling ties for the Union Pacific railroad outside Omaha, her father had "built up a hatred" for the Irish that "smoldered the rest of his life." He thus met his new bachelor Irish neighbors in the Bear Paw Mountains south of Chinook with cool suspicion. Gradually his reserve thawed, and one day shortly after the death of Lillian's brother Louis from a ruptured appendix, he confided in the sympathetic Irishmen that the family would wait until spring or summer to meet the annual residency requirement on their second homestead, the old John Muir ranch two miles west. One of the men, James Berry, then betrayed this confidence and jumped Miller's claim. When Miller challenged him, the story goes, Berry held him by the beard and threatened him with an ax. A lengthy lawsuit followed, and according to Miller, after her father lost, he appealed and eventually won his case before the U.S. Supreme Court in about 1899. The case appears in neither federal nor state casebooks, and perhaps Miller exaggerated its legal importance because the conflict was a traumatizing ordeal for her family. Berry and his friends terrorized Lillian's mother, poisoned family animals with strychnine, cut fences, and turned livestock onto crops. After his legal defeat, Berry left the country. Berry's compatriot Frank McCadden stayed in the area, and he and Miller remained "arch enemies all their lives."[29]

In fact, incident after incident of confrontation reported in the *Chinook Opinion* involved people of different backgrounds: a Hispanic versus an Irishman (Lopez and Rowler, the latter going unpunished after a jail-break); a "half-breed" beaten to death by an "employee of the Spokane house" (presumably white since his race goes unmentioned); and John Sanborn, an Indian tried for horse stealing by John Robinson, a white whom Sanborn in turn accused of selling liquor to Indians. There was the four-year quarrel between reservation sub-agent William Allen, a white man (tarred and feathered about ten years earlier by unnamed members of the Indian community), and his brother-in-law, Charles Perry, a "half-breed" reservation store-keeper whom the newspaper describes as "well-educated, and rather wealthy," a disagreement that ended in Allen's death by

Lillian and her mother Elizabeth "Lizzie" Miller, c. 1896. Lillian remembered strong female bonds on her childhood sheep-ranching frontier near Chinook, Montana.
Photo courtesy Linda Haugen, Chinook, Montana.

two of Perry's bullets. In June 1899, at a small train station east of Chinook, "several section men" for the railroad, presumably white, "made an armed assault on a bunch of Japanese laborers." In another reprehensible incident in September 1900, confirming Russell's portrait of Landusky, cowboys attacked a "halfbreed" camp near that town in order to assault the women. When one man, Thomas Upee, defended his wife, three cowboys killed him by beating his head in with a rock. Given that the region as a whole was not prone to rampant violence, the virulence of some of these incidents suggests that ethnic or racial tensions were among the more explosive sources of disagreement.[30]

Even if it did not explode into violence, general indications of prejudice were evident: a sign announcing "No Niggers, Chinamen or Kickers Wanted" hung on the wall of Frenchy Bouchard's restaurant in Harlem, Montana, thirteen miles east of Chinook. (The term "kicker" seems to be a synonym for troublemaker used on both sides of the boundary.) The *Chinook Opinion* introduced a list of Chinese customs under the heading "The Queer Chinaman." That same newpaper's obituary of Thomas O'Hanlon, reputedly a "King among men" and the "father of Chinook," includes mention of his brother and sons but says nothing of the children's Indian mother. Local headlines suggested local prejudices as well: "Why the Japs are Employed," "Indians Are Ugly." Ethnic humor was well received, though we cannot tell in what underlying spirit. We know that the town hall hosted "entertainments" including "farces, Irish, black face and Chinese comedy" that "kept the audiences in laughter." The region's large Irish population was evidently not offended. Ethnic humor may even have facilitated the acceptance of differences. In some cases, though, it merely justified an inequitable social structure, as the newspaper's mordant humor over the neighboring Indians' destitution makes clear: "A band of the 'Noble Red Men' and their better halves, and their usual accompaniment of papooses and dogs, were in town this week," wrote the editor breezily, "and as a result there isn't a piece of red cloth, broken dish or any other old thing that a squaw could carry, left in the back yards—as a street cleaning bureau they are a success." In these and other newspaper items from 1899 to 1902, the social hierarchy was clearly ordered, at least in part, by notions of race and ethnicity.[31]

The Indians at Fort Belknap apparently returned the compliment to local whites. If the reservation's agent in 1903, W. R. Logan, could dismiss the local merchants as "a pack of coyotes" who worked the crowd at reservation payday (to collect from their Indian customers), one can imagine what epithets the Indians themselves might have had for their white neighbors. The Indians had ample justification for dark humor. A short list of targets would include James N. Sample, the reservation's white assistant farmer for a few years, a moral busybody whose removal the Indians petitioned for in 1901 on grounds of general incompetence; agent Morris L. Bridgeman, a drunkard eventually tried and convicted for establishing a thorough system of fraud and graft during his tenure from 1900 to 1902; C. R. Barton, the reservation's licensed trader and Bridgeman's handmaiden; and James Pond, the interpreter who signed Bridgeman's bogus vouchers. Even Logan, a man of good character and good intentions, drew criticism from the Indian council. In their own defense, Indians rallied against predatory whites, and in 1892, the Fort Belknap Indian police arrested a non-reservation settler who was foraging on the reservation for firewood (for which the Indians and especially the squaw men received bitter excoriation in the *Chinook Opinion*).[32]

In this volatile atmosphere, inter-Indian enmities thrived as well. Fort Belknap residents today claim that reservation factionalism has been exaggerated, and according to the reservation agent in 1898, two prominent Gros Ventre leaders accepted the Assiniboine as full partners in the reservation.[33] Nevertheless, much evidence suggests that during the reservation's early decades, the Gros Ventre and Assiniboine at Fort Belknap were at times deeply divided. The two tribes were old adversaries whose alliances and enmities with one another varied over time. They sometimes adopted each other's dances or ceremonies, and as the Sioux and the whites assaulted their lands, they sought the benefits of alliance. At the same time they maintained different beliefs and separate tribal identities, and largely separate communities on the reservation, the Gros Ventre at Hays, the Assiniboine at Lodgepole. While the Gros Ventre seemed competitive, eventually eager to prosper in white culture, and anxious to set themselves apart from the Assiniboine, the Assiniboine portrayed themselves as more tolerant, communal, and culturally conservative. "Gros Ventres put others down—Assiniboines and breeds," asserted a young Assiniboine woman in the 1970s. "We never did that."[34]

Gros Ventre and Assiniboine did at times compete for resources. When they became particularly worried about Assiniboine competition, the Gros Ventre strategically employed the U.S.–Canadian border, an artifact of white invasion, to distinguish themselves from the reservation's other groups. In 1898, a group of Gros Ventre asked that the Assiniboine and the "Red River half breeds" be removed from the reservation, and during land allotment proceedings in 1922 the Gros Ventre argued that most of the Assiniboine were in fact "Canadian" usurpers of lands that rightfully belonged to the Gros Ventre. In an ironic reversal of Sitting Bull's efforts to use the medicine line to establish Canadian identity, the Gros Ventre now used it to strip another tribe of its claims.[35]

North of the border, Maple Creek newspapers revealed a degree of schizophrenia on the subject of race and ethnicity undetectable in Chinook. Human interest items in the *Signal* and the *Ranching News*, founded in 1902, and their successor, called the *Maple Creek News*, played to an audience who viewed minority peoples as exotica captured for white English-speaking people's mental cabinets of curiosities. One week there might be an excerpt of popular fiction entitled "The Métis: Historical Romance of the Canadian West," the next, the report of a "pow-wow" in Maple Creek, attended by members of the "fair sex" (a term that leaves no doubt about their race) and their "escorts," describing entertainment by "aborigines" of "picturesque appearance . . . noble savage[s] arrayed in feathers and paint with sheep bells on [their] nether limbs" who danced to the "delightful and soul-entrancing" rhythms of the tom-tom. Other columns described life "Among the Jews—News Notes about Them from Around the World," or recounted the "Picketts," a "colored" minstrel show of "comedy sketches and banjo playing." Such articles leave the impression that race issues were anthropological, while others were a simple matter of the civil code, as when "Lee Yonk and Woy Cong" were "fined $30 each for serving liquor without a license in their restaurants."[36]

Behind this portrait of bemused tolerance in southwest Saskatchewan lay the harsher realities of multicultural conflict. Former resident Mable Rudd was reported to be a victim of the "White Slave traffic" in Vancouver's Chinatown, while a local columnist quipped in 1903 that "Japanese were not required in Maple Creek, so they departed," leaving the reader to wonder under what duress (and what other groups might be deemed "not required"). An "American" (and therefore presumably white) stole two sets of buffalo horns from a depot Indian peddling his wares in Maple Creek, handing him an obviously counterfeit ten-dollar bill and jumping back onto the train with a "horse laugh." (Local law was in this case color-blind. The Mounted Police soon had the thief "admiring the landscape at Swiftcurrent from behind bars," noted the reporter.) Social tensions also appeared in the benign neglect that comes with racial segregation. In the 1890s, one Violet Moorhead, apparently unaware of or unable to call upon local Métis midwives of good reputation, lost her first child in Maple Creek's old International Hotel because of the incompetence of a drunken nurse named Mrs. Stuttaford.[37]

Mounted Police reports, published annually in the Canadian Sessional Papers, corroborate the presence of racial and ethnic tensions north of the border, though the evidence is not extensive. In the 1880s and '90s most reports recount the Indian-Métis activity one might expect before Canadian Indian removal was complete. Métis and Indians, now marginal and hungry people in a changing economy and culture, were frequent parties to criminal activity, most often thievery and livestock killing. As a preventive measure, in the early part of 1886 Superintendent McIllree ordered his constables to escort all "half-breeds" they did not know to headquarters. Yet the Métis gradually adapted, and by 1890 another superintendent reported that some of the area's well-to-do Métis were considered "among the most respected people in the community."

If the Métis seemed to stir mixed emotions among their neighbors, the police found that whites often harbored unfounded and excessive fear of Indians. A settlement of Austrian and German Jews at Josephsburg, west of Maple Creek, were so "deeply impressed with improbable stories told them of the Indians" that they required a police constable of their own for the winter of 1889. In 1896, when a Métis interpreter for the Mounted Police suggested establishing an Indian reserve in the Cypress Hills, Superintendent M. H. White-Fraser reported "some uneasiness" in the district over the proposal, and himself declared that it would be "greatly damaging."[38]

One might conclude that Indians and Métis were the Mounties' main troublemakers. On closer reading, however, the Mounted Police reports suggest a more complex web of social tensions. By 1904, Josephsburg residents had come to fear not Indians but other whites. Unscrupulous cattlemen occasionally rounded up the Germans' unbranded cattle and sold them as mavericks—in one case despite direct appeals in both German and English by the owner and his son. Admittedly, diversity may not have been the only cause of friction, as Josephsburg's denizens appeared to have had trouble with everybody, including each other: Superintendent Gagnon commented in 1895 that the "settlement is composed almost entirely of Germans, who seem to be continually getting into hot water with each other, and need some looking after." In 1895, another group of whites falsely accused Indians of cattle theft in hopes of removing them from the area, apparently because they simply did not like their presence.[39] Turning the tables, in 1905 an Indian in Josephsburg who was attempting to recover his horses (stolen by a Métis thief) had reason to fear a German, who, having bought the horses from the horse thief, faced down the previous owner with a shotgun.

The full consequences of increasing diversity in the Maple Creek district, however, are not in the vocabulary of Mounted Police reports. Beyond the Indians, Métis, and Josephsburg Germans, few ethnic groups received mention. A party of "Chinamen" tried to "smuggle themselves" across the international boundary in 1895. A "German born in Southern Russia," who alleged that three men robbed him of $155, became so hopelessly tangled in contradictions at their trial in Medicine Hat, his apparent confusion perhaps compounded by the difficulties of translating his obscure German dialect, that he lost his case. Most often, though, the characteristics of plaintiffs and defendants in Mounted Police reports remain veiled by such anonymous epithets as "settler," "employee," "suspect," "perpetrator," or "noted crook." The clearest association of crime to racial and ethnic tensions came from Superintendent Moodie, who in 1910 wrote that such infractions showed a "marked increase in this district." The Maple Creek News concurred: "The old timer cannot help observing the marked increase in crime throughout the district in the last few years," noted the editor in 1910. It was "no doubt accounted for," declared Superintendent Moody, "by the great influx of immigrants," all those Germans, Scandinavians, Russians, Rumanians, Chinese, and Americans, "pouring in from all directions."[40] As local residents saw it, increased diversity was taking its toll.

South of the border, no one pronounced with magisterial authority on the effects of diversity or, beyond folklorists, gave an overview of conflict. No watchful government agency left its record, like a gauge measuring social tension. Instead, the records on the U.S. side of the border capture only the violent eruptions of what must have been, underneath, a society under some pressure. The loudest of these, one which was to leave its mark on the course of national history, was the *Winters* decision.

Local folklore is strangely silent about *Winters*. Neither of Blaine County's local histories—Janet Allison's vivid, story-filled celebration of the lives of the area's most prominent settlers and A. J. Noyes's loosely threaded tales of colorful renegades and "plainsmen"—mentions it. Nonetheless, the facts are straightforward and well known. On June 26, 1905, the United States government, representing the Indians of the Fort Belknap Indian Reservation, filed a complaint in Montana district court against twenty-one Chinook defendants. The charge against the defendants was unlawfully obstructing and diverting the waters of the Milk River and its tributaries away from the Fort Belknap Indian reservation, causing "great and irreparable damage" to the Indians' agricultural and stockraising operations. The battle lines were drawn over water, the West's most precious resource. When the court granted an injunction against the defendants, the defendants appealed to the Ninth Circuit court of appeals in October 1906. When the Indians won again, the defendants appealed once more, to the U.S. Supreme Court, which heard the case in October 1907 and handed down its eight-to-one decision in January 1908, in which the Indians won again. There could be no more appeals.[41]

The legal consequences of *Winters v. United States* were simple and profound. It established what lawyers now call the "Indians-always-win" doctrine, or, in the words of U.S. Supreme Court justice Joseph McKenna, "By a rule of interpretation of agreements and treaties with the Indians, ambiguities occurring will be resolved from the standpoint of the Indians." "The Indians had command of the lands and the waters" before the whites came, Justice McKenna asserted. "Did they give up all this? Did they reduce the area of their occupation and give up the waters which made it valuable or adequate?" In this case, in the opinion of the court, they did not. "The lands were arid and, without irrigation, were practically valueless." Never mind that Plains Indians had managed well for a long time without water rights, until they were expected to become farmers. The Indians were a special case, the court made clear, falling under neither of the two water rights doctrines then recognized under U.S. law, riparian and prior appropriation. Lawyers being lawyers, the court's intent—how much water do Indians get and for what purposes?—has been contested ever since.[42]

Beneath the public debate over the decision and its significance lie the hidden currents of Northern Plains conflict. Such currents escape the reductive and often ambiguous elegance of court decisions. They escape, too, the entertaining stories of heroes and personal confrontation that comprise local folklore. Because humans act as free agents, they move within a web of contingencies whose outcome is not clear, but rather presents the range of possibilities of local conflict: the way in which individuals, local circumstances both social and physical, and large and powerful institutions combine to shape the course of events. We might think of these currents as the strata beneath the surface tensions of life in the arid and multicultural West. In the *Winters* case, they are deeply embedded.

First, the lay of the social landscape is deceptively simple: white settlers versus local Indians. Yet the composition of these groups and how they came together holds some surprises. Defense attorneys Edward C. Day and James A. Walsh, in arguments before the Ninth District Court of Appeals in San Francisco, portrayed the defendants as "diligent" home and community builders who could not maintain their properties or, they suggested, their "communities of civilized persons" (which to any contemporary reader meant non-Indians) without irrigation. Twenty-one defendants were listed, including three corporations, the Matheson Ditch Company (with fifteen stockholders), Cook's Irrigation Company (with about twenty-eight stockholders), and the Empire Cattle Company.[43]

The defendants were hardly corporate barons. One, Minnie Carles Gannaway, was a thirty-five-year-old seamstress and mother, a Quaker, and wife of the reservation teacher at Fort Belknap, Robert Gannaway. Her children played with their Indian neighbors. Another, L. Ereaux, was of mixed Indian and white blood, although not on reservation rolls, but nevertheless requested a lease of ten thousand reservation acres for grazing in 1901. The Empire Cattle Company, a recent and evidently short-lived presence in the area, was the only large corporation in the group. The rest appear to have been sheep, cattle, and horse ranchers of various means and connections. Some were cooperating neighbors with moderate assets: John Matheson was a Scots Presbyterian from Ontario who after years of failure had finally successfully dammed a tributary of the Milk called the North Fork. Matheson persuaded his neighbors to sign on to this bigger project, which included a lengthy ditch. Bertha, Lydia, Ezra, and Andrew Reser were members of the same family listed as separate defendants. Bertha and Lydia taught school on the Fort Belknap reservation, and their father, Wyman L. Lincoln, was an Indian agent at Old Fort Belknap from 1878 to 1887 and, ironically, the first advocate of Indian agriculture there. Andrew Reser, whom the Indians dubbed "Poggie-Scope" or "Crooked Nose," was for a time the reservation farming instructor, later a Chinook blacksmith.[44]

Moses Anderson, whose name the case bore in its early stages, was a horse rancher with a history of violent "feuding," not with Indians but with his Anglo-surnamed neighbors.[45]

The eponymous Henry Winter, misspelled "Winters" in the case docket, was the only defendant in the case who was listed in *Progressive Men of the State of Montana*, a self-congratulatory catalogue published in Chicago in about 1901. He appears there as "Henry Winters . . . among the prosperous and extensive stockgrowers of Choteau County," with "ten ranches and over 4,000 acres of land in the Chinook area, where he settled in 1889," and "imbued with those sterling characteristics which have made the German-Americans so important a factor in the development and progress of our republic." Winter seasonally advertised a shearing pen for local wool growers, and he invested in new equipment, including a "Fairbank boiler from Toledo, Ohio." But by the time of *Winters v. United States*, his rising star had fallen. He was fined $121.80 in 1899 for ignoring a livestock quarantine. Then he spent August 1903 to July 1904 in prison for shooting and butchering a steer belonging to a Helena cattle outfit. This last crime may have come as no surprise to local residents; he had apparently boasted of "having stolen cattle on several occasions." The verdict, however, caused "general surprise," according to the local editor, since Winter was "one of the most prominent sheepmen" in the county, worth "upward of $50,000."[46]

As for the Indian and government side of the lawsuit, it was neither a straightforward alliance nor a clear case of Indian advocacy. William R. Logan, the Fort Belknap superintendent who initiated the suit, was without question more of an Indian advocate than his predecessor, the bibulous and corrupt M. L. Bridgeman. His motivation for bringing charges seemed to stem from his strong advocacy of Indian farming. But by the time *Winters* had reached the Supreme Court, prominent Gros Ventre had complained that Logan was stealing Indian cattle for his own ranch and generally ignoring the people's wishes.[47] What may seem in the history books an impressive defense of Indian rights was apparently not so impressive to the Indians themselves. Reservation Indians were divided on the issues as well. Beyond traditional Gros Ventre–Assiniboine tensions, the two groups often disagreed about resource management and how reservation Indians should make a living. The Assiniboine, who were less enthusiastic farmers than the Gros Ventre, might take lumber that the Gros Ventre intended to use for flumes, or use their survey stakes for kindling, or try to take Gros Ventre fields in petty land wars. Moreover, irrigation was the white agents' initiative. Though many Indians favored it, some, with good reason, eventually viewed its elaborate requirements as an expensive drain on tribal resources with inadequate return. It was hard for them not to be skeptical. Lack of adequate farming equipment, poverty, disease, cultural resistance to white ways, a weak voice in reservation affairs, and the shifting whims of nineteen different superintendents between 1887 and 1920 perpetually frustrated Indian efforts to make a living.[48] The Indian-government party was sufficiently divided to make Logan's action a radically transforming one: no Logan, no lawsuit.

The second complication, apparent in the first, was the importance of contingent events in shaping this history. Irrigation along the Milk River was only a partially cooperative enterprise in these early days. If some settlers, such as John Matheson, were cooperators, a decidedly divisive, competitive, and even criminal streak ran through others on the list of defendants. Henry Winter resisted quarantines and rustled cattle because he wanted to, not out of need. Though the opposing parties in *Winters v. United States* were far-from-inevitable groupings, through circumstances they pitted reservation residents against settlers, not even entirely Indians versus whites. Indeed, by comparison, conflicts among white settlers were at a much higher pitch in the summer of 1905.

Water in the West is the great complicator. Local newspaper accounts reveal just how complicated the context for the *Winters* case was. In April 1905 a group called the Milk River United Irrigation Association "wined" and "dined" itself in Havre and wrote to President Theodore Roosevelt about the urgency of a federal irrigation project on the Milk. Then in June, W. M. Wooldridge, the local irrigation maven claiming to speak for a group of local irrigators, protested against federal assistance, which he saw as a threat to the cooperative and "self-reliant" nature of local irrigation. The valley, he noted, had divided into competing "interests," arguing over whether existing water rights should or should not be determined by the courts, and over federal versus local development schemes.[49] To centralize or not to centralize. It was the classic federalist-versus-anti-federalist debate of western, and indeed American, history.

Chinook area irrigators set themselves against the Milk River Irrigation Association. One angry resident complained that through an error in calculation, upriver crop land was "burning up . . . while the water goes on down the stream to the—you expect we're going to say Indian dam, but" no, continued the irate writer, the Harlem ditches were the offender, "running full of water" while the Indians "ran out but a few hundred inches." In early September, F. H. Newell, chief of the Bureau of Reclamation, conveyed to the secretary of the interior a plan for compromise between opposing valley factions. At the end of the month the Harlem Irrigation Company filed suit against a group the newspaper called "all the water users around Chinook" to adjudicate water rights in the Milk River valley. Even "many of the defendants" had "conflicting claims" and so were "not working together preparing for the trial." By December, Canadian interests in the watershed were in court against the United States to determine their share. The irrigation plan had turned into an argument among branching roots, each hoping to suck water from the other.[50]

Finally, nature itself played a vital role in the circumstances surrounding the *Winters* case. Local records suggest a remarkably benign social atmosphere in the 1890s, when competing irrigation systems were built up along the Milk River, put in place with little rancor thanks to adequate annual precipitation. Settlers and Indian agents, respectively, prepared the way for vast irrigation works, each apparently without concern over the other. Parties from both groups sought federal aid, with every expectation of getting it. In 1898, Fort Belknap agent Luke Hays outlined an elaborate irrigation proposal to the commissioner of Indian affairs. The reservation hired a well-respected New York engineer to carry out these plans. Hays, like a boy in a sandbox, became buoyant with a ludicrous vision of the Indians as a cheerful, hardy peasantry hauling wheat to a local flour mill.[51]

Meanwhile, area settlers were irrigating in large numbers. "The day is not far distant when every foot of irrigable (and it is nearly all that kind) land in this broad valley will be under irrigation," announced the *Chinook Opinion* encouragingly in 1891.[52] Thirty-six parties had filed for water rights on the Milk River by 1898, with the *Opinion* trumpeting the names of these progressive citizens. Oddly enough, this included the residents of Fort Belknap. "Good Indians," sang the headline just five years before the *Winters* case began. "Good," according to the article's first sentence, meant "self-supporting." "The government is now building them an extensive irrigation system that will bring a large area under cultivation and provide homes for all" with "plenty of water," the paper reported.[53] This goodwill was based upon the false premise of abundant resources. Only the Great Northern Railway seemed prescient about scarcity. The company, which had petitioned Congress regarding its own plans for an eleven–mile-long channel from St. Mary's Lake that would increase the flow of the Milk River threefold, struck at its competitors. Hired saboteurs destroyed a settler's competing irrigation works in June 1890.[54]

The rest of the area's residents apparently believed that nature would provide. Skies would open, ditches would run full. Poor man, rich man, Indian, settler, all would run the race and all would have prizes. They were in for a rude awakening. To say that 1905 was a dry year is an understatement. The records of the U.S. Weather Bureau are missing the area's rainfall data for six of those twelve months, an unofficial record kept at the O'Hanlon Mercantile in Chinook showed the lowest annual rainfall since the record began in 1881—a scant 6.76 inches. In June, William Logan warned the commissioner of Indian affairs: "So far this spring we have had no water in our ditch whatever. Our meadows are rapidly parching up." The

Indians' crops would be lost "unless some radical action is taken at once to make the settlers above the Reservation respect our rights." Government observers had predicted the shortage. The 1890 census reported that the Milk River drainage basin embraced little mountain runoff, supplying water to irrigate only "a small percentage of the land."[55]

As anyone who has spent time beneath the fickle western skies knows, drought on the Great Plains is impossible to predict and impossible to control, and its effects are profound. What were the consequences of the drought occurring when it did along this stretch of the Milk River? Without drought coinciding with Superintendent Logan's pressure for farming rather than livestock raising on the reservation, events might have played out very differently. In fact, in 1906, "one of the wettest Mays ever recorded in northern Montana" left "so much water" that the ditch companies "suspended hostilities." Through opposing sides in a lawsuit cut the complex fault lines of Northern Plains society, environment, and happenstance.[56]

Following the usual course for western waters, before long the federal government asserted its hold on local water resources. The United States and Canada signed a treaty on the Milk River watershed in 1910. Milk River irrigators entered into an agreement with the Department of the Interior in 1911, meeting strict stipulations for water use and allowing federal construction to begin on the Milk River reclamation project.[57] Henry Winter was gone from Chinook by 1910, along with five others on the list of twenty-one *Winters* defendants. Fifteen remained, undaunted. The concentration of irrigators shifted, somewhat mysteriously, between 1902 and 1919: the number of acres irrigated from the Milk River dropped nearly 20 percent, and those on Snake Creek dropped nearly 60 percent, but those on other tributaries increased almost 250 percent. Both the *Winters* decision and the Department of Interior ruling included the Milk River's tributaries, which thus exposed irrigating settlers to prosecution. The threat of drought, we must conclude, pushed them to higher ground for more reliable, more plentiful water. Even so, irrigation works did not come close to meeting the newspaper booster's euphoric prediction: in 1919, 162 Blaine County farms, or only about 9 percent of the total, were irrigated.[58]

While the roiling waters of enterprise washed over the Milk River valley, the Maple Creek–Eastend–Cypress Hills watershed irrigators north of the border remained relatively amicable. The area's only notable water litigation occurred in the small town of Shaunavon, just east of Eastend, in 1918, over an ineffective drainage system that flooded a neighboring hotel basement.[59]

The watchful Canadian state had sent out its controllers early, preventing a battle between local and state interests. Out on the high ground of the countryside, beginning in 1912, two small bands of government men working under engineers Hugh Duffield and M. H. French roamed the ditches and ditch sites in wagons, sleeping in white canvas tents, inspecting and shoring up what they called the "haphazard" irrigation works that dotted the Cypress Hills. In the winter of 1913 they organized over two hundred independent and apparently noncommunicative irrigators who "have very little idea of what is being done . . . even in close proximity to them" into the Cypress Hills Water Users' Association.[60] What government emissaries and nature could not resolve, moderate human demand did. As in the Bear Paw drainage to the south, Cypress Hills runoff was "intermittent." Mr. French calculated probable shortages in the event of successive dry years. What they could store during wet years, he decided, would meet any potential demand during dry ones. He did not calculate the effect on their south-of-the-border neighbors, though his scheme, he wrote, would eventually require "all available water" from the Frenchman River, which ran through Eastend to the Milk River, and from Battle Creek, the stream John Matheson and his associates around Chinook called the North Fork. Actual development, he admitted, was "niggardly" and crude. Demand, or at least irrigation development in the Cypress Hills–Maple Creek district, was in 1913 considerably less than the demand upon the Milk River and its tributaries. With otherwise similar social and environmental conditions, even small differences in circumstances set these two areas apart.[61]

What, then, can we conclude about conflict in this corner of the West? Saloon and street violence, labor unrest, ethnic strife, social hierarchies, state and local interests, water wars, the code of the stiff upper lip— all were elements of Northern Plains life. As a case study in conflict, the region fails at mythology, neither celebrating its outlaws as prominently as other western places nor fitting neatly into the Canadian "harmonious settlement" idea. As well, it fails as the battleground for a dramatic contest between the controllers and victims of capitalist development. People tended not to act individually but in factions or small groups, according to desires or social prejudices that allied them with a race, an ethnic group, a cowboy ethos, or an economic interest. At the same time, the communal rhythms of the Old World and of the nomadic Indian groups were gone— features such as class structure, an ancient web of rights and obligations, or a settled mode of production that organized people on the land. If this "homogeneously diverse" borderland, lacked one overriding, potentially violent ethnic, nationalist, or racial conflict, individual cases of pettiness, theft, murder, and greed nonetheless abounded.[62] The place was disturbingly reminiscent of the setting for Walter Van Tilburg Clark's classic Western novel *The Ox-Bow Incident*, a moral universe where there is no monopoly on brutish, exploitive, hateful, or weak behavior.

"The day of the Highland or Lowland or English villages is past," wrote English social commentator Elizabeth B. Mitchell of Western Canada in 1914. If a "Dane or a Galician or an American, dropped down next you a year ago, may be a good kind neighbour," she averred, he "can not be quite the same as a man of your own dialect and religion and ways, the son of a man who crossed the 'waste of seas' with your father, and who used to work the next croft on the far off 'misty island.'" Understandably, she noted, "there are jealousies and misunderstandings between Canadians and Americans and Englishmen" in Saskatchewan; "much more is it difficult for these to co-operate with French-speakers or 'foreigners.'" If Mitchell romanticized the Old World past just a bit, she tried not to romanticize the Canadian present: "Mine is no gallant tale of camp foray and jingling bridle," she asserted unapologetically. Conflict here, she suggested, was a different kind of story, requiring a different language. "The modern country settler is a fighting man, too, but the weapons of his warfare are different, and his enemy is not a bodily presence."[63]

Plains people struggled unequivocally, as Mitchell suggested, not only for nature but *with* nature. It took most of their energy. Cooperation and conflict, the yin and yang of settlement, move in harness together. Social and environmental struggles were inextricably linked. Each human atom fought for position in the prairie universe. They came to the turn-of-the-century borderland, wrote Mitchell, portraying the elements of nature as personae in a medieval morality play, "to wrestle long and hard with Frost and Drought and Solitude and Poverty."[64] In the first decade of the twentieth century, a new flood of humans would become a force as powerful as any element of nature.

CHAPTER EIGHT

THE COSMOPOLITAN THRONG

Belvina Williamson, a newcomer from Iowa, was typical. She and her family were explorers "as adventurous as Christopher Columbus," she wrote, not yet knowing just how apt her ocean metaphor was as the train car packed with the Williamsons' livestock, wagon, and sorghum barrels full of dishes and linens launched onto "uncharted seas to an unknown land." Her older sisters, Ora and Ovidia, were wide-eyed at their prospects: "Will there be Indians?" Ovidia asked with concern. "Aw, who's afraid of Indians!" scoffed their brother. It was 1910, and already their imaginings of Montana were of a mythical Old West, and, as it turned out, an equally mythical new one.[1]

The Williamsons, like many others, first saw the land from the "immigrant car" window of the Great Northern Railway. Others saw it from the Canadian Pacific "colonist car," the saddle, the wagon seat, the Missouri River steamboat, or the dusty cab of a Model T. Their hearts rose. Grass. Space. Hope. A few moments passed. Then their hearts sank as they absorbed the desolation of the landscape. "Why, oh why," one newcomer mourned, "did we come out here?"[2] People were known to turn on their newly dust-covered heels and go back to where they came from.

Even by 1910, the borderland was not a place that yielded positive first impressions. Gullies and coulees sloped into a gently undulating earth. Light heaves roiled the surface. Low vegetation rose from the ground, all sage and cacti and short grasses. The groves of cottonwood and willow that bordered the few rivers, and the small evergreen and poplar forests of the nearby mountains, were remote islands of shade. Stretches of thick gumbo clay dotted the landscape, and dirt mounds marked the entrances of a prairie dog town. In coveted locations a knee-high creek washed downward over the prairie's swells and hummocks. Signs of human beings were dwarfed in the hugely visible landscape. Everywhere was quiet, endless earth, the big sky, and a constant wind that one either submitted to or despaired of.[3]

But they came, and they came in large numbers. Between about 1908 and 1918, the semi-arid lands of the Northern Plains became North America's bargain basement. Governments, railroads, land speculators, and local promoters on both sides of the international boundary still had a prairie to sell, and they did it with the slick efficiency of snake-oil salesmen who actually believed in their own patent medicines. They made dry squares of land, the saltine crackers of the North American continent, sound like manna from heaven. People could not seem to get there fast enough. They came from everywhere, a second generation of settlers, and they wanted to be farmers.

After a discouraging start in which the land was outshone even by Jumbo the elephant, prospects for immigration in western Canada finally brightened when in 1897 Prime Minister Wilfred Laurier's new Liberal government appointed a settlement zealot named Clifford Sifton minister of the interior. Under Sifton, an aggressive, tireless, and ingenious promoter, the number of immigrants to the prairie began to rise, aided by a general European exodus to North America with complicated causes. The Canadian Pacific successfully targeted several desirable groups of immigrants, especially Americans, while discouraging others. Whoever Sifton thought would make the best farmers, Sifton wanted: hearty peasants over urban workers, Ukrainian and Russian Dukhobors (a persecuted Christian sect whose name means "spirit wrestlers," whose passage to Canada was paid for by novelist Leo Tolstoy) over Jews, blacks, Italians, or even non-farming English. Sifton simplified homestead procedures, promoted irrigation schemes, and provided for numerous colony migrations.[4]

The CPR became a fountain of paternalistic schemes. It created towns (often before the rural population could fill them), expanded its rail services, started hundreds of demonstration farms, launched a three-million-acre irrigation project in Alberta, and generally developed natural resources.[5] Over the next two decades the boosters, though nursing and aggravating prejudices as an ever more ethnically assorted horde took up the land, finally got their wish. Immigration to Canada outpaced natural increase. CPR land sales quadrupled from 1901 to 1902, beginning a boom that lasted, with peaks and valleys, until the 1920s.[6] The Great Northern's efforts, with a more North American–based scheme, followed a similar trajectory of success.

Historians have documented this promotion well. Much of it was pure hokum. With "direct and simple language," one booklet lured its prospective dupes: "Heat prostrations are unknown in Montana. . . . Montana 'chinooks' make the winters pleasant. . . . Grief and grouches don't grow well in Montana. . . . Every Montana farmer carries a checkbook," and, more soberly, "Blatant brag and bluster won't do—the world wants the facts." Subtle it was not, but it worked. Only in the North American West could a place that perhaps was undeserving of one settlement boom have experienced a second.[7]

Most insidious was the promoters' appeal to scientific truth and new technology, a credo in which North Americans on both sides of the border were eager to believe. In the wake of the Southern Plains drought of the 1890s came the dry farming movement, the fools' gold of dirt. The method was enthusiastically touted by a Vermont-born farmer named Hardy Webster Campbell, who in 1907 began promoting a supposedly climate-immune agenda of deep plowing, subsoil packing, and summer fallowing, and a Canadian named Angus Mackay, who had developed similar ideas in the 1890s. A crowd of promoters soon followed: the Montana Agricultural Experiment Station; the Great Northern, Northern Pacific, and Canadian Pacific railroads; the Montana State Board of Agriculture, Labor, and Industry; the Dry Farming Congress, which by 1912 had drawn huge audiences at annual meetings in cities from Denver to Lethbridge, Alberta; federal and provincial governments; and local investors in dry farming experiments. Their emissaries fanned the countryside, thumping the bible of "scientific" dry-land agriculture like so many gospel revivalists.[8]

Legislation was soon enacted to satisfy the demand. In the United States, the Enlarged Homestead Act of 1909 expanded the unit of free land from 160 to 320 acres. In Canada, the Dominion Lands Act of 1908 boosted the 160–acre free homestead system, a copy of the U.S. program, by offering settlers another 160 acres of contiguous Dominion lands or "purchased homesteads" at a low price. More people would take up homesteads between 1900 and 1920 than in all of the late nineteenth century.[9] The dry-farming boom, engineered by the corporate, scientific, and governmental elite, had begun.

By 1910, Jim Hill himself was promoting what he called his "great adventure" in every hamlet and farm in Dakota, Montana, and Washington State. Though he was in his early seventies, Hill's vigor was undiminished. With a bow tie, three-piece suit, pince-nez, and huge white beard, he became an agricultural revivalist, stumping from the backs of trains and out of buckboards, pointing his finger to the skies at state and county fairs. He sold the prairie as no one had done before. He preached the gospel of homestead settlement. He hauled soil from Montana and elsewhere to his St. Paul laboratories for experimentation. He sent out "seed improvement" trains to spread the news of new techniques to the people. He advocated irrigation. He promoted the deep plowing, subsoil packing, frequent harrowing, and summer fallowing that was to make the desert bloom. Hill offered cash prizes at the annual Billings Dry Farming Congress for the best crops grown on dry land. Great Northern station platforms sprouted little glass display cases full of heavy-headed Montana wheat. He lifted from the transborder whirlpool of talent a native Ontarian and former professor of animal husbandry named Thomas Shaw, invariably referred to as Professor Shaw, and made him the Great Northern agricultural expert. By 1910, Shaw managed forty-five experimental company farms in Montana. Hill was careful to call his program "scientific farming" and demanded that others do so, too. The word dry he thought, was bad for business.

So, even as the name Jim Hill became a national household word synonymous with "damned monopolist" for his attempts at collusion and consolidation, struck down by the Supreme Court in 1904, Hill launched one of the most impressive campaigns to champion the small farmer in American history. Albro Martin, Hill's worshipful biographer, devotes to this monumental effort a mere 4 pages in a 615–page tome. Those who have dared criticize it Martin dismisses as "professional controversialists." But the Montana writer and journalist Joseph Kinsey Howard, always ready to call a spade a spade, recognized Hill's proselytizing as the kind of manic hopefulness it was. Hill was a bookish farmer's son, a visionary and a backcountryman at heart, whose essential qualities are captured in this anecdote: Passionate about the smallest details of his railroad's operation, Hill was said to travel it incognito in a $15 suit. On one such occasion in the town of Belton, Montana, Hill was being served a steak at Mrs. Appgar's cabin, a popular stopping place for travelers along the line. When Mrs. Appgar revealed to her customer why she charged such a reasonable price for the meat—she attributed her low costs to the largesse of a Great Northern baggage man who threw it off the rail car without charge—Hill in turn told her who he was and said he would "put a stop to that." "Well," replied Mrs. Appgar, undaunted, "I'm damn sorry to meet you." Hill must have liked her humor. The baggage man continued tossing, and the meat stayed cheap.[10]

Jim Hill was legendary for both his rustic charisma and his relentless and passionate striving, two qualities that he combined to the utmost in his Great Northern promotional scheme. "There was in him something of the bravura of northwestern plainsmen, who had been known," noted Howard, "to walk deliberately and unnecessarily into a blizzard or into murderous hail, mocking the gods of storm, testing their own stamina." This time, Hill was leading thousands after him.[11]

Hill had plenty of help in his role as prairie Moses. Unlike in Canada, the United States had few naysayers in the mix of interested parties. The federal government, largely due to the efforts of Montana senator Joseph M. Dixon, not only passed the Enlarged Homestead Act in 1909, but followed with the Three-Year Homestead Act of 1912, which reduced the waiting period for ownership from five to three years. Montanans produced their own promotional blizzard. From 1909 to 1914, the Montana Bureau

Sub-agent and sub-collector of customs John J. English waiting for business, Dominion Lands Office, Maple Creek, Saskatchewan, 1906. The rush of newcomers became so large by 1910 that the agent quit in disgust until he secured a salary increase.

Photo courtesy Glenbow Archives, Calgary, Alberta.

of Agriculture, Labor and Industry published three editions of *The Resources and Opportunities of Montana*, a shameless varnishing of what it claimed was the "unvarnished truth" about the agricultural possibilities of the state. Hundreds of booster clubs and land companies peddled local land. Meanwhile, within the company Max Bass, the general immigration agent, appealed with some success to Mennonites, German Baptists, and other groups beginning in the 1890s.[12]

Jim Hill got his wish. The land rush was astounding. The dry country began absorbing people like blotting paper. Droves of them—in Model T's reeking with cooking grease, in little Maxwells with repaired axles, in piled-high Studebaker wagons, and of course on the railroads, stepping dazed from emigrant cars, standing expectantly amidst trunks, clocks, manure, flying feathers, wagons, and sewing machines, waiting trackside for a "locator" to take them to their square of paradise.[13] Coney Island on a summer Saturday or the great hall at Ellis Island in 1902 might have compared favorably to the atmosphere at Montana's Great Northern stations in 1912.

Historians have chronicled the rush as well as they have its promoters. Between 1909 and 1919, Montana homestead entries sextupled, up from just over five million acres in 1909 to almost thirty-five million acres in 1919.[14] Packed with people such as Belvina Williamson and her family, the railroad brought more than a thousand emigrant cars into northern Montana in the first quarter of 1910 alone. In the Chinook vicinity, land was entered under the Enlarged Homestead Act at the rate of sixty filings a week. "In one evening during the spring of 1910," notes historian Mary Hargreaves, "250 landseekers arrived on the train to Havre, 50 other having already stopped along the route west from Glasgow." The U.S. land office in Havre, the town just west of Chinook on the Great Northern line, again recorded 250 homestead entries on a single day in March 1913, when the total for the month reached 1,600. The Blaine County directory of farm properties and tax valuations lists no homesteaders in its 1909–10 edition; by 1915–16 the number of farmers listed as homesteaders was 1,407, or 30 percent of the total, virtually all on public lands.[15]

The scene north of the border was no different. In February 1910, the Maple Creek Board of Trade began receiving letters from "a large number of U.S. farmers," many of whom apparently followed up on their queries. In March the Maple Creek newspaper reported "the large number arriving on Tuesday night taxed the hotels to their limit and they were only the vanguard." Maple Creek had invited them. In 1909 its board of trade sent out 20,000 fliers to "all parts" of the United States singing the praises of southwest Saskatchewan to prospective homesteaders. By 1910 the number of Americans using United States stamps to post their letters in Maple Creek was large enough to warrant a public scolding in the newspaper. By June, Maple Creek's Dominion lands office agent was so overworked, he quit in disgust until he received a salary increase.[16] If the devastating winter of blizzards in 1906–07 had caused many livestock operations to fold, this was a human blizzard of even greater consequences.

Ranchers marked its coming with the acceptance they might reserve for a malevolent force of nature. "Ranching in this part of the province will soon be a thing of the past," pronounced Mounted Police superintendent J. V. Begin about the Maple Creek district in 1912. "Ranchers are going out of business. Most of the land has been opened up for homesteaders. Old ranch grounds are gradually being cut up by farmers. Stock cannot anymore roam over the country as hitherto." Chinook area residents recalled the same phenomenon. "See, after 1910," said sheep rancher James McCann, "homesteaders just walked in here and took every acre." "Hell," remarked another, "when this country filled up with dry farmers the range was gone." If reports of the ranching industry's death were somewhat exaggerated, one thing was clear: a new and diverse population had begun to arrive on both sides of the border.[17]

Though Belvina Williamson and her siblings did not know it, the twentieth century in North America was about to become the century of identity—emphasizing the cultural and political labeling not only of nations, but of racial, ethnic, and political-interest groups. Which raises a question: Just who did these rapidly converging, dislocated, optimistic, border-crossing, wildly diverse newcomers and old-timers think they were? Canadians? Americans? Westerners? A grab bag of ethnic groups? There is no simple answer. Most did not say. For these people, as for most of their contemporaries, we make an educated guess based on the writings of the few who did report. They were exploiters and users of a land they both loved and hated; ranchers who felt crowded and farmers who felt isolated, Indians and Métis who felt both; a people without a collective history who quickly developed a local mythology; people of many nations who seldom celebrated nationalism.

For those who did record their thoughts, their recollections varied. Mac Montgomery, the cigar-smoking uncle of journalist M. R. Montgomery, did not remember much diversity in turn-of-the-century Chinook. His lasting impression of the town where his brother and sister-in-law settled in 1898 was that it had two unusual people: a Jew who rolled cigars for a living (whom the 1910 census listed as M. Sahke, Russian cigar maker, age sixty-one), and a Catholic priest from the Fort Belknap reservation. Of an evening, he recalled, they could be seen walking around town together, two bachelors with only each other to talk to. Everybody else, apparently, were "usual people."[18]

Mac Montgomery may have had a commonplace impression of Chinook's townspeople, where American-born whites indeed outnumbered other groups. But his snapshot was not an accurate portrait of the Northern Plains as a whole. First, a Catholic priest was not a rare sight throughout Montana, which was predominately Catholic. Second, the "usual" people were strikingly diverse. And when the homestead rush began in earnest after 1908, it made a moderately heterogeneous set of communities even more so, especially on the Canadian side of the line. Perhaps a more accurate picture emerges from the impressions of another newcomer named George Shepard, arriving in Maple Creek from England in the full force of the homestead rush.

It was a far cry from his native Kent. The town streets were gritty, there was no butcher to the Queen, no seaport, no retired archery courts, no lush hops-filled countryside, and ironically, no Buffalo Bill's Wild West Show with sights to pop an English child's mouth wide open. Even so, Shepard was impressed as he stood on the sidewalk of Maple Creek in 1913. He and his brothers, sons of a butcher, made the trip to town almost weekly, he claimed, from their homestead sixty road-miles to the south near the U.S. border. Their father had been driven out of business by the Chicago meat-packing industry in 1906, and in an if-you-can't-lick-'em-join-'em spirit, the whole family shipped off to Canada to farm. Maple Creek, recalled Shepard, was "the metropolis of the whole region enclosed by the international border, the Alberta boundary, the South Saskatchewan River—east to the areas served by Gull Lake and Shaunavon." The cow town of the 1890s had a new face, with cement sidewalks in the business district, a sewage system, a water pipeline to the Cypress Hills, four grain elevators, four churches, a cemetery, a hospital, and a bank. And though Shepard could only begin to guess at the origins of this community's identity, he knew it was a hive of activity.[19] "In the evenings, the sidewalks were crowded with a cosmopolitan throng of people. There were cowboys and ranch women dressed in colorful attire. There were fancy surries and top buggies favoured by businessmen taking their families out for a drive. Every train on the transcontinental line stopped for coal and water. The tourists, disgorged on the plank platform, gazed open-mouthed at the cowboys, the range attire, and the buffalo-horn hatracks offered for sale by local Indians."[20] After twenty years the depot Indians were still there, a testament to perseverance.

Among this "cosmopolitan throng" were many types that Shepard neglected to mention but which were already familiar by the 1890s: Mounties in uniform and former Mounties become ranchers; Scandinavians, Poles, a Lithuanian notorious in poker circles for his wife, who circled the table with a babe in arms interweaving her Lithuanian lullaby with the names of the cards other players held. Nova Scotians, Ontarians, and Manitobans of various occupations. English and Irish of every class and station had arrived, some of whom had lived in the United States, Australia, or eastern Canada. There were numerous Scots farmers and ranchers, a native Spaniard who had arrived via San Francisco, and Métis families of expert trappers, scouts, fiddlers, and midwives. Quebecers included stockmen, a legendary axman named French George, and a lawyer and his wife from Montreal. A French storekeeper and a German rancher who were veterans of opposing armies in the Franco-Prussian war were now neighbors. Other notables included a Chinese restaurateur, owner of the King George on Pacific Avenue and the Royal (names chosen, perhaps, for what he viewed as a British-born culture) on Jasper Street; the two wealthy, peripatetic French Tenaille brothers building estates with wine cellars in the wide-open spaces; and Americans in great variety, from Michigan, Minnesota, North Dakota, Kansas, Montana, Vermont, and elsewhere, ranging from cowboys and buffalo hunters to farmers and hotel keepers.[21]

In the mix were some remarkable absences. Blacks and Hispanics were either extremely few in Maple Creek or went unmentioned, with the exception of someone referred to as "Nigger Malley" who "did the washing and was general help for the early police"—by 1913 perhaps long gone—and occasional visitors such as the traveling black baseball team called the Dixie Minstrels.[22] Mormons, who settled farther west in Cardston, ignored the district. Ukrainians, too, who arrived in large blocs in other parts of the Canadian West, were not in evidence. Hutterites came, but not until the 1950s. Most of the local Indians, of course, had since left. The small band of Cree on the Nikaneet Reserve and the hangers-on selling trinkets at the train station were a tiny remnant of the once-dominant local culture. The Northern Plains were boiling with strangers, a murky palette of interpenetrating classes and cultures across the dun-colored land.

By 1913 Chinook, too, was a cosmopolitan center. Mingling on its streets were the "Denison Dutch," a group of German-American sheep ranchers and their families from Denison, Iowa, including Lillian Miller and her family, who settled in the Bear Paw Mountains south of Chinook in the 1890s, and many other Germans besides; Basque sheep herders and Swiss stonemasons; Irish, English and Scots; English Canadians, including a former Hudson's Bay Company trapper and the Thompson family, who had come south during the Métis uprising of 1885; French Canadians; two groups of Mennonites, one called the "Minnesota Settlement" and another drawn from Kansas and Oklahoma; the VandeVen's dirt-poor Dutch settlement called Hollandville; numerous Scandinavians, Norwegian, Finnish, Swedish, and Danish; mixed bloods such as the children of Irish-born merchant Thomas O'Hanlon, who married an Indian woman, a common occurrence here in the 1880s; a few Chinese, including Lee Cum, a longtime area restaurateur and roundup cook with a taste for gambling; a smattering of Turkish and Japanese railroad laborers; a sprinkling of Russians; a Hungarian farmer; Italian miners; and a French woodworker.[23]

Eastend, too, to use novelist Wallace Stegner's phrase, became a "far from unanimous town." Unlike the well-established settlements of Maple Creek and Chinook, Eastend was just coalescing in 1913. As a gathering place, it was among the oldest in the region, having been the site of a Métis village, a short-lived Hudson's Bay Company post, a Mounted Police outpost, and a post office for early ranchers. Now, with a branch of the CPR going through to Lethbridge, Alberta, it was transformed as quickly as the turn of a kaleidoscope. A loose collection of outback Maple Creek ranches became a branch line boomtown. The ranchers who had gathered in postmaster Ben Rose's log house on mail days to chat and play poker over coffee and who organized the occasional dance among some forty men and six or eight married women were suddenly joined by railroad crews, a flood of wheat-sowing homesteaders and their families, and a town full of marginal professional types. The town was surveyed and building started that fall; the CPR's southern branch arrived in May 1914.[24] The ecstatic founders of this new Canadian town were a pair of eager Americans who had owned the Z-X ranch in Eastend since 1902, a couple of honky-tonk grandees from Butte, Montana, invariably referred to in local history books as a duo, "Messrs. Strong and Enright."[25]

Three booming towns. It was a difficult mixture to grasp. Eastend's confused identity was characteristic of the entire region, where newcomers rushed headlong into an already mobile, already diverse population. What might we call John Linder, a German-born former Illinoisan who in 1870 drove an ammunition wagon in the Franco-Prussian war, spent the years 1888 to 1894 in Chinook, Montana, drove a covered wagon to the Cypress Hills in Canada in 1894, where he lived for sixteen years, and eventually moved the forty miles north to Maple Creek? Or Robert Seymour, an Irish-born railroad foreman who worked for the Canadian Pacific and the St. Paul, Minneapolis and Manitoba lines and lived in Canada, Minnesota, and North Dakota before he settled in Chinook in 1888? Or Mable Horse Man, age seven in 1910, equal parts Gros Ventre, Swedish, Yankton Sioux, and Irish, who spoke English and was listed as "Gros Ventre Indian" in the 1910 census? Or Enemy Girl Jones, age forty-eight in 1910, born in Canada to a Gros Ventre father and an Assiniboine mother (presumably the "enemy" for whom she was named), whose first language was Assiniboine and who lived on a U.S. reservation populated in equal numbers by Gros Ventre and Assiniboine?[26]

More important, what did they call themselves—German, Irish, Catholic, Gros Ventre, American, Canadian, Westerner, Northern Plainsman, rancher? Or, at some point, Maple Creeker, Fort Belknaper, or Chinookite? When and how did that sense of identity develop? From which parts of the social constellation did it emerge—family, nationality, race, religion, gender, occupation, environment? What, if anything, bound them all together? As Stegner put it, "There was no way for any of us to know exactly who we were." Many North American groupings have had a strong sense of community—a Puritan city on a hill, a free-roaming Plains tribe, a Mormon hive, a Scots-Irish Appalachian backcountry community, the Quebecois, or even a small-town Illinois collection of failed Kentucky squatters or a plantation of South Carolina slaves. This place lacked the homogeneity of anything but its hopes.[77]

Statistics tell part of the story. We know that the Chinook area was becoming home to a growing number of ethnic groups. We also know that the Indians at Fort Belknap, always a divided population, remained so. By 1908, the Fort Belknap population totaled 1,256: 37 percent Assiniboine, 36 percent Gros Ventre, and 23 percent of mixed race or multitribal parentage, astonishingly few of whom (20 of 260, or about 7 percent) bound Gros Ventre and Assiniboine blood in kinship. The Gros Ventre were concentrated in the Little Rockies on the southern part of the reservation, while their traditional enemies, the Assiniboine, lived nearer the agency headquarters to the north. While these Indians were not a strong presence in Chinook, they certainly mingled with area whites. The agency superintendent remarked in 1911 that "a number of white men have married members of the tribes" and reported with some consternation in 1913 that "Indians can buy liquor easily in towns nearby."[28] Blacks, again, were few. With the black Tenth Cavalry gone from Fort Assiniboine, soon followed by everyone else when the fort closed in 1911, blacks numbered only eighteen in Chouteau County in 1910 and only two, both men, in Blaine County in 1920. Hispanics appear to have been scarce as well but had no separate listing in the census.[29]

We know that in Maple Creek, too, the change was striking in the decade after 1901, when the census put the town's population at 785 people, more than 80 percent of them of British origin. (It is impossible to tell how many were of Canadian or American origin, since they were not listed separately.) By 1911 the town had grown to 936 people, almost equally divided between males and females, with only 30 percent of British origin. There were significantly more Germans, Scandinavians, Russians, Rumanians, Chinese, and a category called "unspecified" (just over 50 percent of the population), many of them presumably Americans, now a large enough group to separate from the British. Religious preferences had grown more diverse as well. Between 1901 and 1911, the number of Anglicans in Maple Creek dropped from roughly a third to 18 percent and the number of Methodists from 25 percent to 18 percent, accompanied by increases in Catholics, Presbyterians, Baptists, Greek Orthodox Church, Lutherans, and "unspecified."

At the same time, the surrounding countryside also had become less British. While detailed statistics are unavailable, Mounted Police reports confirm the population shift as a general one. "The new settlers comprise many Americans, chiefly from Dakota and Illinois," noted Superintendent Cuthbert in 1907. "Settlers are pouring into the district from all directions, but more particularly from the United States," observed Superintendent Moodie in 1910. Homestead entries in Maple Creek that year, he wrote, had reached 1,535. In 1915 they were still coming, until by 1916 there was "little land left open for homesteading."[30]

Of course, the population diversity of the North American continent in 1910 was increasing generally as well. The ethnic and racial categories of any census raise fascinating and problematic questions about identity as a social phenomenon, and we must make do here with the limitations of the evidence.[31] Nevertheless, what made this frontier especially striking were two things: the high overall diversity of the region in a North American context, and the striking increase in diversity in the Maple Creek area by 1920.[32]

How do we understand the overall diversity of the borderland? We might take as a benchmark of high population diversity New York City in 1910, after more than a decade of heavy foreign immigration. Measured by categories of birthplace (American-born and so on), and separating blacks as a significant racial group, the New York City diversity index (a measure based on the number of ethnic groups and their respective concentrations in a given area) is 18. Columbus, Ohio's, is 7, and the state of Mississippi's at only 4 in the same year (Mississippi was 56 percent black, with no foreign-born group equaling as much as 1 percent of the population). Diversity indices for the Maple Creek and Chinook regions for these three decades, 1890–1920, average nearly 4 points above those of the United States and Canada as a whole. And if the Fort Belknap reservation diversity figure of 11 is any indication–its population divided roughly into thirds among Gros Ventre, Assiniboine, and mixed bloods or other tribes–diversity among native populations, often overlooked, was also relatively high.[33]

The Maple Creek region's religious diversity is equally high, averaging four points above the Canadian norm. The Chinook area figure averages twenty-one points below the United States norm for religious diversity, possibly because U. S. data on religion was based on forms sent to religious bodies rather than the census. Only the largest and most well organized groups would have identified and recorded their membership for the census survey in an unsettled hinterland—hence the dominance of Catholics, who were long-standing residents thanks to the region's missions.[34]

Such high diversity in medicine line country is hardly surprising. The railroads, after all, were hotly advertising the West across the ocean, and the native peoples were a significant presence. The distinct pattern of change in the region's diversity is not unexpected, either. Between 1890 and 1921, the Maple Creek region significantly increased in diversity, from around 12 in 1891 to 8 in 1901 to about 15 in 1921, while the Chinook region, higher in diversity to begin with, changed only slightly, averaging around 15. Demographically, then, if not culturally, the medicine line was fading to a wisp. The region on both sides of the border were becoming either Americanized or more similar in character. This shift occurred at the expense of native peoples throughout the region, and at the expense of the British in southwest Saskatchewan. The diversity index offers at least some explanation of Mac Montgomery's nonchalant view of the similarities among the "usual people" of Chinook. Montgomery did not recognize the area's diversity perhaps because it had been there so long and its rough edges had worn off, perhaps because it involved out-of-town enclaves, and perhaps because it included so many Indians, easily disregarded by the casual white visitor. He likely would not have dismissed it so lightly, this evidence tells us, had he been a hundred miles to the north.

In the end, the anecdotal evidence and statistical data converge. Diversity became the norm in North America's last agricultural land rush. The sievelike quality of the border—the imprecise migration records and shifting categories that give its statisticians fits—found no exception here. How often might someone identified in official statistics as an "American" in Canada be originally from yet a third place, or perhaps even born in Canada and returned there after a stay in the States? We know that an estimated 2 million Americans entered Canada with the purpose of settlement between 1901 and 1931. In 1908, a peak year, 97 percent of these chose Canada's western provinces. In 1911, 21 percent of residents in the Moose Jaw, Saskatchewan, census district encompassing Maple Creek were American-born. And the United States, of course, was in the midst of one of the largest foreign influxes in its history.

Flouting the simplicity of the surveyors' lines, the Northern Plains became what appeared outwardly to be a multicultural borderland of remnants, immigrants, old-timers, newcomers, the uprooted, and the invaded, a mix designed to confound generalization. Many subgroups within the population held common threads—ethnicity, religion, place of origin. But as a whole, people mingled on the grassland like the largely non-native species they were, with little sense of common history and, so it seemed, little need for the political bonds of nationhood. Yet for over thirty years this social miasma developed its own shifting geography of cooperation and conflict, association and independence. Their tensions were not those of a borderland, but of a spectacular flood of strangers.[35]

A ll roads lead to Maple Creek," announced the *Maple Creek News* in 1909, especially from "the land of the Stars and Stripes." As time passed and population diversity increased, the patrician tendencies that colored the Canadian side of the border faded. Eastend, situated halfway between Chinook and Maple Creek, displayed the Americanization of southwest Saskatchewan like town colors. "Pop" Strong, one of the town's two American founding fathers, springs from the pages of local history with the improbable passions of a Sinclair Lewis character. Always dressed in collar and tie—"strange for a ranch owner," recalled Ray Baker, a boyhood playmate of Strong's son Pete—Strong was the "ultimate capitalist, always exhorting us to become merchants and 'own our own,'—even if only a peanut stand." Occasionally the town replaced something English with something characteristically Canadian—giving up tennis for curling, for example—but Americans were everywhere.[36] These included Bill Anderson, a Minnesotan who, as proprietor of the poolroom and barber shop, was at the center of community social life and gossip; J. D. "Slippers" Prestidge, a Texas cowpuncher, the region's outstanding bronc rider; W. J. Leaf, a Minnesota Swede, who ran the general store next to the pool hall; and the many members of the Minnesota Society, who, if anything like the Stegners, "never thought of [them]selves as anything but American" or hybrid Canadian-Americans.[37]

On the U.S. side of the line, incoming Canadians were swallowed in the general influx. (Chinook was not sending out fliers to Canada.) A few insular ethnic communities sprang up along the border: the Dutch at Hollandville, Lutheran Scandinavians at Turner and Hogeland, northeast of Chinook, and three Mennonite groups near the border. But the society was remarkably open. A Nazarene minister who held a revival in the border community of Cherry Ridge in 1914 won enough converts to build a Nazarene church there.[38]

Canadians and Americans, in fact, were less distinguishable from each other than were newcomers and old-timers, farmers and ranchers. The farmers flooding in were rarely viewed as participants in the local land ethic. Except for the occasional appearance of dry-farm boosterism, the language reserved to describe farmers is more subdued, more critical than that used for ranchers. Ranchers and journalists might give a farmer credit for having a good work ethic, but no one spoke of the fellow with "farming in the blood" or the "dry farm way of life." A writer for the Maple Creek *Ranching News* in 1903 neatly summarized the conventional wisdom about farming that persisted for decades on both sides of the border: "No man can get a bare living on 160 acres of prairie in this semi-arid district" he wrote; "Agriculture is out of the question, except in a minor way, or by expensive irrigation."[39]

Cornelius Zeestraten, the quiet father in Mary Weeks's account of her Dutch immigrant ancestors' dry farm north of Chinook, was living proof of this statement. Zeestraten's experience suggests that local farmers in the 1910s led lives of quiet desperation. The dry farming saga Weeks wrote is one of the most vivid of local documents. It is so overimagined, in fact, that Zeestraten comes across as a figure from a melodrama, obscuring his true feelings. We know less what he thought than what Weeks, inferring from relatives' stories, believed he should have thought. In Weeks's dramatic rendition, Cornelius plows the earth with reverence. He squeezes a handful of his "rich loam," drapes the reins "loosely over his shoulders," makes the sign of the cross and cries, "Giddap." He is not a complicated human being but a cliché, the "perfect picture of a pioneer." Beyond the role-playing, however, it is clear that Cornelius Zeestraten was simply a farmer on a bad farm that would not yield, and his family lived in a miserable state. One disaster followed on another in impossible succession. The milk cows were lost. The dugout and later the frame house were poorly built and cold. There was no money to buy coal. Debts mounted at the Bogy Mercantile in Chinook. Land, house, and cattle were mortgaged. Family relations were tense. The crops failed. By any standard, this farm sounds like hell on earth. Nor was it atypical. By the 1930s, few small dry farms had survived as a dependable single strategy of land use.

Borderland farmers intended to do what tens of thousands of others from the Southern Plains to the northern prairies did: plant flax or wheat and sell it as a cash crop on the grain markets of St. Paul or Chicago or Montreal. Less clear, however, is what the people in this locality were thinking when they did this, or how the place affected them over time. When Weeks writes of how Zeestraten "surrender[ed] to nature," threw a dart at a map, and returned to Wisconsin, we are no closer to understanding Cornelius Zeestraten or his view of nature.[40] It is difficult to compare Zeestraten with those in similar localities across the West. Historian James Malin and others, for example, have argued that foreign immigrants were more inclined to love the soil for its own sake than were Americans, who were, as Malin put it, "always ready to sell at a profit."[41] Zeestratens had come for a "new life," much as the ranchers had—to establish a home, acquire property, and "work for [him]self." Other dry farmers, such as Norwegian immigrant Bill Helgeson, who planned to "prove up" and move on, came with speculation in mind. In either case, who could learn to feel at home or love the land? Cornelius Zeestraten left no record of his sentiments. Another Hollandville resident, however, recalled one such homesteader who in 1927 may have expressed for his peers what Cornelius did not: "I finally got enough money to get out of this country and I'm goin'!"[42]

Farmers such as Zeestraten did not write romantically about their world. If they wrote at all, as Canadian George Shepherd did, it was (by Shepherd's own description) to "escape to the heroic past" of the rancher.[43] The farmer in his shack, a dogged plower, a sedulous flycatcher, was not viewed as an intimate partner with the land. He had none of the rancher's open-air routines. He tore up earth, planted, killed pests, and waited. "Honeyocker," "scissorbill," he was called, words spat out as if a home-

A homesteader in Hollandville, north of Chinook, Montana, anticipating that dry-land farming techniques would produce prosperous farms during the homestead rush of the 1910s.
Photo courtesy Montana Historical Society, Helena, Montana.

steader and a hock of saliva were one in the same. The onus on farmers was twofold: first, that some were greedier than ranchers, ecological carpetbaggers trying to break in the country to a new form of land use, sell out for a profit, and leave. The Jeffersonian myth of the virtuous yeoman carried little force here. Second was that they wanted to transform the countryside in radical ways—section it, fence it, pulverize and plow it, tame it beyond recognition. There may be some truth to these criticisms, though if Wallace Stegner pronounced his father "brainlessly and immorally destructive" of the natural environment, it was a truth few farmers admitted for the historical record.[44] Compared to the error and incompetence that mar the record of early ranchers, however, an even more destructive and self-destructive disjunction between high hopes and semi-arid land reality runs through local farming documents.

By 1910, local ranchers became venerated as "old-timers" partly to distinguish them, the literature suggests, from the lesser species who came after them. With few exceptions, the Southwestern Saskatchewan Old Timers' Association in Maple Creek does not consider anyone who arrived in the area after about 1900 an "old-timer" nor anyone after about 1906 a pioneer. "I feel duty bound to include this couple among our pioneers," begins the entry for Dr. Frederick Dawson in Maple Creek's book of distinguished early settlers. Dawson, who arrived in 1908, was not even a farmer, yet his inclusion had to be justified by his "many years of faithful service."[45] Early ranchers became the Pilgrims of these plains, an exclusive club that closed almost as quickly as it opened. If not all ranchers were pioneers, certainly the sacred term pioneer meant only ranchers.

The language of local farmers reflects less interest in the natural environment than that of the ranchers. Farming requires waiting; time fell heavy upon them. And in their waiting they were not outdoor enthusiasts. "I had so much time on my hands that I became a pretty good card player," wrote an Eastend homesteader who "had no money," "and not too bad at checkers, either." "The shortage of money, the hard winters in cold houses, the dry years and the loneliness was a very depressing thing for some," recalled Iladell Anderson of her homestead childhood near the border south of Eastend. One evening during dinner her father found their neighbor's hat floating in the well. The neighbor, aptly named Mrs. Running, soon to leave on a trip to Ontario to relieve her melancholy, had excused herself from the table where her three children sat with the Andersons, put on her coat and hat, and drowned herself behind the house. Mrs. Running was likely the victim of more than wind and weather. But by the 1910s, local attitudes toward the landscape were becoming more troubled. Ranchers felt "crowded"; farmers felt lonely.[46]

Regional literature is a testament to difficulty for rancher and farmer alike. Over the thirty years between 1890 and 1920, local writers developed a strong element of gallows humor and bitterness about nature's unwillingness to bend to human efforts. The bitterest words inevitably came from the dry-land farmers of the 1910s, who took on an almost impossible agricultural task and suffered from the most unreasonable expectations of any settlers. "Oh, prairie land, sweet prairie land," wrote a local poet named Hattie Smiley from the vantage point of her tiny house, fourteen feet on a side, just north of the U.S.-Canadian border. She borrowed the cadences of an old English hymn about "Beulah Land," as had many westerners before her, to parody the song's usual celebration of Edenic bliss. Instead of "O Beulah Land, sweet Beulah Land, / As on thy highest mount I stand," Smiley writes,

As on some little mound I stand,
I look away across the plains,
And wonder why it never rains,
And notice what the people stand,
Who come here to this prairie land.

"The prairie chickens flit and fly," she adds, "And find no place beneath the sky, / Where they can warm their poor cold feet, / While hunting for a bite to eat."[47] Nature, as it often does in literature, mirrored humanity.

"The prairie," wrote another disturbed dry-land resident, this time on the U.S. side of the border, is "a composition of emptiness stained with sweat, dust and despairing tears," a place where "making a living . . . . was a sickness, an infection."[48] The area's sheltered hills, coulees, and chinook winds favored some residents with a more forgiving environment than many other parts of the Great Plains, and tempered the local attitude. But any part of this land was a temperamental prize. As years passed and second- and third-choice land was taken up, residents' relationship with the land increasingly resembled that of a wild-animal tamer or a bewildered lover—devoted, frustrated, hopeful of something in return for one's efforts, wishing for more cooperation and fewer violent outbursts.

At about that time, just before the first train had run through town in 1914, the Stegner family arrived in Eastend, jouncing into town on Buck Murphy's stagecoach from Gull Lake after the long train trip from Iowa. Young Wally Stegner spent his boyhood there and later used some portion of his literary capital remembering it, lighting the map with the glow that only brilliantly reimagined places acquire. Reading Stegner's *Wolf Willow*, part memoir, part history, part novella, one feels transported across a great divide, out of our own time, in which a sense of place, of belonging somewhere, has been greatly diminished.

Wolf Willow is no pastoral idyll. Its setting is a borderland, a frontier, by definition a place of tension and transition, with heightened questions of identity. Stegner's Saskatchewan is in many ways part of the encroaching urban industrial movement that would soon overtake the twentieth century with a centrifugal, delocalizing force. Its people are themselves migrants, a restless collection of opportunity seekers. Yet his personal narrative returns us to a time when local environments, both social and natural, still exerted a powerful influence, even among a wandering Great Plains population that might easily give the impression of ball bearings let loose on a flat surface.

The Stegners came to join Wallace's father, George, camped in a derailed dining car and harboring his perennial great expectations. There were no streets, hardly even houses. What they did find soon enough, Wallace Stegner noted in retrospect, was a "wild mix of people and cultures." "My impression, and I have only memory to corroborate it," he recalled in a letter, "is that there were more Americans than any other kind of people there, but the Americans themselves were different kinds."

Texas cowpunchers, already on the fade when we arrived, who had moved north through the plains to Montana and then Canada; farmers, many of them Scandinavian by origin, who worked into the Northwest by a sort of migration route through the Dakotas and Montana; and various exotics like Jakie Klein, the butcher, who was American Jewish of some variety, and another storekeeper, Miller, of the same wandering-Jew species. The Syrians, whose name was Haddad, might have been American for a while . . . . the ministers were prevailingly Scottish Presbyterians without any American intervals. There were a certain number of English whom we thought of as Cockneys, and a few professional people—barristers and doctors— who were mainly drunks and who disappeared fairly fast, by death or departure. There were some metis families whom we didn't know well because they were Catholic and didn't seem to attend either school or Sunday School. There were a couple of Chinese . . . Dukhobors— Ukrainians I guess—whom we never saw in Eastend. . . . [The] English families that tried to import tennis were few and transitory, mainly the drunken professionals and real estate sharks."[49]

Wallace Stegner in an Eastend, Saskatchewan, swimming hole, at about age 6, c. 1915. He later called his Saskatchewan boyhood that of a "sensuous little savage."
Photo courtesy Mrs. Mary Stegner.

Wallace Stegner had a child's acute awareness of social distinctions on the Canadian side of the line. He arrived in what he later called the "new nontown" of Eastend at age five, twenty years later than little Lillian Miller and her sheep-ranching parents south of the border.[50] But like her, he came at a time when social diversity was at its peak, arriving north of the line after 1909 with the second wave of homesteaders. While Miller believed that "being a little girl" in her family meant that she must be "always sheltered and never too uncomfortable," Stegner was a self-described "sensuous little savage" seeking full exposure. One sees him in photographs, a small child grinning from a rough country swimming hole or with his shoulder behind his larger, tougher brother, Wally being a sickly child who aspired toward the accomplishments of his rougher associates. He found the town's tea-sipping, tennis-playing English families intolerable snobs; one could hear the sardonic edge in his voice, even at age eighty-one, when he recalled the Huffman family and their pretensions to gentility. Instead, Stegner relished the dirt: "I caught lice from the half-Indian kids I played with," he remembered. "I learned dirty words and dirty songs from the children of construction workers and from the Z-X cowpunchers. With others, I was induced to ride calves and engage in 'shit fights' with wet cow manure in the Z-X corrals."[51]

The tough ethos also had its harder edge. "Cultural distinctions we recognized," Stegner recalled, "and sometimes prejudices of a certain raw kind. . . . It was Jews, 'Chinks,' 'halfbreeds,' and others outside the standard American-Canadian patterns who inspired it." Differences among people were points for comment or caricature. "Everybody had two names," Stegner noted, "the one his parents had given him and the one the community chose to call him by": Skinny, Lefty, Preacher Kid, Jew Meyer, Slippers, Runt.[52] Another Eastend resident, in describing a woman whose appearance he disliked, demonstrated the frontier talent for description: "She had a figure like a busted couch, a voice like the noise produced when a man files a bucksaw, and her face was a plastic surgeon's dream of raw material." Against anyone perceived as an outsider, "the folk culture sponsored every sort of crude practical joke, as it permitted the cruelest and ugliest prejudices and persecutions," added Stegner. "Systematically," he recalled, "the strong bullied the weak." Mah Li, a Chinese cook, was "abused in imaginative ways ever since he arrived back at the turn of the century." Once Stegner saw cowboys make him lick a doorknob at fifteen degrees below zero, tearing the skin off his tongue. Like Miller with Set-Em-High, Stegner in childhood innocence wanted to be Mah Li's friend and also had received a gift from him, a magpie that could say "O Five," the Stegners' laundry mark. Yet Stegner's need for acceptance in the cruelties and posturings of his social millieu often overrode his impulse for friendship; he "would have been ashamed not to take part in the teasing, baiting, and candy-stealing that made [Mah Li's] life miserable," including killing (with his own gun) two of Mah Li's white ducks.[53]

Eastend's social tensions were typically not nationally based. "Between Americans and Canadians, as such," Stegner noted, differences "hardly mattered." In the heavily American and Canadian Eastend, hidebound English residents were the more likely objects of ridicule. They had "accents," drank tea instead of coffee, and were perceived—with some justification according to Stegner—as generally incompetent farmers or frontiersmen.[54] Name calling and cruelties circumscribed an unforgiving social code, the "code of the stiff upper lip," Stegner called it, unaccepting of those perceived as cowardly, timid, or outside the norm, admiring of "good shots, good riders, tough fighters, dirty talkers, stoical endurers of pain," and white Americans and Canadians.

Stegner's *Wolf Willow* provides as well a deep insight into the farmer's world, as it records his intimacy with the earth during his Saskatchewan boyhood and the absolute failure of his parents to understand the land or make a living on it. Despite Stegner's self-deprecating quip that he was the "Herodotus of these Hills," his is the local homesteaders' loudest voice. Stegner distinguishes, as did his family's winter and summer houses, between town and homestead. The town of Eastend, at the edge of a foothills-prairie environment, was the concerted product of both nature and its founding fathers, J. C. Strong and J. E. Enright. Like medieval walls, the looping green coils of the Frenchman River and the curving ditch and the straight lines of Strong and Enright's irrigation flume enclosed Stegner's town, a sanctuary from the bare, windswept existence of the homestead to the south, a notion that would recur in his writing. Across the smooth surface of the Frenchman stood the Strong and Enright dam, a wooden structure supported by pilings and buttresses, and the ditch and flume snaking from it were as natural to the boy as the river itself. "I loved that dam and the main ditch," Stegner recalls. "Almost as much as the river they defined my world of town." He learned to swim in the ditch, walked its banks to school, caught and killed ermine and mink near its pilings. The memories this human-inflected nature impressed upon the child were visceral ones of sound and smell, a mixture of artifact and wild growth: "There was a lovely summer sound the ditch made, flowing softly against its banks and waving the long grasses like hair," Stegner writes; the smell of the wolf willow shrub that perfumed the riverbank, "pungent and pervasive . . . has always meant my childhood." Nature is something used and lived in, neither good nor bad, neither friend nor enemy, but part of the contrasts and contradictions and practices of life itself.[55]

Such familiarity with the landscape was generally shared and endured from the 1890s to the 1910s, in part because environmental hardship persisted in full force in the region's everyday life. The place was a backwater, as Stegner realized when he moved to the "big town" of Great Falls, Montana, in 1920, wearing elkhide moccasins on his feet and gawking at indoor plumbing. Through often brutal contact with nature, Stegner, like Miller, understood untempered terror, torpor, cruelty, and frustration. In the long, shade-starved days on the family's isolated homestead, forty miles south of Eastend, he watched glue-slimed flies drag their tiny bodies across hot flypaper, never reaching freedom, his mother telling him they were a parable for the family's own predicament as dry farmers. He remembered killing scores of gophers, being an "expert in dispensing death," shooting generally "at anything that moved," and one especially fascinating, terror-inspiring tussle with a weasel that fought back at the boy and his pitchfork with primitive ferocity. George Stegner, facing total failure on a dry-land farm, "did not grow discouraged," Stegner recalled; "he grew furious" at such a betraying and obstinate country. Young Wallace sometimes found himself in the path of that fury.[56]

By the 1910s, Stegner suggests that the expectations of the settlers were more bent on conquering nature than working with it. When Stegner writes about the prairie homestead, close association with nature veers between partnership and competition. The homesteaders pressed for some sign of their own authority and security against nature's vastness and power. "More satisfying than the wagon trail, even," he writes, "because more intimately and privately made, were the paths that our daily living wore in the prairie. I loved the horses for poking along the pasture fence looking for a way out, because that habit very soon wore a plain path all around inside the barbed wire. . . . I scuffed and kicked at clods and persistent grass clumps, and twisted my weight on incipient weeds and flowers, willing that the trail around the inside of our pasture should be beaten dusty and plain, a worn border to our inheritance."[57]

It is hard to say whether the area's commercial expectations increased over thirty years, as this passage might suggest. Stegner does not press the point. The overlay of the adult writer becomes especially complicated. Critical as he is of his family's "blindly destructive" efforts at farming, he finds even their partly destructive intimacy with nature potentially redeeming.[58] His paths are a metaphor honoring the difficult task of making a place not only out of raw nature, but within the coordinates that civilization had laid down for the newcomers. On one hand, the railroad and the homestead grid signified the impersonal world of resource colonialism—commerce, world markets, new technology, abstraction, and anonymity. On the other hand, the wagon roads, horse trails, and footpaths were "an intimate act, an act like love" worn in the "earth's rind" that can only be made by people who really live in a place, a virtuous rural intimacy "denied to the dweller in cities." "It was an unspeakable satisfaction to me when after a few weeks I could rise in the flat morning light that came across the prairie in one thrust, like a train rushing down a track, and see the beaten footpath, leading gray and dusty between grass and cactus and the little orange flowers of the false mallow that we called wild geranium, until it ended, its purpose served, at the hooked privy door." In Stegner's prairie world a home-steader both needed and resisted nature to make the place his own. And though Stegner later recognized the ecological insanity of the dry farming movement—he remembered his father as always wanting to "make a killing and end up on Easy Street"—his path makers are a comfortable and com-forting image of balance and understanding, the appealing half-truths of an immensely talented writer.[59]

The farmers introduced to the area as well a new element of public relations and reliance on popular authorities in one's relationship to nature, and they irrevocably changed the character of the local sense of place. Competing with the landscape for primary attention were interests and organizations that would tell settlers where they were and what to do there. Farmers were likely to have settled here in response to propaganda. They lis-tened to James J. Hill and distant "experts" who arrived on farming trains and distributed literature about how to dry farm. They spoke of "proof of what the Professors" said.[60] In contrast to the German-American sheep ranchers of the 1890s, who arrived naive and educated themselves by trial and error as a local group, much of the behavior in the farming settlement of the 1910s was shaped in absentia and in abstraction. According to Blaine County agricultural extension agency records, dry farmers planted what they thought would sell for the greatest short-term profit, forgoing a diver-sified approach, including livestock, that would make "farming more per-manent" and demand close attention to local conditions.[61]

Yet nature never lost the upper hand. For these newcomers along the medicine line, farmers as well as ranchers, the persistent remoteness and unforgiving environment supplied even into the twentieth century what the region's converging and polyglot cultural history often did not: a local identity. It was neither Canadian nor American, but a sense of belonging to a particular place and a specific landscape. As Stegner declared, "I may not know who I am, but I know where I am from." From the physical place of the Northern Plains grew community and identity. "What this town and its surrounding prairie grew from, and what they grew into, is the record of my tribe."[62] Stegner did not mean the local Odd Fellows club, the grain coop-erative, the Presbyterian church, or the pool hall, a sum of affiliated parts. Nor, in a place without history, did he mean the past. He was speaking of the land, and it lay in the fundament of the self. It was a landscape of sights and smells and associations imprinted with the indelible stamp of child-hood memory.

Behind increasing frustration and failure, even among whites, was this constant frame of reference. Regardless of whether nature was the object of blame or praise, it was to some degree part of a human geometry, or vice versa. People and their activities did not stand outside nature but in it; all measurements were taken in the relationship of one to the other. The landscape that local residents appreciated or decried was a pastoral one, neither a wilderness nor a potential factory. It was infused with assumed connections. Stegner's bird sits on a fence post, and "[a]ll diameters run through him; if he moves, a new geometry creates itself around him," just as the human being feels "how the world still reduces me to a point and then measures itself from me."[63] Such people were the direct descendants of Charlie Russell's 1890s cowboy, who is part range animal. If whites fell short of the Indian notion of a biological polity, in which they were on an equal footing with nature, neither were they fully competent or wholly devoted instrumentalists who viewed nature in a purely manipulative or commercial way. The landscape, for many, became a set of sights and smells and experiences burned into memory. "Desolate? Forbidding? There was never a country that in its good moments was more beautiful," wrote Stegner, the child grown up, in his mid-forties, revisiting his childhood home. Like Stegner, local poets refer lovingly to "pleasant valleys" and "nature's loveliness," the place where "one could feel so close to God" or find the "space to grow in." "Everybody from Eastend is full of homesickness for the place," wrote Stegner in 1971 to Cora Brummitt Carlton, who grew up with him there. "The statement is so true," she replied.[64]

Some of that landscape, of course, is covered over, lost. It cannot be recaptured. The social world, particularly, has changed—the strange diversity of early settlement, the varieties and nuances of speech, the squeaking of wooden wheels, the constant presence of horses and their trappings, the hunting hounds as large as antelope that paced many ranches, the tang of game lying bloody in a wagon bed in front of the general store. But much of the landscape survives; colors, scents, textures, and sounds that persist from the early twentieth century. The smells are pungent—sage, wolf willow, dust, approaching rain, the sweat and feces of livestock and horses, the whiff of gasoline near an outbuilding. Wind whips the hair, nips the eyelids. Flies and mosquitoes whine and dive toward the ears. The open space is gaping, the curve of the road steadying, the Bear Paws or the Cypress Hills a distant blue image on the undulating horizon. To know these things was, and still is, to know the place. They meant home.

CHAPTER NINE

"WE CAN PLAY BASEBALL ON THE OTHER SIDE"

L ost between Harlem, Mont., and the Canadian line," read the advertisement, "grain sack marked J. H. Betz, containing piano leg for old
style piano. Will finder please notify and receive reward." Betz, a
Montanan, ran the ad in the Eastend, Saskatchewan, *Enterprise*,
December 7, 1916. Probably the least of his concerns was that he ran it in
a foreign country.[1]

From the looks of it, the Montana-Saskatchewan border is still a place
where you could lose a piano leg and then hope that somebody from the
other side of the line might find and return it though finding a piano leg
here would take longer now, at the turn of the twenty-first century, than it
would have in 1916, at the height of the homestead boom. In Betz's time,
notices of cross-border visits of friends and relatives were frequent news
items in the local papers. "Messrs. John Ryan, J. H. Sheetz, L. N. Bunteen
and John Regan of Chinook, Montana, arrived in town Monday," reads a
typical Maple Creek notice of cross-border traffic. "They came across country in an automobile." Notes a 1903 *Chinook Opinion*, "Stock speculators
of Maple Creek, N.W.T., have been looking over the stock market here-
abouts," the word *stock*, of course, referring to livestock. "Breeds and
Indians" from Canada "peddled wolf and coyote pelts" in Chinook in 1901.
"Oliver Tingley, of Big Sandy, is at the Maple Creek race meeting, which
opens today, with the thoroughbreds which he recently brought out from
the east," read the *Opinion* in 1901. "He will take in the Regina meet before
his return." Shortly after that, Chinook-area resident A. J. Barrett raced his
horse Good Eye throughout western Canada.

People did cross-border business—in cattle, sheep, horses, land, opium,
and, during Prohibition, in whiskey. They shared traveling peddlers and
entertainment troupes. They traveled back and forth for visits, supplies,
picnics, and ball games, crossing the border freely, (unless they had livestock), without stopping at a port of customs.[2] "Settlers in southern

Saskatchewan did much of their business in Montana," one homesteader wrote. "Gas and goods were cheaper, limitations on border crossings less stringent and mileage no greater." "It was not uncommon in those days," wrote another, "to find work across the Border." They settled, back and forth, on either side, or had ranches on both sides of the border. They compared racehorses. They inconveniently had babies on cross-border trips. And, not least, they played baseball.[3]

For anyone expecting notable cultural differences along this border, George VandeVen is happy to disabuse them of the idea. His readiest memories of cross-border and town and country familiarity involve baseball, particularly the homesteaders versus townies rivalry. "We beat Chinook so bad they didn't even know they was on the same field," he chuckled, still proud of the homesteaders' mighty pitching and hitting. He recalled these games in the summer of 1998, just after we had opened one of three barbed-wire gates en route to the United States–Canada border, making our way through cow pastures in his Dodge Sierra pickup. As we neared our destination, we silently devised a method for opening and closing gates, a risky enterprise where George would lean his eighty-five-year-old shoulder into a large pole wrapped with wire, and I would hold my breath and uneasily pull a heavy wire loop latch off over the top of it and pray that I would not lose a finger. George's hands were so large they looked as if they knew how to farm all by themselves. He would point them at the horizon and remember a game, homesteaders against homesteaders, the players drawn from both sides of the boundary line. One of them was a Mountie.

Nothing signified the increasing unity of the borderland better than baseball. Lewis and Clark, after all, had played ball with Nez Percé. By the 1890s, many Americans would have described baseball as the "American game."[4] And certainly the American side of the border was enthusiastic about the sport. The Chinook newspaper published regular reports of the local team's games and related items, including a list of "baseball proverbs" for the philosophical fan. The game was played in every school district, from the Missouri benchlands to the border.[5]

Moreover, baseball has long been an arena in which Canadians measure their relative independence from American influence, a debate that was heating up during the Maple Creek–Chinook settlement period. Baseball was a "southern intruder," a disgusted Toronto *Globe* writer grumbled in 1905, against which "cricket fights an uphill battle to preserve old world culture on the frontier."[6] Baseball, for many Canadians, was a symptom of creeping Americanization. Yet Canada had its own claims on the sport, dating at least from the occasion of King George's birthday in Beachville, Ontario, in 1838, at which some form of baseball was the game of choice to celebrate the king's victory over Ontario's democracy-minded rebellion of

The Maple Creek baseball club, 1903.
Photo courtesy Southwest Saskatchewan Old Timers' Museum, Maple Creek, Saskatchewan.

1837. This was one year before the apocryphal invention of baseball in Cooperstown, New York. Long before the Canadian Pacific Railway penetrated the prairie, baseball in its many nineteenth-century forms was popular in Ontario and along the Red River. And the Canadian West embraced the sport with enthusiasm. By 1917, Climax, Saskatchewan, and Corral Coulee, Montana, two tiny communities that had sprung up between Chinook and Maple Creek, played "hotly contested games every weekend." In June 1919, a baseball tournament in Shaunavon, the nearest large town east of Eastend, included teams from Havre and Chinook, south of the border, as well as Maple Creek, Moose Jaw, and six other Saskatchewan towns. Along the border, Americans had no monopoly on the "national sport."[7]

Records from southwest Saskatchewan not only reveal who was playing baseball—Americans, native Canadians, and immigrants alike—but suggest that people loved it. They played it at every picnic, at every sports day, at every nationalist Canadian celebration. Often there were doubleheaders.[8] On Victoria Day 1909, the "Fat Men vs. Lean" game in Maple Creek prompted the liveliest reportage:

> Bill Green, weighing 253-1/2 pounds without his suspenders, stepped into the pitchers box with due dignity, took a fore and aft reef in his trousers, spat on the ball, swung his glass arm around two or three times, and then looked "Dink," who was behind the bat, square in the eye. "Dink" rubbed his right [hand] over the place where his hair ought to have been and gave the signal for an out-drop. . . . For the hungry tribe the "Swede" in the box looked handsome but harmless.[9]

In a small community where everyone knew everyone else, such name-calling and exaggeration were the stuff of close association based on mutual respect and understanding. In the informal setting of the district picnic, baseball was a democratic affair. Everyone played—men, women, and children. "In the summer there were ball games on Sunday afternoons,"

Maple Creek Curling Club, 1902, Maple Creek, North-West Territories. A European sport more prevalent on the Canadian side of the boundary.
Photo courtesy Medicine Hat Museum and Archive, Medicine Hat, Alberta.

recalled a woman from near the border, "where everybody was welcome and everybody who wished to play did so, it never mattered how many were on the teams."[10]

Eastend eventually became a curling town, but baseball played an important part in its history. The first person ever buried in Eastend was killed in a baseball game, and as there was no cemetery, his death necessitated one. The player was Anton Rustad, hit by a pitch in a game between the hamlets of Lowell and Eastbrook in May 1914. Eastend at the time was little more than a ranch with pretensions, but the trauma of Rustad's death allegedly resulted in a ban on baseball "for some time," according to the local history book. If there was a ban, it was quickly lifted. By June the Eastend team was practicing three times a week. In 1915 local businesses closed for two hours to see their team lose 9–7, to Antelope Butte.[11] An old homesteader from the Missouri River benchlands, expressing a last wish, saw baseball as his ultimate reward:

> The time is here about or when
> Our ages are past three score and ten.
> I hope when we cross that great divide
> We can play base ball on the other side.[12]

"We can play base ball on the other side." The writer meant heaven, of course, but the phrase described the borderland itself, and its promise of freedom and new beginnings.

One afternoon in the tiny town of Govenlock, a few miles above the U.S. border, a man named Jack Hoffman sought to test the powers of baseball. As George Shepherd tells it, Jack was playing in a game between the married men and the bachelors. Jack was playing for the bachelors, but everyone was soon in for a surprise. Midgame, Jack's abandoned wife from Montana arrived in Govenlock seeking her long-lost husband. "The game proceeded," Shepherd continues, "with Jack in the married men's team and the bachelors so demoralized that the married men won the game. Though "Mrs. Hoffman stayed and we came to like her a lot," in a game freighted with the metaphors of "going home" and being "safe," Jack Hoffman had literally sought a change of identity, a new beginning as a freer man.[13] Baseball, says George VandeVen, knew no border.

Nor did many of the local relationships. George likes to describe the area's transborder cosmopolitanism in another brief sketch of his childhood days on the Montana side of the line north of Chinook. As a toddler in the mid-1910s, George spent all his time at his father's coal mine, meeting the people who came to Hollandville from a wide surrounding area to buy the VandeVens' coal. They came from the new settlements and homesteads that since 1910 had come to fill the dry, flat borderland between the Cypress Hills and Chinook. "A lot of them," he recalled, were from the Canadian side of the line: Germans, Mennonites, Scandinavians, Russians, Dutch, Swiss, Belgians, English, Irish. They would line up and set out flared grain boxes, narrower on the bottom, to be filled. Some were returning from Chinook with a truck or wagon piled with groceries and supplies, which they'd empty out to fill with coal. A donkey pulled coal carts up a railroad track out of the mine. "It was quite a place to grow up because at one time I could speak about five languages," he said. "I could swear in five languages, too," he added with amusement—a level of erudition of which his mother was not terribly fond. The newcomers were only continuing the kind of cultural mixing that had gone on since the early settlement period, but now their relationships, interethnic as well as interracial, increasingly stretched across the border.[14]

The unpretentious English, for one, now outnumbered their elite countrymen, and they sometimes adapted in extremis. Arthur Knight, remembered in the local history book as an "Englishman with a wonderful singing voice," was not otherwise known for his cultural pretensions. He collected his neighbors' threshing screenings and ate them as porridge, a diet he supplemented with cooked gophers.[15] There were many like Knight, if less eccentric, who followed all manner of personal inclinations. H. S. "Corky" Jones, who arrived in Maple Creek as an eighteen-year-old from the Isle of Wight in 1898, embraced his new surroundings so thoroughly and with such intelligence that while earning a living at various menial jobs he became a brilliant self-taught scholar in local history, geology, and paleontology. He talked to what Indians he could find about local history, and attended their powwows. He found old foundations on his ranch, searched out an old Métis named Jean Laframboise, and learned where the Métis had lived in the nineteenth-century prairie equivalent of town houses—buildings thirty to forty feet long and fourteen feet wide divided into twelve-foot-long family units, each with a stone fireplace and chimney. He built violins heard on the BBC and at Métis gatherings alike, and collected enough dinosaur and mammal bones to fill the basement of the Eastend school. Like Jones, the elites, here as in Chinook, tended to be self-made successes who came West with loose change and little else.[16]

With contact came composite identity—people of mixed race and ethnicity, familiar with and somewhat tolerant of the ways of others. Residents such as Mable Horse Man or Enemy Girl Jones were of mixed ancestry. Others, such as George VandeVen and Charlie Russell, were pluralists by desire and experience. During his youth as the most arcadian of cowboy idealists, Russell had lived with the Canadian Blackfoot for six months in the 1880s (a "tough time," he admitted) and later became an advocate for the homeless Canadian Cree in northern Montana. He did not claim to fully understand Indian cultures, but visibly admired them: his artwork is filled with them, his regular dress included a Métis-style sash, and he and his friends frequently donned Indian costumes, escaping in their imaginations from an increasingly populated and complex world. "The robe will be spred and the pipe lit," he would write to more than one friend; "when the grass grows long in the trails betwine our camps it is not good."[17] With Indian metaphors he would draw his readers back toward arcadia and personal freedom.

Although Russell's voice is distinctive, Chinook and Maple Creek were full of storytellers with a regional sound. While today the region's English, spoken or written, has little Indian or Métis influence, it does have a distinctive brisk northern accent

Métis women and children. Métis women were often midwives in the Maple Creek, Saskatchewan area.
Photo courtesy Medicine Hat Museum and Archive, Medicine Hat, Alberta.

—rolled Scots *r*'s and broad Scandinavian vowels melded in a way that seems to mimic the broad, rolling landscape. A few differences stand out: in Saskatchewan they "stook" the wheat, in Montana they "shock" it. South of the border had "rodeos," north of the border "stampedes." Saskatchewan had "remittance men" or "mud students," well-to-do sons of British families who paid to learn the fundamentals of ranching; Montana, at least in the Chinook area, did not. Nevertheless, many terms—"coulees," "sloughs," "bench lands," "wolfers" (bounty hunters), "chinooks," "bootleggers," "democrats" (a light horse-drawn wagon with high, narrow wheels)—were used in common.[18] In tape recordings of early settlers, one would have to listen very carefully to distinguish a Cypress Hills inhabitant from a Bear Paw resident by speech alone.

Large, ethnically mixed audiences also shared various kinds of music. The Northern Plains did not produce on either side of the border anything as distinctive as the Mississippi delta blues. People favored popular songs of the time and nationalist music of various kinds. A Cypress Hills woman, for example, a native-born Canadian, recalled the "old time music and Norwegian waltzes" that the Svennes brothers played at her house for the "American and Scandinavian families in the district." She and her father, of German and English descent, played, too, but she remains silent about whether or how musicians influenced one another. Distinctive, however, were the Métis fiddlers, who influenced dance music on both sides of the border. Continuing a tradition of native fiddle music dating from the late 1600s and 1700s, when French fur traders and later Irish and Scottish lumberjacks, trappers, and homesteaders introduced the fiddle to the backcountry, they played a spirited, sawing blend of French, Scottish, and Indian music with a sound reminiscent of Cajun fiddling. "As you pushed your way into the house the din was terrific," said George Shepherd of a Métis fiddler at a Cypress Hills ranch house. "A local Métis named Whitford was sawing away on a violin as though he would saw it in two, sweat streaming down his face and beating time with his moccasined foot. Added to this were the shouts of the dance callers." Some Métis fiddlers, such as Mary Trotchie from the Chinook area, were women. We do not know what stylistic differences may have distinguished players or bands across the border. We do know the music and the dancing were intense.[19]

Like the dances, many social gatherings were occasions for cultural mixing. Métis fiddlers played at white dances; Indians and whites occasionally mixed at large events. Nationalities were forgotten or benignly celebrated. And everywhere farmers mixed with ranchers. Vernon Gale, a son of English parents raised in the Cypress Hills area, recalled "such a wide variety of racial backgrounds," yet believed that he and his acquaintances "didn't know that there were such words as 'racial discrimination' because we were all . . . Canadians."[20]

Even as the fluidity of the border did create individuals and occasions of mixed culture, on neither side did all this mixing create what we would call a "multicultural" society, where groups were equally entitled to power, wealth, or social acceptance. This is hardly surprising, given the racial prejudices and tensions in both the United States and Canada at the time. Post–Civil War American race relations had reached a new nadir in the early twentieth century, between whites and blacks as well as among ethnic groups. World War I heightened British Canadian racism against French Canadians and the immigrants, whom they called "enemy aliens." On the Northern Plains one had to look no further than native groups to find grave social imbalances. Fort Belknap Indians lived with the strange duality of physical segregation and the expectation of cultural assimilation. While Indians often worked for whites as ranch laborers, whites never worked for Indians, except as the emissaries of white culture on the reservation. Métis were accepted as scouts, jockeys, musicians, and shingle mill operators, and were thought worthy of listings in local histories, yet were not exempt from racial slurs. "This Métis friend had many good qualities," we learn of Isador Laframboise in the Maple Creek history book, "tho at times dimmed by lesser ones learned from other races." Canadians, by reputation more tolerant of differences and less demanding of ideological uniformity, committed their sins against difference, too. A dominant Anglo-Canadian-American culture reigned, influenced but not overtaken by myriad mingling cultures.[21]

If anyplace bore out Alexis de Tocqueville's maxim that Americans were "forever forming associations," the borderland was one of these. "In the city men shake hands and call each other friends," wrote Russell in one of his prairie aphorisms, "but its the lonesome places that ties their harts together." In Maple Creek, Chinook, and Eastend alike, the divisions born of pluralism diminished with association, created less for ideological reasons than to provide escape from the isolation of ranch and homestead life. Between 1890 and 1920 the borderland sprouted clubs, organizations, and affiliations assiduously. In one nineteen-month period the town of Eastend organized more than twelve voluntary organizations. Even on the Canadian side of the line, government was no substitute for camaraderie.[22]

Some were business organizations formed for commercial advantages. Their names filled the local newspapers. In the Chinook area, cooperative irrigation projects mushroomed along the Milk River, along with an early Stockgrowers' Association, Chinook Business Men's Association, Commercial Club, cooperative Farmers' Round-up Association, and North Chouteau County Wool Grower's Association.[23] The Maple Creek area produced the Whitemud Pool Round Up association early on, and later, partly under the aegis of the provincial government's Co-operative Organization Branch, there was a Southern Saskatchewan Wool Growers' Association, Stockgrowers' Association of Saskatchewan, Maple Creek Creamery Association, hospital board, Board of Trade, and a Public Works Commission. Wheat pool cooperatives attracted members in the 1910s and burgeoned after World War I on both sides of the line—in Saskatchewan under the guidance of American organizer Aaron Sapiro.[24]

These organizations were proof that the old frontier mythology of self-reliance and individualism was deeply embedded in an increasingly collective society in the North American West. Moreover, views of modernity and self-reliance straddled the border. American and Canadian attitudes toward the twentieth century's shifting social and political agendas were singularly divided between conservative individualists and progressives who welcomed a new society. Rube Gilchrist, a lanky Nova Scotian who arrived in the Cypress Hills in the spring of 1900, seemed more like a dissenting American individualist when he described his neighbors as "hardy, self-reliant descendants of the original pioneers, who are very capable of looking after themselves; we don't like people from the outside coming into the hills to try and look after us." Meanwhile, on the American side of the line, the Chinook prophet of cooperatives welcomed the collectivism that was transforming the dispersed and localized society on which the Western

CHINOOK
Literary Society
Opera House
Chinook Orchestra
Coming Men of America
Modern Woodmen of
  America
Ancient, Free, & Accepted
  Masons
Willing Workers Society
Independent Order of Odd
  Fellows
Eastern Star of Montana
Ladies' Aid Society
Episcopal Ladies' Guild
Laurel Lodge of the
  Daughters of Rebecca
Chinook Baseball Team
Gun Club
Royal Neighbors of America
  Knights of Fidelity
Chinook Equal Suffrage
  Club
Society of Montana Pioneers
  (statewide)
Commercial Club
St. Timothy's Guild
Chinook Aerie of Eagles
Democratic Party
Republican Party

MAPLE CREEK
[Robert] Burns Club
Opera House
Maple Creek Brass Band
Old Timers' Society
Modern Woodmen of America
Ancient, Free, & Accepted Masons
Quadrille Club
Independent Order of Odd Fellows
Canadian Order of Foresters
Ladies' Aid Societies
Horse Breeder's Association
Maple Creek Curling Club
Maple Creek Baseball Club
Maple Creek Dramatic Company
Maple Creek Agricultural Society
Ancient Order of United Workers
International Brotherhood of Maintenance of Way
Pioneer Loyal Orange Lodge
Royal Templars of Temperance
Women's Total Abstinence Society (including a
  "babies' league")
Lacrosse Club
Medicine Hat Brotherhood of Trainmen (affiliations)
Women's Hospital Aide Society
Skating Rink Company
Royal Templars and Temperance Lodge
Orange Lodge
Overseas Club
Maple Creek Boy Scouts
Maple Creek Club
Board of Trade
Liberal Party
Conservative Party

American myth of self-reliance was based: "Combined interest is the coming rule of the day," wrote W. M. Wooldridge in 1903, and he was right, though it was not to come for twenty-odd years.[25]

Most organizations, though, were purely social—the stuff of small-town novels. A list of Chinook and Maple Creek clubs 1890 to 1915, invites a comparison of the people who formed them:[26]

Canadians, too, were apparently "forever forming associations." The Canadian town has a distinct Scots flavor, with its Orange Lodge and Robert Burns and curling clubs. Its Quadrille and Overseas clubs suggest a European-minded populace, as does the sport of tennis, played and reported in local news. The Maple Creek Club, fashioned after an English gentlemen's club, complete with a reading room and electric lights, had no genteel counterpart among Chinook's saloons. The Chinook Commercial Club had its twin in Maple Creek's Board of Trade. The egalitarian Equal Suffrage Club strikes the note of classic American reform, yet Saskatchewan granted women the vote in 1916, only sixteen months after Montana.[27] Other evidence, too, runs contrary to national stereotypes. Maple Creek's Total Abstinence Society drew public criticism from one area Scotsman who wished to "guard against the curtailing of liberty and freedom" and, in the language of Toryism or classical republicanism, advocated simple "self control" over drink.[28] Judging from this list, Chinookites appear to be nineteenth-century associative American townspeople emerging into the corporate interests of a new twentieth-century society, while Maple Creek residents seem to be remnants of the British Empire, acquiring a mixture of collectivist twentieth-century interests and American laissez-faire liberalism.

This organizational impulse in southwest Saskatchewan may have been an outgrowth of the American Progressive movement toward collective activity and reform, and thus a sign of "Americanization." (Foreign investment in Canada was at this time rapidly become more American than British.) It may also have been that class association fit easily into the British and Canadian political tradition. Clearly, both influences were at work.

Religious affiliation was another remarkably neutral meeting ground. To paraphrase writer Norman Maclean's comment that "there was no clear line between religion and fly fishing" in his Montana Scots Presbyterian family, there was no clear line between religion and socializing in this corner of the Northern Plains. Religion had the aura of a social occasion, comfortable as a feather mattress; it started out that way by necessity. An itinerant Baptist preacher packed the Chinook town hall in 1890, despite a dearth of Baptists.[29] In what seemed a proverb of regional worship, the same Baptist preacher found himself seated around a table in the Montana Hotel dining with a Congregationalist minister and a Catholic priest. Like it or not, people of different faiths found themselves sharing not only dinner tables but church services and rooms to hold them in. "The Scandinavians, Germans, Ontario men, Englishmen, and run-of-the-mine Americans, even the Syrian grocer and his family, became Presbyterians because that was where the only social action was," recalled Wallace Stegner of Eastend's religious community.[30]

While some isolated themselves from this easygoing mingling—the Mennonite communities who arrived in the 1910s, for example, and in the 1950s the Hutterites near Maple Creek—what another early resident recalled as an "ecumenical spirit" characterized the region throughout the settlement period.[31] When a Methodist minister organized a log church in the Cypress Hills in 1894, this same resident recalled, two of the axmen who built it were "Mr. Dan Braniff, a staunch Roman Catholic, and my Uncle John Cumberland, the son of a proud Presbyterian family." Thomas O'Hanlon's brother Henry, another visionary Irish Catholic town father of Chinook, was a close friend of John Matheson, a Chinook-area Canadian Scots Presbyterian. "Your father thinks I practice a kind of idolatry," O'Hanlon solemnly told the Matheson children one day. But his Catholicism did not hinder the two men's friendship. Their mutual interests in horses, farming, and ranching innovations overrode any religious estrangement.[32] Among such people, old religious identities remained compatible with their new identities as cooperative frontier residents.

At the same time, ecumenicism had its limits on both sides of the line. Missionaries to the Indians had arrived early, and native religion was suppressed at Fort Belknap. Reservation superintendents advocated "eliminat[ing] any doubtful features" of ceremonial dances suggesting "anything more than innocent amusement," generally "curtailed" the frequency and duration of dances, and tolerated no "tortures" or "sun dances." Occasional religious tensions existed among new settlers as well. Even the game of baseball could not overcome a disappointing incident in the 1920s when a Cypress Hills teacher recalled that her "four Catholics were not allowed to go to a Protestant picnic" to play ball.[33]

Canadians most often experienced tensions between French Catholics and Anglo Protestants. The issue of teaching religion in schools bitterly divided Manitoba in the 1890s. Canadian Protestants went so far as to create by parliamentary bill in 1925 the United Church of Canada (unofficially in existence since 1908), a melding of the Methodist, Congregationalist, and Presbyterian churches whose partial motivation was solidarity against Catholics and non-Protestant immigrants. Though the Catholics north of the border rarely complained for the record, it was probably easier to be a Catholic in Montana, where they made up a percentage of the population twice that of the United States as a whole, the reverse of the situation in Saskatchewan.[34]

The hub of the area's social life, however, was neither religion nor voluntary association, but the picnic—an age-old custom of rural life. "What kept these people going?" askes a chronicler of one local family history. "It wasn't religion; I never saw any of them in church."[35] It was picnics, he suggests. On both sides of the border, every neighborhood or school district held picnics, drawing people from across thirty square miles or more. They ranged from outdoor feasts to religious meetings, weekly winter dances with midnight "lunches" that went on until dawn, ball games, food eaten down by a swimming hole, and full-blown rodeos. "Box socials," annual "stampedes" or rodeos, "sports days," Christmas pageants: these were the chief outlets for people's passions, the backbone of their self-image. "When a storm hit enroute to someone's home for a dance," wrote one veteran of southwest Saskatchewan social events, "no one turned back for home, but each one of the men in the sleigh would take turns walking ahead of the horses to make sure they were on the right road." He recalled attending thirty-two dances in a single winter. "We would rather dance than eat," wrote one participant, lavish praise considering how high eating was on the list of activities in medicine line country. There was no "age gap," no "element of social status," but great "camaraderie," recalled another.[36]

If picnics were occasions at which folks could learn to accept other cultures, they were also opportunities for citizens to become explicitly nationalized—turned into Canadians or Americans. Official celebrations such as Victoria Day and Dominion Day in Canada and the Fourth of July in the United States were big events, sometimes lasting two days. In his short story "Goin' to Town," Wallace Stegner describes one such event. The boy in the story, Stegner hmself, stands on his homestead "looking southward toward the impossible land where the Mountains of the Moon lifted above the plains, and where, in the town at the foot of the peaks, crowds would now be eating picnic lunches, drinking pop, getting ready to go out to the ball field and watch heroes in real uniforms play ball. The band would be braying now from a bunting-wrapped stand, kids would be tossing firecrackers, playing in a cool grove." By about 1910, however, the patriotic content of these holidays was almost beside the point. With Americans eagerly attending Victoria Day picnics, such gatherings became a forum for powerful local interests. Prominent community members occasionally threw big holiday dance parties—the Gaff family's rancher-farmer dance of 1913 and the Lohman ball in Chinook, for example—that people recalled with immediacy fifty years after the fact. By 1907, as sheep began to overtake cattle on local ranges and the area's wealthiest citizens tended to be sheep ranchers, Chinook held the annual "Non-Ah Float Ball," a two-day affair of dances, orations, food, and baseball to celebrate the close of the wool season. The Murraydale

Stampede and Picnic, held in the Cypress Hills, became a showcase for the best international rodeo competitors, and an ardent interest of many residents.[37]

If national celebrations were presumably occasions at which the bonds of nationhood were formed among diverse people, minority groups also participated in large public celebrations. In footraces, the "Indian race" preceded the "cowboy race" at the Victoria Day celebration at Maple Creek in 1910, for example (there was no mention of Indians who were also cowboys), and an "Indian pow-wow" was incorporated into the annual Murraydale Stampede. Minority groups also held their own gatherings. The Chinese celebrated Chinese New Year, a weeklong occasion during which they greeted other townspeople with "gong gay fa toy," or "happy new year."[38] The Indians held Sun or Grass Dances (despite reservation agents' efforts to prohibit or curtail them), which, like rodeos or ball games, were transborder events. White observers remember watching wagon trains of Indians from the Nikaneet reservation in the Cypress Hills headed south to Fort Belknap, returning three weeks later trailing out for what seemed a mile or more with additional hangers-on and dozens of dogs.[39]

Such tribal or cross-tribal gatherings were bittersweet. They reminded Indians of their losses even as they revived their sense of identity. "My heart is sad," said Chief Little Bear, a Cree from Canada, at a Fort Belknap Grass Dance gathering in 1903. "I see my people that were once as numerous as the mosquito and whose sting was a sharp as the buffalo gnat have fallen like the leaves shaken from the dry branch of the cottonwood tree." In such striking similes he continued, describing the Indians he saw before him as emblems of a tragic loss of identity, who sat "like a death-feigning opossum, too drunk to know whether this is a grass dance or a ping-pong party."[40] Sitting Bull had been right: after thirty years of living with the medicine line and its consequences for their cultures, many Indians believed that they were no one at all.

In contrast to Indians, non-native women found themselves free participants in all aspects of regional social and economic life. Males and females did most things in partnership. Women were accepted as economic and physical helpmates and were granted suffrage during this period. Ida Chadwick's recollection of her family relationships on a homestead south of Maple Creek in the 1910s are typical: at age seven, she "had to help Mother a lot," while her mother "helped Dad in the fields, discing, cultivating or plowing with the horses." "By the time I was fourteen," recalled Natalie Sorge Forness, "I worked outside like a man." She and her future husband courted while hauling their separate wagonloads of grain to the hamlet of Ravenscrag near Eastend. Women were not afraid to take on men, nor were they criticized when they did. Eva Gaff, a tough, capable and much-admired early settler on Battle Creek south of the Cypress Hills, once knocked down a hired hand for beating a horse.[41]

However much women may have liked or disliked their rough labors, they also relished a more exclusively female world. They remember female camaraderie with delight, and the absence of it with regret. Lillian Miller's autobiography, recalling her childhood south of Chinook, swells with affection when describing the network of females in her life. Like Miller, Alice Tantow Dalke from the Cypress Hills recalled nostalgically a childhood when "every woman was a friend."[42] Women found some useful part of their identity in being women, and liked it.

Men—Henry Clark, for example—were often not so lucky. Compared to the vivid female sense of identity, Clark and his male brethren shared an enforced typology, what Stegner called the "code of the stiff upper lip" universal to the West.[43] On this frontier, the code was already part mythology, even to its adherents. It was rarely talked about. Clark captures it in an anecdote about himself as a young boy on an Eastend-area farm. At age five or six, he was slow to grasp the male code to which he was being introduced. "'The West is where men are men and women are just a nuisance,'" he heard from his father's cronies, a phrase that baffled him for two years until he thought he had met a "man's man" in Harry Willis. Willis rode up one day while the Clarks were visiting at Ben Rose's ranch,

> and asked Ben to shoe his saddle horse's front feet. A pair of shoes was found, but they were too narrow at the back or open end. Ben said he had no forge, but Harry took the shoes one at a time, laid them on his chest and with his bare hands, bent the cold steel and shaped those shoes to fit. I had at last seen what it meant to be a man and made a mental note that if I was going to be a man, I would have to bend horseshoes on my chest.

But after some reflection, young Clark decided that maleness in the form of mere brute strength was not so attractive. "On the way home I asked Dad why Mr. Willis had such big arms, chest, neck and muscles. Dad said that when a boy, Mr. Willis used to row the dories for the fishermen off the Nova Scotia coast. I decided that if that was the way it made you look, I was never going to row a dory."[44]

In the early days, before the railroads and new settlement, the Mounties, the Sioux, and the U.S. Army made survival along the medicine line a game among nations. After 1890, though, many sources of identity competed with nationalism. Though Canadians elsewhere adopted anti-American slogans and held genuine fears of what they called America's "continentalism," or designs on the Canadian West, the nation-state became only one lens though which borderland events were viewed. Borderland residents even used national identity to promote a broader international sense of community.

In 1916, when the young Canadian town of Eastend was still founding clubs at a fantastic rate, a large group of area residents formed, for example, the Minnesota Society. Competing for membership with the Dauntless Society (for Christian charity and benevolence), the Musical and Social Club, the Yeomen's Society, the Gun Club, the baseball team, the Dancing Club, the Odd Fellows, the Kennel Club, and the Masonic lodge, its appeal was uncertain. But the Minnesota Society drew considerable attention. At its first annual banquet and dance, the 125 guests included "not only a reunion of the Minnesota people," but the "whole community" in order to "enhan[ce] the social welfare and stimulat[e] the sentiment of good feeling which has always prevailed here," reported the newspaper. And rather than stand on a sense of enduring national identity, they toasted the king; they toasted their adopted land; they toasted Canadian citizenship.[45]

Like Bill Helgeson, it seemed that many wanted to be Canadians *and* Americans. A Norwegian immigrant who worked for a time in Saskatchewan, and then twenty miles northeast of Chinook from 1912 to 1914 in the dry-farming town of Turner, Montana, Helgeson described assimilation as a form of wisdom given him by a Norwegian American on the boat to America: "Get away and stay away from the Norwegians as soon as you can and have nothing to do with them. They will just keep you as long as they can, work you hard and pay you as little as they can get by with. . . . Go to work for Americans or anybody else, and see how they or other people live and work." Once on the Northern Plains, Helgeson lived by this dictum. "By staying away from Norwegians, I learned how to talk English fast . . . and learned American ways and customs." The fact that he was in southern Saskatchewan at the time did not seem to matter. Canada and the United States were for him one general English-speaking culture. In fact, he felt "more like a Canadian or American" than a Norwegian, he wrote proudly.[46]

In 1914, the world shifted. Suddenly, World War I lay across the cross-border culture like a fuse, reviving forgotten or faded nationalisms. On August 4, 1914, Canada, as part of the British Empire, went to war with Germany. One of Saskatchewan's five cavalry units was based in Maple Creek and was called overseas in 1915. Unlike the Boer War of 1898, in which Canadians also fought, this was a large-scale war of modern nations, a war of endurance that hinged on economic and industrial production and pitted national against national.[47] Canadians rallied around a national cause, while the United States remained neutral until 1917. The old medicine line abruptly reemerged.

People in southwest Saskatchewan watched young men leave for Europe. By the spring and summer of 1915 the Eastend newspaper was reporting war casualties and the establishment of a local branch of the Canadian Red Cross, and had begun publishing residents' letters from the front. A Seattle newspaper called the *German Press* became contraband. Children suddenly became aware of affiliations they "hadn't really known we had." "Here's to the American eagle," the Canadian boys taunted the American-born Stegner boys. "He flies over mountain and ditch, But we don't want the turd of your damn bird, You American son of a bitch." If more severe acts of xenophobia occurred in Eastend or Maple Creek, they left little trace. But Canada and the prairie provinces generally were full of ethnic sanctions and reprisals. Prime Minister Robert Borden's Union party government disenfranchised pacifists, conscientious objectors, and those from an "enemy" country who had become naturalized after 1902 or habitually spoke an "enemy" language. Nearly eight thousand "enemy aliens" in the prairie provinces spent time in internment camps.[48]

When the United States finally entered the war, anti-German nationalism swept the United States as well. Dan Cushman, who spent the war years in the town of Zurich, ten miles east of Chinook on the Great Northern line, remembered in his otherwise lighthearted memoir, *Plenty of Room and Air*, just how powerful and alarming it was. Anyone suspected of pro-German sentiments received unkind treatment. One afternoon, as the Cushmans stood by, Chinook townspeople threatened to hang an "old rancher named Herman Boldt . . . but instead they made him get down on his knees in front of the court house and kiss the flag."[49] Such incidents were common. Public feeling approached a kind of hysteria undocumented in Maple Creek or Eastend. One rancher whom Cushman remembers as a "small and dapper, pleasant and obliging" man about forty years old who claimed to be Danish was suspected as a German spy because, as a bachelor who lived near the railroad, he would be able to notify Germans of passing troop trains.[50] While he was apparently never harmed, he and others suffered false suspicions.

At the same time, the temperance movement sweeping both nations came to the border. Illegal liquor trafficking across the border became a cottage industry. The timing of the region's various prohibition laws was critical. Montana's took effect in 1918, two years before national prohibition of the manufacture, transportation, or sale of intoxicating liquor into the United States took effect.[51] Saskatchewan had already gone "dry" on the last day of 1916, when it closed all liquor dispensaries, but allowed the manufacture of liquor in Saskatchewan and its import and export. A provincial referendum prohibited its import to Saskatchewan in 1921, while export to Quebec and British Columbia, where prohibition had failed, remained legal.

With prohibition, the medicine line took on its old coloration of a legal distinction to be exploited. The village of Robsart, just west of Eastend, became an export center of illegal liquor to Havre and Chinook, and southern Saskatchewan became a lively hub for hijacking, bootlegging, and illicit distilling. Dreamers such as Wallace Stegner's father, George, seizing upon liquor trafficking as one more chance to make a fortune, went jouncing over the back roads at night in their Model-T's full of booze, headlights beaming out a new borderland vision of prosperity.[52]

Perhaps Dan Tenaille, the French aristocrat who brought zoo animals and French linen wallpaper to the prairie, serves as a kind of border Everyman. In wealth and nationality, Tenaille was unusual, but behind the rich trappings Tenaille's aspirations were simple: a life close to the land in a spacious countryside. According to his daughter, Marie Anita Tenaille Henriot, who in the 1970s wrote a vividly intimate sketch of the family's Saskatchewan history, Dan Tenaille loved "rural life [and] animals." Before coming to Canada, he visited "several properties" in eastern France with his mother, one with "large pastures, woods, lakes, surrounded by walls" for keeping in antelope. But "the simple sight of those walls drove Dan to flight," his daughter wrote. "He dreamed of vast, open spaces and he informed his mother that he was fond of going to Canada." "La vie libre," he called it.[53]

La vie libre. It was a life countless residents imagined for themselves, cowboys such as artist Charlie Russell and his "big range," which he dotingly referred to (in the long American tradition of feminizing nature) as a "beautiful girl that had many lovers"; homesteaders such as Cornelius Zeestraten, toiling for a "deed to his property" so he could "work for [him]self";[54] and Gros Ventre and Assiniboine mourning the loss of their hunting days.[55] The free life held many meanings for the region's people: open country, spiritual satisfaction, property, prosperity, escape from a world of unacceptable expectations. Even in his exoticism, Tenaille was commonplace, one among the "wild mix of people and cultures" that colored local life.

Sitting Bull crossed the medicine line in 1877 seeking la vie libre, and crossed again in 1881 forced to give it up. A generation later, Dan Tenaille left his beloved "vast, open spaces" twice. The first time, in 1904, he left to serve in the French reserve army and, as it turned out, play tennis among a "beehive" of young ladies, where he met and married the woman with whom he returned to Eastend. The second time, in 1912, he left for good. Crowded out by farmers, he said, he went south to clear a plantation on the Caribbean island of Santo Domingo, where he perhaps learned to swear in Spanish. But Tenaille's legacy carried with it the peculiar borderland ambiguity of his Eastend life. While still in Saskatchewan, in 1911 he organized the A squadron of the Twenty-seventh Light Horse Division of the Canadian army. At the outbreak of World War I, as a major in the Twenty-seventh, he left Santo Domingo in the service of Canada. He was conscripted to command a company in the Fifth Overseas Battalion of the Canadian Expeditionary Force, and, in courageous service, was killed in 1915 in the northwest of France. In an appropriately multicultural ending, he was buried in France in a Canadian cemetery.[56]

The nationalist feelings along the border proved neither divisive nor long-lived. Compared to the American Southwest, where nationalist and assimilationist sentiments exacerbated Anglo-Hispanic tensions, this borderland retained a friendly atmosphere, simply because its population, though diverse, did not divide along the clear fault lines of linguistic and racial difference.[57] Perhaps this was because for most people in the region, as for Frenchman Dan Tenaille, identity was complex—a blend, often self-conscious, of where they were at the moment and who they had been before. They all wanted to *become* something, and still retain part of where they had come from. In the lives on the borderland, the real divide was not the border. It was the line that divided past from future—the line of hope, and, as in baseball, a game without a clock, it seemed to stretch into infinity.

CHAPTER TEN

NATURE'S "INCIVILITIES"

Wallace, the Stegners' youngest boy, lay hot and delirious beside his mother, Hilda, in the Eastend, Saskatchewan, schoolhouse, his streaming nosebleed staining their clothes and bedding. The room, which normally housed the third and fourth grades, was swollen with sickness. Victims of the Spanish influenza epidemic of 1918 lay crammed into the four-room brick building, including much of the town and many of the strongest men remaining on the home front during World War I. The virus preferred the lungs of strong, young adult men, bolstering the theories of those who blamed the epidemic on German-propagated germ warfare.[1]

Stegner's father, George, a bull of a man who had once played professional baseball and was now trying to grow wheat on dry land, lay sweating and chilling in the men's ward. A few volunteer nurses and one exhausted, drunkard doctor named DeSerres, whose more competent colleagues were tending to the war wounded, ministered with soup and Epsom salts. The sick sang songs together and called out jokes to boost morale. Trains stopped running. The town was quarantined. The school janitor brought a bobsled to work daily to haul the dead to the town cemetery, a place apparently so bleak and unappealing that Hilda Stegner expressed the wish that if she died, she wanted to be buried "anywhere else."[2]

Death and sickness had come in many forms to the Saskatchewan hinterland during its short tenure. "It began crude," as Stegner described it years later in *Wolf Willow*, "but it began strenuous."[3] By the time the epidemic hit that autumn, the year 1918 had already brought illness and death to several local residents. In January, thirty-year-old Joseph Stauber froze to death in his shack on the high plains. Before he succumbed, neighbors had found him crawling on the floor in circles on frozen arms and legs, his dog lying stiff under the bed. In February, Mrs. Tony Klein, the Jewish butcher's wife, visited the Mayo Institute in Minnesota for treatment of an illness the *Eastend Enterprise* did not disclose. In June, the derelict Dr. DeSerres's baby daughter, Jeanette, an "exceptionally bright and winsome babe," according to the newspaper, died from drinking carbolic acid, used to bathe the horses' feet.[4]

Judging from the local newspapers, accidents, drownings, severe illness, and disease, which often occurred far from professional or competent medical assistance, were fairly common occurrences. The newcomers expected hardship. They were used to untimely deaths—the sudden, fatal kick of a horse, or a ruptured appendix thirty miles from town over impassable roads. They were used to inhospitable weather—blizzards, hailstorms, heat, drought, wind, prairie fires, plagues of grasshoppers—biblical conditions seemingly custom-made by a vengeful climate. "And after all this the Lord smote him," as the line from 2 Chronicles goes. Andrew Garcia's "melting pot of hell" was also, for many, an "environment from hell."[5]

Some had been felled by hardship. A group of Iowans on the American side of the line, for example, were so discouraged by the hot, dry summer of 1890 that all but two families had abandoned their new settlement of Box Elder, south of Chinook. The German Jewish settlement of Josephsburg, northwest of Eastend, in 1891 underwent an "almost complete exodus," as Mounted Police superintendent Jarvis described it, only to be replaced by Germans fleeing still other failed farms in North Dakota. The early Métis settlement near Chinook left no monument other than a large boulder, rolled to the top of a hill to mark the grave of the group's Italian Jesuit priest. Then there were the cattle ranchers who suffered through the "Big Die-Up" of 1886–87 and finally sold out after the snowy winter of 1906–07, and the hard-luck group at Hungry Hollow in the Bear Paw Mountains south of Chinook, starved out in the 1890s. The ill-starred Hollandville community, north of Chinook—George VandeVen's stomping ground—which drought and bad luck would transform from a village to a ghost town in just ten years, was by 1918 on the edge of defeat.[6] The list goes on.

But for the settlement population, which by the fall of 1918 had reached about five hundred in Eastend, devastating pestilence was new. From September 1918 to the spring of 1919, the Spanish influenza virus reminded the world of the stealthy power of germs, and of human powerlessness before them. Carried by the soldiers of World War I, the influenza pandemic flared up as if from nowhere and roared across continents like a prairie fire. It was an international catastrophe. This new and virulent strain of the disease claimed at least 21 million people, far more than those killed in the war itself. In the United States alone some 550,000 died, more than the number of Americans killed in both world wars, Korea, and Vietnam combined.[7] For borderland residents, the epidemic, like the farming, was fierce.

While records from Chinook leave a sketchier impression of the epidemic's effect on the U.S. side of the border, they suggest little difference from its impact on Eastend. The Blaine County Emergency Hospital, a makeshift establishment in the Annex Hotel, recorded 107 patients and 11 deaths between mid-October and late December. Schools, churches, theaters, and pool halls were ordered closed to slow the virus's spread; saloons remained open during these few remaining weeks before the Eighteenth Amendment, prohibiting the manufacture, sale, or transport of intoxicating liquor, took effect. In Eastend, influenza had killed at least 1 percent of the population by spring, and by one estimate 10 percent, sixty people or more—enough to lead Ruby Huffman on a campaign to "beautify" the cemetery.[8] She and her neighbors could do little else.

Farther north, the Alaska-Yukon border was effectively a wall of ice against the microbial advance of flu into northwest Canada. A cordon sanitaire on the Chilkoot and White Passes kept flu carriers from entering the Canadian Yukon at least until the spring of 1919. By contrast, what was the Montana-Saskatchewan border but a field of intermittent prairie dog holes?[9] Besides, there were returning soldiers and other contacts with the pandemic on both sides of the border. From October through December, influenza mortality rates reached six-tenths of one percent of the population in Saskatchewan, eight-tenths of one percent in Montana. Public health policies made little difference to borderland victims.[10] The arrival of the flu yanked local life off its redemptive upward arc of progress and back into the tragedies of ordinary history. Nature, not culture, had the upper hand.

In the face of hardship, any hardship, most borderland newcomers had expected to prevail. These were people who could extract a thorn from the knee in a howling blizzard and bend pieces of iron bare-handed. Though some were bound to fail, settlers came to the Northern Plains with the confidence born of a long tradition of European expansion. Both the United States and Canada were, after all, offspring of the British Empire, upon which the sun never set. "God may defer His temporal reward for a season," wrote Alexander Whitaker, a preacher at the English Jamestown colony in 1613, "but be assured that in the end you shall find riches and honour in this world and blessed immortality in the world to come."[11] Jamestown's founders mostly died in their homes or soon returned to England. Yet three hundred years later, these Northern Plains settlers did not talk very differently from their Virginia advance guard. "I predict an enormous volume of trade in 1916 . . . from . . . the big crop which must result this fall," said one pundit of local conditions, pulling out something called a "prosperity chart" before the Eastend Board of Trade. It was the same refrain every year—part propaganda, part faith, not just in God but in the notion of rational human progress.[12]

Cultural confidence, the kind the British Empire once had, or the kind displayed by these North American settlers, boosters, and promoters, appears impenetrable from a distance. Close up, one expects to find the doubters, the naysayers, the deep thinkers, the pessimists. Willa Cather wrote in the opening of *My Antonia* of the eradication of confidence on the open plains. "Between that earth and that sky I felt erased, blotted out," says her newly arrived narrator; "I did not say my prayers that night: here, I felt, what would be would be."[13] In her fiction, Cather infuses the landscape with the limits of the human condition. She foreshadows what is to come in her novel about exile and struggle. On the Northern Plains, however, life followed a different order. If this was a land "primed for fatality," the people did not start out knowing it.[14] They met their landscape with head-on energy and optimism. "In its flatness you are a challenging upright thing," wrote Wallace Stegner. "It is a country to breed mystical people, egocentric people, perhaps poetic people. But not humble ones . . . It was not prairie dwellers who invented the indifferent universe or impotent man." Here was hope, optimism, self-importance.[15]

Gros Ventre chief and daughter, Fort Belknap, Montana, 1906.
Photo courtesy Dept. of Library Services, American Museum of Natural History (Neg. No. 338933).

These settlers afforded their optimism partly at the expense of having no local sense of the past. In 1907, the *Chinook Opinion* had recalled for its readers' entertainment the "great plague of London" of the fourteenth century, one of the many boilerplate "world news" items that filled each issue. Yet for terrifying pandemics, in 1918 they needed to look no farther than their own backyards.[16]

K ills the Best, a Gros Ventre Indian girl, was about Wallace Stegner's age in 1918. (She was eleven, he was nine.) She lived in the United States on the Fort Belknap Indian reservation, about seventy miles south of Eastend. She may have gotten the flu that autumn—there were about eighty cases recorded at the two reservation boarding schools—but if she did, she apparently wrote nothing about her experience. Her father, Dan Sleeping Bear, was, like Stegner's father, self-supporting, with his own piece of reservation land. He and her mother, Strike the Enemy, had each been married twice, and Kills the Best was the fourth of five children. She would likely have gone to the St. Paul's Catholic mission school on the reservation, a stone building about forty miles south of the Milk River, where a girl with the name Sleeping Bear, probably her aunt, was among the first pupils in the 1880s. The Sleeping Bears were a prominent Gros Ventre family, yet cooperative with whites. A man named Sleeping Bear, probably Kills the Best's grandfather, was a chief with large herds of horses and cattle. In 1894, he went with a small Fort Belknap delegation to Washington, D.C., to ask the commissioner of Indian affairs for more economic assistance. In a photograph of the delegation he appears in the back row, behind Assiniboine men in buckskins and bone breastplates, a small, handsome man wearing a suit. He eventually started his own trading post on the reservation in competition with white traders.[17]

During Kills the Best's childhood, Fort Belknap was a small constellation of windswept settlements (it still is). The ratio of horses to people was about ten to one. The ratio of cultivated acres to people was less than two to one. There were three Catholic churches—one at the reservation agency on the Milk River, twenty-five miles east of Chinook; one at St. Paul's mission, forty miles south near the town of Hays (predominantly Gros Ventre), on the reservation's southern border; and one near Hays at Lodgepole (a mostly Assiniboine village). Two traveling Indian Presbyterian ministers had modest missions as well, for the tenth of the population who were non-Catholic. There was a large, low, log dance hall in Hays, built to be round like lodges or outdoor camp circles, with a wooden floor and an entrance big enough for the horses that were given away during the festivities. Including St. Paul's, opened in 1887, there were three private schools: the Lodgepole

Day School, and the dilapidated Fort Belknap Boarding School at the agency, the sight of which caused one reservation agent to be "simply made sick." Some of an earlier generation of children had attended the famous distant Indian schools in Carlisle, Pennsylvania, and Fort Shaw, Montana, to which parents were now "very much opposed." The reservation schools were not terribly popular, either. The mission school produced "lots of run-aways," and intruders had recently entered the girls' dormitory at the agency school. People lived in log houses in winter—a reservation agent described them as "abominable huts . . . with dirt roofs and the poorest of floors"—and skin lodges in summer. Despite a high incidence of disease (including rampant tuberculosis), medical service was poor and unreliable. There was no hospital.[18]

If Kills the Best Sleeping Bear did get the flu, she did not die of it. Fort Belknap agency superintendent A. H. Symons wrote in his annual report covering the year 1918 that no reservation children, and only 36 adults of the 349 who got the flu, died, roughly 2 percent of the Fort Belknap popu-lation. The agency physician was judged to have "handled the case[s] com-paratively well," with one trained and three practical nurses and the doctor from Harlem hired to help. Compared to other reservations, Symons judged, they got off lightly. But if some Indian groups suffered greater loss-es, the Gros Ventre, along with the Assiniboine and others who made up the Fort Belknap population of some 1,200, still experienced larger losses than the non-Indian populations around them.

Indians and European diseases have an old and acrimonious relation-ship, and the influenza of 1918 was no exception to this history. By 1918, the Gros Ventre were steeped in white culture: religion, farming, language, food, economy. Even by the nineteenth century, Plains Indians were expe-rienced purveyors of beaver and buffalo to eastern natives and white fur traders. The Gros Ventre stopped growing their own tobacco when they began trading for it, in about 1800.[19] And of things neo-European, the one most familiar to them was disease. The U.S. Public Health Service report-ed that 17 percent of Montana Indians (24 percent nationally) caught the flu between October 1, 1918, and March 31, 1919. The mortality rate was 7 percent (9 percent among Indians nationally), about three times as high as that in the nation's big cities. In six months, more than 2 percent of U.S. Indians died in the great pandemic—a mortality rate comparable to that of the general population during the Civil War.[20]

Unlike their white counterparts in Eastend and Chinook, the Indians at Fort Belknap had a long and painful cultural memory of local epidemics. D. Sleeping Bear, presumably Kills the Best's father, wrote a paper (now in the Fort Belknap Tribal Archives at Fort Belknap College) called "How Small Pox Came to the Gros Ventre." It is a story not easily forgotten.

Smallpox, the most devastating of European legacies to native populations, arrived among the Gros Ventre in the late eighteenth century, shortly after the horse entered their culture. For the Gros Ventre, 1780–81 was the first year of contagion. They and many other tribes had heavy losses. In a scene that repeated the experience of other native groups, when a war party of raiding Assiniboine, Kenisteno, and Ojibwa came in upon a Gros Ventre village, they were surprised to find rising from the lodges not warriors, as they had anticipated, but the heavy stench of death.

In a twist of fate, this first epidemic soon proved a boon to the Gros Ventre tribe as a whole. As they retreated southwestward against the advance of the better-armed Cree and Assiniboine, they gained the ground north of the Upper Missouri River from the Shoshone, who were even more weakened from the disease. But their good fortune was short-lived.[21] The Gros Ventre suffered a second epidemic in 1801, a third in 1829 and more in the 1830s. In 1856, the steamer *Clara* carried smallpox up the Missouri River, killing up to one-fourth of the remaining Gros Ventre. In 1869–70, 741 more died of smallpox. In about a hundred years, the tribe shrank to one-sixth its former size, from a population of 600 warriors and perhaps 3,000 or more people to a total population of approximately 600. So passed the century in a series of macabre visitations.[22]

The Gros Ventre had such deep cultural memories of devastating epidemic diseases that they devised stories around them. Kills the Best is likely to have known from her father the story of smallpox and skunks, from the days when the Gros Ventre still rode the banks of the Milk River in hunting parties. In 1939 The Boy, an elder Gros Ventre born in 1870, told it to an anthropologist.[23]

In the days of Gopher and Prairie Dog Old Man, The Boy began, a large party of Gros Ventre warriors, allies of the Blackfoot, went east on a war raid against the Shoshone, Assiniboine, and Sioux. A little below the confluence of the present-day Milk and Missouri Rivers, in north-central Montana, they came upon two corpses in a tree wrapped in the blankets of white men. Delighted, the men unwrapped the blankets and cut them up for leggings. By sunrise, however, one of their party was dead. Panic-stricken, the remaining warriors fled toward their main camp. Most died on the way, killed by an enemy more powerful than the Sioux. "That is a bad sickness," cried the older people, who knew of smallpox, when the remnant party arrived. "It all but kills off the tribe once it starts," they warned, and urged the tribe to disperse. The twelve bands that made up the camp scattered, hoping to thwart an epidemic. For many it was too late. At least half of the Gros Ventre would die.

Then they discovered the power of skunks over Atsa:. In Gros Ventre belief, Atsa: was the malevolent bearer of illness, particularly epidemics. He was predictably unattractive, with scaly skin, long nails, and bushy hair; he was unwashed and unkempt, and wore a hungry look. He lingered near encampments during solar eclipses looking for victims. Understandably, no one liked him, nor offered him food or tobacco.

This time, however, after the Gros Ventre dispersed, according to The Boy, one man and his large family cleverly thwarted Atsa:'s efforts. Having plenty of meat for provisions, they sneaked away from their band into a thick patch of brush along the Milk River. The aroma of a windward skunk carcass did not deter them from their chosen campsite: they considered stench an inconvenience to which they would soon grow accustomed. As time passed, however, and no one died of smallpox, they began to attribute their well being to the reeking skunk. They killed more skunks and hung them around the camp in every direction. Atsa:, they decided, did not care for "Chief Stripe." While they knew that the Plains Cree used skunk fluid for many medicinal purposes, the Gros Ventre did not. The hanging-carcass preventative was apparently their own innovation.

By 1918, local settlers understood almost nothing of the area's native peoples or their scourges. The exploits and cultures that immediately preceded the settlers here "would all have been news to us," Stegner noted. "[T]he world when I began to know it had neither location nor time, geography nor history," he lamented of his Eastend boyhood. "In general the assumption of all of us, child or adult, was that this was a new country and that a new country had no history." Frontier children learned about themselves through utterly foreign examples—the pastoral English countryside of their schoolbooks, tales of relatives' exploits in the American Civil War, or stories of their European fathers and grandfathers. From the Eastend schoolhouse echoed not the past dramas of their local coulees, but tales of Greece and the green hills of England, informing the bemused schoolchild who romped among jackrabbits and buffalo berry that he was heir to swans and phoenixes. "I was educated for the wrong place," as Stegner put it. "Education tried, inadequately and hopelessly, to make a European of me."[24]

Because of this local amnesia, the countryside was filled with ghosts that seemed to exist only for small circles of people, a past that many of the next generation of schoolchildren, Indian and white, would know nothing about. Few whites made a point of teaching children or newcomers about the Indian wars. There were no grammar school history lessons on the defeated Sioux, the crushed Nez Percé, the unflappable Mounted Police inspector Walsh, or even the resolute American general Miles, who had crossed this ground. Wallace Stegner's father, like others nimbly inventive, told his son that the crumbling Métis chimneys outside Eastend were "Indian signaling chimneys," one of half a dozen local interpretations, Stegner recalled, "all of them wrong."[25]

A shipment of sheep from Maple Creek stockyards, next to a pen of buffalo bones in the foreground, September 20, 1889.
Photo courtesy Southwest Saskatchewan Old Timers' Museum, Maple Creek, Saskatchewan.

Of a local past being rapidly forgotten, there were haunting reminders, such as the arm that fell out of Indian burial rags secured in a tree when young Mabel Perrett, unsuspecting, poked at the mysterious bundle with a stick. Ten-year-old Arthur Newby remembered the mounds of buffalo bones he could traverse like stepping stones "without touching the ground," and which in an 1889 photograph heap like eerie driftwood along-side a crammed-full sheep pen, a kind of bleached ghost herd haunting the bleating mass that had replaced it. The Métis chimneys, so creatively mis-understood, stood like ancient ruins at Eastend, while the old telegraph line between Fort Assiniboine, just west of Chinook, and the Mounted Police post near Eastend at Battle Creek, used until 1891 to help keep the region's peace, was reduced by 1893 to a booby trap of downed wires and rotting poles, "a source of danger both to stock and to persons riding or driving" by. The great distances and continual migrations, added to the abstract com-modities that the commercial capitalist economy made possible, allowed borderland settlers a kind of detached existence, abstracted from the place they now occupied. Unlike the Gros Ventre, Eastenders and other white prairie newcomers lived in one place and often thought and acted in the language of another. Stegner called it a life of "uncrossable discontinuity."[26] It was not the border that divided people, but their separate pasts.

A woman Stegner remembered only as Miss Mangan, one of Eastend's two schoolteachers and the town's chief pretender to culture and sophistication, illustrated the settlers' miseducation and their humble place in the biosphere better than she could have imagined or would have admitted. Mangan, Stegner recalled, was sadistic and snooty, and the object of resentment and ridicule among the townspeople. She was "nasty-nice," he related in an interview, a woman of malevolent falsity. She had once made young Wallace bend over a water fountain until recess as punishment for taking an unauthorized drink, and one day frightened a Mrs. Gilchrist into a breakneck trip to the doctor by sending a Gilchrist child home with "pediculosis." The infuriated mother later discovered it was only a case of common head lice. Here was a self-righteous snob who, in Stegner's words, "held herself above all superstition," a self-styled "city girl condemned to the trans-Siberian provinces." Yet during the epidemic, driven beyond the constraints of public persona, she nipped liquor in her sickbed, not a spit wad's arc from her regular post as arbiter of knowledge and propriety.

As the story circulated through town, the wicked Miss Mangan provided Stegner with his fondest memory of the flu. In the view of many Eastenders, her pretentions to superiority ranked with those of their neighbors who insisted on tennis, a game ill-suited for a "bald-assed frontier." For all her airs, the Ontarian Miss Mangan was not above taking what her fellow residents, who favored ethnic pejoratives, would have described as "a little Dutch courage." For Stegner, Miss Mangan provided a way to take pleasure in the disorder the 1918 influenza epidemic had brought to his world. It was as if nature were putting society's injustices right.[27]

The epidemics urged others toward theory, and the autumn of 1918 had its share. Folk remedies abounded. A university sophomore in New Brunswick drank hydrogen peroxide to kill flu germs. Chinese residents in Seattle and Alberta let blood, the Albertans by scratching their wrists with pennies. From San Francisco to Calgary to Chinook, people donned masks, which were largely ineffectual. A Manitoba Indian woman drank rendered skunk fat—she had missed the prescription for external use when a trapper gave it to her brother. A Vancouver window washer sprinkled powdered sulfur into his shoes every morning for protection.[28]

In Eastend, the favored preventives and remedies were chewing tobacco and whiskey. Wallace Stegner, anxious to compensate for what he viewed as embarrassing attributes for a frontier boy—small size, scrawny limbs, and a talent for book learning—would have tried tobacco had he been able to get it. Feeling soft, he perpetually wished for redemption into semibar-barism: "I wanted to be made of whang leather," he later wrote, referring to the tough strips of hide that tied a bedroll to the saddle. Local tobacco provenders—the East End Restaurant, Hazzard and McCloy's barber shop, Haddad's general store, Patterson's drugstore—sold out their supplies quickly in the rush for "chaw" and whiskey that accompanied the flu's arrival. The town streamed tobacco juice, to no avail.[29] The virus still favored the segment of the population most likely to be enthusiastic for such remedies: robust adults between twenty and forty years of age. Their bodies were at their prime to combat localized injuries with intense inflam-mation, which in this case translated into an intense general inflammation from trachea to alveoli.[30] For Eastenders, then, this was a malady with a sense of irony. Being made of whang leather was for once a liability.

In their efforts to find cures and preventive measures, borderland set-tlers also had the pretensions of science. By 1918, they had crossed the threshold of modernity: they were thoroughly entrenched in a worldwide market economy, utterly dependent on the railroad, and increasingly scien-tific in their approach to agriculture. One foot was becoming planted in fos-sil-fuel technologies and utilitarian thinking, or what Max Weber called "means-end" rationality—actions determined by their useful results rather than by their social acceptability.[31] They were anchored by the logic of cap-italist agriculture and encouraged by American and Canadian credos of progress and economic growth. Just north of Eastend in Maple Creek, a brief history and scientific review of influenza appeared in the local news-paper. "As it is such an old disease," the unnamed author noted, "doctors have naturally learned a great deal about its prevention and treatment." The preventive measures prescribed were simple: "[K]eep away from those infected," eat nourishing foods, dress comfortably, get lots of sleep, and live "in the open air and in bright, well-ventilated rooms." Suggested "cures" were "rest, warmth and quiet," aspirin, and antiseptic. South of the border, the *Chinook Opinion* reported that free immunizations with an unproved flu vaccine were available in the nearby town of Havre.[32]

At the same time, in terms of local behavior, the other foot remained firmly planted in folk beliefs, trial and error, and culturally useful myths familiar to their medieval forebears, whose saints built monasteries beneath holes in the heavens where they saw angels passing to and fro.[33] Science itself was often little more than an article of faith. Their dry-land strategy of deep plowing was no more a proven agricultural technique than tobacco was good medicine—even less so than festooning the area with skunk carcasses. Yet if their influenza remedies were not quite science, neither were they quite religion. The God of Eastend's Anglicans, Presbyterians, Catholics, and Jews was not the Puritan God who, with Atsa:-like agency, personally pulled down every dog who drowned in the rivers of Massachusetts Bay. Like the natives whom they displaced, the settlers of the North American West relied on their own angels of faith and imagination in a natural world that remained, to a large degree, beyond their control.

In truth, no preventive or cure was very effective against the 1918 epidemic. The influenza vaccine had no immunologic value.[34] Quarantines were difficult to maintain. The flu, like the Great War, made people think in new terms. Unlike the war, however, the Spanish influenza did not turn them toward political nationalism, but served instead as a grim reminder of the universal human bond to the earth, and of the continuities of history that the region's settler's seemed blind to. Their upward arc of progress, their ethos of social and economic growth, was clearly not the only design that moved the raw materials of nature. They suddenly found themselves in the same microbiological vortex that the Indians of this region had entered nearly a century before. Wallace Stegner remembered that the flu "was the agency that drove a lot of people away, even before drought and dust storms." "The whole town was sick," he recalled. "There were all kinds of families busted." Like the smallpox epidemics of the previous century, the flu left a powerful cultural imprint. Stegner's words echo the Gros Ventre's, mourning the dead after a smallpox epidemic: "The trees along the Milk River," said the Indian, "were just loaded with bodies."[35]

In biblical fashion, though, there was more to come—another avenging angel sounding another trumpet, breaking another seal, unleashing another plague. "The first woe has passed; behold, two woes are still to come." If Hilda Stegner wanted to be buried "anywhere else," she would soon be in a position to get her wish, and it would not be because of the flu.[36]

L ike the mingling rivulets of separate cultures come to water the fields of promise, neighbors in medicine line country were strangers forced into communion. The land itself was an untried, alien place to wrest into submission. And at this intersection of unknowns, the most unfamiliar to his circumstance was the dry farmer of the 1910s. For his expectations there was no cure but experience.[37]

On an August morning in 1919, a rust-colored ferruginous hawk riding the high ventilation of a summer chinook, watching an errant gopher make its final, fatal excursion, perhaps senses impending disaster in the landscape. Straight below lies a farm, a brown constellation of shack, privy, and woodpile connected by dirt paths. Just beyond is a ring of packed dirt, a firebreak against prairie fires. The ring sits inside a pasture fence, which in turn sits inside a rectangle, two squares miles hard to distinguish as the western half of Section 3, Township 1, Range 24, lying along the

Canadian–U.S. border. Alongside runs the edge of a fifty-acre wheat field, once planted with flax that colored the field with blue, because Dakota folklore taught that flax was a good crop for a newly broken field. Now, though, it is the dull tan of stunted, water-starved summer wheat. At the field's southeastern corner stands a black iron obelisk to mark the international border, slightly larger than the U.S. and Canadian survey stakes that divide the region into a vast checkerboard of squares.[38]

The hawk wheels south. Pickings are slim. Tracks worn from the iron wheels of a democrat wagon make a path to a shallow coulee at the boundary line. During a wetter year a clayey sludge of earth and water might sit here, bordered by the tiny yellow blossoms of silverweed. The tracks join a trail south to Hydro, Montana, a tiny, boldly named religious settlement of Kansas and Oklahoma Mennonites and a few Nazarene fundamentalists. Past Hydro, the trail, known as Bagan Road, passes other buildings—houses, post offices, churches—and more squares of earth planted in wheat where the hawk might try later for prey. Other than the Mennonites, little distinguishes this landscape from the one north of the border. The square fields spread from the boundary line intermittently on both sides as if they have been unfurled, challenging the huge geometries of horizon and sky on the broad, flat ocean of prairie.

These fields seem the culmination of a progress as natural as the ascent of civilization itself, the dry farmer growing wheat on plains with an average thirteen inches of annual moisture. Theirs was the common land-use succession in the North American West, from native to newcomer, miner to rancher to farmer, and its assumptions seemed to be the inspiration for the triumphant columns in the local newspapers. Success! Optimism! told as a familiar expansionist creation story of hard work and progress.[39]

But while this creation story has set its characters in place, it does not prescribe who will succeed and who will fail. Local newspapers, Canadian and United States, champion general confidence, touting the goal of "steady growth," the success of "the man who can regulate the water," "development at a rapid rate," and unity in the "pursuits that tend to the common good and growth of the country." Jim Hill and the Canadian Pacific had nothing on the local press for fantastical promotions. Once again, the bald land beckoned. According to one editor's hyperbole, with enough effort area farmers would someday "export turkeys to Turkey and grease to Greece."[40]

By contrast, longtime residents apparently attempted to pass along environmental wisdom to newcomers with the art of understatement. In 1914, newcomer George Shepherd rattled along toward the hills in an "old democrat one blistering hot day" with a longtime Cypress Hills rancher. The land was parched. "Is this a dry country?" Shepherd asked. "Oh, no," replied the laconic old-timer, " 'bout like this year." Some old-timers, despite their misgivings, were hospitable to new homesteaders. "Though as settlers we might have been considered interlopers, we were invited," George Shepherd recalled of the "last big old-timers' dance" at the Gaff ranch, an occasion designed to bid farewell to "the days of the open range."

But most homesteaders proved impervious to local advice. The Zeestratens, the luckless Dutch family that settled north of Chinook in 1910, harbored the typical delusionary confidence of their fellow home-steaders. Newly arrived, they borrowed for living quarters a two-room sheepherder's shack from an experienced sheep rancher and irrigator named Arthur Benton. One of the Zeestratens took up occasional work on the Benton ranch. If Benton gave no advice, it was not through lack of opportunity, yet one reads the painful account of the Zeestratens' attempts to jury rig a household water supply, which was continually tainted either with alkali from wells or with cow urine and "wrigglers" from a dammed-up slough.[41] "Everybody was going to make a million dollars," one rancher recalled of this impenetrable dry-farm optimism; "that's the way it was, the thought there would be no failures."[42]

The Teodor VandeVen family on their dry-land homestead at Hollandville, a tiny Dutch settlement north of Chinook, Montana, in the 1910s, during the second and last homestead rush on the borderland.
Photo courtesy of the Montana Historical Society,

Some viewed the dry farmer with sympathy: "You see these dry land farmers they were moved in there and they didn't know what they were up against right from the start," recalled one old-timer. "These people will come here," fumed another, placing the blame on the unspoken forces of promoters and nature, "led by false representation, and when they have tried and failed they will be broke, paupers. . . . No greater crime could be committed than the one now being carried into effect."[43]

Others, however, stuck with their initial contempt. "[Y]ou got an entirely different class of people come in when they homesteaded the land," said one rancher; "the dry land farmers."[44] They were seen as fools and unfriendly usurpers. A sheepman could find a lost sheep on their places, "either killed or dressed or in their corrals," and "doggone," another said, it "got so pretty near every fellow come out and want to run you off." The homesteaders, after all, plowed up the open grazing lands north of the Milk River and south of the Cypress Hills. "[F]rozen out north of here by dry land farmers," recalled one sheep rancher tersely. "See," said another, "after 1910 homesteaders just walked in here and took every acre." One of the ranchers' "favorite sayings," according to local folklore, was that "the white man took the country away from the Indians, and then the home-steader took it away from the white man." The sentiment that "they didn't know how to farm in those days and the area up there was a rolling country not adapted to farming too well" was widely shared.[45]

People had, in fact, cautioned one another about the climate for years. "Cropping," the Maple Creek Mounted Police superintendent noted in 1894, was "in the majority of seasons . . . simply a waste of time and money." "I had seen the oats grow in favorable seasons in the tracks of the roundup wagons," said another man who had traversed the entire country-side from Maple Creek to the Missouri River as a freight hauler and ranch-er since the 1880s, "but could not believe that such land would ever grow crops in paying quantities."[46] Andrew Caswell recalled being told by an Indian, in the 1890s, "Someday the white man go like this," and then the Indian blew the grains of sand off his palm, leaving only bare skin.

But if the ranchers predicted the homestead failure, they could not (or in some cases deliberately did not) help to prevent it. Despite some friend-ly interactions, the absence of affection between most ranchers and the new dry farmers undoubtedly dampened the free exchange of local folk-lore. A retired rancher named Flynn from Zurich, a few miles west of Chinook, every year answered the question. "What kind of a year is it going to be, Mr. Flynn?" "Dry," he would say, as writer Dan Cushman told it. This was a man "who despised the homesteaders; he wanted them all bankrupt, frozen out, burned out, starved out, scattered by the wind." "Dry," he would say, looking long at the horizon. Flynn "made his voice husky dry as he said it. 'Dry-y, dry-y, dry-y-y.'" He couldn't know that in 1917 he would finally be right.[47]

The drought fell like a hammer. Annual rainfall, which averages about thirteen inches, dropped to below ten inches during 1917, '18, and '19. And even though the price of wheat hit a high of about $2 a bushel in the wartime boom of 1918, it fell in peacetime to $1 a bushel in 1921, while wheat yields in the region fell to below ten bushels an acre. Quickly the dry farmers blew away like grains of sand, as the Indian had prophesied. Though it has become almost lost to Great Plains history in the shadow of the larger Dust Bowl disaster of the 1930s, the dry farming failure of the late 'teens and early 1920s was catastrophic. The numbers alone command attention: between 1917 and 1920, the population of Blaine County decreased by 16 percent, from an estimated 10,800 to 9,057. Between 1919 and 1925, approximately two million acres of Montana farm land fell out of production. Eleven thousand farms, about 20 percent of the state's total, were abandoned.[48] In southwestern Saskatchewan, more than a third of the two hundred townships in the Maple Creek–Eastend area census division lost population between 1921 and 1926. In 1926 alone, fifteen thousand farms were abandoned in Saskatchewan and Alberta; nearly five hundred of them were in the Maple Creek–Eastend area, almost 80 percent of the number abandoned in 1936, at the height of the Dust Bowl. George and Hilda Stegner and their two sons, who lived summers in that homestead on the boundary line, found no way to make a living. After one spectacular wet year in 1915, when George Stegner could carry his six-foot frame into his field and disappear from view, all was lost.[49]

"We had come to a new country with limited means," wrote one Chinook-area dry farmer, "which [were] too soon dissipated through . . . the malicious action of Nature itself." "Nature," he concluded, "has treated [man] with more incivilities and actual punishment than could ever be dreamed of in the minds of man." [50] To his mind nature, not culture, was the culprit. But there had been drought in the early 1890s, and still the homesteaders had persisted. Why had this mass failure to thrive on the land come so late? Surely culture, as well as nature, was now to blame?

The answer to these questions is complex. Governments, railroads, land speculators, and promoters were certainly implicated on both sides of the international boundary. Just as the epidemic of germs illustrated how abstracted local people were from their land and its history, the epidemic of homesteaders engendered a remarkable failure of communication, a massive breakdown of local tradition and sense of place. Social philosopher Alexis de Tocqueville located one explanation for such endemic discontinuity, which he found everywhere in nineteenth-century America, in American society itself. American society, he believed, was based on democratic individualism and economic independence. "Such folk," he noted of Americans,

> owe no man anything and hardly expect anything from anybody. They form the habit of thinking of themselves in isolation and imagine that their whole destiny is in their own hands. Thus, not only does democracy make men forget their ancestors, but also clouds their view of their descendants and isolates them from their contemporaries. Each man is forever thrown back on himself alone, and there is danger that he may be shut up in the solitude of his own heart.[51]

This may fairly describe the solitary homesteader who froze to death in his isolated shack, or the dry farmer on his square of prairie, each indebted for his own 320 acres. As Elizabeth Mitchell noted of 1914 Saskatchewan, this was no Old World village of ancient rights and obligations. The disruption of local influences and institutions had allowed the disaster to happen.

Yet individualism did not entirely characterize the people of medicine line country. Here, too, Tocqueville may help explain more fully the course of events on the Northern Plains. Tocqueville identified the threatening presence of government (to which one would add corporate interests) in cases of an "undertaking beyond the competence of one individual citizen"—occasions when centralized power might "wholly usurp the place of private associations" and, in Tocqueville's prescient metaphor, "leave the helm of state to guide the plow."[52] Just as important in explaining the dry farming disaster was the considerable inclination of these people to form interest groups and cooperative associations, an essential art, as Tocqueville argues, of a good and intelligent society. Historian Bernard DeVoto once described the true Western individualist as the one at the end of a rope whose other end was held by a bunch of cooperators. If the social and economic systems here were fundamentally individualistic, they were also highly associative. The Zeestratens, for example, like other groups of dry farmers, lived in a village of fellow Dutch émigrés, among whom they made strong associations and even class distinctions. Yet association is not the same thing as sound social policy or behavior, and it can, in fact, align people into opposing or self-reinforcing interest groups. Democracies, as James Madison noted long ago, experienced the "mischiefs of faction."[53]

So it happened in the Chinook–Maple Creek region, blind to the international boundary. A powerful commercial elite had guided the plow too freely, and local association could or would not temper it. Local factions, rather than a home-grown sense of the commonweal, dominated the society, and nature dominated them all. Unlike "aristocratic nations" in which, Tocqueville observed, "families maintain the same station for centuries and often live in the same place," this was a collection of assorted and dislocated people experimenting on new ground.[54] The place was, in fact, the creation of strangers in a strange land, seen from the air as an intermittent checkerboard of cracked and stunted wheat fields, two-rut roads intersecting at right angles, gray board structures yielding to the enormous weight of the perduring wind and sky, the inscription of distant decisions, glyphs of an imported social and economic order.

When the Miller family of sheep ranchers lost a son to a ruptured appendix in the 1890s they chose to send the body "home" to Iowa for burial. His tearful, desperate mother and seven-year-old Lillian sat on a snowy hilltop, watching the wagon carrying the body disappear over the "last high point in the white landscape." The image of this departure captures the profound dislocation of their experience. Like the Millers, a large minority of the settlers between 1890 and 1920, and a large majority of dry farmers, would watch years of effort, loved ones, and high expectations vanish into nothingness. "Stevenson and Shelley," wrote a local poet, "Sang praises to the wind," but "Neither poet never stood / Upon this bare brown hill / And watched, through dust and tears, / That ruthless monster hurl my pregnant fallow / Against a neighbour's thirst-paddled fence."[55] In that whiteness was the social and emotional abyss of people for whom there was no automatic, time-worn sense of place, no easily won sense of who or especially where they were.

As for the land, it covered over the homestead boom. Hollandville has vanished, perhaps lost even to the archaeologist. A few ranchers repossessed the range. On the United States side, abandoned homesteads were sold "for little or no money," remembered one rancher, wishing he had bought more.[56] Despite these ranchers' interest, regional optimism, at least for the time being, was blunted. In 1859 explorer John Palliser called this region a desert. In 1880 a Canadian botanist declared it a garden. A more obscure man named Angus McMillan, walking through the Milk River valley in 1886 on his way to the western Montana gold fields, allegedly described the treeless plain as a "terrible country," and now, after thirty-five years of promotion and optimism, there was an entire countryside emptying of people who finally agreed with him.[57]

James J. Hill died in 1916, presumably content in the midst of a land rush he had created. Yet there is a sense of foreboding in his 1910 *Highways of Progress* that his stump speeches belie. On a highway, Hill wrote, "[e]ach [nation] moves, through history, toward what we call progress and a new life or toward decay and death." This is not the unguarded optimism of nationalist propaganda or the satisfied pronouncement of a smug elder statesman of successful railroad entrepreneurism. Here is the cautionary voice of a Henry Adams or a Frederick Jackson Turner, warning his fellow citizens that the nation is going to hell in a handbasket. The national debt, Hill complained, was rising with dangerous and unprecedented abandon; the days of "unlimited expansion" onto largely unexploited lands was drawing to a close; the ruinous waste and abuse of "a national patrimony" of natural resources threatened the nation's well-being. In this peculiarly mixed message, the sixty-year-old doctrine of Manifest Destiny was turned into a jeremiad, a lament for the closing of what Hill called "the era of unlimited expansion."[58] The Northern Plains communities of Chinook, Eastend, and Maple Creek were the products of a latter-day land rush, a remnant of the great era of national expansion. They were a technologically engineered frontier on marginal land. Hill complained of national debt, but he, like the CPR, mortgaged the lives of people who could little afford it against a vision of small farms on dry land. Despite their bravado, Hill and his fellow promoters knew such communities were at risk. They knew it, yet they denied it.

Lillian Miller's brothers, Chris and Henry, sold their sheep ranch in 1958, nearly 350,000 acres deeded and leased. An absentee land lord eventually split it up and sold it. Lillian, after graduating from Stanford, lived in Dennison, Iowa. The Zeestratens folded in 1920. In that year their crop was flattened by a hailstorm two days before the harvest. But it was the three years of drought preceding this that broke them. These tireless people, who had once made their living by draining a lake in a Dutch reclamation project, now fled Montana because of its lack of water. As if accepting some randomness or chaos in the cosmic order that might account for their ill fortune, they threw a dart at a map and moved to where it landed, back to Wisconsin. "I remember when they left," George VandeVen recalled, "and never heard from 'em after."[59]

From the people's point of view, it mattered little which side of the border they were on. There remained no medicine line across which lay a new hope for the future. As with the influenza, government response to the mass misfortune was minimal. Rex Adkins's family left a coulee north of Ravenscrag for Montana in 1927 to "make a new start." "[W]hat we found just across the border," he noted, "was four years of drought which ruined a dry land farmer." James Welch, a writer of Gros Ventre–Blackfoot ancestry, whose stories evoke the boarderland's most haunting questions, put it in his 1979 novel, *The Death of Jim Loney*, set in Fort Belknap: "It wasn't the end of the world . . . but you could see it from here."[60]

WALLACE STEGNER AND THE NORTH AMERICAN WEST

In the spring of 1920, thirty-nine years after Sitting Bull's departure, Wallace Stegner's family left the place he would someday call the "capital of an unremembered past." The family caravan, a democrat wagon followed by a yellow-spoked, black and brass Model-T Ford, rattled down the old road, abandoning six years on the Saskatchewan prairie. From the Stegner's winter home in Eastend, they headed across the border toward Great Falls, Montana. There they would escape crop failure and begin a new life with indoor toilets, lawns, and streets with names, and where within a year, in some divinely orchestrated mundane perversion of artistic apprenticeship, Wallace Stegner would mow Charlie Russell's lawn.

They stopped at their failed summer homestead for a final farewell. Its southern edge ran blankly along the international boundary line, a frontier of now uncultivated sprouting wheat. They walked around touching things for the last time, feeling like ghosts. They gazed at tumbleweeds. They stayed the night. They shut the gate on the empty pasture, "enclosing our own special plot of failure from the encroaching emptiness." Young Wallace watched as two neighboring abandoned homestead shacks, dubbed "Pete" and "Emil" by the Stegners as if they were characters in a morality play, fell behind them and into the horizon like boats lost at sea.[1]

Those shacks and thousands like them were the only monuments of this fledgling society. Others more recently abandoned still stand, haunting the prairie. Their image has become a metaphor for foolish and hopeful enterprises in an unforgiving land, an image finally for the Dust Bowl. Wallace Stegner knew that this folly and hope knew no national boundary. "With nothing in sight to stop anything," he wrote of his family's final crossing, "along a border so unwatched that it might have been unmapped, something really had stopped there; a crawl of human hope had stopped." Stegner was a border creature, as all novelists are, attracted to the margins, intersections, transformations, tensions, and ambiguities of life. He wrote about the Mormons, the line of aridity that sets the West apart, exposure and sanctuary, town and country, the United States and Canada, history and fiction, fathers and sons, East and West. *Crossing to Safety*, his late-in-life novel of Vermont, is a borderland, pure and simple. He found in the West the "geography of hope," what he wished to be a clear-eyed, unromantic promise born of direct experience with the land, a continental gift unrelated to America's national myth of a cowboy's frontier or the Canadian rejection of that myth. A hope for constant improvement, for "community responsibility," for attachment to the land that even in misery and failure and disappointment, crossed the border.[2]

In history, the political border matters. Stegner knew this as surely as did Sitting Bull. "The 49th parallel ran directly through my childhood, dividing me in two," Stegner declared. "I missed becoming Canadian by no more than an inch or two of rain." "In actual fact," he wrote in *Wolf Willow*, sounding his most Canadian,

> the boundary which Joseph Kinsey Howard has called artificial and ridiculous was more potent in the lives of people like us than the natural divide of the Cypress Hills had ever been upon the tribes it held apart. For the 49th parallel was an agreement, a rule, a limitation, a fiction perhaps but a legal one, acknowledged by both sides; and the coming of law, even such limited law as this, was the beginning of civilization in what had been a lawless wilderness. Civilization is built on a tripod of geography, history, and law, and it is made up largely of limitations.[3]

Stegner never examined the border's history systematically. Its restrictions remained, for him, amorphous and subtle, more irritating and inexplicable than consequential. But he knew it mattered. It mattered as the medicine line, as the last political symbol of hope for nineteenth-century plains natives, and as the reason rival governments and visionary capitalists deliberately established parallel worlds of settlement along it. It faded into something to overcome or ignore, despite the political and cultural divisions the border signified, and in contrast to the twentieth-century Mexican border, it made its mark as something astoundingly weak, weaker than the local forces of nature and culture and the larger forces of capitalism and British-based nations. It was, perhaps more than any other, the place where exclusively national stories become an intertwined story of the North American West.

Early on in my pursuit of the border, I wrote a letter to Wallace Stegner. My topic had confounded me, as well as most of the non-native people who had lived there. It had confounded them as an alien environment, harsher than they expected. It had confounded me as a borderland. Where I expected the meaty contrasts of two nations, with distinctive cultures and traditions, I found instead a surprisingly parallel and ultimately intertwined past, not without the distinctions of two nations, but hardly defined by them either. "Dear Mr. Stegner," I wrote, "I have begun a comparative history of U.S. and Canadian frontier communities [and] the more I learn about these places, the more I find myself wishing for your advice." I followed with two pages of rather relentless questions: "You wrote in *Wolf Willow* that you weren't sure whether you were Canadian or American. Were there clear ways in which one could know?" "Were there clear cultural differences or conflicts (such as the issue of gun-toting?)" "Was national identity a matter of concern to you and your schoolmates or your parents?" He wrote back some good answers: "I think your Chinook-Eastend-Maple Creek parallel is a good one, and should be revealing. . . . But what you call the 'murky palette' of interpenetrating cultures is more apparent to a modern historian than it was to a boy living in the midst of it. For all I knew, that was the way the world was. . . . We all—Jews, Canadians, Americans, English, Syrians—were a pretty equal democratic mix." There was too much to discuss in letters, he said. Could we "work out a meeting in June?"[4]

As I wound along the road into California's Altos Hills above Stanford University, home of the writing program Wallace Stegner created, toward the Stegners' house, I was struck by how much the grassy hills and the breathtaking vistas out toward the Pacific Ocean reminded me of the Cypress Hills rising above the ocean of prairie around Eastend. A long country road that could have led to a ranch house curved up to a modest, inviting, modernist-style home from which came the sound of someone playing something like Chopin or Brahms. Mary Stegner answered the door and thought I was a writing fellow. No, I said, just a historian. The Stegners put me immediately at ease, his voice as rich and melodious as her piano. On a long, curved couch surrounded by bookshelves and a spectacular view out a picture window, we spent three lovely hours rummaging through old files of correspondence and photographs, reviewing every character from the Eastend pool hall to the border homestead, perusing an Eastend insurance company map circa 1920, and discussing Canada and America, the West and failure. Stegner seemed to love talking about Saskatchewan, a mixture of regret, pain, affection, and amusement passing over his broad Scandinavian face. By the end of our conversation, the indelible mark that the prairie landscape of his childhood had left on him was palpable. "If I am native to anything," he has written, "I am native to this."[5] He knew not just that it was humble and unrefined, but that it was valuable. It was a place he understood from his deepest experience, a place that thrust him in the midst of a harsh natural world and attached him to it forever. By the time of our meeting I suspected that my contrasting nation-states were only one useful lens for understanding the past, that other categories such as the environment and the wild mix of people could be just as important. Now I knew so. Although human beings destroy and abuse it, nature is still in charge—more powerful than nations, more fundamental than literary careers or artistic greatness.

Stegner's parents lost their struggle on the borderland. But as a border denizen, their son ultimately won what Milan Kundera has called the struggle of memory against forgetting. From the dry dust of a father's failure and Jim Hill's empire dream, Wallace Stegner created a kingdom of words, an enduring legacy that those who know and love the West, Canadian and American, enter with awe and familiarity, a dwelling place as spacious and grand as the West itself. "A Westerner is less a person than a continuing adaptation," he wrote, "less a place than a process." Or, "[t]he West has had a way of warping well-carpentered habits, and raising the grain on exposed dreams." But he counseled patience: "Some are born in their place, some find it, some realize after long searching that the place they left is the one they have been searching for. But whatever their relation to it, it is made a place only by slow accrual like a coral reef." He recognized that making a rooted past and present based on intimate understanding of a land and a place is a long, slow, and still enormously incomplete process—something that Sitting Bull understood and that relative newcomers to North America have never been very good at. "[N]ot unhopeful," he wrote ruefully, affectionately of Eastend. "Give it a thousand years."[6]

Several years after my meeting with Wallace Stegner, after years of disquieting mental wrangling over the borderland's struggle for life against death, I went to the border just to stand on it, perhaps to find its medicine. As we drove north in George VandeVen's pick-up, George reiterated that in his youth the locals "never paid no attention to the line." Homestead-era people, he said again, "didn't even know the border was there." In a manner of speaking, they didn't. "While I lived on it," Wallace Stegner once wrote, wondering at the unselfconscious ignorance that surrounded his childhood, "I accepted it as I accepted Orion in the winter sky. I did not know that this line of iron posts was one outward evidence of the coming of history to the unhistoried Plains, one of the strings by which dead men and the unguessed past directed our lives."[7] Like Stegner, VandeVen did not speak for history. He spoke for those who lived it. He emphasized the necessity behind ignoring the border. "It was neighbor help neighbor," he said. "Didn't matter what your religion was or where you came from." "The Canadians were Americans too," added Anne Schroeder, my other octogenarian guide, with some finality. The history of this borderland divides not along one medicine line, I thought, but several dividing pursuit from sanctuary, desolate reality from persisting hope, environmental indifference and ignorance from a sense of place, tribe from tribe, past from future. And although the term "medicine line" nearly disappeared from the local vocabulary by 1900, it captures, better than does the political U.S.–Canada border, the conundrum of identity and the mess of cultural and environmental contact that people there experienced.

Eventually we made it to the old medicine line. George VandeVen, Anne Schroeder and I walked out from the truck about fifty feet, like astronauts tethered to a ship. We stood along the line for a while, gazing down the border fence. The wind nipped gently at our clothes. The American fence was down, looking like something a hawk dropped. The Canadian fence looked small, receding to the vanishing point in each direction. Without it, I thought, the scene would look primeval. Indeed, not much has changed here since the 1930s. Even by the 1920s, the dwindling numbers of farmers began paying closer attention to their landscape. Those who remained—who by the 1970s numbered about one-fourth the original peak settlement population of 1920—tended to blame themselves for failure. They tried to adapt, taking up mixed ranching and farming. They began to strip farm, summer fallow, take on other jobs, irrigate, purchase livestock, and resign themselves to periodic drought. Today, on the north side of the border, cropland is not an uncommon sight. Large-scale government-subsidized farming around Eastend—mainly feed grains and hay—forms a pattern of rectangles, visible on a satellite map from outer space. Blaine county, with fewer subsidies, is still comparatively bare.[8]

The railroads still pass through Chinook and Maple Creek. The nicest hotel in Chinook, the Chinook Inn, sits just south of the embankment, at the end of the main street lined with bars. It is clean, plain, fairly new. The beds vibrate when the trains pass by, just as they would have in the 1890s. The towns and the countryside itself are quieter now, the rush for land long over. The novelist Richard Ford lives a few blocks from the statue of Charlie Russell in a house purchased while wandering through on a hunting trip. In 1998, he showed me a photo of a one-room schoolhouse he planned to replicate on the empty northern flats where George VandeVen was raised— a fittingly spare life's canvas for an itinerant writer who once favored the postmodern, anti-Stegnerian watchword, "anywhere but here." He chooses permanence in the very place where Stegner first felt its absence. Bob Sharples, who sold Ford his house, runs the Chinook Motor Inn. He doubles as a real estate agent to make a better living. But the rush now is out-ward, he agrees, away from land and family enterprises that no longer prom-ise a way to make a living. The children do not know that when they ask their parents, "Now how I am supposed to make a living?" they echo Sitting Bull's words of more than a century ago.[9]

The purpose of nations and their boundaries is less certain than it was when Sitting Bull and Louis Riel criss-crossed this land. Canada is less politically stable, perhaps, even than it was at the time of its union in 1867, its east-west unity fragile, its fate uncertain, its strongest bond perhaps its anti-Americanism. The 1994 North American Free Trade Agreement and new trans-border relationships called "globalization" have also weakened this boundary. It is conceivable that Maple Creek and Chinook could one day be a part of the same nation. A lot of prairie people, said a retired bor-der patrolman, think it might "make more sense if we drew a line north and south, and got rid of Ottawa and Washington altogether." Echoing the wishes of the nineteenth-century Sioux, the Blackfeet Indians have already pressed the point. In the winter of 2000, Alberta and Montana Blackfeet asked Canadian federal officials to allow them to ignore the U.S.–Canada border, as do the Mohawks who have such a crossing in New York State. "We are segregated by a line," said chief Peter Strikes With a Gun of the Peigan Blackfeet, when more than forty Blackfoot leaders met in Great Falls to discuss the problem. "It has taken away our relationship," which dates from the eighteenth century. The Blackfeet do not like having guards han-dle their sacred medicine bundles every time they cross the border, or pass through it on a vision quest.[10] After more than a century, they still under-stand what they want. History, like the global, national, and regional "lines of civilization," tells us who we are. So, sometimes, does ignoring history—in that vast open space without borders where the gesture of belonging, the certainty of hope and failure, the best medicine, does not depend upon a line.

Prologue: Through the Looking Glass

1. Details of the surrender are from the *St. Paul and Minneapolis Pioneer Press*, July 21, 1881, from their anonymous reporter on the scene. Other details of the surrender and the days leading up to it are in Edwin H. Allison, *The Surrender of Sitting Bull* (Dayton, Ohio: Walker Lithograph and Printing, 1891), reprinted in Doane Robinson, ed., *South Dakota Historical Collections* 6 (1910-12): 231–70; and three newspaper accounts: *Bismarck Tribune*, June 3, 17, and August 4, 1881; *Chicago Times*, June 11, 1881; and further articles in the *St. Paul Pioneer Press*, June 17 and 25, July 13, 18, and 20, and August 3, 4, 7, and 14, 1881. See also Robert M. Utley's excellent biography, *The Lance and the Shield: The Life and Times of Sitting Bull* (New York: Henry Holt and Company, Inc., 1993), chs. 17 and 18, which I have drawn from here.

2. *Légaré v. United States*, Records of the U.S. Court of Claims, General Jurisdiction, no. 15713, nov. 4, 1889.

3. *St. Paul Pioneer Press*, July 21, 1881; John C. Ewers. "When Sitting Bull Surrendered His Winchester," in *Indian Life on the Upper Missouri* (Norman: University of Oklahoma Press, 1968), 175–81.

4. *St. Paul Pioneer Press*, July 21, 1881.

5. *St. Paul Pioneer Press*, August 3, 1881.

6. *Bismarck Tribune*, August 5, 1881. Last quote from James Creelman, *On the Great Highway: The Wanderings and Adventures of a Special Correspondent* (Boston: Lothrop Publishing Co., 1901), 301, quoted in Utley, *Lance and Shield*, 247.

7. Dee Brown, *Bury My Heart at Wounded Knee: An Indian History of the American West* (New York: Holt, Rinehart, Winston, 1970), 426.

8. See accounts of Sitting Bull's death in Brown, *Bury My Heart at Wounded Knee*, 436–38; and Utley, *Lance and Shield*, 296–302.

9. See Jack Nisbet's *Sources of the River* (Seattle: Sasquatch Books, 1994), a lively account of the explorations of British fur-trader David Thompson, esp. 76.

Chapter 1: Drawing the Line

1. Meriwether Lewis and William Clark, *The Journals of the Expedition under the Command of Capts. Lewis and Clark*, ed. Nicholas Biddle (New York: The Heritage Press, 1962), 1:140, 142 (May 24–27, 1805). See also Stephen E. Ambrose, *Undaunted Courage: Meriwether Lewis, Thomas Jefferson, and the Opening of the American West* (New York: Simon and Schuster, 1996), 226.

2. Wallace Stegner, *Wolf Willow: A History, a Story, and a Memory of the Last Plains Frontier* (Lincoln and London: University of Nebraska Press, 1955), 84. In an essay that paints sharp distinctions between the American and Canadian Wests, Dick Harrison argues that Stegner focuses on local rather than national meanings of the border partly because medicine line country was an atypical, "very local experience." I wrote this book partly to test that assumption. See "Frontiers and Borders: Wallace Stegner in Canada," in Charles E. Rankin, ed., *Wallace Stegner: Man and*

Writer (Albuquerque: University of New Mexico Press, 1996), 195.

3. W. J. Twining, chief astronomer, United States Boundary Commission, in *Reports Upon the Survey of the Boundary between the Territory of the United States and the Possessions of Great Britain from the Lake of the Woods to the Summit of the Rocky Mountains* (Washington, D.C., 1878), 7, 19–21, "Report of the Chief Astronomer, W. J. Twining," 74–75. Part of the reports are published in U.S. Doc. 1719, 44th Congress, 2d session 1876–77, Senate Executive Documents, vol. 2, exec. doc. no. 41.

4. James Willard Schultz, *My Life as an Indian* (Boston: Doubleday 1907), 10–12. Schultz came to Fort Benton at age seventeen in about 1876, a young upstate New Yorker having an adventure before his expected return to the military academy at West Point. He never returned East to live. Schultz remained in the West and became a fur trader, member of the Blackfeet tribe, and guide, and one of the great chroniclers of late-nineteenth-century Montana and the borderland territory.

5. Ibid.

6. Twining, *Reports Upon the Survey of the Boundary*, 8.

7. Michael P. Malone and Richard B. Roeder, *Montana: A History of Two Centuries* (Seattle: University of Washington Press, 1976), 56–57.

8. Twining, *Reports Upon the Survey of the Boundary*, appendix A, "Report of Captain James Gregory," 275–83; appendix B, "Report of First Lieutenant Greene," 339. George Mercer Dawson, *British North American Boundary Commission Report on the Geology and Resources of the Region in the Vicinity of the Forty-Ninth Parallel* (Montreal: Dawson Brothers, 1875), 295.

9. "The Convention of 1818," in *Treaties, Conventions, etc. between the United States and Other Powers, 1776–1909* (Washington, D.C., 1910), I: 612–58. For a summary, see "The Treaty of Ghent and Negotiations that Followed, 1814–1818," ed. S. E. Morrison, *Old South Leaflets* (Old South Association, Boston, n.d. [c. 1937]), no. 212, 15–16.

10. John E. Parsons, *West on the 49th Parallel: Red River to the Rockies, 1872–1876* (New York: William Morrow and Company, 1963), 8.

11. Stegner, *Wolf Willow*, 87–88.

12. Dawson, *British North American Boundary Commission Report*, 295; Lieutenant Francis Vinton Greene, assistant engineer for the United States Boundary Commission of 1872–74, quoted in Parsons, *West on the 49th Parallel*, 110; *The Papers of the Palliser Expedition, 1857–1860*, ed. with an introduction and notes by Irene M. Spry (Toronto: The Champlain Society, 1968), cx, cxiv, 421–22, 538–39; Twining, *Reports Upon the Survey of the Boundary*, 5, 7, 26, 281; James Hector and Henry Youle Hind, quoted in Alec H. Paul, "Human Aspects of the Canadian Plains Climate" in *Prairie Forum* 9 (fall 1984), 203; Angus McMillan family history, cited in Janet S. Allison, *Trial and Triumph: 101 Years in North Central Montana* (Chinook, Mont.: North Central Montana CowBelles, 1968), 1–2.

13. Lewis and Clark, *Journals*, 1:142.

14. *Papers of the Palliser Expedition*, xxxviii, cviii, cix.

15. "Map Shewing Prof. Macouns Route for 1880," Public Archives of Canada, National Map Collection, NMC17678; *Papers of the Palliser Expedition*, cxv; Doug Owram, *Promise of Eden: The Canadian Expansionist Movement and the Idea of the West* (Toronto: University of Toronto Press, 1980), 149–67.

16. David M. Emmons, *Garden in the Grasslands: Boomer Literature of the Central Great Plains* (Lincoln, Neb., 1971); Mary Wilma M. Hargreaves, *Dry Farming in the Northern Great Plains, 1900–1925* (Cambridge, Mass.: Harvard

University Press, 1957), 277, and ch. 7, "Promotionalism and the Movement."

17. Twining, *Reports Upon the Survey of the Boundary*, 6–7; Stegner, *Wolf Willow*, 81, 87; Parsons, *West on the 40th Parallel*, 25, 33.

18. Twining, *Reports Upon the Survey of the Boundary*, "Report of the Chief Astronomer W. J. Twining," 74–75; Stegner, *Wolf Willow*, 88–90; Parsons, *West on the 49th Parallel*, 32. Major Reno's character is well drawn in Evan S. Connell, *Son of the Morning Star: Custer and the Little Bighorn* (New York: Harper and Row, 1984), 9–10.

19. Twining, *Reports Upon the Survey of the Boundary*, "Report of the Chief Astronomer W. J. Twining," 86; appendix A, "Report of Captain James Gregory," 265, 275, 277, 282–85; appendix B, "Report of First Lieutenant Greene, U.S. Engineers," 335, 339–40, 348; Stegner, *Wolf Willow*, 91–96.

20. George McDougall to A. Morris, October 23, 1875, Provincial Archives of Manitoba, A. G. Morris Papers, MG/B1/1136, quoted in Hugh A. Dempsey, "The Fearsome Fire Wagon," in Hugh Dempsey, ed., *The CPR West: The Iron Road and the Making of a Nation* (Vancouver and Toronto: Douglas & McIntyre, 1984), 56.

21. "Land Ordinance of 1785," reprinted in *Documents of American History*, 9th ed., ed. Henry Steele Commager (Englewood Cliffs, N.J.: Prentice-Hall, 1973), 123–24; Paul W. Gates, *History of Public Land Law Development* (Washington, D.C.: Zenger Publishing), 59–65, 219–30.

22. For the outlines of the debate on the nature of Jeffersonian republicanism, see Lance Banning, "Jeffersonian Ideology Revisited: Liberal and Classical Ideas in the New American Republic," and Joyce Appleby, "Republicanism in Old and New Contexts," *William and Mary Quarterly* 43 (January 1986): 3–34. Jefferson to Edmund Pendleton, August 13, 1776, *The Papers of Thomas Jefferson*, ed. Julian P. Boyd (Princeton: Princeton University Press, 1950), I:492.

23. Allan G. Bogue, "An Agricultural Empire," in Clyde A. Milner II, Carol A. O'Connor, Martha A. Sandweiss, eds., *The Oxford History of the American West* (New York: Oxford University Press, 1994), 289; Richard White, *"It's Your Misfortune and None of My Own": A New History of the American West* (Norman: University of Oklahoma Press, 1991), 139.

24. *Lord Durham's Report on the Affairs of British North America* [1839], ed. Sir Charles Lucas (New York: Augustus M. Kelley, Publishers, 1970), 2:209–10, quoted in Chester Martin, *"Dominion Lands" Policy* (Toronto: McClelland and Stewart, 1973), 119.

25. *The Globe* (Toronto), July 15, 1862; Charles Tupper, *A Letter to the Earl of Carnavan by Charles Tupper in Reply to a Pamphlet Entitled "Confederation"* (n.p., October 19, 1866), Public Archives of Canada, 42.

26. Lucas, *Lord Durham's Report*, 212.

27. Manitoba Act, *Statutes of Canada*, 33 Vic., ch. 3, s. 30, quoted in Martin, *"Dominion Lands" Policy*, 9.

28. Martin, *"Dominion Lands" Policy*, 12–13.

29. Joseph Kinsey Howard, *Strange Empire: A Narrative of the Northwest* (St. Paul: Minnesota Historical Society Press, 1994 [1952]), 75, 93–94, Martin, *"Dominion Lands" Policy*, 17–18.

30. James C. MacGregor, *Vision of an Ordered Land: The Story of the Dominion Land Survey* (Saskatoon, Sask.: Western Producer Prairie Books, 1981), 1–4; Dominion Lands Act, 1872, *Statutes of Canada*, 35 Vic., ch. 23, reprinted in Thomas, ed., *The Prairie West to 1905: A Canadian Source book* (Toronto: Oxford University Press, 1975, 89–90. See Martin, *"Dominion Lands"*

Policy, 8–9, for a discussion of the political effects of McDougall's survey on the Macdonald government.

31. Don McLean, *Home from the Hill: History of the Métis in Western Canada* (Regina, Sask.: Gabriel Dumont Institute, 1987), 28, 37, 50–51; quotation from Toby Morantz, "The Fur Trade and the Cree of James Bay," in Carol M. Judd and Arthur J. Ray, eds., *Old Trails and New Directions* (Toronto: University of Toronto Press, 1980), 48. This policy was extremely successful. Until 1821, however, when in competition with the Canadian North West Company, XY Company, and others, the Hudson's Bay Company also employed indentured servants from Scotland and the Orkney Islands on seven-year contracts, a system that gave them a high degree of control over a cheap labor force. When business competition ended, however, the large pool of unemployed Métis were more profitable, since much of the work was seasonal and they could be laid off when not needed.

32. Howard, *Strange Empire*, 71, 84, 93–95. Howard's account of the rise and fall of the Métis nation is vivid and almost Homeric in its portrayal of a heroic and oppressed people.

33. MacGregor, *Vision of an Ordered Land*, 13–14, mentions this Métis unit of measurement, noting that it only applied to level land.

34. For the Métis point of view, see Maclean, *Home from the Hill*, 83. For the surveyors' side of the incident, see MacGregor, *Vision of an Ordered Land*, 5–7. Howard, *Strange Empire*, 98, 166, describes Riel and this incident.

35. The Manitoba Act, *Statutes of Canada*, 33 Vic., ch. 3 (1870), reprinted in Thomas, ed., *The Prairie West to 1905*, 77–79; Martin, "Dominion Lands" Policy, 20–23. Mackenzie, quoted in the debate on the Manitoba Act, *Parliamentary Debates* (1870), 1287–96, excerpted in Thomas, *The Prairie West to 1905*, 80; McLean, *Home from the Hill*, 102, 105; Macdonald to John Rose, February 23, 1870, Saskatchewan Archives Board, Regina. For a summary of the Métis land crisis during the 1870s see Gerald Friesen, *The Canadian Prairies: A History* (Lincoln: University of Nebraska Press, 1984), 195–201.

36. MacGregor, *Vision of an Ordered Land*, 21, 34, 45, 65.

37. Gates, *History of Public Land Law Development*, 420–22; Martin, "Dominion Lands" Policy, 16. For specific comparisons of other borrowing between U.S. and Canadian law in the West, see the excellent collection *Law for the Elephant, Law for the Beaver: Essays in the Legal History of the North American West*, edited by John McLaren, Hamar Foster, and Chet Orloff (Pasadena, Calif.: The Ninth Judicial Circuit Historical Society, 1992), particularly Hamar Foster and John McLaren, "Law for the Elephant, Law for the Beaver: Tracking the Beasts," 1–22, and David R. Percy, "Water Law of the Canadian West: Influences from the Western States," 274–91. On Powell see Donald Worster, *An Unsettled Country: Changing Landscapes of the American West* (Albuquerque: University of New Mexico Press, 1994), 1–30 and his forthcoming biography of Powell.

38. Frederick Jackson Turner, "The Significance of the Frontier in American History" in *The Frontier in American History* (Tuscon: The University of Arizona Press, 1986), 3, 12.

39. Richard Hofstadter, *The Progressive Historians* (Chicago: University of Chicago Press, 1968), Part II, ch. 4, "The Frontier as an Explanation," is still one of the most insightful of myriad Turner critiques. Two recent re-evaluations are Patricia Nelson Limerick, *The Legacy of Conquest: The Unbroken Past of the American West* (New York: W. W. Norton & Company, 1987), 20–27, and William Cronon, *Nature's Metropolis: Chicago and the Great West* (New York: W. W. Norton & Company,

1991), 31, 46–54. Cronon sees usefulness in Turner's notion of "free land" as abundant natural resources, as opposed to his erroneous conflation of "free land" with the conquest of "savagery," 402, n. 115.

40. Lucien Febvre, "*Frontiere*: the Word and the Concept," in A *New Kind of History: from the Writings of Lucien Febvre*, ed. Peter Burke, trans. K. Folca (New York: Harper & Row Pub., 1973), 208–11; Fernand Braudel, *The Identity of France: vol 1., History and Environment*, trans. Sian Reynolds (New York: Harper & Row Pub., 1989), 310.

41. Turner, "Significance of the Frontier," 3.

42. Febvre, "*Frontiere*," 214–15; Sahlins, "Natural Frontiers Revisited," *American Historical Review*, 1445; Turner, "Significance of the Frontier," passim.

43. Edmund Burke, *Burke's Politics: Selected Writings and Speeches of Edmund Burke on Reform, Revolution, and War*, Ross J. Hoffman and Paul Levack, eds. (New York: Alfred A. Knopf, 1949), 304, quoted in John Conway, "An Adapted Organic Tradition," *Daedalus*, 117 (fall 1988): 383.

44. Martin, "*Dominion Lands*" *Policy*, 120.

45. MacGregor, *Vision of an Ordered Land*, 49, 50.

46. Twining, *Reports upon the Survey of the Boundary*, 19; MacGregor, *Vision of an Ordered Land*, 78.

Chapter 2: "The Melting Pot of Hell"

1. Robert P. Higheagle Manuscript, Walter Stanley Campbell Collection, University of Oklahoma, box 104, folder 21, 41.

2. Andrew Garcia, *Tough Trip through Paradise, 1878–1879*, ed. Bennett H. Stein (Sausalito: Comstock Editions, 1967), xvi, 3, 56, 131, 249, 363–64. Garcia's travels took him just south of medicine line country, but he refers repeatedly to the Fort Benton–to–Canada orbit of trade, of which medicine line country was a part, and the Assiniboine, Gros Ventre, Blackfoot, Sioux, Métis, and Nez Percé who floated through it in the 1870s. Stein attributes the phrase "melting pot of hell" to Garcia in the introduction. Although they sometimes fought, Indian women also aided one another in Garcia's tough gang-war world. A Gros Ventre woman in an Assiniboine camp took in the Nez Percé woman In-who-lise, Garcia's future wife, after she escaped the battle of the Bear Paws just south of present-day Chinook, where the Nez Percé surrendered to General Miles in October 1877 (pp. 126, 263).

3. James Morrow Walsh Papers, "An Account of the Sioux Indians 1876–1879" or "To My Dear Cora," anonymous letter to his daughter Cora, with editing notes, May 1890, Provincial Archives of Canada, M705 (microfilm), at the Public Archives of Manitoba, Winnipeg.

4. Andrew C. Isenberg, *The Destruction of the Bison: An Environmental History, 1750–1920* (Cambridge: Cambridge University Press, 2000), 34, 40. *Manuscript Journals of Alexander Henry and David Thompson*, ed. Elliot Coues (Minneapolis, 1897), 2:516, 530, cited in David G. Mandelbaum, *The Plains Cree: Anthropological Papers of the American Museum of Natural History*, vol. 37, pt. 2 (New York City, 1940), n. 1 165–67, 171, 179–81; John C. Ewers, *The Blackfeet: Raiders on the Northwestern Plains* (Norman: University of Oklahoma Press, 1958), 6–7.

5. Edwin Thompson Denig, *Five Indian Tribes of the Upper Missouri: Sioux, Arickaras, Assiniboines, Crees, Crows* (Norman: University of Oklahoma Press, 1961), orig. pub. in the *Forty-Sixth Annual Report*, Bureau of American Ethnology, Smithsonian Institution (Washington, D.C., 1930 [1854]), xxx, xxxi, 77. P. Richard Metcalf, in *The New Encyclopedia of the American West*, ed. Howard Lamar (New

Haven: Yale University Press, 1998), 298, calls Denig "the most prolific and knowledgeable student of the upper Missouri Indians in the nineteenth century."

6. Denig, *Five Indian Tribes of the Upper Missouri*, 25.

7. Richard White, "The Winning of the West: The Expansion of the Western Sioux in the Eighteenth and Nineteenth Centuries," *Journal of American History* 65 (September 1978): 319–43.

8. Mandelbaum, *Plains Cree*, 183, 187; Denig, *Five Indian Tribes of the Upper Missouri*, 71–72.

9. E. Wagner Stearn and Allen E. Stearn, *The Effect of Smallpox on the Destiny of the Amerindian* (Boston: Bruce Humphries, 1945), 75; W. J. McGee, *The Siouxan Indians*, vol. 15 for 1893–94 (Washington, D.C.: U.S. Bureau of American Ethnology, 1897), 196; *Original Journal of the Lewis and Clark Expedition*, ed. Reuben Gold Thwaites (New York: Dodd, Mead, 1905), 7:90–91.

10. *Original Journal of the Lewis and Clark Expedition*, vol. 1, quoted in Stearn and Stearn, *Effect of Smallpox*, 74; see White, "The Winning of the West," 325, for this argument regarding the Sioux; Denig, *Five Indian Tribes of the Upper Missouri*, 114–15; Mandelbaum, *Plains Cree*, 187. Denig asserts that the Cree were severely hit by the smallpox epidemic of the late 1780s. Mandelbaum, however, argues that they were probably less affected than more sedentary or larger-grouped tribes. Denig, from 1837 to 1855 a trader at Fort Union, an American Fur trading post about 250 miles east of the Chinook–Maple Creek area, suffered smallpox there and had two Indian wives (concurrently). He wrote his manuscript in 1855–56. In 1949, FBI handwriting experts identified the manuscript as Denig's.

11. Olive Patricia Dickason, "Historical Reconstruction for the Northwestern Plains," in R. Douglas Francis and Howard Palmer, eds, *The Prairie West: Historical Readings* (Edmonton: Pica Press, 1985), 46–48. For an explanation of Blackfoot names, see Hana Samek, *The Blackfoot Confederacy 1880–1920: A Comparative Study of Canadian and U.S. Indian Policy* (Albuquerque: University of New Mexico Press, 1987), 11.

12. Regina Flannery, *The Gros Ventre of Montana: Part I, Social Life* (Washington, D.C.: Catholic University of America Press, 1953), ch. 1, "Historical Background"; John G. Carter, "Notes on the History, Social and Ceremonial Organization of the Prairie Gros Ventres (Atsina)," ms., American Museum of Natural History Department of Anthropology, 1–4; Denig, *Five Indian Tribes of the Upper Missouri*, 63–64; Dickason, "Historical Reconstruction," 48; Mandelbaum, *Plains Cree*, 183, 187. Neither the anthropologist Robert Lowie ("The Assiniboine," *Anthropological Papers of the American Museum of Natural History*, vol. 4, pt. 1 [New York, 1909]) nor Denig comments on the deterioration of Assiniboine-Cree relations. The Cree, though established on the plains, still returned occasionally, perhaps seasonally, to eastern marshes and forests as late as 1820. By 1845, however, when Father de Smet visited them, they were thoroughly entrenched as a Plains tribe.

13. Sylvia Van Kirk, "Fur Trade Social History," in Francis and Palmer, eds., *The Prairie West*, 79–81; her book, *Many Tender Ties: Women in Fur-Trade Society in Western Canada, 1670–1870* (Winnipeg: Watson and Dwyer, 1980), covers the subject more extensively.

14. Joseph Kinsey Howard, *Strange Empire* (St. Paul: Minnesota Historical Society Press, 1994), xxv, 56.

15. James Willard Schultz [Apikuni], *Blackfeet and Buffalo: Memories of Life among the Indians*, ed. and with an introduction by Keith C. Seele (Norman: University of Oklahoma Press, 1962), 43.

16. For this point of view, see Joseph Kinsey Howard, *Montana: High, Wide and Handsome* (Lincoln: University of Nebraska Press, 1983 [1943]), 21–29; also Isenberg, *Destruction of the Bison*, 107–08, 112–13, 137.

17. Denig, *Five Indian Tribes*, 96.

18. Wallace Stegner, *Wolf Willow: A History, a Story, and a Memory of the Last Plains Frontier* (Lincoln and London: University of Nebraska Press, 1955), 95; Gerald Friesen, *The Canadian Prairies: A History* (Lincoln: University of Nebraska Press, 1984), 42, 131; Dan Flores, "Bison Ecology and Bison Diplomacy: The Southern Plains from 1800 to 1850," *Journal of American History* 18 (September 1991): 480–83; Dewdney speech at Battleford, November 27, 1879, *Saskatchewan Herald*, December 15, 1879, quoted in Beal and Macleod, *Prairie Fire, the 1895 North-west Rebellion* (Edmonton: Hurtig, c. 1984), 63–64; Mounted Police commissioner A. G. Crozier to deputy minister of the interior, April 21/May 7, 1880; Crozier to commanding officer, Fort Walsh, October 14, 1880; Crozier to commissioner, Cypress Hills, February 8, 1881, in Public Archives of Canada, Indian Affairs, RG 10, vol. 3652, file 8589, pt. 1. The Sioux One Bull remembered, as did others, plentiful game during the first years of the tribe's Canadian hegira, in Walter Stanley Campbell, Collection, University of Oklahoma, box 105, notebook 12, p. 15. There is no analysis equivalent to Flores's for the Northern Plains, although Douglas B. Bamforth discusses differences among Plains subregions in *Ecology and Human Organization on the Great Plains* (New York: Plenum Press, 1988), ch. 5.

19. I am indebted to Peter C. Mancall, author of *Deadly Medicine: Indians and Alcohol in Early America* (Ithaca: Cornell University Press, 1995), for educating me on this subject.

20. From Bertrand W. Sinclair, *Raw Gold* (New York: Dillingham, 1907), excerpted in Dick Harrison, ed., *Best Mounted Police Stories* (Edmonton: University of Alberta Press, 1978), 30–36.

21. Paul F. Sharp, *Whoop-up Country: The Canadian-American West, 1865–1885* (Norman: University of Oklahoma Press, 1955), 58. Stegner, *Wolf Willow*, 75–79; John W. Bennett and Seena B. Kohl, "Movement and Renewal: An Anthropological History of the Last Great Westward Migration to the Canadian-American West, 1890–1920," manuscript, Washington University, St. Louis, ch. 3, "The Canadian-American West: Historical Backgrounds."

22. W. S. Gladestone to Katherine Hughes, August 11, 1910, in Gladestone File, Alberta Provincial Library, quoted in Sharp, *Whoop-up Country*, 35. Thomas F. Schilz, "Brandy and Beaver Pelts: Assiniboine-European Trading Patterns, 1695–1805," *Saskatchewan History* 37 (1984): 98.

23. Gerald Friesen, *The Canadian Prairies: A History* (Toronto: University of Toronto Press, 1984), 166–67. Ch. 8 contains a nice summary of the Mounties as part of Macdonald's nationalism. The Mounted Police Act, Statutes of Canada (1873), in Lewis G. Thomas, ed., *The Prairie West to 1905: A Canadian Sourcebook* (Toronto: Oxford University Pess, 1975), 153.

24. D. M. McLeod, "Liquor Control in the North-West Territories: The Permit System, 1870–1891," *Saskatchewan History* 16 (Autumn 1963): 81–89; R. C. Macleod, *The NWMP and Law Enforcement, 1873–1905* (Toronto: University of Toronto Press, 1976), 32.

25. Albert L. Sperry, *Avalanche* (Boston: Christopher House 1938), 34. For the Mounted Police pay scale, see the Mounted Police Act, Statutes of Canada (1873), 155–56. On Dickens, see Macleod, "Dickens," in the *Dictionary of*

Canadian Biography (Toronto: University of Toronto Press, 1966–), 9:261–62. Public Archives of Canada, MG 29, F-52, Diary of Constable R. N. Wilson, 1881–88", quoted in Macleod, *The NWMP and Law Enforcement*, 32–33.

26. Thomas J. Bogy to J. H. McNight, January 16, 1878, McNight Papers, private collection, quoted in Sharp, *Whoop-up Country*, 129.

27. Schultz, *Blackfeet and Buffalo*, 64; Macleod, *The NWMP and Law Enforcement*, 40–41. Sharp, *Whoop-Up Country*, 102–06, gives the stereotypical view of Canadian law enforcement on the Northern Plains during this period, moderated by a historian's recognition of abetting circumstances.

28. Dun and Bradstreet, Inc., records, "Montana, vol. 1, 228, Baker Library Special Collections, Harvard Business School.

29. Louis Riel,*The Collected Writings of Louis Riel*, 8 December 1875–4 June 1884, Gilles Martel, ed., vol. 2 (Edmonton: University of Alberta Press, 1985) 243–54.

30. Sharp, *Whoop-up Country*, 45.

31. Garcia, *Tough Trip Through Paradise*, 53, 55–56. Cecil Denny, *Riders of the Plains: A Reminiscence of the Early and Exciting Days of the Northwest* (Calgary: Herald Company, Limited, 1905), 54.

32. Richard Gwyn, *The 49th Paradox: Canada in North America* (Toronto: McClelland and Stewart, 1985), 20–21, 24, 29–31; Robin Winks, *Canada and the United States: The Civil War Years* (Baltimore: Johns Hopkins University Press, 1960), 238–40.

33. Samek, *The Blackfoot Confederacy*, 158–59; Sharp, *Whoop-up Country*, 36–38; Macleod, *The NWMP and Law Enforcement*, 9, 35.

34. Bernard D. Fardy, in *Jerry Potts*, Paladin of the Plains (Langley, B.C.: Mr. Paperback, 1984), 35, gives the recipe; Schultz, *Blackfeet and Buffalo*, 56.

35. Carter, "Notes on the History, Social and Ceremonial Organization of the Prairie Gros Ventres," 31–32.

36. Garcia, *Tough Trip through Paradise*, 243–44, 247.

37. See John C. Ewers's ethnological study *The Blackfeet: Raiders on the Northwestern Plains* (Norman: University of Oklahoma Press, 1958), 258–59, for liquor-related mortality statistics gleaned from several sources; and "Report of the Commissioner of Indian Affairs," 1873, 252, cited in Ewers, 259. Samek, *Blackfoot Confederacy*, discusses the effects of liquor on the Blackfeet briefly, 40, 158–61. See also Hugh A. Dempsey, *Crowfoot: Chief of the Blackfeet* (Norman: University of Oklahoma Press, 1972), 77–81, 103, 116, 127; and Fardy, *Jerry Potts*, 35, 43, though his statistic about the Bloods, like the entire book, is not footnoted. Schultz, *Blackfeet and Buffalo*, 56–57.

38. Dempsey, *Crowfoot*, 78, 81, 116.

39. William Francis Butler, *The Great Lone Land: a Narrative of Travel and Adventure in the North-West of America* (London: S. Lowe, Marston, Lowe & Searle, 1872) 243; William K. Powers, *Sacred Language: The Nature of Supernatural Discourse in Lakota* (Norman: University of Oklahoma Press, 1986), 202, 209; Mitford M. Matthews, ed., *Dictionary of Americanisms on Historical Principles* (Chicago: University of Chicago Press, 1966), vol. 2.

40. Author's Correspondence with Michael Doxtater, Mohawk turtle clan, Cultural Education Specialist for the American Indian Program at Cornell University, Feb. 15 and June 9, 2000, and Bill Asikinack, Professor of Indian Studies at the Saskatchewan Indian Federated College, February 17, 2000. On langauge groups see Charles L. Cutler, *O Brave New Words!: Native American Loanwords in*

Current English (Norman: University of Oklahoma Press, 1994), 25, 27. "Annual Report of Superintendent L. N. F. Crozier, 1880," 30–34, in Walsh Papers, Provincial Archives of Canada, microfilm box M705, Public Archives of Manitoba collection, 333–41; "An Account of the Sioux Indians 1876–1879," Walsh Papers, passim.

41. Edward E. Barry, "The Fort Belknap Indian Reservation: The First Hundred Years, 1855–1955," Montana State University Library, Bozeman, Montana, 176. John F. Finerty, *War-Path and Bivouac or Conquest of the Sioux* (Norman: University of Oklahoma Press, 1961 [1890]), 278. In "Common Ground, Different Dreams: The U.S.-Canada Border" *National Geographic* (February 1990): 121, Priit J. Vesilind attributes the hero quotation to Sitting Bull without citation.

42. Howard, *Strange Empire*, 49; A. L. Haydon, *Riders of the Plains* (London: A. Melrose; Toronto: Copp Clark, 1910), 95; L. V. Kelley, *The Range Men* (Toronto: W. Briggs, 1913), 143. See also *The Oxford English Dictionary*, 2nd ed. (Oxford: Clarendon Press, 1989), 550.

43. "Robert P. Higheagle Manuscript; Walter Stanley Campbell Collection, University of Oklahoma, box 104, folder 21, p. 41.

Chapter 3: Sanctuary

1. This evidence is from firsthand Indian accounts in *The Custer Myth: A Source Book of Custeriana*, ed. W. A. Graham (Mechanicsburg, Penn: Stackpole Books, 1995 [1953]), including "Kill Eagle's Story of His Stay with the Hostiles, "54–55, "The Narrative of Mrs. Spotted Horn Bull," 86, "Interview with Sitting Bull," 70 (*New York Herald Tribune*, November 16, 1877), and "The Story of the Cheyenne Warrior Wooden Leg," recorded by Dr. Thomas B. Marquis, 104. See also *Black Elk Speaks: Being the Life Story of a Holy Man of the Oglala Sioux*, as told through John G. Neihardt (Lincoln: University of Nebraska Press, 1961), 108–09, and "The Moving Robe Woman Interview," *Lakota Recollections of the Custer Fight: New Sources of Indian-Military History*, comp. and ed. Richard G. Hardorff (Lincoln: University of Nebraska Press, 1991), 92–95, n. 9.

2. Robert M. Utley, *Lance and the Shield: The Life and Times of Sitting Bull* (New York: Henry Holt, 1993) 43, 82; Francis Paul Prucha, *The Indians in American Society from the Revolutionary War to the Present* (Berkeley: University of California Press, 1985), 17–21; Jerome A. Greene, *Yellowstone Command: Colonel Nelson A. Miles and the Great Sioux War, 1876–1877* (Lincoln: University of Nebraska Press, 1991), 4–5.

3. Greene, *Yellowstone Command*, 5; "Interview with Sitting Bull," in Graham, *The Custer Myth*, 68; Utley, *Lance and the Shield*, 115–16, including newspaper quote.

4. Utley, *Lance and the Shield*, 116, 126–28, 131; "Interview with Sitting Bull," *The Custer Myth*, 68.

5. "Kill Eagle's Story of His Stay with the Hostiles," "Interview with Sitting Bull," "Hump's Story of the Custer Fight," "Low Dog's Account of the Custer Fight," Hamlin Garland, "General Custer's Last Fight as Seen by Two Moon," in Graham, *The Custer Myth*, 54, 70, 75, 78, 103. Also, Thomas B. Marquis, *Wooden Leg, a Warrior Who Fought Custer* (Lincoln: University of Nebraska Press, 1931), 237; *Black Elk Speaks*, 131, and Ian Frazier, *Great Plains* (New York: Farrar, Straus, Giroux, 1989), 180.

6. Jerome A. Greene, *Yellowstone Command: Colonel Nelson A. Miles and the Great Sioux War, 1876–1877* (Lincoln: University of Nebraska Press, 1991), 1–4, 14,

18, 24; Utley, *Lance and the Shield,* 165.

7. An exception is Roger L. Nichols, *Indians of the United States and Canada: A Comparative History* (Lincoln: University of Nebraska Press, 1998).

8. Walter Stanley Campbell Collection, "Stanley Vestal", Division of Manuscripts, Western History Collection, University of Oklahoma Libraries, "Old Bull Tells . . . ," box 105, notebook 11.

9. Greene, *Yellowstone Command,* 66, 88, 89; Stanley Vestal, *Sitting Bull, Champion of the Sioux: A Biography* (Boston: Houghton-Mifflin, 1932) 191–93; Campbell Collection, "Old Bull Tells . . . ," box 105, notebook 11.

10. See Greene, *Yellowstone Command,* 97, ill. 15. In this account, I have relied on Nelson A. Miles, *Personal Recollections and Observations of General Nelson A. Miles* (Chicago: The Werner Company, 1896), 221ff; Campbell [Vestal], *Sitting Bull,* 194–202, 203; Greene, *Yellowstone Command,* 94 n. 4, 100–6, 112; and Miles to Mary Miles, December 15, 1876, in Virginia W. Johnson, *The Unregimented General: A Biography of Nelson A. Miles* (Cambridge: The Riverside Press, Houghton Mifflin Company, 1962), 118–19.

11. Greene, *Yellowstone Command,* 120; Utley, *Lance and the Shield,* 174–75.

12. Greene, *Yellowstone Command,* 179; Utley, *Lance and the Shield,* 175, 179, 181–82.

13. James Morrow, "An Account of the Sioux Indians 1876–1879" anonymous letter to his daughter Cora, May 1890, Walsh Papers Provincial Archives of Canada, M705, at the Public Archives of Manitoba, Winnipeg. Joseph Manzione, *"I Am Looking to the North for My Life": Sitting Bull, 1876–1881* (Salt Lake City: University of Utah Press, 1991), 45.

14. The leaders' mixed emotions are evident in Walsh's account of his first meeting with Sitting Bull in the Hunkpapa camp in Walsh papers, "An Account of the Sioux Indians." The war quote is attributed to a member of Four Horns' band.

15. This and the following account are drawn from "An Account of the Sioux Indians," Walsh Papers.

16. Ibid.

17. Miles, *Personal Recollections,* 19–24, 30–33; Dumas Malone, ed., *Dictionary of American Biography,* (New York: Charles Scribner's Sons, 1933), 12:614–16. See also the two biographies of Miles: Johnson, *Unregimented General,* ch. 1 (quotation from page 12, taken from Oliver Otis Howard's *Autobiography*), and Newton F. Tolaman, *The Search for General Miles* (New York: G. P. Putnam's Sons, 1968), ch. 2.

18. John Fredrick Finerty, *War-Path and Bivouac,* 269, 230.

19. Greene, *Yellowstone Command,* 21.

20. Johnson, *The Unregimented General,* 345, 350, 351, 353, quotation from Sen. John Sherman to Miles, Washington D.C., April 3, 1890, Miles Collection; Robert M. Utley, *Frontier Regulars: The United States Army and the Indian, 1866–1890* (New York: Macmillan P., 1973), 220, 289; and Mark H. Brown, *The Flight of the Nez Percé,* (Lincoln: University of Nebraska Press, 1967); 420. Brown accuses Miles of "selfish glory-grabbing."

21. Utley, *Frontier Regulars,* 188–218, traces the failure of Grant's Peace Policy; see Greene, *Yellowstone Command,* 120, 228, and ch. 1 for a discussion of the tactical approach to the Sioux campaign.

22. For Custer's view of Indians as savages "whose cruel and ferocious nature far exceeds that of any wild beast of the desert," see Evan S. Connell, *Son of the Morning Star* (San Francisco: North Point Press, 1984), 168. Miles to Mary Miles, November 6, 1876, quoted in Johnson, *Unregimented General,* 128–29.

23. Miles, *Recollections*, 17–18, 103; Nelson Appleton Miles, *Serving the Republic: Memoirs of the Civil and Military Life of Nelson A. Miles, Lieutenant-General, United States Army* (New York: Harper & Brothers, 1911), 164–68; Tolman, *Search for General Miles*, 105–10, 116, 120; Tolman goes so far as to liken Miles's view to that of French anthropologist Claude Lévi-Strauss's that, in Tolman's words "the mental equipment of primitive man, past or present, has generally been equal to that of the most civilized man," but argues that Miles was "too early for his theories about equal rights for Indians to be taken seriously." Miles devoted three chapters of his *Personal Recollections* to his sympathetic view of the "Indian character" and circumstances.

24. Quoted in Greene, *Yellowstone Command*, 206 n. 8.

25. Miles, *Serving the Republic*, 164–68.

26. "Members of N.W.M.P. Engaged in 1873 and 1874," M.89.28.7, Medicine Hat Museum and Art Gallery, Medicine Hat, Alberta; R. C. Macleod, *The Northwest Mounted Police, 1873–1919* (Ottawa: Canadian Historical Association, 1978), 22–25; C. Frank Turner, *Across the Medicine Line* (Toronto: McClelland and Stewart, 1973), 20–27; Sir Cecil Edward Denny, *The Riders of the Plains; a Reminiscence of the Early and Exciting Days in the Northwest* (Calgary: The Herald Company, Limited [c 1905]), 23.

27. "An Account of the Sioux Indians," Walsh Papers; miscellaneous documents, n.d., Walsh Papers, M705.

28. Miscellaneous documents, n.d., Walsh Papers, M705; "An Account of the Sioux Indians," Walsh Papers.

29. J. M. S. Careless, "Frontierism, Metropolitanism, and Canadian History," *Canadian Historical Review* 35 (1954): 17, and *Frontier and Metropolis: Regions, Cities, and Identities in Canada before 1914* (Toronto: University of Toronto Press, 1989). The classic works on the role of the metropolis in Canadian history include Harold Adams Innis's *Problems of Staple Production in Canada* (Toronto: The Kyerson Press, 1933), and "Significant Factors in Canadian Economic Development," *Canadian Historical Review*, 18(1937): 347–84. See also Ramsay Cook, "Frontier and Metropolis: The Canadian Experience," in Ramsay Cook, *The Maple Leaf Forever: Essays on Nationalism and Politics in Canada* (Toronto: Macmillan, 1971), 166–75; Alan F. J. Artibise, *Winnipeg: A Social History of Urban Growth, 1874–1914* (Montreal: McGill-Queen's University Press, 1975); and Carl Berger, *The Writing of Canadian History: Aspects of English-Canadian Historical Writing 1900–1970*, 2nd ed. (Toronto: University of Toronto Press, 1986) an excellent study of Canadian historiography and its struggle with the question of national identity. William Cronon's *Nature's Metropolis: Chicago and the Great West* (New York: W. W. Norton, 1991) is a recent example of the Canadian metropolitan thesis put to good use in explaining the rise of Chicago and its hinterlands. Quotations from Douglas LePan, "The Country without a Mythology," in A. J. M. Smith, ed., *The Book of Canadian Poetry* (Chicago: University of Chicago Press, 1957), 8, and Sacvan Bercovitch, "New England's Errand Reappraised," in John Higham and Paul Conkin, eds., *New Directions in American Intellectual History* (Baltimore: 1979), 85.

30. Samek, *Blackfoot Confederacy*, 19; Indian Act of 1876, Statutes of Canada, 39 Vic., ch. 18 (1876), and the parliamentary debate on the Indian Act, House of Commons *Debates* (1876), 342, 749–51, reprinted in Thomas, ed., *The Prairie West to 1905*, 85–88; Miles, *Recollections*, 345; R. M. Scott to Walsh, Walsh Papers, August 15, 1877.

31. Macleod, *The NWMP and Law Enforcement*, 26, table 1. Public Archives of Canada, Dufferin Papers, reel A-406, Dufferin to Kimberly, December 24, 1873, quoted in Macleod, *The NWMP and Law Enforcement*, 18. Walsh to the Department of the Superintendent, April 24, 1878, Walsh Papers, M705.

32. Miscellaneous documents, including Walsh, letter from Wood Mountain, April 4, 1880, Walsh Papers M705.

33. Finerty, *War-Path and Bivouac*, 265; Macdonald to Lorne, November 24, 1879, Public Archives of Canada, Lorne Papers, 195–96, quoted in Macleod, *The NWMP and Law Enforcement*, 30; Louis Riel, *The Collected Writings of Louis Riel*, gen. ed. George F. G. Stanley (Edmonton: University of Albera Press, 1985), 2:212. Others wrote in a similar vein: "There is, to my mind, no possible doubt but that influence is being brought to bear to keep 'Sitting Bull' in Canada," complained Commissioner Irvine to the minister of the interior, Public Archives of Canada, microfilm, RG 10, vol. 3652, file 8589, pt. 1.

34. The history of the relations between native peoples and the British and Canadian governments is too extensive to cover here. A book expressing native discontentment over their treatment is Eric Robinson, *Infested Blanket: Canada's Constitution and Genocide* (Winnipeg: Queenston House Pub., 1985).

35. Lt. Col. Winton, Secretary to the Governor General, to the Privy Council, February 11, 1881, Public Archives of Canada, Indian Affairs, RG 10, vol. 3652, file 8589, pt. 1.

36. Finerty, *War-Path and Bivouac*, 245, 265; Library of Congress, William T. Sherman Papers, vol. 47, "Sherman to Miles," February 9, 1878, quoted in Manzione, "*I Am Looking to the North*," 114; Walsh to Irvine, October 31, 1880, and February 8, 1881, Public Archives of Canada, Indian Affairs, RG 10, vol. 3652, file 8589, pt. 1; document written by Walsh, July 19, 1879, and "An Account of the Sioux Indians," Walsh Papers.

37. Utley, *Lance and the Shield*, 213–15; Manzione, *Looking to the North*, 135, 151; Library of Congress, William T. Sherman papers, Sherman to Sheridan, March 9, 1879, quoted in Manzione, 113.

38. Utley, *Lance and Shield*, 66–67, 75, 101, 138, 162; Marquis, *Wooden Leg*, 179; and also "Low Dog's Account of the Custer Fight," *The Custer Myth*, 74. Numbers of troops versus warriors vary somewhat. See "Philo Clark's 1877 Battlefield Survey," "General Sheridan's Comments," and "Comments by General J. B. Fry on Godfrey's Narrative," *Century Magazine*, January 1892, in *The Custer Myth*, 116, 117, 151.

39. "Mohammed" quote from journalist John F. Finerty, *Chicago Times*, August 1, 1879. Matthew W. Stirling, *Three Pictographic Autobiographies of Sitting Bull*, Smithsonian Miscellaneous Collections, vol. 97, no. 5 (Washington, D.C.: Smithsonian Institution, 1938), and Alexis A. Praus, *A New Pictographic Autobiography of Sitting Bull*, Smithsonian Miscellaneous Collections, vol. 123, no. 6 (Washington, D.C., Smithsonian Institution, 1955). Also see Campbell, *Sitting Bull*, plates between 266 and 267. Marquis, *Wooden Leg*, 383.

40. "The Story of Sitting Bull: Was He A Winnipegger?," Jan. 3, 1891, copy of newspaper clipping, n.p., Public Archives of Canada, Indian Affairs, RG 10, vol. 3691, file 13, 893; Sitting Bull's first biographer W. Fletcher Johnson, *Red Record of the Sioux: The Life of Sitting Bull and the History of the Indian War of 1890–'91* (Philadelphia: Englewood Publishing Company, 1891); Jerome Stillson in the *New York Herald*, and Charles Diehl in the *Chicago Times*, Oct. 22 and 23, 1877; "pompous" quote from James McGlaughlin, annual report, August 15, 1883, in

Commissioner of Indian Affairs, *Annual Report*, 1883, 48–49; see also *My Friend the Indian* (Lincoln: University of Nebraska Press, 1989); Raymond J. DeMallie, forewords to Vestal, *Sitting Bull*, xvii, xviii, and Vestal, *Warpath: The True Story of the Fighting Sioux Told in a Biography of Chief White Bull* (Lincoln: University of Nebraska Press, 1934); and Mike Fraga, review of Manzione, "*I Am Looking to the North*," in *Western Historical Quarterly*, 23, (February 1992): 95–97. The most meticulously researched and insightful biography to date is Robert Utley's *Lance and the Shield*.

41. See Utley, *Lance and the Shield*, chs. 15–19. "An Account of the Sioux Indians," Walsh Papers.

42. The transcript of Irvine's council is in NWMP, *Annual Report*, 1877, 35–41. Irvine's personal account is quoted in Turner, *North-West Mounted Police*, vol. 1, 326–30.

43. The book originally appeared as Eric Nicol, ed., *Dickens of the Mounted: The Astounding Long-lost letters of Inspector F. Dickens NWMP, 1874–1886*, (Toronto: McClelland & Stewart Inc., 1989), and is catalogued that way in Harvard's Widener library, where I borrowed it. See pp. 53, 62, 101, 119–21, 150–53. See also Roderick Charles Macleod, "Francis Jeffrey Dickens," *Dictionary of Canadian Biography*, vol. XI (Toronto: University of Toronto Press, 1982), 261–62.

44. From Elspeth Cameron's introduction to *Canadian Culture: An Introductory Reader* (Toronto: Canadian Scholars' Press, 1997), 8. On giving ammunition to the refugee Sioux, see letter from L.N.F. Crozier to Dep. Min. of the Interior, May 3, 1880, Public Archives of Canada, Department of Indian Affairs, RG 10, vol. 3652, file 8589, pt. 1. On Sioux receiving no food from Canadians, see Campbell Collection, box 104, notebook 12, interview with Chief One Bull, and box 105, notebook 35, interview with Two Bull. See also J.M. Walsh to James Macleod, July 25, 1879; L.N.F. Crozier to the General to the Privy Council, February 8, 1881; Lt. Col. Winton, Secretary to the Governor General to the Privy Council, February 11, 1881, Public Archives of Canada, Department of Indian Affairs, RG 10, vol. 3652, file 8589, pt. 1.

45. "Jokes Told by Sitting Bull," Campbell Collection, box 104, file 12, w. The file does not say who actually told the jokes to Campbell, but comes at the end of several stories told by One Bull.

46. See Fowler's chart of "humour," H.W. Fowler, *A Dictionary of Modern English Usage*, 2d ed., rev. by Sir Ernest Gowers (New York: Oxford University Press, 1965), 253. "Jokes Told by Sitting Bull," Campbell Collection, box 104, file 12, w.

47. Crozier quote from telegram, May 3, 1881, Leif N. F. Crozier to Lieutenant Colonel Dennis, Public Archives of Canada, Indian Affairs microfilm, RG 10, vol. 3652, file 8589, pt. 1. My overview of the general diplomatic situation comes from the Walsh Papers, MG6, A1, Provincial Archives of Manitoba, Winnipeg, 1–611; records and correspondence regarding Sitting Bull and the American Sioux on microfilm, Indian Affairs, Public Archives of Canada, RG 10, vol. 3691, file 13, 893, and RG 10, vol. 3652, file 8589, pt. 1; *NWMP Annual Reports*, 1877–1881. Utley, in *The Lance and the Shield*, covers the highlights in chs. 15–17.

48. Lt. R. M. Hoyt to Post Adjutant, Cheyenne River Agency, November 20, 1877, RG 74, Bureau of Indian Affairs, Letters Received, Cheyenne River Agency, National Archives and Records Administration, M234, roll 130, frame 418. See also Harry H. Anderson, "A Sioux Pictorial Account of General Terry's Council at Fort Walsh, October 17, 1877," *North Dakota History* 27 (July 1955): 93–116. Both are cited in Utley, *Lance and the Shield*, 373, n. 22.

49. Quotes from "Excerpt from book by Wood," 466–75, in Walter Stanley Campbell Collection, Division of Manuscripts, Western History Collections, University of Oklahoma Libraries, box 113, file 6.

50. Classic works discussing national character are Louis Hartz, *The Founding of New Societies: Studies in the History of the United States, Latin America, South Africa, Canada, and Australia* (New York: Harcourt, Brace & World, Inc., 1964); Frank Underhill, *In Search of Canadian Liberalism* (Toronto: Macmillan of Canada, 1960); Paul F. Sharp, *Whoop-Up Country: The Canadian American West, 1865-1885* (Norman: University of Oklahoma Press, 1955); W.L. Morton, *The Canadian Identity* (Madison: University of Wisconson Press, 1961); and Seymour Martin Lipset, *Continental Divide: The Values and Institutions of the United States and Canada* (New York: Routledge, 1990).

51. On Canadian versus U.S. Indian policy toward the refugee Sioux see Manzione, "*I Am Looking to the North*," (introduction; Christopher C. Joyner, "The Hegira of Sitting Bull to Canada: Diplomatic Realpolitik, 1876–1881," *Journal of the West* 13 (April 1974); 6–18; Gary, Pennanen, "Sitting Bull: Indian without a Country," *Canadian Historical Review* 51 (June 1970): 123–40.

52. McClean, *Home from the Hill: A History of the Métis in Western Canada* (Regina: Gabriel Dumont Institute of Native Studies and Applied Research, 1987) 88, 101–02, 164–67; Thomas Flanagan, *Riel and the Rebellion: 1885 Reconsidered,* 2nd ed. (Toronto: University of Toronto Press, 2000), 9, and *Louis "David" Riel: "Prophet of the New World,"* rev. ed. (Toronto: University of Toronto Press, 1996), 33–35. Flanagan's excellent work convincingly argues that Riel's messianic religious fervor was more responsible for the 1885 Rebellion than government negligence of the Métis, since the Canadian government was responding to Métis grievances.

53. Flanagan, *Louis "David" Riel,* 46–49, 54.

54. Ibid., 56, 58, 63. On Riel's insanity, see Howard, *Strange Empire,* 322–24, and Douglas Owram, "The Myth of Louis Riel," in R. Douglas Francis and Howard Palmer, eds., *The Prairie West: Historical Readings,* (Edmonton: Pica Press, 1985), 163–81. Owram traces Riel's transformation in historiography.

55. Ibid., 111, 113–15; Riel, *Collected Writings,* 2:218–19, 220 n. 4., 220–21, 221 n. 1.

56. Riel, *Collected Writings,* 2:246 n. 2; Flanagan, *Louis "David" Riel,* 116–18, 120, 122.

57. McLean, *Home from the Hill,* 164–65. Joseph Kinsey Howard, *Strange Empire: A Narrative of the Northwest* (New York: Morrow, 1952), 355, 359, 367, 383. See also Riel, *Collected Writings,* 2:220, n. 4; for Crowfoot quote Bob Beal and Rod Macleod, Prairie Fire: The 1885 North-West Rebellion *(Edmonton: Hurtig, 1984),* 67–68. *While only a fraction of them participated in the rebellion, the Indian population between Ontario and the Rockies was estimated at 40,200 in the 1870 Census of Canada. The Métis numbered 9,800 in Manitoba, where most of them lived.*

58. On Big Bear, Crowfoot, and the Blackfeet, respectively, see Beal and Macleod, *Prairie Fire,* 64–65, 67–68, 281; Crowfoot quote from John McLean, *Canadian Savage Folk* (Toronto: William Briggs, 1896), 380. Gabriel Dumont's account of the battle of Fish Creek, April 1885, states this composition of native forces, which Dumont numbered at two hundred. McLean, *Home from the Hill,* 206–07, 213–18. Flanagan, *Riel and the Rebellion,* 100. For summaries of historiographical arguments about the Rebellion, see McLean, *Home from the Hill,* ch. 7, esp. 228–29; Beal and Macleod, *Prairie Fire,* ch. 7; and Gerald Friesen, *The Canadian Prairies, A History*

(Lincoln: University of Nebraska Press, 1984), 227.

59. Indian Commissioner Edgar Dewdney to Commissioner of Indian Affairs, North-West Territories, January 2, 1880, Canada Sessional Papers (no. 4), 1880, pt. 1, report of the deputy superintendent-general of Indian affairs, 1879, p. 88.

60. Friesen, The Canadian Prairies, 227.

61. The best account of the Nez Percé flight is Brown, Flight of the Nez Percé.

62. "An Account of the Sioux," Walsh Papers; Brown, Flight of the Nez Percé, 407–8, 428.

63. Campbell Collection, Old Bull on Nez Percé, box 106, notebook 5; Manzione, Looking to the North, 99–100; John P. Turner, The North-West Mounted Police, 1873–1893 (Ottawa: Edmond Cloutier, 1950), 342. Old Bull estimated the refugee Nez Percé numbers at about one thousand, Turner at about three hundred, and Walsh at about "98 men, 50 women and about as many children and 300 horses."

Chapter 4: If You Build It, Will They Come?

1. James J. Hill, Highways of Progress (New York: Doubleday, Page and Company, 1910), vii, 248; Henry David Thoreau, Walden, or, Life in the Woods (New York: The New American Library, 1960), 83.

2. Michael P. Malone, James J. Hill: Empire Builder of the Northwest (Oklahoma City: University of Oklahoma Press, 1997), 3. The most marvelously written, if least probing, of Hill's biographies is Stewart H. Holbrook, James J. Hill: A Great Life in Brief (New York: Alfred A. Knopf, 1955), 187.

3. Holbrook, James J. Hill, 7, 20, 32, 38–39, 45, 61. The Horatio Alger reference is on 18.

4. Pierre Berton's novelistic account of the building of the CPR, The Last Spike: The Great Railway 1881–1885 (Markham, Ontario: McClelland and Stewart/Penguin Books Canada, 1989 [1971]), 13–28, contains a lively description of the syndicate's decision to change the route, a decision for which the precise chemistry remains a mystery. W. A. Waiser, in his manuscript "A Willing Scapegoat: John Macoun and the Route of the CPR," argues persuasively that the naturalist John Macoun, on whose glowing testimonial of the land's fertility the southern route is often blamed, was merely a prop. The CPR syndicate's real motivation, he argues, was to successfully compete with the Northern Pacific.

5. Holbrook, James J. Hill, 70–71; Toronto Globe, May 3, 1881, quoted in Berton, The Last Spike, 19; Albro Martin, James J. Hill and the Opening of the Northwest (St. Paul: Minnesota Historical Society Press, 1991 [1976]), 243–44; see Heather Gilbert, Awakening Continent: The Life of Lord Mount Stephen. vol. 1: 1829–91 (Aberdeen: Aberdeen University Press, 1965), 101–02, on Stephen's butler.

6. There are nearly as many views on the change of route as there are writers about it. For a sampling see F. G. Roe, "An Unsolved Problem of Canadian History," Canadian Historical Association Annual Report, 1936, 65–77; Berton, The Last Spike, 18–28; Waiser, "A Willing Scapegoat: John Macoun and the Route of the CPR,"; Harold Adams Innis, History of the Canadian Pacific Railway (Toronto: University of Toronto Press, 1971), 291; Doug Owram, Promise of Eden: The Canadian Expansionist Movement and the Idea of the West, 1856–1900 (Toronto: University of Toronto Press, 1992), 161–65.

7. Martin, James J. Hill, 14–18, 207; Holbrook, James J. Hill, 11. Martin's sympathetic biography of Hill borders on hagiography. Malone and Holbrook are more balanced.

8. Chester Martin, *"Dominion Lands" Policy* (Toronto: McClelland and Stewart Limited, 1973) 35, 37.

9. Ralph W. Hidy, Muriel E. Hidy, and Roy V. Scott, with Don L. Hofsommer, *The Great Northern Railway: A History* (Boston: Harvard Business School Press, 1988), 59, 72, 85.

10. This apt phrase comes from Martin, *"Dominion Lands" Policy*, 36.

11. Loretta Fowler, *Shared Symbols, Contested Meanings: Gros Ventre Culture and History, 1778–1984* (Ithaca: Cornell University Press, 1987), map 3, "Reduction of reservation lands assigned to the Gros Ventres, 1855–95," 69.

12. Hill to Allen Manvel, January 9, 1893, quoted in Martin, *James J. Hill*, 411.

13. Quoted in William Cronon, *Nature's Metropolis:* Chicago and the Great West (New York: W. W. Norton, 1991) 92. Cronon discusses this transformation in the vast countryside that became Chicago's hinterlands, a countryside that included the northern plains. Thoreau, *Walden*, 83. *Compact Edition of the Oxford English Dictionary* (New York: Oxford University Press, 1971), 1:1308.

14. Innis, *History of the Canadian Pacific Railway*, 97–98; Hidy, *The Great Northern Railway*, 28–29; Gilbert, *Awakening Continent*, 262, 68–70, 78–79.

15. Malone, *James J. Hill*, 38, 41, 108; Martin, *James J. Hill*, 281, 318–19, 378, 394, 436–37; Gilbert, *Awakening Continent*, 254.

16. John A. Eagle, *The Canadian Pacific Railway and the Development of Western Canada, 1896–1914* (Kingston, Ontario: McGill-Queen's University Press, 1989), 5–8.

17. Eagle, *The Canadian Pacific Railway*, 9–12; Holbrook, *James J. Hill*, 78–80. The reference to Ross J. M. Egan is in T. D. Regehr, "Letters From End of Track," Hugh A. Dempsey, ed., *The CPR West: The Iron Road and the Making of a Nation*, (Vancouver: Douglas & McIntyre, 1984). 39–40.

18. Leonard Bertram Irwin, *Pacific Railways and Nationalism in the Canadian-American Northwest, 1845–1873* (New York: Greenwood Press, Publishers, 1968 [1939]), 172–85.

19. Gerald Friesen, *The Canadian Prairies: A History* (Lincoln: University of Nebraska Press, 1984), 173–74; Irwin, *Pacific Railways and Nationalism*, 206–17.

20. Stephen to Macdonald, November 13, 1880, Public Archives of Canada, quoted in Martin, *James J. Hill*, 240.

21. Gilbert, *Awakening Continent*, 70, 262, 77 (the CPR contract from the *Journals of the House of Commons of Canada, 1880–81* is reprinted in appendix I); Innis, *History of the Canadian Pacific Railway*, 97–98.

22. Martin, *"Dominion Lands" Policy*, 37; Stephen to Macdonald, December 29, 1884, Macdonald Papers, "Stephen" 269, Stephen to Macdonald, July 12, 1887, Macdonald Papers, "Stephen" 270, and Macdonald to Tupper, Tupper Papers 319, March 17, 1885, quoted in Gilbert, *Awakening Continent*, 167, 175, 215. On Canadian disunity, and provinces using the CPR as a lever to force concession from the federal government, see Gilbert, *Awakening Continent*, 136.

23. Eagle, *The Canadian Pacific Railway*, 3; Gilbert, *Awakening Continent*, 182–85; Don McLean, *Home from the Hill*: A History of the Métis in Western Canada (Regina: Gabriel Dumont Institute of Native Studies and Applied Research) 236; Innis, *A History of the Canadian Pacific Railway*, 274, 291–92. As Innis put it, the "acquisitive characteristic" of eastern Canada had pulled the project through, and the "stability" and business acumen of the CPR company's management had left it in a "satisfactory financial condition."

24. John G. Moore to Hill, September 3 and December 24, 1893, quoted in Martin,

James J. Hill, 411. Martin identifies Moore as Hill's financial associate on 394, though a typographical error lists him as "John N. Moore." W. L. Morton, in an overly general fashion, explores the consequences of these parallel east-west infrastructures in "The Significance of Site in the Settlement of the American and Canadian Wests," *Agricultural History* 25 (July 1951), 101. Along the border, he concludes, environmental conditions were virtually identical. Different metropolitan and political controls, he argues, accounted for any social "variations," of which he finds only one: stronger central controls in the Canadian West produced ultimately "stronger protest movements." Because new technologies removed the isolation of earlier eras, he adds, they obviated the Turner thesis of frontier democracy.

25. Arthur Barlowe, quoted in David B. Quinn, *The Roanoke Voyages, 1584–1590*, (London: Hakluyt Society, 1955), 108, in turn quoted in Edmund S. Morgan, *American Slavery, American Freedom: The Ordeal of Colonial Virginia* (New York: W. W. Norton and Company, 1975), 27. *Collier's Weekly*, June 1, 1901; *Atlantic Monthly*, December 1906; *Literary Digest*, September 15, 1923, on roll 1, Great Northern Railway Company, Advertising and Publicity Department, magazine and newspaper advertisements, 1884–1970, microfilm edition, Minnesota Historical Society. The *Literary Digest* appeal is particularly touching, considering that failed homesteaders were leaving the area in droves by 1923. Pamphlet entitled *Canada West*, by B. Davies, Canadian government agent in Great Falls, Montana, issued by the minister of the interior, Robert Rogers (Ottawa, 1912).

26. Stephen to Macdonald, February 26, 1882, Macdonald Papers, "Stephen" 267, and Macdonald to Tupper, July 25, 1883, Macdonald Letter Book, 22.218, quoted in Gilbert, *Awakening Continent*, 95–96, 134.

27. Canadian House of Commons, *Debates*, May 4, 1885, quoted in Patricia E. Roy, "A Choice Between Evils: The Chinese and the Construction of the Canadian Pacific Railway in British Columbia," in Dempsey, ed., *CPR West*, 30–31. D. J. Hall, "Clifford Sifton: Immigration and Settlement Policy," *The Prairie West: Historical Readings*, R. Douglas Francis and Howard Palmer, eds. (Edmonton: Pica Press, 1985), 292.

28. Owram, *Promise of Eden*, 166; Gilbert, *Awakening Continent*, 107, 109; Statistics taken from the *Historical Statistics of Canada*, M. C. Urquhart and K. A. H. Buckey, eds., graphed in Kenneth H. Norie's excellent article, "National Policy and the Rate of Prairie Settlement," in Francis and Palmer, eds., *Prairie West*, 239.

29. Quoted in Martin, *James J. Hill*, 411. Malone, *James J. Hill*, 169, 173, 175, 181; Joseph Kinsey Howard, *Montana: High, Wide, and Handsome* (Lincoln: University of Nebraska Press, 1983 [1943]), 167.

30. Hugh A. Dempsey, "The Fearsome Fire Wagon," in Dempsey, ed., *CPR West*, 60, 57.

31. Benton *Weekly Record*, May 19, 1883, North-West Mounted Police Report, 1884, quoted in Dempsey, *CPR West*, 10, 62; John Maclean, *The Indians of Canada* (London: Charles H. Kelley, 1892), 78.

32. Butler, *The Great Lone Land*, 241.

33. Uncited official quoted in Martin, *"Dominion Lands" Policy*, 87.

Chapter 5: Which Side Are You On?

1. The area of Chouteau County is listed as 17,459,200 acres (27,280 square miles) in the *Eleventh Census of the United States, 1890*, Report on the Statistics of Agriculture in the United States (Washington, D.C., 1895). Population figures are taken from *Compendium of the Eleventh Census, 1890*, Part I, Population, 258,

which lists the Chouteau County population at 4,741 and, interestingly, excludes Indians without saying so; *Twelfth Census of the United States, 1900*, part 1, Population, table 19, "White, Negro, and Indian Population, by Counties: 1880 to 1900," 547, which lists 3,723 Indians in Chouteau County in 1890; and *Eleventh Census of the United States, 1890* (Washington, D.C., 1894), Report on Indians Taxed and Indians Not Taxed in the United States, 98, listing 952 Assiniboine and 770 Gros Ventres, 35 of other groups.

2. The descriptions in this imaginary journey are pieced together from the following sources: the reminiscences of Jay Rhodes, a foreman on the TU ranch in the early 1890s, in A. J. Noyes, *In the Land of Chinook or the Story of Blaine County* (Helena, Mont.: State Publishing Company, 1917), 52–57; Blaine County Operator-Road Map, 1984; Alvin J. Lucke Map of Blaine County, Montana Historical Society, SC 1363; *Compendium of the Eleventh Census of the United States, 1890*, part 1, Population, 258; Margaret Fulton, "Memories of Early Walsh and Graburn," booklet (n.p., n.d.), Maple Creek Old Timers' Museum (MCOT), Maple Creek, Saskatchewan; articles in the *Chinook Opinion Jubilee Centennial Edition*, 1964, including Mrs. A. H. Lohman, "Early Days"; A. D. Newby, "Year of 1902 and 1903"; Margaret Griffin Spencer, "Upper Clear Creek Area"; anon., "Lloyd, Montana"; Harry L. Burns, "Yantic-Lohman Community"; Ruth Reser Gill, "Long Ago . . ." (1954); anon., "Keaster"; Herbert Kimball, "Cleveland and Surrounding Area 1890 to 1910"; and Mildred Monson, "Bear Paw Jack." Also, Lillian M. Miller, "I Remember Montana," ms., Montana Historical Society, Helena, Montana (this contains excellent descriptions of terrain, vegetation, and wildlife in the Bear Paw mountains area in the 1890s); Mrs. A. S. Lohman, "The A. S. Lohman Story," ms., Blaine County Public Library; Murdoch Matheson map, "Chinook—Early 1890s," in Janet S. Allison, *Trial and Triumph: 101 Years in North Central Montana*, (Chinook, Montana: North Central Montana CowBelles, 1968), 24–25.

3. Rudyard Kipling to Francis F. Fatt, Dec. 9, 1910, reprinted in the *Medicine Hat News*, 1998, and on netreader.com/community/medicinchat/stories/historical/kiplingsreply.html.

4. John A. Eagle, *The Canadian Pacific Railway and the Development of Western Canada, 1896–1914* (Kingston, Ont.: McGill–Queen's University Press, 1989), 3; Gwen Pollock, comp., *Our Pioneers* (Maple Creek, Sask.: Southwestern Saskatchewan Old Timers' Association, n.d.), 4. Harold A. Innis's methodologically pathbreaking economic and political history of the CPR, *A History of the Canadian Pacific Railway* (Toronto: University of Toronto Press, 1971 [1923], is also a rich source of information. The crew outside Maple Creek, if not American, was at least working for the American firm of Langdon and Shepard, CPR general contractor from 1882 to early 1883. See T. D. Regehr, "Letters from End of Track," in Alan H. Dempsey, ed., *The Iron Road and the Making of a Nation* (Vancouver: Douglas & McIntyre, 1984) CPR West, 38. Gill, "Long Ago . . . ," *Chinook Opinion Jubilee Edition*; Pollock, comp., *Our Pioneers*, 4; *Census of Canada 1891*, ms. Maple Creek School District A, Assiniboia West, North-West Territories, August 17, 1891–October 14, 1891, microfilm T-6426, National Archives of Canada, Ottawa.

5. "Map Shewing Mounted Police Stations & Patrols Throughout the North-West Territories During the Year 1891," *Report of the Commissioner of the North-West Mounted Police Force* (Ottawa, 1892); *Report of the Commissioner of the North-West Mounted Police Force*, Superintendents' Reports, A Division, Maple Creek, for 1890, appendix J (Ottawa, 1891); 1891, appendix H (Ottawa, 1892); 1893, appendix G (Ottawa, 1894), which contains a description of the landscape along the interna-

tional boundary; Anon., "Ranching in the Cypress Hills and Area," ms. M85.1.102, MCOT. Indians' names are taken from appendix BB, "Return of Criminal and Other Cases Tried in the North-West Territories . . . 1893," in "Report of the North-West Mounted Police," *Sessional Papers of the Parliament of the Dominion of Canada, 1894*, 213–215. Fort Walsh gravestones are mentioned in George Shepherd, "Pioneer Cow Town," *Leader-Post*, March 24, 1943, SHS 135, Saskatchewan Archives Board.

6. Anon., "Keaster," *Chinook Opinion Jubilee Centennial Edition*; Fort Assiniboine Records, Montana Historical Society microfilm 281, "Returns from U.S. Military Posts, 1800–1916," Roll 42, Fort Assiniboine, Montana, May 1879–December 1891, (National Archives of the United States, Washington, D.C.).

7. On Harry Bettington, see Ann Saville, ed., *Between and Beyond the Benches: Ravenscrag* (Eastend, Saskatchewan: Ravenscrag History Book Committee, 1983), 120. Much Canadian scholarship has proclaimed the harmonious settlement of the Canadian West, where "peaceful, law-abiding ranchers, farmers, and government-encouraged colonists" turned to organized justice and Mounted Police protection rather than to "the rifle over the door," in the words of G. F. G. Stanley. For a perceptive critique of this argument, see D. H. Breen, "The Canadian Prairie West and the 'Harmonious' Settlement Interpretation," *Agricultural History*, 47 (January 1973): 63–75.

8. Appendix BB, "Return of Criminal and Other Cases Tried in the North-West Territories from 1st December, 1890, to 30th November, 1891," *Report of the Commissioner of the North-West Mounted Police Force* (Ottawa, 1892), June 2, August 17, 1891; *Chinook Opinion*, June 12, 1890.

9. Comparing U.S. and Canadian census data is a tricky task. The United States categorizes by birthplace, and the Canadian by "racial origin," which lumps together British, Canadians, and Americans. Birthplace information is available on manuscript censuses, which I compiled for Maple Creek. U.S. religious data is incomplete and imprecise, based on respondents' answers to forms sent to religious bodies, whereas Canadian data on religion is gathered on the manuscript census forms. For population figures, I used: *Eleventh Census of the United States, 1890*, Population, vol. 1, table 33 (ms. burned); *Compendium of the Eleventh Census, 1890*, Part 1, Population, tables 13, 16, 496, 533; *Third Census of Canada, 1891*, table V; and MS, Maple Creek School West, North-West Territories; *Twelfth Census of the United States, 1900*, vol. 1, Population, part 1, tables 1, 19, 34; *Fourth Census of Canada, 1901*, vol. 1, Population, tables 7 and 11; *Thirteenth Census of the United States, 1910*, ms., Chouteau County districts: Fort Belknap Reservation Indian Population, Fort Belknap Reservation White Population, Chinook, Cleveland, Reidel, Warrick, Wayne, Lloyd, Clear Creek, Madras, Divide, Maddux, Coburg, Paradise Valley, Zortman, and Harlem; *Fifth Census of Canada, 1911*, vol. 2, table 7, and Special Report on Area and Population, table 1; *Fourteenth Census of the United States, 1920*, vol. 3, Population, tables 9 and 12 for Indian population, 586, and ms. census for Blain County School districts 1, 2, 3, 6, 8, 20, 28, 29, 43; *Sixth Census of Canada, 1921*, vol. 1, Population, tables 26 and 27; Vol. 2, table 53, division 4, 336. For figures on religion, I used: Department of the Interior, Census Division, *Abstract of the 11th Census, 1890*, 2nd ed., table 2, 260 and *Compendium of the Eleventh Census, 1890*, part 1, Population, table 2, 29; *Third Census of Canada, 1891*, vol. 1, table 4, 328. U.S. *Bureau of Census Special Reports, Religious Bodies: 1906*, part 1, Summary and General Tables, table 4, 334; *Fourth Census of Canada, 1901*, vol. 1, Population, table 10, 278-9; and MS, Maple Creek School District A, Assiniboia West, North-West

Territories; *U.S. Bureau of the Census, Religious Bodies: 1916*, part 1, table 63; *Fifth Census of Canada, 1911*, vol. 2, table 2, 138; *U.S. Bureau of the Census, Religious Bodies: 1926*, vol. 1, table 32; *Sixth Census of Canada, 1921*, vol. 1, table 38, 718.

10. *Eleventh Census of the United States, 1890*, Population, vol. 1, table 33; *Twelfth Census of the United States Census, 1900*, Population, part 1, 249, and table 19, 547. County population figures apparently do not include Indian population, which I added to calculate percentages.

11. *Census of Canada 1891*, ms., Maple Creek, School District A, Assiniboia West, microfilm T-6426. Métis freighters and their families totaled 94, North-West Mounted Police 83. On Chief Little Mountain, see the *Benton Weekly Record*, May 19, 1883, quoted in Alan H. Dempsey, "The Fearsome Fire Wagon," in Dempsey, *The CPR West*, 62. On the Cree and Métis dispersal, see Alan D. McMillan, *Native Peoples and Cultures of Canada* (Vancouver/Toronto: Douglas and McIntyre, 1988), 84, and David G. Mandelbaum, *The Plains Cree: Anthropological Papers of the American Museum of Natural History*, vol. 37, pt. 2 (New York City, 1940) map figure 1; "Nikaneet Indian Reserve," in Saville, *Between and Beyond the Benches*, 302–04.

12. Harry Otterson, "Thirty Years Ago on the Whitemud River, or The Last of the Open Range," ms. (Glenbow Archives, Calgary, Alberta), 14; Tenaille Documents, R-E458, Saskatchewan Archives Board.

13. Little Frenchman Creek may be the Frenchman river or its tributary.

14. Anonymous, portions courtesy the Stewart family, "Dan Tenaille," *Range Riders and "Sodbusters,"* 816–17; Tenaille Documents, Saskatchewan Archives Board. Tobogganing anecdote from Betty Harrison, "Jacques Terraine Garissere," Saville, *Between and Beyond the Benches*, 482. Garissere held the stopwatch. The documents do not reveal the Tenaille source of wealth.

15. Tenaille Documents, Saskatchewan Archives Board. "Guy Armand Thomas De Cargouet."

16. "Jacques Terraine Garissere," "Joe Chourrout," "Pete and Edna Mae Chourrout," and "Anton Lognos," in Saville, *Between and Beyond the Benches*, 482, 478–79, 286. "Jean Claustre," "Joseph T. Renaud," and "Michael Oxarat," in Pollock, comp., *Our Pioneers*, 73, 484; "The McRae Family," in Joyce Nuttall, ed., *From Sage to Timber, A History of the Fort Walsh, Cypress Hills (West Block), and Battle Creek Areas* (Maple Creek, Sask.: Merry Battlers Ladies Club: 1993), 118.

17. "Joe Chourrout" and "Jacques Terraine Garissere" in Saville, ed., *Between and Beyond the Benches*, 478, 482.

18. J. H. Price, who settled near the town of Knowlton in southeast Montana in the 1890s, was one such man. Dan Fulton, "Failure on the Plains," *Agricultural History*, 51(Jan. 1977): 52. Photographer Evelyn Cameron's heritage is traced in Donna M. Lucey, *Photographing Montana, 1894–1928: The Life and Work of Evelyn Cameron*, (New York: Knopf, 1990), 12–14. *Chinook Opinion*, October 10, 1901.

19. Anonymous, "A Bit of England on the Prairies," in Barry Broadfoot, *The Pioneer Years, 1895–1914: Memories of Settlers Who Opened the West* (Toronto: Doubleday, 1976), 129–34.

20. "Frank and Marion (Phillips) Barroby," "F. Donald and Gladys H. (Keddell) Corry" and "Barrett Corry," and "The A X Story," in *Between and Beyond the Benches*, 532–33, 540, 541, 120, 164. Author's notes from Eastend Museum, where a number of the Corrys' photographs are on display.

21. Medicine Hat Museum and Art Gallery photographic collection, PC 395.73. *Maple Creek News*, August 4, 1910, August 3, 1911. C. Blythman won in 1909, 1910,

and 1911. Billiards report in issue of April 29, 1909.

22. "Myles Cooper Bolton," "James Bolingbroke," and Ruth Masters, "Masters Family," in *Between and Beyond the Benches*, 269, 152, 287–88; Wallace Stegner, *Wolf Willow: A History, a Story, and a Memory of the Last Plains Frontier* (Lincoln: University of Nebraska Press, 1955), 294.

23. On December 21, 1894, the 10th U.S. Cavalry, a black unit, established its headquarters at Fort Assiniboine. Fort Assiniboine Records, Montana Historical Society, December 30, 1894.

24. *Chinook Opinion*, May 22 and June 12, 1890; Allison, *Trial and Triumph*, 52; *Report of the Commissioner of the North-West Mounted Police Force* 1894, appendix G, A Division, 121, and 1895, appendix F, A Division, 112; Miller, "I Remember Montana", 95. Miller notes that the Millers' summer sheep range was "close to the Canadian line."

25. *Report of the Commissioner of the North-West Mounted Police Force, 1894,* appendix G, A Division, 115, includes Superintendent G.B. Moffatt's comments on the border from a trip there in June 1893.

26. Anon., "Horace Greeley" (biography) and "Questionnaire re the late Horace Greeley," (n.d.), Saskatchewan Archives Board, SHS 24 (Greeley served in the Territorial Assembly from 1898 to 1905).

27. Albert L. Sperry, *Avalanche*, (Boston: The Christopher Publishing House, 1938), 35; "Notes on the History, Social and Ceremonial Organization of the Gros Ventres of the Prairie, Saint Paul Mission on the Fort Belknap Reservation, Montana," as told to John G. Carter by General Hugh F. Scott, informants Running Fisher, John Buckman, and Bernard Striker, ms., American Museum of Natural History Department of Anthropology, esp. 25; Edward E. Barry, "The Fort Belknap Indian Reservation: The First Hundred Years, 1855 to 1955," ms. (Montana State University, Library, Bozeman, Montana), esp. pp. 79–88; Beth Mundt, "The Mundt Family," ms., 1968, Blaine County Public Library. Mundt records the memories of George Mundt, a Bear Paws sheep rancher's son, including comments on Indians and black troops.

28. Arthur Poulin, "Phydime and Aline Poulin," and anonymous, "Elise (LeRoy) and Ernest Piquard," in *Between and Beyond the Benches*, 568–69, 166–67. Stegner, *Wolf Willow*, 294. A sampling of the Englishmen mentioned illustrates the point: Harry Bettington sold out and moved to the West Coast in 1910; Myles Bolton died in a train accident in 1909, whereupon his widow sold the ranch to an American; the Masters family left in 1922; the Corrys put their ranch up for sale in 1919 in order to spend the winter in England and return in the spring, and moved permanently to Vancouver Island in 1933; Spencer Pearse lasted until 1941, when he sold out and moved to British Columbia; Frank and Marion Barroby retired to Medicine Hat, Alberta, in the 1940s. References as cited above, except Corrys, *Eastend Enterprise*, October 2, 1919. "A Bit of England on the Prairies," in Broadfoot, *The Pioneer Years, 1895–1914*, 134.

Chapter 6: A Living or a Way of Life?

1. Charles M. Russell, "The Story of the Cowpuncher," in *Rawhide Rawlins Stories*, (Kalispell, Mont.: Bud Morris, 1967 [1921]), 41. Of the many books on Russell, see Larry Len Peterson, *Charles M. Russell, Legacy : Printed and Published Works of Montana's Cowboy Artist* (Helena, Mont.: Twodot, 1999), and Brian W. Dippie, ed., *Charles M. Russell, Word Painter: Letters 1887–1926* (Fort Worth: Amon Carter Museum, 1993).

2. See A. J. Noyes, *In the Land of Chinook, or The Story of Blaine County*, (Helena,

Montana, 1917), 121, 123; "Interview with the Gilchrist Family," March 1963, Southwest Saskatchewan Old Timers' Museum.

3. Dippie, ed., *Charles M. Russell*, 1, 2, 100. Dippie describes the unfenced Milk River valley of the late 1880s and early '90s as Russell's refuge from the over-crowded Judith Basin to the south.

4. Hugo Maguire, quoted in Gwen Pollock, *Our Pioneers* (Maple Creek, Sask., South Western Old Timers' Association, n.d.), 62–64.

5. "Reminiscences of Erwin Miller and Lillian Miller Westin," Montana Historical Society (MHS), 12; anonymous, "Hacking It on the Grub Line," quoted as an oral history in Barry Broadfoot, *The Pioneer Years, 1895–1914: Memories of Settlers Who Opened the West* (Toronto: Doubleday, 1976), 18–20.

6. Anonymous, "The Lost World of Cypress Hills," in *Our Pioneers*, 2.

7. Anonymous, "Ranching in the Cypress Hills and Area," M.85.1.102, Saskatchewan Archives Board, 2, 6.

8. "It had lightened [sic], fire balls jumped from one long horn to the other, for cattle were not dehorned in those days, they needed that protection for the wolves," noted an anonymous writer describing Lillian Miller's brother Henry's "fling into the romantic world of the cowboy" as a night herd. It did not charm the sheepman's son as it did Bennett's cowboy. "He referred to it as 'the night I wanted to go back to Iowa.'" Anonymous, "The Denison, Iowa, Germans," Blaine County Public Library.

9. John W. Bennett, *Northern Plainsmen: Adaptive Strategy and Agrarian Life*, (Arlington Heights, Ill.: AHM Publishing Corp., 1969), 176–79, 197, 180; John Bennett and Seena Kohl, *Settling the Canadian-American West, 1890–1915* (Lincoln: University of Nebraska Press, 1995), 26.

10. Mrs. Charlie Scott, "Mr. Philip Ross, Mrs. Evelyn Miller Ross," in Pollock, *Our Pioneers*, 85.

11. Margaret Fulton, "Memories of Early Walsh and Graburn," (n.p., n.d.), Southwestern Saskatchewan Old Timers' Association archive, Maple Creek, Sask., 22.

12. Anonymous, "The Denison, Iowa, Germans," ms., Blaine County Public Library, Chinook, Montana.

13. Fulton, "Memories of Early Walsh and Graburn," 36. "The farmers found it was not a farming country in the chinook belt," wrote Ernest Perrin, Winnie Perrin Hancock's nephew, in Ann Saville, ed., *Between and Beyond the Benches: Ravenscrag* (Eastend, Saskatchewan: Ravenscrag History Book Committee, 2nd printing, 1983), 80.

14. See, for example, "Reminiscences of William Davies," MHS, 3–4; "Reminiscences of Murdock Matheson," MHS, 4–5; "Reminiscences of Chauncey Flynn," MHS, 1, 3; and the *Chinook Opinion*, September 12, 1901, which reported under the category of "how times change" that long-time captain of the Bear Paw cattle pool, Frank Plunkett, "has sold his cattle and recently invested in sheep." Such examples are too numerous to list here. In Mrs. Roger (Hearther) Beierbach's account of conversations with Mr. Ray Faulkner and Mr. Graham Parsonage, "Ray Faulkner's Trails Travelled," in, *From Sage to Timber*, 54. Faulkner, a Cypress Hills rancher, traded horses for cattle. The horses, in a typical transborder incident, were rounded up from the Montana range. *Maple Creek Ranching News*, August 20, 1903. George Stewart, "Agricultural Development of the *Maple Creek* District," *Maple Creek News*, October 2, 1963, Saskatchewan Archives Board.

15. *Chinook Opinion*, January 10, 1901; *Maple Creek News*, September 23, 1909, January 6, 1910; Sally Foreman Griffith, *Home Town News: William Allen White and*

the Emporia Gazette (New York: Oxford University Press, 1989), 142–44. The booster's job, according to Griffith, was to promote "morality, unity, harmony, and progress" (160). She supports her argument from White and the *Emporia Gazette*, but the evidence—to patronize local businesses, to sacrifice for the common good of the community could just as easily have come from the *Chinook Opinion* of the same period, 1890 to 1920. The *Maple Creek News* and *Eastend Enterprise* had a similar but milder booster ethos.

16. Interview with William Ross, MHS OH 294, tape 1, June 8, 1982, Laurie Mercier, interviewer.

17. Map of Blaine County, February 7, 1952, Land Holdings of Miller Bros., Inc., in Blaine County Museum, Chinook, Montana; "Reminiscences of Erwin Miller and Lillian Miller Westin," MHS, 2.

18. Sherm Ewing, *The Range* (Missoula: Missoula Press Publishing Company, 1990), 244. The book is an engaging set of oral histories of regional ranchers collected in the 1980s by a Yale- and Cornell-educated American who became an Alberta rancher in 1955. "Reminiscences of James McCann," MHS, p 8.

19. Author interview with Olive Ramberg Satleen, Sweet Nursing Home, Chinook, Montana, August 8, 1986. Tape in possession of author.

20. Anonymous, "Denison, Iowa, Germans," Blaine County Public Library; Ewing, *The Range*, 240, quoting Alex Johnston, a Lethbridge, Alberta, research station scientist.

21. See *The Grain Growers' Guide*, August 3, 1910

22. Sister Genevive McBride, O.S.U., *The Bird Trail* (New York: Vantage Press, 1974), ch. 6. See chapter 8, "In the Wilderness Once More," in Don McLean, *Home From the Hill: A History of the Métis in Western Canada* (Regina, Sask.: Gabriel Dumont Institue of Native Studies, 1987), 240–46 and passim. Whether the Métis had a distinctive view of nature is uncertain, because, as McLean suggests, individual Métis or Métis families seem to have blended white and Indian cultures to different degrees over a broad spectrum of possible attitudes and practices. Quotation from the author's interview with Irene Grande, Helena, Montana, August 1998, tape in the author's possession.

23. Dee Brown, *Bury My Heart at Wounded Knee: An Indian History of the American West* (New York: Holt, Rinehart & Winston, 1970), 439–44; Robert Wooster, *Nelson A. Miles and the Twilight of the Frontier Army* (Lincoln: University of Nebraska Press, 1993), 188; Loretta Fowler, *Shared Symbols, Contested Meanings: Gros Ventre Culture and History, 1778–1984* (Ithaca: Cornell University Press, 1987), 58–60, 137.

24. A description of lodge skins appears in "History of Gros Ventre Tribe of the Blackfeet Indians," ms. by an anonymous Gros Ventre Indian, Blaine Country Library, Chinook, Montana; "Superintendent's Annual Narrative Report, Fort Belknap Agency," 1911, Bureau of Indian Affairs, National Archives of the United States, roll 45, section II, "Health"; The Male to M. L. Bridgeman, November 1, 1901, quoted in Barry, "The Fort Belknap Indian Reservation: The first Hundred Years, 1855–1955," ms. (Montana State University Library, Bozeman, Montana)," 98 n. 52. Fowler argues that the Gros Ventre of Fort Belknap devised strategies for maintaining their sense of tribal identity in the face of white disruption and interference. She does not, however, include their views of nature or the landscape in her discussion. See Fowler, *Shared Symbols*, 131–40, 142; Regina Flannery Herzfield, field notes, August 13 and 15, 1940, and July 8 and August 2, 1948, Department of Anthropology, Catholic University of America, Washington, D.C.,

quoted in Fowler, *Shared Symbols*, 98.

25. See Paul Voisey, *Vulcan: The Making of a Prairie Community* (Toronto: University of Toronto Press, 1988), 32. Voisey frames his discussion of an Alberta community in the early twentieth century by weighing out the contending influences in rural life—metropolises, eastern and old world customs and institutions, and the new environment. Every action must be traced to some point of origin. I would argue, instead, that each resident's occupation, temperament, interactions, and events make a mess of many such tracings. Because it frames life in a rigid dichotomy, as if having to prove Frederick Jackson Turner right or wrong once and for all, wondering to what *degree* people transplanted old traditions and created new ones is the dullest avenue to the inner meaning of Northern Plains frontier experience.

26. Harold Longman, "Rube Gilchrist," copied from the *Leader Post*, August 23, 1954, Saskatchewan Archives Board.

27. See "Reminiscences of Chauncey Flynn," MHS, 8–9.

28. A third diary by V. L. Bogy kept from 1874 to 1879, at the MHS, dates from the pre-settlement period; the diary of Chinook merchant Henry O'Hanlon was lost in a fire at the O'Hanlon Mercantile. Others, in private hands, may exist.

29. "Diary of Lorana Marshall," 1899, 1902–07, 1912, 1917, 1918, ms., Saskatchewan Archives Board, R-E458. The Marshalls' most recent prior residence had been Malta, Montana, east of Chinook. Sadie Marshall Henley, "The Marshall Story," in *From Sage to Timber*, 117.

30. "Diary of Mrs. Robert Hancock, nee Winnie Perrin, 1906–1907," ms., m86.37, Southwest Saskatchewan Old Timers' Museum, Maple Creek, Saskatchewan. According to the South Western Saskatchewan Oldtimers' Association book *Our Pioneers*, 50, 76, Winnifred Perrin (1875–1963) was born to a farming family in Aylesford, Kent, England, joined her brothers in Canada, and lived for fifty years in a log cabin on Piapot Creek. She met her husband, Robert, during his service as a Mounted Policeman in the 1890s. For explication of the garrison mentality, see Northrop Frye, *The Bush Garden: Essays on the Canadian Imagination* (Toronto: Anansi, 1971), and Margaret Atwood, *Survival: A Thematic Guide to Canadian Literature* (Boston: Beacon Press, 1972).

31. A. D. Newby, "Year of 1902 and 1903," *Mrs. Wendell Byrd, "Travel Troubles,"* *Chinook Opinion Golden Jubilee Edition*, booklet, (Chinook, Montana: *Chinook Opinion*, 1964).

32. Quoted from Janet S. Allison, *Trial and Triumph: 101 Years in North Central Montana* (Chinook, Montana: North Central Montana Cow Belles, 1968), 11. I use the term *community* here to mean, as Wendell Berry recently defined it, "a locally understood interdependence of local people, local culture, local ecomony, and local nature." See Wendell Berry, *Sex, Economy, Freedom and Community* (New York: Pantheon Books, 1993), 120.

33. I borrow these categories of ranching styles from Terry G. Jordan, *North American Cattle-Ranching Frontiers: Origins, Diffusion, and Differentiation* (Albuquerque: University of New Mexico Press, 1993), 202, 210–12, 226–27. This is a comprehensive yet admirably detailed coverage of the striking diversity of ranching frontiers.

34. Simon Evans, "The Origin of Ranching in Western Canada: American Diffusion or Victorian Transplant," *Great Plains Quarterly* 3 (1983): 90, 93, figure 5–5. Both Jordan and Evans stress the Cypress Hills' uniqueness, Jordan arguing that the Anglo-Texan influence was weak, Evans arguing that it was significant in comparison to northern Rocky Mountain foothills ranching. John W. Bennett in

Northern Plainsmen only obliquely suggests the cultural roots of Cypress Hills area ranching. He stresses these ranchers' roughness, mobility, adventurousness, independent-mindedness, and anti-sheep mentality characteristic of the Anglo-Texan system, but consistently turns his discussion toward local adaptation and away from inherited folkways. See chapter 6 of his book, 180–82, 192–200. See also John W. Bennett, *Of Time and the Enterprise. North American Family Farm Management in a Context of Resource Marginality* (Minneapolis: University of Minnesota Press, 1982), 40–41.

35. *Our Pioneers*, 73, 58, 59. A typical entry about such Scots ranchers is that of Mr. and Mrs. John Lawrence, from which this quote is taken.

36. *Chinook Opinion*, September 1890; George Shepherd, "The Cypress Hills of Saskatchewan," ms., Saskatchewan Archives Board; *Fourth Census of Canada 1901*, vol. 2, "Natural Products", table 34, which lists 71,460 sheep and 101,017 cattle in Assiniboia West; *Twelfth Census of the United States, 1900*, "Agriculture", part 1, table 35: neat cattle total 85,987, sheep 931,233, up from 156,102 neat cattle and 216,581 sheep in 1890 (see *Eleventh Census of the United States, 1890*, vol. 3, "Report on the Statistics of Agriculture," tables 8 and 10); "The Reminiscences of Erwin Miller and Lillian Miller Westin," Montana Historical Society Oral History Project, MHS SC1515, 2.

37. "Reminiscences of Chauncey Flynn," Montana Historical Society Oral History Project, MHS SC1517, October 21, 1972, Jeffrey J. Safford, interviewer, transcription, 1; "Reminiscences of James McCann," MHS, 1. McCann also recalled his father's experience south of Chinook in the 1890s, where "for a little while" he "run cattle but then the sheep moved into the country so thick that they couldn't hardly run cattle and everybody was running sheep," including his family.

38. Robertson Davies, *World of Wonders* (Hammondsworth, Eng.: King Penguin, 1985 [1975]), 606.

39. Lillian M. Miller, "I Remember Montana," reminiscence, ms. (Montana Historical Society, Helena, Montana) 127, 130–31, 110–12, 153; Clyde Reichelt, "The Remarkable Miller Brothers of the Bear Paws," *Great Falls Tribune*, December 7, 1958.

40. See Donna M. Lucey, *Photographing Montana, 1894–1928: The Life and Work of Evelyn Cameron* (New York: Alfred A. Knopf, 1991), xi.

41. Miller, "I Remember Montana," 19–21, 24–5.

42. Miller, "I Remember Montana," 77, 76, 147–48, 64–65; Lucey, *Photographing Montana*, 78.

43. Otto Moir, *Robsart Pioneers Review the Years*, ed. Robsart Committee (privately published, 1955).

44. The best account of the winter of 1906–07 in this region and its disastrous consequences for the local cattle industry is in Harry Otterson, "Thirty Years Ago on the Whitemud River, or The Last of the Open Range," ms., Glenbow Archives, Calgary, Alberta. As do I, Wallace Stegner relies heavily on this account in *Wolf Willow*, especially in the chapters "Specifications for a Hero," 137–38, and "Genesis," a fictionalized account drawn from Otterson's manuscript.

45. Otterson, "Thirty Years Ago on the Whitemud River"; "Ranching," in Lyle LaRox, ed., *Range Riders and Sodbusters* (North Battleford, Sask., 1984), 22, which acknowledges that "this winter put nearly all the big ranching enterprises out of business."

46. Dippie, *Charles M. Russell*, 71.

Chapter 7: What Are We Fighting For?

1. Isaac Cowie, *The Company of Adventurers: A Narrative of Seven Years in Service of the Hudson's Bay Company During 1867–1874 on the Great Buffalo Plains* (Toronto: William Briggs, 1913), 435; Charles M. Russell, "Johnny Reforms Landusky," in *Rawhide Rawlins Stories* (Kalispell, Mont. Bud Morris, 1967 [1921]), 54.

2. Janet S. Allison, *Trial and Triumph: 101 Years in North Central Montana*, (Chinook, Montana: North Central Montana CowBelles, 1968), 3; Charles M. Russell, illustrated letter to "Kid" Price June 1, 1917, reprinted in A. J. Noyes, *In the Land of Chinook or The Story of Blaine County* (Helena, Montana, 1917, 127; stories told by Bob Stuart and K. Lowery, Russell's Chinook buddies, in ibid., 123–26. Russell, *Rawhide Rawlins*, 54.

3. Noyes, *In the Land of Chinook*, 34–35; on Lamkin, see *Chinook Opinion*, October 26, 1899.

4. Noyes, *In the Land of Chinook*, 34–35, 115–19 (he quotes at length F. M. "Daddy" Marsh's and Billy Skillen's narratives of Kid Curry); Mrs. A. S. Lohman, "Early Days," *Chinook Opinion Jubilee Edition*; *Chinook Opinion*, September 24, 1903. On western outlaws and violence, see Richard Maxwell Brown, "Violence," in Clyde A. Milner II, Carol A. O'Connor, and Martha A. Sandweiss, eds., *Oxford History of the American West* (New York: Oxford University Press, 1994), 399.

5. Richard White, *"It's Your Misfortune and None of My Own": A New History of the American West* (Oklahoma City: University of Oklahoma Press, 1991), 330.

6. *Chinook Opinion*, May 30, June 6, July 11, 1901; Noyes, *In the Land of Chinook*, 118.

7. *Chinook Opinion*, July 11, June 6, 1901.

8. See Edwin Thompson Denig, *Five Indian Tribes of the Upper Missouri*, ed. and with an introduction by John C. Ewers (Norman: University of Oklahoma Press, 1961), 89–94, and Richard Maxwell Brown, *No Duty to Retreat: Values and Violence in American History and Society* (Norman: University of Oklahoma Press, 1994). Brown summarizes his argument in "Violence."

9. Dashiell Hammett, *Red Harvest*, quoted in Barnaby Conrad III, *Ghost Hunting in Montana: A Search for Roots in the Old West* (New York: Harper Collins West, 1994), 265.

10. See David M. Emmons, "The Price of 'Freedom': Montana in the Late and Post-Anaconda Era," *Montana, the Magazine of Western History* 44 (autumn 1994): 66–73.

11. The only local accounts of the strike I found were in Allison, *Trial and Triumph*, 47–50, and the *Chinook Opinion*, April 19, April 26, and May 3, 1894. See also Ralph W. Hidy, Muriel E. Hidy, and Roy V. Scott, *The Great Northern Railway: A History* (Boston: Harvard Business School Press, 1988), 139–43. Quote from "A Defense of the C.P.R. Land Policy," unattributed oral history in Barry Broadfoot, *The Pioneer Years, 1895–1914* (Toronto: Doubleday, 1976), 239.

12. Quoted in James M. Minifie, *Homesteader: A Prairie Boyhood Recalled* (Toronto: Macmillan, 1972), 42–43, and referred to as a standard joke in Barry Broadfoot, *Next-Year Country: Voices of Prairie People* (Toronto: McClelland and Stewart, 1988), ix.

13. *Chinook Opinion*, February 18, March 8, March 10, 1904. Bernard DeVoto captured Westerners' resentment of their colonial status in his many writings. His phrase for western antifederal feeling was simply "Get out and give us more money," quoted in Wallace Stegner, *The American West as Living Space* (Ann Arbor: University of Michigan Press, 1987), 9. For other historians' recent versions of this

sentiment, see William Deverell, "Fighting Words: The Significance of the American West in the History of the United States," *Western Historical Quarterly* 25 (summer 1994): 197.

14. *Chinook Opinion*, November 8, 1900, and the "Twin City Twinkles" column by "David," June 21, 1900. On Saskatchewan politics and government programs to aid farmers, see J. William Brennan, "Wooing the 'Foreign Vote'. Saskatchewan Politics and the Immigrant, 1905–1919," *Prairie Forum* 3 (spring 1978): 61–77; on the Provincial Rights Party, see L. D. Courville, "The Conservatism of the Saskatchewan Progressives," in R. Douglas Francis and Howard Palmer, eds., *The Prairie West*: Historical Readings, (Edmonton: Pica Pica Press, 1985), 518–20.

15. On Hungry Hollow, see Allison, *Trial and Triumph*, 91.

16. Letter from Kid Tibbits to Joe Gussenhaven, 1946, copy in Blaine County Library.

17. Quoted (uncited) in a brochure, "Fort Walsh National Historic Park," a Canadian Ministry of the Environment publication (1987). *Chinook Opinion*, April 23, 1903, October 22, 1903.

18. Ann Saville, ed., *Between and Beyond the Benches: Ravenscrag* (Eastend, Saskatchewan: Ravenscrag History Book Committee, 2nd printing, 1983), 276–77.

19. *The Morning Leader* (Medicine Hat, Alberta), Saturday, December 6, 1924, transcription in Medicine Hat Museum and Art Gallery, M89.28.4.

20. On recent gender theory and the West see Susan Lee Johnson, "'A Memory Sweet to Soldiers': The Significance of Gender in the History of the 'American West,'" *Western Historical Quarterly* (November 1993): 495–517.

21. *Maple Creek News*, July 21, 1910, and April 27, 1911.

22. Elizabeth B. Mitchell, *In Western Canada before the War: Impressions of Early Twentieth Century Prairie Communities* (Saskatoon: Western Producer Prairie Books, 1981 [1915]), 195.

23. Ibid., 195, 5, 20.

24. Local resident Arthur Benton supposedly sought refuge from Wyoming violence in the 1890s. See Allison, *Trial and Triumph*, 74.

25. Mitchell, *In Western Canada before the War*, 5.

26. Diversity in 1901 Chouteau County, measured on a diversity index at 18, equals that in New York City in 1910. See Ch. 8, n. 32.

27. Lillian M. Miller, "I Remember Montana," reminiscence, ms. (Montana Historical Society, Helena, Montana) 2, 34, 156–58.

28. Ibid., 38, 40–41, 43–44, 167, 168, and passim; Waldine Miller Lindquist, daughter of Lillian Miller, telephone interview with the author, June 12, 2000.

29. Ibid., 164.

30. *Chinook Opinion*, May 30, 1901; June 27, 1901; May 9, 1901; March 27, 1902; and July 17, 1902; June 8, 1899; November 22, 1900.

31. *Chinook Opinion*, October 3, 1901; July 20 and 27, 1899; August 3 and 30, 1899; December 19 and 26, 1901. *Maple Creek News*, September 9, 1909, contains an anonymous letter from someone opposing the new sewer system who calls himself "a kicker," an expression apparently common in the transborder Maple Creek–Chinook region.

32. *Chinook Opinion*, April 28, 1892.

33. Notes from author's telephone conversation with Preston Stiff Arm of Fort Belknap, July 1990. Fowler also heard this view on the reservation; see Loretta Fowler, *Shared Symbols, Contested Meanings*, 2. On competition for resources, see Edward E. Barry, "The Fort Belknap Indian Reservation: The First Hundred Years,

1855–1955," ms (Montana State Library, Bozeman, Montana), 86. On Gros Ventre objections to Assiniboine and others' presence see Luke C. Hays to the commissioner of Indian affairs, August 21, 1898, series 2, Federal Records Center, Seattle, cited in Barry, 93 n. 9, and Fowler, 92.

34. Fowler argues this in *Shared Symbols, Contested Meanings*. See her last chapter, "Conclusions," 233–53, and trace the argument and its variations over time through pages 48, 54, 70–71, 215–17, 207–09, 230, and 208. Quote taken from Fowler's tape-recorded field interviews, 1979.

35. Ibid., 204.

36. *Ranching News*, May 4, 1904; *Maple Creek News*, April 8 and 29, May 6, 1909.

37. *Ranching News*, August 20, 1903; *Maple Creek News*, August 12, 1909. On Violet Moorehead, see Gwen Pollock, comp., *Our Pioneers* (Maple Creek, Saskatchewan: Southwest Saskatchewan Old Timers' Association, n.d.), 67.

38. See, for example, *Sessional Papers* no. 17, 1888, "Annual Report of Supt. Antrobus"; *Sessional Papers* no. 28, 5–6 Edward VII, 1906, "Annual Report of Supt. R. B. Deane," 20, 21; *Sessional Papers* no. 7, 1887, appendix C, "Annual Report of Supt. McIlree"; *Sessional Papers*, 1897, appendix H, "Annual Report of Inspector M. H. White-Fraser, A Division," 178.

39. *Report of the Commissioner of the North-West Mounted Police Force 1895*, appendix A, "Annual Report of Supt. Severe Gagnon," 25; *Sessional Papers* no. 13, 1890, appendix L, "Annual Report of Inspector Sanders," 118; *Report of the Commissioner of the North-West Mounted Police, 1904*, "Annual Report of Supt. R. B. Deane," 17; *Reports of the Royal Northwest Mounted Police*, 4–5 Edward VII, 1905, appendix A, "Annual Report of Supt. R. B. Deane," 19; *Chinook Opinion*, May 30 and June 27, 1901.

40. *Report of the Commissioner of the North-West Mounted Police Force, 1895*, "Report of Supt. Gagnon," 24–25; *Sessional Papers* no. 28, 5–6 Edward VII, 1906, "Annual Report of Supt. R. B. Deane," 19; *Sessional Papers* no. 28, 1 George V, 1911; "Annual Report of Supt. J. D. Moodie," 144; *Maple Creek News*, January 20, 1910.

41. Allison, *Trial and Triumph*, passim; Noyes, *In the Land of Chinook*, passim; *Winters v. United States*, (1908), in *U.S. Supreme Court Reports*, vol. 207, "Cases and Points," 37.

42. *Winters v. United States*, (1908). See Norris Hundley Jr.'s excellent article "The 'Winters' Decision and Indian Water Rights," *The Western Historical Quarterly* 13 (January 1982): 17–41, for the legal context and debate surrounding the decision. I am grateful to Neil Leifer for his expert advice on Indian law.

43. *U.S. Supreme Court Reports*, vol. 207, "Cases and Points" 37, *Winters v. United States* (1908), transcript of record, U.S. Circuit Court of Appeals for the Ninth Circuit, November 20, 1906, "Answer of defendants," 14–18.

44. *Twelfth Census of the United States, 1900*, "Population," Montana, Chouteau County, Fort Belknap Indian Reservation, microfilm T623, roll 910, National Archives; "Robert Boyd Gannaway," by Caroline Gannaway Lafrantz, ms., Blaine County Library; Barry, "The Fort Belknap Indian Reservation," 97, ix, 65; [Ruth Reser], untitled history of the Reser family in Montana, ms., Blaine County Library. Ruth, Bertha, and A. H. Reser are found in the *Twelfth Census*, Montana, Chouteau County, Chinook Township, sheet no. 6; Ezra and Lydia (nearly illegible) Reser are in the same census, sheet no. 5. See also A. H. Reser blacksmith shop advertisement, *Chinook Opinion*, May 15, 1890; Allison, *Trial and Triumph*, 55.

45. *Chinook Opinion*, September 21, 1899, refers to Moses Anderson, "charged with assault in a branch of" a "feud" called the "paradise Valley Whitecapping out-

rage." Also involved were William McGrew of Clear Creek, charged with shooting his neighbor Albert Davey; John Birds and William B. Lithgo, tried for the murder of Claus Nichols in the Bear Paw mountains; and perhaps two other men named Frank Nessler and Frank Andrews.

46. *Chinook Opinion*, September 21, 1899; Norris Hundley Jr., "The 'Winters' Decision and Indian Water Rights," *The Western Historical Quarterly*, 13 (January 1982): 17 n 2; *Progressive Men of the State of Montana* (Chicago: A.W. Bowen & Co., Engravers and Publishers, n.d. [1901]), 1877–78; *Chinook Opinion*, June 15, 1899. Hundley correctly notes that Winter's name is written as "Henry Winter" in the *Twelfth Census*, suggesting a clerical error in the court records, which add an *s* to the last name. The name also appears as "Winter" in the *Chinook Opinion*; see, for example, June 8 and 29, 1899. Winter's trial and prison sentence are reported in the *Chinook Opinion*, August 27, 1903, his release in the July 28, 1904, edition. The incident is corroborated in Miller, "I Remember Montana."

47. W. R. Logan to the commissioner, August 14, 1902, February 23, 1905, July 21, 1909, series 2, Federal Record Center, Seattle, quoted in Barry, "Fort Belknap Indian Reservation," 111 n. 6, 114 n. 12. The title "agent" was changed to "superintendent" in 1904. On complaints against Logan see Sleeping Bear et al. to McNichols, January 27, 1907, file 154–21040–1908, Fort Belknap Agency Central Files, cited in Fowler, *Shared Symbols*, 80 n. 90.

48. Fowler, *Shared Symbols*, 90–91; Barry, "Fort Belknap Indian Reservation," 86, 91–92, 175 viii–ix, 142–50. By 1920, a group of Assiniboine asked for prompt cessation of work on irrigation projects.

49. *Chinook Opinion*, April 20 and June 29, 1905.

50. *Chinook Opinion*, July 27, August 17, September 7, and 28, and December 7, 1905.

51. This was the scheme of agent Luke Hays. See Barry, "Fort Belknap Indian Reservation," 90–94.

52. *Chinook Opinion*, May 7, 1891.

53. For the list of irrigators, see Barry, "Fort Belknap Indian Reservation," 124–25. T. C. Burns, an early Chinook-area irrigator, for example, is extolled repeatedly. See *Chinook Opinion*, May 7, 1891, where Burns is invoked: "One of the best signs of the times is the determination of our settlers to get water over their ranches. . . . We're on the right track now, so don't get discouraged." The Indian article is in *Chinook Opinion*, August 31, 1899.

54. *Chinook Opinion*, June 26 and November 6, 1890; February 19, 1891.

55. Rainfall record 1880 to 1969, Blaine County Museum, Chinook, Montana, recorded 1880–1932 by the Thomas O'Hanlon Company, 1933–1969 by the Milk River Elevator and Speers Implement. Quote from William R. Logan to Francis E. Leupp, June 3, 1905, Fort Belknap Indian Agency Papers, box 20, Records of the Bureau of Indian Affairs, RG 75, Federal Archives and Records Center, Seattle, quoted in Hundley, "The 'Winters' Decision and Indian Water Rights," 20. On the Milk River drainage basin, see *Eleventh Census of the United States, 1890*, "Report on the Statistics of Agriculture in the United States," 163.

56. See Donald Worster, "The Warming of the West," in *An Unsettled Country* (Albuquerque: University of New Mexico Press, 1994), 98–102; *Chinook Opinion*, May 31, 1906.

57. Vested Water Right Owners v. Department of the Interior, United States Reclamation Service Milk River Project, January 28, 1911, amended Aug. 16, 1911, in Contracts, book 1, Blaine County Courthouse, Chinook, Montana.

58. R. L. Polk & Co.'s Chouteau County and Fort Benton, Havre and Chinook Directory, 1909–1910 (Butte and Helena: R. L. Polk & Co., n.d.).

59. Eakins v. Town of Shaunavon, 1918, Western Weekly Reports, Supreme Court trials, vol. 1, 566–71.

60. "Report of R. J. Burley on the Maple Creek District," Sessional Papers no. 25, 1914, "Annual Report of the Department of the Interior," vol. 2, part VII, "Irrigation," 18–20.

61. Compare a total of 8,320 irrigated acres in the eastern Maple Creek district in 1913 (10,194 in 1912) to the Milk River and tributaries' 56,597 irrigated acres in 1902 and 108,555 irrigated acres in 1919. See M. H. French, Inspecting Engineer, "Crop Report for the Year 1913," Sessional Papers no. 25, 1915, vol. 2, part 3, "Irrigation", 78–80; and "Report of M.H. French, on the Eastern Maple Creek District," Sessional Papers no. 25, 1914, "Department of the Interior," "Irrigation," 26. Hugh Duffield's 1914 report on the western district gives no figures for irrigated acreage. He investigated 113 irrigation schemes, compared to 100 for French. See Duffield's report, Sessional Papers no. 25, 1914, "Department of the Interior," "Irrigation," 28. For Milk River figures, see Fourteenth Census of the United States, 1920, vol. 7, "Irrigation and Drainage, Montana," table 7, 201.

62. The borderland's complexity parallels recent historiographical trends to reduce the dominance of nationalist history, even if medicine line country fails to precisely fit new categories analysis. "By the end of the 1960s," John Higham recently noted, "the study of national character and the respect for national myths was collapsing." The "new paradigm of the 1970s and 1980s has celebrated the authenticity of small or submerged communities rather than the uniqueness of any great community." Higham, "The Future of American History," Journal of American History, (March 1994): 1298. See as an example Ronald Takaki, A Different Mirror: A History of Multicultural America (Boston: Little, Brown and Company, 1993). He posits ethnic and racial "borders," social versions of European-style frontiers appropriate to the U.S. border with Mexico but not Canada. Recent studies of capitalist development in the West include Donald Worster, Rivers of Empire: Water, Aridity, and the Growth of the American West (New York: Pantheon Books, 1985), and William Cronon, Nature's Metropolis: Chicago and the Great West (New York: W. W. Norton and Company, 1991). In each, the West undergoes a lamentable and universal capitalist distancing of people from nature, either at the hand of "a coercive, monolithic, and hierarchical system, ruled by a power elite" (Worster, 7) or the "geography of capital" (Cronon, 340), only part of the story here.

63. Mitchell, In Western Canada Before the War, 161.

64. Ibid., 35–37.

Chapter 8: The Cosmopolitan Throng
1. Belvina Williamson Bertino, The Scissorbills: A True Story of Montana's Homesteaders (New York: Vantage Press, 1976), 18–19.

2. Lillian M. Miller, "I Remember Montana," reminiscence, ms. (Montana Historical Society, Helena, Montana), 42.

3. Such descriptions occur repeatedly in area documents. See, for example, Miller, "I Remember Montana," passim, and Wallace Stegner, Wolf Willow: A History, a Story and a Memory of the Last Plains Frontier, (Lincoln: University of Nebraska Press, 1955) ch. 1.

4. Gerald Friesen, The Canadian Prairies: A History (Lincoln: University of

Nebraska Press, 1984), ch. 11 on immigrant communities, 1870–1940; *Encyclopedia Britannica*, CD-ROM version, on Dukhobors; and D. J. Hall, "Clifford Sifton," *The Prairie West: Historical Readings*, R. Douglas Francis and Howard Palmer, eds., (Edmonton: Pica Pica Press, 1985), 295.

5. Max Foran, "The CPR and the Urban West, 1881–1930, Hugh A. Dempsey, ed., *The CPR West. The Iron Road and the Making of a Nation* (Vancouver: Douglas & McIntyre, 1984), 89–105.

6. Chester Martin, *"Dominion Lands" Policy* (toronto: McClelland and Stewart Limited, 1973), 85.

7. See K. Ross Toole, *Twentieth-Century Montana: A State of Extremes* (Norman: University of Oklahoma Press, 1972), 49; Mary Wilma M. Hargreaves, *Dry Farming in the Northern Great Plains, 1900–1925* (Cambridge, Mass.: Harvard University Press, 1957), 277. For an account of the similar promotional movement on the central U.S. Plains in the 1870s, see David M. Emmons, *Garden in the Grasslands: Boomer Literature of the Central Great Plains* (Lincoln, Nebraska, 1971).

8. See, for example, *The Resources and Opportunities of Montana* (Helena, Mont.: Department of Agriculture and Publicity, 1914), 69–80.

9. Martin, *"Dominion Lands" Policy*, 162, 232; Richard White, *"It's Your Misfortune and None of My Own": A New History of the American West* (Normandy: University of Oklahoma Press, 1991), 433.

10. Albert L. Sperry, *Avalanche* (Boston: The Christopher Publishing House, 1938), 36–37.

11. Albro Martin, *James J. Hill and the Opening of the Northwest* (St. Paul: Minnesota Historical Society Press, 1991 [1967]), 552–55; Hargreaves, *Dry Farming* (the exhaustive and definitive book on dry farming) 179, 158; Ralph W. Hidy, Muriel E. Hidy, and Roy V. Scott, *The Great Northern Railway and the Opening of the Northwest* (St. Paul: Minnesota Historical Society Press, 1991), 103–07; and Joseph Kinsey Howard, *Montana, High, Wide, and Handsome* (Lincoln: University of Nebraska Press, 1983 [1943], ch. 16, "The Dream of Jim Hill."

12. Michael P. Malone and Richard B. Roeder, *Montana: A History of Two Centuries* (Seattle: University of Washington Press, 1976), 183; Toole, *Twentieth-Century Montana*, 49; Hidy, Hidy, and Scott, *The Great Northern Railway*, 103.

13. See Martin, *"Dominion Lands" Policy*, 116–26, 157, 161–65; Kenneth H. Norrie, "National Policy and the Rate of Prairie Settlement," in Francis and Palmer, eds., *Prairie West*, 237–56; and a special issue of *Agricultural History* 51(January 1977), that includes several dry-farming articles, including Hargreaves, "The Dry-Farming Movement in Retrospect" and Den Otter, "Adapting the Environment: Ranching, Irrigation, and Dry Land Farming in Southern Alberta, 1880–1914."

14. Hidy, Hidy, and Scott, *The Great Northern Railway*, 103.

15. Howard, *Montana*, 169–70, 186; Hargreaves, *Dry Farming*, 447; *R.L. Polk & Co's. Directory for Blaine County*, 1910–11 and 1915–16.

16. *Maple Creek News*, January 5, May 26, 1910. "Here is Maple Creek's opportunity," the editor wrote in classic booster fashion. *Maple Creek News*, February 17, March 3, and June 9, 1910.

17. Hargreaves, *Dry Farming*, 85–87, 144–46, 150–51; *Canada Sessional Papers*, 1913, "Report of Superintendent J. V. Begin, Maple Creek, 1912," 98; "Reminiscences of James McCann," transcript, SC 1518, October 21, 1972, 26, and "Reminiscences of Murdock Matheson," transcript, SC 1520, October 22, 1972, 15, Montana Historical Society Oral History Project.

18. M. R. Montgomery, *Saying Goodbye: A Memoir for Two Fathers* (New York:

Alfred A. Knopf, 1989), 10; "Thirteenth Census of the United States 1910," ms., Chouteau County, Chinook School District 10.

19. George Shepherd, *West of Yesterday*, ed. and with a commentary by John H. Archer (Toronto: McClelland & Stewart Limited, 1965), 71; *Maple Creek News*, August 14 and 28, October 2, 1963; *Free Press Prairie Weekly Farmer*, June 29, 1955; unidentified newspaper, January 11, 1951, Saskatchewan Archives Board; Joyce V. Griffith, "Health Care in Maple Creek from 1875–1982," Southwest Saskatchewan Old Timers' Museum, ms., March 1982.

20. Shepherd, *West of Yesterday*, 71–72.

21. The list is compiled mostly from biographies in Gwen Pollock, comp., *Our Pioneers* (Maple Creek, Saskatchewan: South Western Oldtimers' Association, n.d.) The Chinese restaurateur, Lee Yook, is mentioned as a victim of robbery in the *Maple Creek News*, January 18, 1912, under the headline "Stole 'Chinks' Cash Register."

22. Pollock, *Our Pioneers*, 46; *Maple Creek News*, August 8, 1912.

23. Ms. file, Blaine County Library, Chinook, Montana, including "Minnesota Settlement," Caroline Erebacher (1964); "Hydro," by Ann Schroeder (1964); "Memories of My Early Days in Montana," by Alice A. Cromley (n.d.). Also, Mary E. Weeks, *Forgotten Pioneers* (n.p., n.d. [1982]), Blaine County Library, Chinook, Montana; *Thirteenth Census of the United States, 1910*, manuscript, Population, Chouteau County, Montana, "Chinook Township school districts (s.d.) 10, 29, 32, 33, and outlying area including Cleveland s.d. 14, Big Sandy s.d. 39, 15, 11, Box Elder s.d. 13, Landusky s.d. 23, Wagner s.d. 35, Lloyd s.d. 24, and Clear Creek s.d. 44; George Mundt interview with Laurie Mercier, Montana Historical Society Oral History Project, OH 794, June 28, 1984; "The Reminiscences of Edwin Miller and Lillian Miller Westin," Montana Historical Society Oral History Project, Jeffrey J. Safford, interviewer, October 21, 1972, transcript, 7. Edwin Miller mentions the Basque sheepherders.

24. Stegner, *Wolf Willow*, 248; Harry Otterson, "Thirty Years Ago on the Whitemud River, or The Last of the Open Range," ms., Glenbow Archives, Calgary, Alberta, 12.

25. "Introducing Eastend Saskatchewan," ms., (n.d.), R-E1020, Saskatchewan Archives Board, Regina; *History and Reminiscences of Eastend and District*, (1955), 2–7, Saskatchewan Archives Board. Wallace Stegner gives Enright and Strong the pseudonyms "Martin" and "Fisher" in *Wolf Willow*.

26. *Our Pioneers*, 62; Bob Seymour, "Seymour Family" (1964), ms., Blaine County Public Library. *Thirteenth Census of the United States, 1910*, ms., "Indian Population, Fort Belknap Agency, Montana," sheets no. 33 and 45.

27. Stegner in a letter to the author, March 13, 1990. For histories that present relatively homogeneous frontier settlements, see Kenneth Lockridge, *A New England Town: The First Hundred Years* (New York: Norton, 1970); David Hackett Fisher, *Albion's Seed: Four British Folkways in America* (New York: Oxford University Press, 1989); John Mack Faragher, *Sugar Creek: Life on the Illinois Prairie* (New Haven: Yale University Press, 1986).

28. Superintendent's Annual Narrative and Statistical Reports, 1907–1938, Fort Belknap Agency, National Archives of the United States, Bureau of Indian Affairs, M1011 call no. RG775, roll 45, statistics accompanying annual report for 1908, and M1011, roll 45. Statistical reports are available for 1907, 1908, and 1920–1935 excluding 1923. Narrative reports cover all but five years between 1910 and 1935. For removal statistics see Loretta Fowler, *Shared Symbols, Contested Meanings*: Gros

Ventre Culture and History, 1778–1894 (Ithaca: Cornell University Press, 1987), 70; *Thirteenth Census of the United States, 1910,* "Population," vol. II, 1153; *Fourteenth Census of the United States 1920,* Population, vol. III, table 12, 586.

29. *Thirteenth Census of the United States, 1910,* "Population," vol. II, 1153; *Fourteenth Census of the United States, 1920,* "Population," vol. III, table 12, 586.

30. *Fourth Census of Canada, 1901,* vol. 1, "Population," table 11, "Origins of the People"; *Fifth Census of Canada, 1911,* vol. 2, table 7, and "Special Report on Area and Population," table 1; *Canada Sessional Papers, 1907–1908,* no. 28, "Annual Report of Supt. C. Constantine, Maple Creek, 1907," 37; *1916,* no. 28, "Annual Report of Supt. F. J. A. Demers, Maple Creek, 1915," 104; *1917,* no. 28, Annual Report of Supt. F. J. A. Demers, Maple Creek, 1916," 102; *1911,* no. 28, "Annual Report of Supt. J. D. Moodie."

31. See Lawrence Wright, "One Drop of Blood," *The New Yorker,* July 25, 1994.

32. Diversity is a major, persistent fact of North American history. Yet in a case where numbers can add rigor to a powerful political and emotional issue, historians have been slow to quantify diversity. It occurred to me that if the data in graphs could be reduced to a single number, an "index," for comparison, it would strengthen their essential purpose—to compare diversity and its change over time—and make for a much easier task.

Since apparently there is no existing diversity index, I invented my own: an equation that measures both the number of groups and the concentration of the largest group in a population. Diversity = y/x if y = number of groups over 1% of the population and x = size (by percent) of the largest group. Least possible diversity = 1 (one group = 100% of population, or 1/1). Maximum possible diversity = 10,000 (100 groups each = 1% of the population, or 100/.01). A practical working standard for high diversity is 20. Numbers throughout are rounded to the nearest whole number. The results are necessarily crude, reflecting not only the values and assumptions of the census takers, but my judgments, too, as well as adjustments for incomplete or mismatched data. Ireland, for example, is a place of separate origin to American census takers, but a part of Great Britain to the empire-loyal Canadians. Race and origin are impossibly tangled categories in both countries, and require finagling with data—separating out blacks and Indians, for example, in indices that otherwise measure a population by birthplace. Indians and Métis appear erratically, as if census takers were unsure of what to do with them. Religious data is hopelessly mismatched. In the United States, deep-seated revulsion against a connected church and state relegated the census of religion to a separate survey sent to existing religious bodies every ten years beginning in 1906 but poorly responded to. In Canada, "religion" is listed on the standard census form, right between "place of birth of mother" and "profession, occupation, or trade," yielding a record as accurate as the population count itself.

Crudeness aside, the index is useful in revealing and comparing demographic change and degrees of diversity in different parts of the nation or continent.

33. Figures calculated from the *Thirteenth Census of the United States, 1910,* vol. 1, "Population," part 1, tables 18, 19, and 28.

34. See "Earliest Protestant Work in Chinook" and subsequent articles on churches in the *Chinook Opinion Golden Jubilee Edition,* 1964.

35. On the movement of populations across the U.S.-Canadian border during this period, see Karel Denis Bicha, "Canadian Immigration Policy and the American Farmer, 1896–1914," Ph.D. thesis, University of Minnesota, March 1963, 129; Sarah Common, "The Flow of Population across the Canadian-United States Border,

1900–1930," M.A. thesis, Queens University, Kingston, Ontario, September 1931, 26; and Marcus Lee Hansen, *The Mingling of the Canadian and American Peoples* (New York: Arno Press and the New York Times, 1970), 246. See also George Stewart, "Agricultural Development of the Maple Creek District," *Maple Creek News*, October 2, 1963. Stewart was eleven when he came to the Maple Creek district with his parents in 1891.

36. Isobelle Dovell, "Curling in Eastend," Ray Baker, "Ernie Baker," in Lyle La Rox, ed., *Range Riders and "Sodbusters"* (North Battleford, Sask., 1984), 98, 255. Wallace Stegner was surprised to find curling the most popular sport in Eastend in the 1950s. See *Wolf Willow*, 296. Robin Welsh, *Beginners Guide to Curling* (London: Pelham Books, 1969), contains a brief history of curling, first played in Canada by early Scottish fur traders and by Scottish soldiers who, restless after the siege of Quebec in 1759, melted down cannon balls and curled on the St. Lawrence River. The Royal Montreal Curling Club was founded in 1807, soon followed by clubs in Michigan and Boston in the 1830s and Wisconsin in the 1840s.

37. "William Anderson," "Eastend Stampede," and "W. J. Leaf, in LaRox, "*Range Riders and "Sodbusters*," 236, 194–195, 574; *Eastend Enterprise*, February 3 and 24, 1916; Stegner, *Wolf Willow*, 84.

38. *Chinook Opinion Golden Jubilee Edition*, 1964.

39. *Ranching News*, August 20, 1903.

40. Mary E. Weeks, *Forgotten Pioneers*, Blaine County Library, 54, 61, 77, 87–88, 94, 178.

41. James Malin, "Rural Life and Subhumid Environment," in Robert P. Swierenga, ed., *History and Ecology: Studies of the Grassland* (Lincoln: University of Nebraska Press, 1948), 213.

42. Weeks, *Forgotten Pioneers*, 21, 53. Norwegian immigrant Bill Helgeson, who described his life north of Chinook in "Homesteading" (Blaine County Public Library, Chinook, Montana), was a typical drifter and speculator: "I had in mind that after I had proved up on my Canadian homestead I would sell it and go to Montana and get a homestead there." George VandeVen, June 28, 1984, Montana Historical Society Oral History Project, OH 796, tape 1, Laurie Mercier, interviewer.

43. Shepherd, *West of Yesterday*, 116–17.

44. Wallace Stegner, "Finding the Place: A Migrant Childhood," in *Where the Bluebird Sings to the Lemonade Springs: Living and Writing in the West* (New York: Random House, 1992), 4, 9.

45. "E.M.T. Notes," "Dr. Frederick Bruce Dawson," in *Our Pioneers*, 34.

46. Walter Hinebauch Sr., in LaRox, *Range Riders and "Sodbusters*," 487. Iladell Anderson, "Gurd Anderson," in *Range Riders and "Sodbusters*," 232. By 1903, according to the *Ranching News*, "the ranching community [was] using the word 'crowded' to describe their present conditions" (August 20, 1903).

47. Mrs. J. A. (Hattie) Smiley, "A Pioneer Song," in Ann Saville, ed., *Between and Beyond the Benches: Ravenscrag (Eastend, Saskatchewan: Ravenscrag History Book Committee, 2nd printing, 1983), 141–42.

48. Anonymous, "Dreams Dry Up During Dry Farm Days," *Chinook Opinion Golden Jubilee Edition*.

49. Wallace Stegner, letter to the author, March 13, 1990.

50. Ibid.

51. Miller, "I Remember Montana," 15; Stegner, *Wolf Willow*, 19; Wallace Stegner, interview with the author, July 7, 1990. Tapes in the author's possession. Wallace Stegner, "Finding the Place," in Clarus Backes, ed., *Growing Up Western*

(New York: Harper Collins Publishers, 1989), 164.

52. Wallace Stegner, letter to the author, March 13, 1990; Stegner, *Wolf Willow*, 128. Some nicknames were accompanied by elaborate stories. The story of Slippers, a Z-X ranch hand from Eastend who once got taken for his boots and hat after a night of carnal pleasures, is recounted in fourteen verses by Eastend homesteader and balladeer Billy Bock, quoted in Edward McCourt, *Saskatchewan* (Toronto: Macmillan, 1968), 67–69.

53. Billy Bock quoted in McCourt, *Saskatchewan*, 65. McCourt remembers Bock's powers of description as a "lightening [sic] bolt [that] always illuminated and frequently devastated the object which lay in its path." Stegner, *Wolf Willow*, 128.

54. Stegner, letter to the author, March 13, 1990.

55. Stegner, *Wolf Willow*, 11–12, 243–44; anonymous, "Introducing Eastend, Saskatchewan," ms., R-E1020, Saskatchewan Archives Board, Regina, Saskatchewan; Map of Eastend, Saskatchewan, Saskatchewan Archives Board, also reprinted in LaRox, *Range Riders and "Sodbusters,"* 31.

56. Stegner, *Wolf Willow*, 280, 275, 277; Stegner, interview with the author, July 7, 1990. The weasel incident also appears in Stegner's story "Butcher Bird," and the gophers and weasel in "Buglesong," *Collected Stories of Wallace Stegner* (New York: Random House, 1989).

57. Ibid., 272.

58. Ibid., 259.

59. Ibid., 272–73.

60. A. J. Noyes, *In the Land of Chinook or The Story of Blaine County* (Helena, Montana, 1917), 143.

61. County Project no. 4, 1919, Blaine County Cooperative Agricultural Extension Agency, 1.

62. Stegner, *Wolf Willow*, 8, 23, 20.

63. Ibid., 19.

64. Stegner, *Wolf Willow*, 8; anonymous, *Range Riders and Sodbusters*, LaRose, ed., 68; Everett Bales, *Range Riders and Sodbusters*, 96–97; Helen Reesor, *From Sage to Timber*, 9. Cora Brummitt Carlton letter to Wallace Stegner, May 16, 1971, in Mr. Stegner's personal files.

Chapter 9: "We Can Play Baseball on the Other Side"

1. *Eastend Enterprise*, December 7, 1916.

2. After about 1915 the increasing number of automobiles made such visits more frequent and casual. An item in the *Eastend Enterprise*, June 17, 1920, reads "R. V. Gregg, Mr. and Mrs. Henry Ostlund, and Mrs. John Huffman are picnic[k]ing this week in Montana." Wallace Stegner, *Wolf Willow: A History, a Story, and a Memory of the Last Plains Frontier* (Lincoln: Unversity of Nebraska Press, 1955), 83–84, ponders the affect of these exchanges. *Maple Creek News*, May 26, 1910; *Chinook Opinion*, August 6, 1903, June 6, 1901, May 30, 1901, July 25, 1901.

3. Fred Alison, in *Range Riders and "Sodbusters* comp. Eastend History Society (North Battleford, Sask., 1984), 227; Elsie Wold, "Elsie and Joachim Jens Petterson Wold," in Ann Saville, ed., *Between and Beyond the Benches: Ravenscrag* (Eastend, Saskatchewan: Ravenscrag History Book Committee, 2nd printing, 1983), 348; On opium smuggling, see *Chinook Opinion*, April 23, 1903. On the capture of a ring of borderland rumrunners see *Eastend Enterprise*, March 4, 1920. See also *Between and Beyond the Benches*, 242–43.

4. By the 1890s tireless baseball promoter A. G. Spaulding had described the

game as America's "national pastime,"a phrase that helped to create a mythology of baseball as a uniquely American sport. See Geoffrey C. Ward and Ken Burns, *Baseball: An Illustrated History* (New York: Alfred A. Knopf, 1994), 40. It seems no coincidence that at the same time, Frederick Jackson Turner was galvanizing another mythology of American uniqueness based on the frontier, a parallel that deserves exploration.

5. *Chinook Opinion*, April 25 and May 23, 1901; Wayne Westover, "Time Keeps Passing," 1964, ms., Blaine County Public Library.

6. Quoted in William Humber, *Cheering for the Home Team: The Story of Baseball in Canada* (Erin, Ont.: Boston Mills Press, 1983), 15.

7. Ibid., 12–13; Anonymous, "North Country Ball," *Chinook Opinion Golden Jubilee Edition*, 1964; *Eastend Enterprise*, June 26, 1919.

8. See, for example, *Maple Creek News*, May 26 and July 7, 1910; and *Ranching News*, May 27, 1909, reporting two baseball games played on Victoria Day, May 24.

9. *Ranching News*, May 27, 1909. The "Fat vs. Lean" contest was in addition to two other more serious games.

10. Gladys (Baynton) Perrin, "John and Evelyn (Reed) Baynton," in *Between and Beyond the Benches*, 374. Novelist Max Braithwaite in *Why Shoot the Teacher* (Toronto: McClelland and Stewart, 1965), described a rural Saskatchewan baseball game this way: "Nowhere else but in a rural school will you find 8 year old girls, 16 year old boys and a teacher playing baseball on equal terms, and playing it seriously." By the 1940s, Saskatchewan was known for producing good female players. See Humber, *Cheering for the Home Team*, 17.

11. Anonymous, "Riverside Cemetery," in LaRox, *Range Riders and "Sodbusters*," 119; *Eastend Enterprise*, July 1, 1915.

12. Westover, "Time Keeps Passing."

13. George Shepherd, *West of Yesterday*, ed. and with a commentary by John H. Archer (Toronto: McClelland & Stewart Limited, 1965), 87.

14. George VandeVen and Anne Schroeder, interview with author, August 6, 1998, trip from Chinook to the U.S.-Canada border; interview with George VandeVen, June 28, 1984, Montana Historical Society, Oral History Project, OH 796, tape 1 of 2, Laurie Mercier, interviewer.

15. "Arthur Knight," in *Between and Beyond the Benches*, 335–36; Stegner, interview with the author, July 7, 1990, describes a gopher dinner with distaste.

16. "Corky Jones," *Range Riders and "Sodbusters*," 530–31. See also Stegner, *Wolf Willow*, 298, 301–03, who regarded the "humble and unpretentious" Jones as the region's truest native intellectual. One self-made man, Rube Gilchrist, owner of one of the largest and longest enduring Cypress Hills ranches, arrived with the remains of forty borrowed dollars. Harold Longman, "Rube Gilchrist biography," *Leader Post*, August 23, 1954, in Saskatchewan Archives Board biography file, Regina.

17. Brian W. Dippie, *Charles M. Russell, Word Painter: Letters 1887–1926* (Fort Worth: Amor Carter Museum, 1993), 25, 47, 121–22; Charles M. Russell letter to Churchill B. Mehard, October 1916, and letter to Maynard Dixon and Frank B. Hoffman, August 21, 1917, in Dippie, *Charles M. Russell*, 229, 240. The "robe and pipe" phrase appears in both.

18. Stegner, *Wolf Willow*, 84; Chester Martin, *"Dominion Lands" Policy* (Toronto: McClelland and Stewart Limited, 1973), 120. "Many townspeople were visitors to the three-day stampede at Havre, Montana, last week" was a typical news item *Eastend Enterprise*, July 10, 1919. The glossary of regional colloquialisms at the back of *Between and Beyond the Benches*, 613–20, is quite useful. Regrettably, Chinook

area documents provide no equivalent.

19. "Edith (Seafoot) Matteson," in *Between and Beyond the Benches*, 136, 302–04. George Shepherd, the *Saskatoon Star Phoenix*, quoted in Leo A. Gaff, "The 'Gaffs' from Scotland to Battle Creek and 'Recollections,'" in *From Sage to Timber:A History of the Fort Walsh, Cypress Hills (West Block), Merryflat and Battle Creek areas* (Maple Creek, Sask.: Merry Battlers Ladies Club, 1993), 74. On native and cross-border fiddle music see "Medicine Fiddle," an award-winning 1991 film by Michael Loukinen.

20. "Mac Moir" and "The People of the Reserve," in *Between and Beyond the Benches*, 136, 302–4; "Vernon Gale" in *Between and Beyond the Benches*, 551.

21. Morton Keller, *Regulating a New Society: Public Policy and Social Change in America 1900–1933* (Cambridge, Mass.: Harvard University Press, 1994), 251, 282; Gerald Friesen, *Canadian Prairies: A History* (Lincoln: University of Nebraska Press, 1994), 354; "Nikaneet Indian Reserve," in *Between and Beyond the Benches*, 301–6. Regional documents contain numerous references to Indian casual labor on area ranches; see Gwen Pollock, comp., *Our Pioneers*, (Maple Creek, Saskatechewan: Southwestern Old Timers' Association, n.d.), 61–62. Gabriel Leveille, son of Mounted Police Inspector Walsh's famed scout Louis Leveille, and celebrated at age nintey-one as Maple Creek's "last living link" with the early Mounted Police, countered such prejudice with the Métis point of view. How did the Mounties look, making their way across the prairie in 1874? "They looked terrible," he said. *Calgary Herald*, July or August 1, 1957, Saskatchewan Archives Board, clippings file, biography.

22. Alexis de Tocqueville, *Democracy in America*, ed. J. P. Mayer, trans. George Lawrence (Garden City, N.Y.: Doubleday & Company 1966 [1848]), 513; Charles M. Russell, letter to Tom Conway, March 24, 1917, in Dippie, *Charles M. Russell: Word Painter*, 233–34; *Eastend Enterprise*, 1914–1916.

23. Allison, *Trial and Triumph: 101 Years in North Central Montana* (Chinook, Montana: North Central Montana CowBelles, 1968), 20, 18; *Chinook Opinion*, Feb. 26, and March 5, 1903, May 23, 1901; Bonifas, "Curtain Going Up," ms., Blaine County Public Library.

24. Saskatchewan Department of Agriculture, "Historical Outline of Agriculture in Saskatchewan as Reflected in Reports of the Department" (Regina, 1955), Saskatchewan Archives Board, vi; Anonymous, "Ranching in the Cypress Hills and Area," ms., Saskatoon Archives Division, Canada Department of Agriculture Publication 1133, Saskatchewan Archives Board, M85.1.102; *Ranching News*, May 19, 1904; *Maple Creek News*, February 10, 1910, September 15, 1910, and November 20, 1913. On Sapiro's efforts in the United States, see Morton Keller, *Regulating a New Economy: Public Policy and Economic Change in America, 1900–1933* (Cambridge, Mass.: Harvard University Press, 1990), 154–56.

25. Harold Longman, "Rube Gilchrist," copied from the *Leader Post*, August 23, 1954, Saskatchewan Archives Board; *Chinook Opinion*, March 5, 1903, reprinted from *The National Homemaker*, January 1903.

26. Sources for the list from Chinook are gleaned from the *Chinook Opinion*, 1901–8; Bonifas, "Curtain Going Up," ms., Blaine County Public Library; John W. Bennett, *Northern Plainsmen: Adaptive Strategy and Agrarian Life* (Arlington Heights, Ill.: AHM Publishing Corp., 1969) 209. Bennett confirms the persistence of voluntary associations and public gatherings in Maple Creek area society (he counted more than thirty-five organizations among Maple Creek's 2,500 people in the 1960s). For Maple Creek, *Maple Creek Ranching News*, 1903–04, *Maple Creek News*, 1909–14.

27. C. Blytheman's provincial tennis matches and winnings are followed in the *Maple Creek News*, 1909–11; *Maple Creek News*, February 8, 1912; John H. Archer, *Saskatchewan* (Toronto: McClelland & Stewart Limited, 1965), 176; Michael P. Malone and Richard B. Roeder, *Montana: A History of Two Centuries* (Seattle: University of Washington Press, 1976), 202–3.

28. Letter from Thomas C. Armstrong, *Maple Creek News*, December 1, 1910. A Thomas Armstrong, born in Scotland in 1879, immigrated to Canada in 1889, is listed in the *Fourth Census of Canada, 1901*, "The Territories," 204, "Assiniboia West, Maple Creek," 11.

29. Norman Maclean, *A River Runs through It and Other Stories* (Chicago: University of Chicago Press, 1976), 1: "In our family, there was no clear line between religion and fly fishing." *Chinook Opinion*, June 26, 1890. That Baptists were few is evident in the "History of Blaine County Churches," *Chinook Opinion Golden Jubilee Edition*, 1964, where the itinerant Baptist preacher is the only Baptist mentioned.

30. *Chinook Opinion*, May 29, 1890; Wallace Stegner, "Finding the Place: A Migrant Childhood," in Clarus Backes, ed., *Growing Up Western* (New York: Harper Collins Publishers, 1989), reprinted in Stegner, *Where the Bluebird Sings to the Lemonade Springs: Living and Writing in the West* (Random House: New York, 1992), 7.

31. On Mennonites, see Caroline Erbacher, "Minnesota Settlement," and Anne Schroeder, "Hydro," ms., 1964, Blaine County Public Library. Bennett, *Northern Plainsmen*, ch. 8 on Hutterites, 246–75.

32. Florence McDougald, "Andrew Cumberland, Eliza Ann Brett," in *Our Pioneers*, 34; On Matheson and O'Hanlon see Allison, *Trial and Triumph*, 93–4; A. J. Noyes, *In the Land of Chinook or The Story of Blaine County* (Helena, Montana, 1917), 27; and "Reminiscences of Thomas A. Ross," Montana Historical Society, 9.

33. Narrative Annual Reports for 1911, 1915, 1916 and 1920, Fort Belknap Agency, Bureau of Indian Affairs (BIA), Superintendent's Annual Narrative and Statistical Reports, 1907–1938, microfilm roll 45, National Archives of the United States. Reservation superintendents described the Indians as mostly Catholics, though they admitted that church attendance was low. Memories of Emma G. Robinson in "Teachers at Fairwell Creek School District," in Saville, *Between and Beyond the Benches*, 251.

34. Archer, *Saskatchewan*, 200; Malone and Roeder, *Montana: A History of Two Centuries*, 269. Their figure is taken from the census of 1906.

35. In his moving recent memoir of small-town American life, *Colored People* (New York: Alfred A. Knopf, 1994), Henry Louis Gates, Jr., marks the transformation of a black community in Piedmont, West Virginia, by its picnics (see especially 211–16); Jack Shepherd, "The Jack Shepherd Story," in *From Sage to Timber*, 210.

36. "Arne Svennes," in *Between and Beyond the Benches*, 111; Wallace Stegner, *The Collected Stories of Wallace Stegner* (New York: Random House, 1990), 84. Rachel (Newton) Decrane, "Reminiscing," in *Between and Beyond the Benches*, 12.

37. Wallace Stegner, *Collected Stories of Wallace Stegner*. (New York: Random House, 1990), 84; Shepherd, *West of Yesterday*, 73; Lillian M. Miller, "I Remember Montana," reminiscence, ms. (Montana Historical Society, Helena, Montana) 204–6; R.L. Polk & Co.'s Chouteau County and Fort Benton, Havre and Chinook Directory, 1909–10 (Butte and Helena: R. OL. Polk & Co., n.d.) and R. L. Polk & Co.'s Chouteau County and Fort Benton, Havre and Chinook Directory 1915–1916 (Butte and Helena: R. L. Polk & Co., n.d.). *Chinook Opinion*, August 1, 1907; *Between and Beyond the Benches*, 174.

38. *Maple Creek News*, May 26, 1910; *Chinook Opinion*, February 18, 1904.

39. Superintendent's Annual Narrative and Statistical Report, 1915, Fort Belknap Agency, BIA, roll no. 45; "Nikaneet Indian Reserve," in *Between and Beyond the Benches*, 304.

40. "Grass Dance Is Celebrated," reprinted from the *Havre Plain Dealer* in the *Chinook Opinion*, July 7, 1903. Little Bear's speech was translated from the Cree "by the Plaindealer Indian correspondent."

41. Ida Chadwick, "Earl and Ida Chadwick" and Natalie Forness, "Adam and Emilie Sorge," in *Between and Beyond the Benches*, 216, 468–69; Leo Gaff, "The Dennis Leo (Bub) Gaff Story," in *From Sage to Timber*, 69.

42. Miller, "I Remember Montana," 41–42, 44, 167, 183; Alice Dalke, "Emil and Caroline Tantow," in *Between and Beyond the Benches*, 236. The Tantows came from North Dakota to settle on the south side of the Cypress Hills in 1914.

43. Stegner, *Wolf Willow*, 130.

44. Henry Clark, "Patsy Clark," in *Range Riders and "Sodbusters,"* 320–22.

45. *Eastend Enterprise*, September 24 and October 29, 1914; February 25, June 10, July 1, and August 12, 1915; January 6 and 20, February 3 and March 9 and 16, 1916.

46. Bill Helgeson, *Homesteading on the Big Flat*, ms., Blaine County Public Library, Chinook, Montana, 1–2.

47. Paul Kennedy, *The Rise and Fall of Great Powers* (New York: Vintage Books, 1989 [1987]), 265.

48. Within nine days of Canada's entry into the war, twenty-four Maple Creek men had volunteered for service. *Maple Creek News*, August 13, 1914; *Eastend Enterprise*, May 20 and August 12, 1915; "Letter From the Front," by Private Frank Whiskin, September 23, 1915; *Eastend Enterprise*, January 14, 1915; Stegner, "Finding the Place," in Backes, ed., *Growing Up Western*, 164–65; Friesen, *The Canadian Prairies*, 352–53.

49. Dan Cushman, *Plenty of Room and Air* (Great Falls, Mont.: Stay Away Joe Publishers, 1975), 191.

50. Ibid., 196–98.

51. Malone and Roeder, *Montana: A History of Two Centuries*, 204.

52. Archer, *Saskatchewan*, 177, 198–99.

53. Tenaille Documents, Saskatchewan Archives Board, R-E458; in French with translation.

54. Charles M. Russell, letter to Harry Stanford, October 17, 1919, in Dippie, *Charles M. Russell*, 285; Mary E. Weeks, *Forgotten Pioneers*, Blaine County Library, Chinook, Montana, 53, 21.

55. Loretta Fowler, *Shared Symbols, Contested Meanings: Gros Ventre Culture and History, 1778–1984* (Ithaca: Cornell University Press, 1987), 197–216. A lament for buffalo days is in "History of the Gros Ventre Tribe of the Blackfeet Indians," anonymous ms., Blaine County Library, Chinook, Montana. The Gros Ventre "were a happy, contented Nation till the Whites came among them," the author wrote "The last of the Buffalo was a few scattered herds in 1885. After that there were none to be found. Then came hard times for the tribe, they lived on the rations the Government gave them."

56. Tenaille Documents, Saskatchewan Archives Board; in LaRox, *Range Riders and "Sodbusters"*, 817; H. S. Jones, "Dan Tenaille," in *Our Pioneers*, 93.

57. Sarah Deutsch, *No Separate Refuge: Culture, Class, and Gender on an Anglo-Hispanic Frontier in the American Southwest, 1880–1940* (New York: Oxford University Press, 1987), 118–19.

Chapter 10: Nature's "Incivilities"

1. Wallace Stegner, interview with the author, July 7, 1990; letter from Wallace Stegner to the author, December 5, 1990. A fictional account of the flu epidemic in Eastend occurs in Stegner's novel *The Big Rock Candy Mountain* (Lincoln: University of Nebraska Press, 1983 [1938]), 278–85, and a nonfiction account in his *Wolf Willow: A History, a Story, and a Memory of the Last Plains Frontier* (Lincoln: University of Nebraska Press, 1955), 290–91. Alfred W. Crosby, America's *Forgotten Pandemic: The Influence of 1918* (Cambridge: Cambridge University Press, 1989), 216, 222.

2. Stegner, letter to the author, March 13, 1990. For a description of the "drunken professional" types in Eastend, see Stegner, *The Big Rock Candy Mountain*, 283. "It occurred to her that everywhere she and Bo had lived there was somebody like Doctor Barber, lost and derelict and painful to see. Were they all over, she wondered, or was it just that Bo took them always to the fringes of civilization where the misfits and the drifters all congregated?" Eastend's two other physicians, N. R. Stewart and B. C. Hardiman, entered World War I; Dr. DeSerres, listed in the first town census of 1914, remained. *Eastend Enterprise*, October 19, 1916; January 25, and April 19, 1917.

3. Stegner, *Wolf Willow*, 246.

4. *Eastend Enterprise*, January 17 and June 13, 1918; *History and Reminiscences of Eastend and District*, 1955, booklet published for the Saskatchewan Golden Jubilee; "Introducing Eastend Saskatchewan," (n.d.), document R-E1020, Saskatchewan Archives Board, Regina.

5. 2 Chronicles 21:18 (RSV).

6. These accounts of failure are found, respectively, in Janet S. Allison, *Trial and Triumph: 101 Years in North Central Montana* (Chinook, Montana: North Central Montana Cowbelles, 1968), 16; North-West Mounted Police Force Reports, 1892, report of Superintendent Jarvis, 1891, and *Sessional Papers*, 1890, North-West Mounted Police Report, appendix L, 1889; Emery Newby, "Year of 1902 and 1903," *Chinook Opinion Golden Jubilee edition*, 1964, 36; Harry Otterson, "Thirty Years Ago on the Whitemud River, or The Last of the Open Range," ms., Glenbow Archives, Calgary, Alberta; and Mary E. Weeks, *Forgotten Pioneers*, Blaine County Library. See also Clyde A. Milner II's excellent essay on identity in Western communities, "The View from Wisdom: Four Layers of History and Regional Identity," in William Cronon, George Miles, and Jay Gitlin, eds., *Under an Open Sky: Rethinking America's Western Past* (New York: W. W. Norton and Company, 1992), 203–22.

7. The best popular history of the influenza of 1918 is Alfred W. Crosby's *America's Forgotten Pandemic*. Figures cited are from page 207.

8. *Chinook Opinion*, October 17 and 24, December 26, 1918; Wallace Stegner, letter to the author, December 5, 1990. *Eastend Enterprise*, January 17, February 14, June 13, and November 14, 1918; Wallace Stegner interview with the author, July 7, 1990. Eastend population given as 350, *Eastend Enterprise*, August 3, 1916, and as 600 in the application for debenture by V. B. Lackey of Eastend to the Local Government Board in Regina, December 20, 1919 (S.A.B., R-421.) Mortality figures for Eastend are sketchy. See Forrest G. Robinson and Margaret G. Robinson, *Wallace Stegner* (Boston: Twayne Publishers, 1977), 27; *Eastend Enterprise*, November 14, 1918, March 6, and July 24, 1919. The Council of the Town of Eastend denied my request for releasing cemetery records for 1918 because of "controversial comments" they contain. Town administrator Cindy Zabolotney, on town letterhead that proclaimed Eastend the "Valley of Hidden Secrets," wrote only that

"the flu epidemic took many lives and the records were very poorly kept." Cindy Zabolotney to the author, November 16, 1990.

9. Crosby, *Forgotten Pandemic*, 251–52; The disease arrived in eastern Montana in late September and in eastern Saskatchewan in late September or early October, and had reached Chinook, Eastend, and Maple Creek by October 24. Eastend residents could have been infected either by germs from eastern Canada or from transborder traffic from Montana. See *Ninth Biennial Report of the Montana State Board of Health for 1917–1918* (Helena, Mont. 1918); Eileen Pettigrew, *The Silent Enemy: Canada and the Deadly Flu of 1918* (Saskatoon: Western Producer Prairie Books, 1983), 60; *Maple Creek News*, October 24, 1918; *Eastend Enterprise*, October 24, 1918; *Chinook Opinion*, October 24, 1918.

10. Figures approximated from the 1916 population figure for Saskatchewan at 647,835 and 3,906 influenza deaths in Saskatchewan for October through December 1918, and approximate 1918 population of Montana at 400,000 (estimated from 376,053 in 1910 and 548,889 in 1920) and 3,222 influenza deaths in Montana for October through December. Mortality figures from influenza for the towns of Eastend and Maple Creek, Sask., and Chinook, Montana, and surrounding areas are unavailable. Local newspapers reported 11 influenza deaths in Blaine County Emergency Hospital, 4 young men dead by mid-November in Eastend (*Eastend Enterprise*, November 14, 1918), 15 dead by early December in Maple Creek, and at least that many more in surrounding districts and among local soldiers overseas (*Maple Creek News*, October 24–December 12, 1918). These figures are undoubtedly low, especially for outlying districts. The Maple Creek newspaper did not publish death totals for fear of alarming people (*Maple Creek News*, October 31, 1918). See *Sixth Census of Canada, 1921*, bulletin 7, 63; *Fourteenth Census of the United States, 1920*, "Population"; *Ninth Biennial Report of the Montana State Board of Health for 1917–1918*, 10.

11. Alexander Whitaker, excerpt from "Good News from Virginia," 1613, reprinted in Louis B. Wright, ed., *The Elizabethans' America: A Collection of Early Reports by Englishmen on the New World* (Cambridge, Mass.: Harvard University Press, 1966), 223.

12. See, for example, an article titled "View in the Milk River Valley, Montana," in the *Chinook Opinion*, December 26, 1901, in which the writer cheerfully predicts a population of 232,500 in the valley residing on forty–acre irrigated farms. Quote is from the *Eastend Enterprise*, November 25, 1915.

13. Willa Cather, *My Antonia* (Boston: Houghton Mifflin Company, 1918), 8.

14. William Faulkner, *Absalom, Absalom!* (New York: Random House, 1964 [1936]), 21.

15. Wallace Stegner, *Wolf Willow*, 8.

16. *Chinook Opinion*, March 7, 1907.

17. Kills the Best is listed on the *Thirteenth Census of the United States, 1910*, manuscript, Fort Belknap Indians, as the daughter, age three, of Dan Sleeping Bear and Strike the Enemy, both Gros Ventre. On Sleeping Bear, see Loretta Fowler, *Shared Symbols, Contested Meanings: Gros Ventre Culture and History, 1778–1984* (Ithaca: Cornell University Press, 1987), 61, 63, 64, 75, 80. Fowler lists Sleeping Bear's age as sixty-six in 1905, making him the right age to be the father of Dan Sleeping Bear, listed as age forty-eight in the 1910 census. Sleeping Bear is not listed in the 1910 census.

18. Fort Belknap Agency Annual Reports for 1911, 1912, 1915, 1918, 1919, and Statistical Report 1920, Bureau of Indian Affairs, Superintendent's Annual Narrative and Statistical Reports, 1907–1938, roll no. 45, National Archives of the

United States; Fowler, *Shared Symbols, Contested Meanings*, 14, 79, 84.

19. Matthew Cocking, *Journal of Matthew Cocking, from York Factory to the Blackfeet Country, 1772–73*, ed. L. J. Burpee, Transactions of the Royal Society of Canada, 3rd series, section 2, vol. 2 (Ottawa, 1909), 111. See also Regina Flannery, *Gros Ventre of Montana*: Part I, Social Life (Washington, D.C.: The Catholic University of America Press, 1953), 61.

20. U.S. *Public Health Service Public Health Reports*, 33 (Washington, D.C.: Government Printing Office, July-December 1918), pt. 2, 2318, and 34 (Jan.-June, 1919), pt. 1, 1008–9; Crosby, *Forgotten Pandemic*, 228.

21. D. Sleeping Bear, "How Smallpox Came to the Gros Ventre," Fort Belknap Tribal Archives, Fort Belknap College, Fort Belknap, Montana; E. Wagner Stearn and Allen E. Stearn, *The Effect of Smallpox on the Destiny of the Amerindian* (Boston: Bruce Humphries, Inc., 1945), 47, 94, 98, 102, 111; Flannery, *The Gros Ventre of Montana*, 9–11, 13, 19–20. Sources differ on the effects of the 1838–40 epidemic on the Gros Ventre; Flannery says they lost fewer than two hundred people, mostly children (20). She cites James H. Bradley, "Affairs at Fort Benton from 1831 to 1869 from Lieutenant Bradley's Journal," in *Contribution to the History of Montana* 3 (Helena, 1900): 201–87. Stearn and Stearn estimate Gros Ventre losses, from an estimated population of three thousand in 1836, as "almost exterminated" and "suffered severely" (94). They cite "De Smet's Letters and Sketches, 1841–42" in *Early Western Travels*, v. 27, ed. R. G. Thwaits (Cleveland: A. H. Clark Co., 1906), and W. J. McGee, *The Siouan Indians*, (Washington, D.C., 1897).

22. Alexander Mackenzie estimated 600 Gros Ventre warriors in 1789, in Flannery, *The Gros Ventre of Montana*, 9; *Eleventh Census of the United States, 1890*, "Report on Indians Taxed and Indians Not Taxed in the United States" (770 Gros Ventre at Fort Belknap agency), 115; and A. L. Kroeber (550 Gros Ventre in 1901), "Ethnology of the Gros Ventre," *Anthropological Papers of the American Museum of Natural History*, vol. 1, pt. 5 (New York, 1908), 146. Stearn and Stearn estimate Gros Ventre numbers at about 3,000 in 1836 in *Smallpox*, 94.

23. John M. Cooper, *The Gros Ventre of Montana, Part II: Religion and Ritual*, ed. Regina Flannery (Washington, D.C.: Catholic University of America Press, 1957), 28–31, n. 28, n. 29; Flannery, *Gros Ventre of Montana*, 34. Flannery dates this story, which The Boy attributed to the time of his great-grandfather, to the epidemic of 1780.

24. Stegner, *Wolf Willow*, 24.

25. Ibid., 28–29.

26. Ibid., 53.

27. Wallace Stegner, interview with the author, July 7, 1990; Stegner, letter to the author, December 5, 1990. The *Eastend Enterprise*, July 3, 1919, confirms the teacher's name as Mangan and her original home as Kingston, Ontario, where she went for summer vacation. For townspeople's views on tennis, see Stegner, letter to the author, March 13, 1990, and Stegner, *Wolf Willow*, 294.

28. Crosby, *Forgotten Pandemic*, 100, 114–15; Pettigrew, *The Silent Enemy*, ch. 5, "Preventatives and Cures."

29. Stegner, *Wolf Willow*, 132. "Whang leather" are short leather strings sometimes attached to a saddle as ties, according to Peter Watts, ed., *Dictionary of the Old West*, (New York: Promontory Press, 1977), 364–65. *Eastend Enterprise*, October 31 and November 14, 1918.

30. Crosby, *Forgotten Pandemic*, 221–22.

31. For an anthropologist's exploration of this topic in the Maple Creek region, see John W. Bennett, *Northern Plainsmen*: Adaptive Strategy and Agrarian Life (Arlington

Heights, Ill.: AHM Publishing Corp., 1969). Bennett concludes that the region's adaptive strategies were a mixture of socially and rationally motivated approaches.

32. *Maple Creek News*, October 24, 1918; *Chinook Opinion*, December 5, 1918.

33. See Lisa M. Bitel, *Isle of the Saints: Monastic Settlement and Christian Community in Early Ireland* (Ithaca: Cornell University Press, 1990), 55.

34. Crosby, *Forgotten Pandemic*, 100, 115.

35. Wallace Stegner, interview with the author, July 7, 1990.

36. Mary E. Weeks, *Forgotten Pioneers*, Blaine Country Library, Chinook, Montana, 177; Revelation 8:12.

37. This idea and some of the material in this chapter appeared in Mary Beth LaDow, "Chinook, Montana, and the Myth of Progressive Adaptation," *Montana: The Magazine of Western History* (Autumn 1989), 10–23.

38. *Cummins Saskatchewan Land Map Series (Showing Names, Locations & Addresses of Owners)*, Saskatchewan Archives Board, map no. B543.63; Stegner, *Wolf Willow*, 274–75.

39. A description of social evolution from wilderness to civilization is in Fredrick Jackson Turner, "The Significance of the Frontier in American History," *Frontier in American History* (Tucson: University of Arizone Press, 1986 [1893]) 11. For an excellent overview of Canadian agricultural efforts and assumptions on the plains during this period, see A. A. Den Otter, "Adapting the Environment: Ranching, Irrigation, and Dry Land Farming in Southern Alberta, 1880–1914," *Great Plains Quarterly* 6 (summer 1986): 171–89.

40. *Chinook Opinion*, August 7 and 14, 1890, March 8, 1900, May 8, 1890; *Maple Creek News*, December 1, 1910, July 6, 1911.

41. Shepherd, *West of Yesterday*, 73–05, 79; Weeks, *Forgotten Pioneers*, 55–56.

42. "The Reminiscences of Harry L. Burns," Montana Historical Society (MHS) Oral History Project, MHS SC1519, interview conducted October 21, 1972, by Jeffrey J. Safford, 10–11.

43. "Reminiscences of Murdock Matheson," MHS, 13; Al. J. Noyes, *In the Land of Chinook, or The Story of Blaine County* (Helena, Montana, 1917), 141.

44. "The Reminiscences of Thomas A. Ross," Montana Historical Society (MHS) Oral History Project, MHS SC1522, interviewed June 2 and December 8, 1973, and May 24, 1974, by Jeffrey J. Safford, 9.

45. "Reminiscences of Erwin Miller and Lillian Miller Westin," MHS, 2; "Reminiscences of James McCann," MHS, 26; "Reminiscences of Murdock Matheson," MHS, 9; "Reminiscences of James McCann," MHS, 26; R.C. Morrison quoted in "The Settlers Came," in Ann Saville, ed., *Between and Beyond the Benches*: Ravenscrag (Eastend, Saskatchewan: Ravenscrag History Book Committee, 1983), 249.

46. *Report of the Commissioner of the North-West Mounted Police 1895*, Annual Report of Superintendent G. B. Moffatt, A Division, Maple Creek, 1894, 111; Joseph Mosser quoted in Noyes, *In the Land of Chinook*, 104.

47. Dan Cushman, *Plenty of Room and Air* (Great Falls, Montana, Stay Away, Joe Publishers, 1975), 222.

48. Mary Wilma M. Hargreaves, *Dry Farming in the Northern Great Plains, 1900-1925*, (Cambridge, Mass: Harvard University Press, 1957), 442; Michael P. Malone and Richard B. Roeder, *Montana: A History of Two Centuries* (Seattle: University of Washington Press, 1976), 218.

49. Gilbert C. Fite, "Great Plains Farming: A Century of Change and Adjustment," *Agricultural History* 51 (January 1977): 249; Rainfall Record

1880–1969, Blaine County Museum, Chinook, Montana; *Climatic Summary of the United States* (U.S. Department of Agriculture Weather Bureau, 1930), eds. R. J. Martin and E. Corbin, bulletin W, section 10—Northeastern Montana, 8; A.H. Joel, J. Mitchell, F. H. Edmunds, and H. W. E. Larson, "Soil Survey Report #9," *Soil Survey of Southwestern Saskatchewan from the Third Meridian on the East to the Alberta Boundary on the West, and from the Top of Township 16 on the North to the International Boundary on the South* (Saskatoon: University of Saskatchewan College of Agriculture, 1931), Saskatchewan Archives Board, 77. Seventy-six of 209 townships in census division 4, or 35 percent, suffered at least 10 percent population loss between 1921 and 1926. See Canada, *Census of the Prairie Provinces, 1936*, 388–91, 400–04. Figures from this are quoted in David C. Jones, *Empire of Dust: Settling and Abandoning the Prairie Dry Belt* (Edmonton: University of Alberta Press, 1987), 257. Census divisions, first established in 1921, are listed in the *Sixth Census of Canada, 1921*, "Census of Agriculture," bulletin No. 9, Saskatchewan, 8–9. For 1926 figures, see C. H. Anderson, *A History of Soil Erosion by Wind in the Palliser Triangle of Western Canada*; Historical Series no. 8 (Ottawa: Canada Department of Agriculture, 1975), 8, 10; Jones, *Empire of Dust*, appendix table 6, 257.

50. Quote from Noyes, *In the Land of Chinook*, 145.

51. Alexis de Tocqueville, *Democracy in America*, trans. George Lawrence, (Garden City, N.Y.: Anchor Books, 1969), 2:508.

52. Ibid., 515.

53. James Madison, "No. 10," in Alexander Hamilton, James Madison, and John Jay, *The Federalist Papers* (New York: New American Library, 1961 [1787–88]), 81.

54. Tocqueville, *Democracy in America*, 2:507.

55. Lillian M. Miller, "I Remember Montana," reminiscence, ms. (Montana Historical Society, Helena, Montana) 43; Anonymous, "Two Faces," in *Between and Beyond the Benches*, 7.

56. "The Reminiscences of William Davies," Montana Historical Society Oral History Project, MHS, SC 1516, transcript of an interview by Jeffrey J. Safford, 4; "The Reminiscences of Harry L. Burns," MHS, 10.

57. *The Papers of the Palliser Expedition*, 1857–1860, ed. with an introduction and notes by Irene H. Spry (Toronto: The Champlain Society, 1968), 421, xxxviii, cviii, cix, cxv. On John Macoun, the Canadian botanist and propagandist for the Canadian government, see W. Kaye Lamb, *History of the Canadian Pacific Railway* (New York: Macmillan, 1977), 79–80, and Doug Owram, *Promise of Eden*: The Canadian expanionist movement and the idea of the West. 1856–1900 (Toronto: University of Toronto Press, 1992), 69.

58. Allison, *Trial and Triumph*, 1–2.

59. James J. Hill, *Highways of Progress* (New York: Doubleday, Page & Company, 1910), 293–97, 327.

60. Author interview with Waldine Miller Lindquist of LaJolla, California, niece of Lillian Miller, June 2000; Clyde Reichelt, "The Remarkable Miller Brothers of the Bear Paws," *Great Falls Tribune*, December 7, 1958; Weeks, *Forgotten Pioneers*, 177; George VandeVen and Anne Schroeder, interview by the author, August 6, 1998.

61. *Between and Beyond the Benches*, 151; *Chinook Opinion*, January 7, 1918; James Welch, *The Death of Jim Loney* (New York: Harper and Row, 1979), 11.

Epilogue: Wallace Stegner and the North American West

1. *Eastend Enterprise*, September 4, 1919; Wallace Stegner, *Wolf Willow: A History, A Story, and a Memory of the Last Plains Frontier* (Lincoln and London:

University of Nebraska Press, 1955), 269, 271-77, 283; Wallace Stegner, "Finding the Place," in Clarus Backes, ed., *Growing Up Western* (New York: Harper Collins Publishers, 1980), 166-69.

2. Stegner, *Wolf Willow*, 283.

3. Ibid., 85, 84.

4. Letter from the author to Wallace Stegner, February 26, 1990; letter from Wallace Stegner to the author, March 13, 1990.

5. Stegner, *Wolf Willow*, 20.

6. Wallace Stegner, "Thoughts in a Dry Land," *Where the Bluebird Sings to the Lemonade Springs: Living and Writing in the West* (New York: Penguin Books, 1989), 55; "Living Dry," op. cit., 57; "The Sense of Place," op. cit., 201; *Wolf Willow*, 85.

7. Stegner, *Wolf Willow*, 85.

8. For farmers' adaptive strategies see Bennett, *Northern Plainsmen*, 236, and Bennett, Of Time and the Enterprise, 43, 38. The one-fourth figure applies to the Maple Creek-Cypress Hills region of southwest Saskatchewan only, not to Blaine County. Allison, *Trial and Triumph*, 175. Almost every local source with reference to agriculture in the late 1910s and 1920s makes these same points. Earth Observation Satellite Company, scene 85269217290X0, path 38 row 26, 7/15/91; Census of Canada 1991, Agriculture, lists Maple Creek crop district, roughly the same area as the Cypress District, with 2,940,686 cultivated acres (figure from the Saskatchewan Department of Agriculture); United States Census of Agriculture 1992 lists Blaine county with 586,725 acres in crop land, and 256,244 acres of harvested crop land from 391 farms (figures from the Montana Department of Agriculture.) See also Bennett, *Of Time and the Enterprise*, ch. 2, on Maple Creek area agricultural history through the 1970s. Local literature has abundant references to the earlier mass failure of dry land farming.

9. Richard Ford, "Good Raymond," *The New Yorker*, October 5, 1998: p. 78.

10. "Blackfeet Hope for Special Tribal Border-Crossing Station," The Associated Press & Local Wire, Feb. 22, 2000; Mark Cooper, "Native Spirits with Ralph Band Official Praises Klein's Support of Border Crossing," *The Edmonton Sun*, Feb. 26, 2000, 8; Howard May, "Alberta Natives Seek Separate Crossing to U.S.," *The Ottawa Citizen*, Feb. 24, 2000, A7. On the decreasing significance of territoriality marked by political boundaries, see Charles S. Maier, "Consigning the Twentieth Century to History: Alternative Narratives for the Modern Era," *The American Historical Review* 105 (June 2000): 807–31.

49th Parallel, 2–3, 5, 6, 7, 9, 214
100th Meridian, 4

A

Adkin, Rex, 211
agriculture, 151–54, 155, 61, 162–66, 166, 169–72, 204–08, 217
alcohol, 30–40, 129, 189–90, 202
Allen, Hugh, 81
American Fur Company, 29, 32
Anaconda Copper Company, 126
Anderson, Iladell, 165
Angus, Richard, 79–80, 82
Apache, 27
Arapaho, 25, 27
Arawak, 25
aridity, 8, 27, 87, 141, 150–52, 162, 165, 205–06, 214
Arikara, 25, 26
Ashinabe, 41–42
Assinboine, 6, 21, 24–27, 30, 31, 42, 49, 69, 77, 85, 94, 112, 137, 143, 159, 190, 198–99
associations, 181–83, 209
Atsa:, 199–200

B

Barroby, Frank, 97
baseball, 174–77
Battle of Bear Paws, 71
Battle of Greasy Grass *see* Battle of Little Big Horn
Battle of Little Big Horn, 43–45, 60
Bear Paw Jack, 100
Beaver Tom, 23, 37
Begin, J.V., 155
Bennett, John, 105–06

Bettington, Harry, 92–93, 97
Big Bear, 68, 69
Big Foot, 113
Black Elk, 43, 45
Blackfeet, 6, 10, 24, 27, 39, 43, 77
Blackfoot, 6, 10, 11, 23, 24, 29, 30, 32, 37, 39, 40, 59, 63, 65, 66, 68–70, 85, 123, 126, 211, 218
distinguished from Blackfeet, 27
Black Hills, 44
Blaine County Museum, 108, 109
Blood, 27
Bolton, Myles, 97
Borden, Robert, 189
borderland *see* medicine line
borders,
significance of, 4–5
Wallace Stegner on, 4, 213
Joseph Kinsey Howard on, 42
boundary surveys, 7–8, 9–11
British, 159, 188, 195
association of, 96–98, 101
Métis and the, 16
remittance men, 97, 179
unrealistic view of landscape, 96–98, 101
British North American Act, 33
Broadwater, Colonel C.A., 36
Brotherton, Major David, x–xii, xv
Bruguier, John "Big Leggins," 46–47
Buffalo Bill Cody, xv, xvi, 156
Buffalo Bill's Wild West Show, xv, 156
buffalo, disappearance of, 29, 30, 85, 201
Buntline, Ned, 104
Bureau of Reclamation, 114, 144
Butler, Captain William F., 40–41

C

Cameron, Evelyn, 119–20
Campbell, Hardy W., 151
Campbell, Walter Stanley a.k.a Stanley
    Vestal, 62, 64
Camp Robinson, 48
Canada
    national myth and, 14, 19, 56, 75,
        87, 130–31, 214
    nationhood of, 15
    Indian policy, 56–59
Canada Firsters, 38
Canadian Indian Act of 1876, 56
Canadian mosaic, 14
Canadian Pacific Railway (CPR), 9,
    74-83, 87, 92, 93, 149–51
capitalism, 107, 162, 214
Carlton, Cora Brummitt, 172
Carter, John G., 39
Cather, Willa, 196
census, 90, 93–94, 133, 145, 155,
    158–60, 208, 241 n9
Chadwick, Ida, 186
Cheyenne, 25, 43, 46, 68
Chief Joseph, 72
Chippewa, 21
Chinese railway laborers, 84
Chinook, 1, 68, 90–93, 107–09, 128,
    189, 211, 217
    associations, 181–83
    Charlie Russell, 103–05, 121–22,
        123
    cultural diversity, 133–37,157–59,
        161-62, 178-79
    Fort Assiniboine, 89
    Fort Belcamp, 89, 80
    immigration, 15
    irrigation, 140–46
    ranching, 116–22
    violence, 123–26, 129–32
chinook winds (defined), 107
Chourrout, Joe, 96
Civil War, 9
Clark, Henry, 187
class distinctions and conflict, 36–37,
    96–97, 126–28, 132, 207, 209
Clifford, Captain Walter, xii
Corry, Barrett, 97
Corry, Donald, 97, 110–11
Corry, Gladys, 110–12

cowboys *see* ranchers/cowboys
Crazy Horse, 48, 64
Cree, 16, 24–27, 30, 38, 40, 59, 68, 69,
    86, 92, 94, 186, 199
Crook, General George, 44–45, 46
Crow, 24, 25, 27, 44, 65
Crowfoot, xiii, 6, 40, 68, 69–70, 85
Crozier, Inspector Lief, 65
cultural diversity, 92–101, 133–40,
    150, 155–62, 167–68, 178–80,
    186, 190
Curry, Kid (Harvey Logan), 124–25,
    132
Custer, General George Armstrong,
    43–45, 50–51
Cushman, Dan, 189, 207–08
Cuthbert, Superintendent, 160
Cypress Hills, 97, 133, 146, 179, 182
Cypress Hills Massacre, 31–33, 37

D

Dalke, Alice Tantow, 187
Death of Jim Loney, The, 211
DeCargouet, Guy A.T., 95
Denig, Edwin Thompson, 24–25, 30
Dennis, John Stoughton, 15–18, 54
Denny, Sir Cecil, 37
DeSerres, Dr., 193
Dickens, Frank, 34, 63
Dickens of the Mounted, 63, 64
disease *see* Spanish influenza and
    smallpox
diversity, 94, 133, 139–40, 147, 158–62,
    167, 181, 191
Dixon, Joseph M., 152
Dominion Lands Act of 1872, 16
Dominion Lands Act of 1908, 151
Dominion Lands Survey, 17
drought, 151, 208, 211
dry farming, 151–54, 155, 162–63,
    170–72, 204–08, 211
Dry Farming Congress, 151
Duffield, Hugh, 146
Dukhobors, 150, 167
Durham, Lord, 14

E

Eastend, 91, 94, 121, 157–58, 177, 181,
    90, 211, 217

associations, 183, 187–88
  English, 97–98
  exodus, 208
  French, 101
  influenza, 194–95
  Wallace Stegner, 166–69, 202,
    213, 216
Egan, Ross J.M., 80
English, John J., 153
Enlarged Homestead Act of 1909, 151,
    152, 154
Enright, J.E., 169
environment/ecology, 8, 116–21, 149,
    165–66, 169–72, 204–08

F

famine, among native peoples, 29
Fenian Brotherhood, 38, 54
Ford, Richard, 217
Foremost Man, 86
Forness, Natalie Sorge, 186
Fort Assiniboine, 68, 89, 98, 133
Fort Belknap, 39, 68, 77, 89, 90, 94,
    101, 106, 112, 136–37, 140–46,
    159, 180, 184, 186, 197–98
Fort Benton, 5–6, 31, 35, 78, 89
Fort Buford, x–xii, 62
Fort Laramie, 44
Fort Laramie Treaty of 1868, 45
Fort Leavenworth, 71
Fort Macleod, 35
Fort Walsh, 24, 63–64
Fort Yates, xii, xiv
French, 184
  Métis and, 16
  association of, 94–96, 101
French, M.H., 146
frontier, defined, 20, 56
frontier thesis, 19–20
fur trade, 16–17, 29–30

G

Garcia, Andrew, 23–24, 37, 39
Ghost Dance religion, xv–xvi, 71, 113
Gibbon, Colonel John, 45
Gilchrist, Rube, 114, 181–82
Gill, Ruth Reser, 90
Grande, Irene, 111–12

Grant, President Ulysses S., 67
Great American Desert, 7–8
"Great Father," 65–66
Great Northern Railway, 77–78, 80–83,
    85, 92, 126–27, 144, 149–52
Greeley, Horace, 98, 99, 100–01
Grenfell, Pasco Du Pont, 79–80
Gros Ventre, 24–27, 41, 77, 101,
    112–14, 137, 143, 159, 190,
    196–200, 202, 204

H

Hammett, Dashiell, 126
Hancock, Winnifred Perrin, 115, 116
Hargreaves, Mary, 154
Harlem Irrigation Company, 144
Havre, 129, 132, 154, 189
Helgeson, Bill, 188
Henriot, Mary A. Tenaille, 190
Hidastsa, 25
Higheagle, Robert, 23, 42
Hill, James J., 12, 73–77, 79–83, 85,
    87, 151–54, 171, 210–11
Hillock, George, 130
Hind, Henry Youle, 84
history, lack of, 197, 200–02
Hoffman, Jack, 177
Homestead Act, 19
homesteaders, 155, 206–10, 211
Honky-Tonk Town, 129
Howard, Joseph Kinsey, 28, 42, 152
Hudson's Bay Company, 9, 16, 17, 27,
    29, 32, 38, 73, 39

I

identity, notions of, 155, 158, 171, 178,
    185–88, 190, 215–16
immigration, 149–62
Indians
  alliances among, 24, 43, 65, 68–69, 72
  disease and, 25–27, 197–200
  humor of, 39, 64
  romanticization of, 53, 55–56, 62, 138
Indian Tribes
  Apache, 27
  Arapaho, 25, 27
  Arawak, 25
  Arikara, 25, 26
  Ashinabe, 41–42

Assinboine, 6, 21, 24–27, 30, 31, 42,
    49, 69, 77, 85, 94, 112, 137,
    143, 159, 190, 198–99
Blackfeet, 6, 10, 24, 27, 30, 32, 40,
    43, 59, 65, 68–71, 77, 218
Blood, 27
Cheyenne, 25, 43, 46, 68
Chippewa, 21
Cree, 16, 24–27, 30, 38, 40, 59, 68,
    69, 86, 92, 94, 186, 199
Crow, 24, 25, 27, 44, 65
Gros Ventre, 24–27, 41, 77, 101,
    112–114, 137, 143, 159, 190,
    196–200, 202, 204
Hidastsa, 25
Iroquois, 41, 42
Kiowa, 25
Mandan, 25, 26,
Mohawk, 41, 218
Nez Percé, 45, 59, 65, 71–72
Oglala, 25
Ojibwa, 12
Omaha, 25, 26
Piegan, 6, 24, 27, 39, 40
Ponca, 25
Shoshone, 27
Siouan, 24
Sioux, ix–xvi, 6, 10, 23–29, 40-49,
    53, 58, 59, 65, 66, 68, 72, 113
influenza of 1918 see Spanish influenza
International Boundary Commission
    Staff, 10–11
I Remember Montana, 118
Iron Horn, 42
Iroquois, 41, 42
irrigation, 127–28, 140–46, 150, 151,
    162, 181

J

Jackson, William Henry, 69–70
Jarvis, Superintendent, 194
Jefferson, Thomas, 2, 6–7, 12, 13
Jones, H.S. "Corky," 178

K

Kennedy, John S., 79–80, 82
Kills the Beast, 197–99
King, Clarence, 19

Kinnick, Belle, 129–31
Kinnick, Bill, 130
Kiowa, 25
Kittson, Norman W., 79–80, 82
Klotz, Otto, 22
Knight, Arthur, 178
Kohl, Seena, 106

L

Laframboise, Isador, 181
Lake of the Woods, 9–10
Lamkin, Horace, 124
Land Ordinance of 1785, 12, 16
Landusky, 123-24, 132, 136
Landusky, Pike, 124
Laurier, Wilfred, 150
Légaré, Jean-Louis, ix–xv
Lewis and Clark, xvi, 1, 2, 27, 41
Lister-Kaye, Sir, 117
Little Bear, Chief, 186
Little Mountain, 85–86
Logan brothers see Kid Curry
Logan, Harvey see Kid Curry
Logan, William R., 142–43, 145
Long, Major Stephen, 7
Looking Glass, 71–72
Louisiana Territory Purchase, 2, 6–7, 9

M

McCann, James, 108
MacDonald, John A., 12, 15, 17, 31–32,
    38, 58, 59, 67, 81–82, 84, 89,
McDougall, John, 40
McDougall, William, 15, 17
McGlaughlin, James, 62
McIntyre, Duncan, 79–80
MacKay, Angus, 151
McKenna, Joseph, 140–41
Mackenzie, Alexander, 1
Maclean, Norman, 183
Maclean, Reverend John, 85
Macleod, Commissioner James, 35
Macoun, John, 9, 75, 84
Malin, James, 163
Mangan, Miss, 202
Manifest Destiny, 14, 20, 55
Manitoba Act of 1870, 15, 18, 67, 69
Maple Creek, 92, 94, 175, 176, 211,
    217

associations, 181-83
cultural diversity, 137–40, 159–62
English, 97, 178
exodus, 208
French, 95-96
immigration, 154–56
language, 179
ranching, 107–09, 116–21
violence, 126–31
World War I, 188
Maple Creek Old Timers' Museum,
    109
Marshall, Lorana, 115, 116
Martin, Albro, 75, 152
Martin, Chester, 15, 18, 21, 75
Matheson, Murdock, 100, 116
medicine line (defined), xiii, xvi, 3, 23,
    40–42
    agriculture, 151–54, 155, 161,
        162–66, 169–72
    associations, 181-83, 209
    baseball, 174–77
    boundary today, 218
    cultural diversity, 92–101, 133–40,
        150, 155–62, 167–68, 178–80,
        186, 190
    Custer, General George, 45
    environment/ecology, 8, 116-21,
        149, 165–66, 169–72, 204–08
    immigration, 149–62
    individualism, 181, 208–09
    Métis/Louis Riel, 66–68, 69–71
    nationalism, 187–89, 191
    national stereotypes, 32, 66
    Nez Percé, 71–72
    prohibition, 189–90
    railroad boom, 73–87
    ranchers/cowboys, 103–11, 116–22,
        155
    religion, 93–94, 183–84
    Sitting Bull crossing, 48-49, 65, 186
    socializing, 184–86
    tension along, 23–24, 66
    term first used, 41–42
    term last used, 217
    unity, 174–78, 180–87
    violence, 123–26, 129–33, 136–37
    Walsh and Miles, 58–60
    whiskey trade, 30–40
    women, 186–87

World War I, 188, 190–91
medicine road, 40–41
melting pot, 14
Mennonites, 73, 84, 154, 157, 177, 205
Métis, 21, 22, 37, 10, 12, 91, 111,
    138–39, 180–81
    border and, 45, 66–68, 69, 71
    fur trade, 16–18, 27–30
    pan-native alliance, 68–69, 70, 71
    rebellion, 70–71, 80
    Red River resistance, 67
    whiskey trade, 38, 39
metropolitan thesis, 56
Miles, Colonel Nelson Appleton,
    45–48, 50-53, 54-60, 66, 69, 71,
    86–87, 113, 127
Milk River see Winters v. U.S.
Milk River United Irrigation
    Association, 143
Miller family, 105, 108, 118, 210, 211
Miller, Lillian, 118–20, 133–35, 157,
    168, 186–87, 211
Miller, Peter, 106
Minnesota Society, 187–88
Mitchell, Elizabeth B., 131, 147, 209
Moir, Otto, 120
Monet, Marguerite, 68
Montana Agricultural Experiment, 151
Montana State Board of Agriculture,
    Labor, and Industry, 151, 152–53
Montgomery, Mac, 155, 161
Moodie, Superintendent, 140, 160
Morgan, J.P., 85
Mounties, 37, 38, 57, 58, 63, 66,
    70–71, 91, 94, 100, 123, 132-133,
    156
    Cypress Hills Massacre, 31-33
    Dickens of the Mounted, 63,
    inception, 31–33
    Mounted Police reports, 138–40, 160
    whiskey trade, 33-36, 40
Mohawk, 41, 218
multicultural, 161, 180
music, 179–80
My Antonia, 196

N

nationalism, 187–189, 191
national myths see United States and
    Canada

nature, attitudes toward, 8–9, 83, 85–87,
    96–97, 104–12, 115–16, 119–20,
    145, 150, 163–66, 170–72, 190,
    196, 205–08, 210–11
Newby, Arthur, 201
Newell, F.H., 144
Nez Percé, 45, 59, 65, 71–72
Nicol, Eric, 63
Nikaneet Reserve, 94
Northern Pacific Railroad, 75, 77,
    81–83, 85, 151
North-West Company, 27
North-West Mounted Police see
    Mounties

O

Oglala Sioux, 25
O'Hanlon, Thomas, 68, 90, 100, 136,
    184
Ojibwa, 12
Ollicut, 72
Omaha, 25, 26
One Bull, 64
organized labor, 126–28
Otterson, Harry, 121
outlaws, Canadian-American
    comparison, 130–32
Oxarat, Michael, 117
Ox-Bow Incident, 147

P

Pacific Scandal of 1873, 81–82
Palliser's Triangle, 8–9, 75
Pearse, Spencer, 97
pemmican, Métis trade of, 17
Peter Strikes With a Gun, 218
Piapot, 6
Piegan, 6, 24, 27, 39, 40
Ponca, 25
Populism, 128
Poundmaker, 6
Powell, John Wesley, 19
Power, T.C., 36
Progressivism, 183
prohibition, 189–90
Pullman Company, 126–27

Q

Qu'Appelle, 94

R

Railroad boom, 73–87
    building of railroads, 73–83
    Plains Indians and, 85–86
    selling of railroads, 83–87
ranchers/cowboys, 103–11, 116–22,
    155, 162, 164–65, 207
Red River carts (defined), 28
religion, 93–94, 183–84
Returns to War, 113
Riel, Louis, 17–18, 27, 36–38, 59
    border/medicine line and, 66–68, 69
    execution, 71, 83
    exile, 67–68
    on class, 36
    on liquor trade, 36
    pan-native alliance and, 68–69
    rebellion, 70–71, 80
    Red River resistance, 67
    Sitting Bull and, 68, 69, 70
Robsart, 189
Rocky Boy Reservation, 94
Rogers, A.B., 75
Rowle, Patsy, 125–126
Rupert's Land, 9, 14, 17, 38
Russell, Charlie, 103–05, 121–22,
    123–24, 136, 178–79, 181, 190,
    213

S

saloons, 123
Satleen, Olive Ramberg, 108
Schroeder, Anne, 1, 216–17
Scott, Thomas, 67
Set-Em-High, 133–34
Sharples, Bob, 217–18
Shaughnessey, Thomas G., 80
Shaw, Professor Thomas, 152
Shepard, George, 156, 164, 177, 180,
    205–06
Sheridan, General, 53, 59
Sherman, General, 53, 59-60
Shoshone, 27
Shultz, James Willard, 5, 29, 35, 37,
    38–40
Sifton, Clifford, 150
Sinclair, Bertrand, 30, 38
Siouan, 24
Sioux, ix–xvi, 6, 10, 23–29, 40–49, 53,
    58, 59, 65, 66, 68, 72, 113

Sitting Bull, ix–xvi, 6, 42, 46–49
  Battle of Little Bighorn, 43–45, 60
  Buffalo Bill Cody's Wild West
    Show, xv
  Canada, in, 65
  crossing the medicine line, 48–49,
    65, 186
  death, xv–xvi
  James Walsh and, 48–49, 62
  jokes, 64
  journalists and, 60–64, 65
  looking glass and, x–xi
  Louis Riel and, 68, 69, 70
  negotiator, 60, 64–65
  Nelson Miles and, 46–48, 52–53
  surrender, ix–xiii, 19, 60, 62
Sleeping Bears (family), 197–200
smallpox, 21, 25–27, 198–200, 204
Smiley, Hattie, 165–66
Smith, Donald A., 79–80, 82
Southern Pacific (railroad), 81
Spanish influenza (1918), 193–98,
    202
Special Survey, 19
Sperry, Albert, 101
Standing Rock Agency, ix, xii, xv, 62
Stegner, George/family, 164, 167, 170,
    171, 190, 193, 208, 213
Stegner, Wallace, xvi, 4, 118, 157, 158,
    164, 166–72, 183, 185, 187, 193,
    196, 200, 202–03, 208, 213–17
Stephen, George, 12, 79–80, 82, 83, 85
Steward, George, 107
Strong, J.C., 169
Symons, A.H., 198

T

T.C. Power & Bro. general store, 99,
    100
Tenaille, Dan, 94–96, 190–91
Tenaille, Jean, 95
Tenth Cavalry, 98, 159
Terry, General Alfred H., 45, 46, 65
Texas Rangers, 66
The Boy, 199–200
Thompson, David, xvi, 1
Thoreau, Henry David, 73, 79
Three-Year Homestead Act of 1912,
    152
Tocqueville, Alexis de, 181, 208–09

Tolstoy, Leo, 150,
Too-hool-hool-zote, 72
trade, axis of, 6, 78–79, 83
Treaty of 1818, 7, 9
Treaty of 1846, 7
Treaty of Utrecht, 2
Turner, Frederick Jackson, 19–20
Twining, W.J., 5–6, 8, 22, 24, 42, 77

U

Union Pacific (railroad), 81, 83
United States
  American myth of, 19, 20, 56, 87,
    115, 130–31, 149, 164, 181–82,
    187, 214
  Indian policy, 44, 51
  Manifest Destiny of, 14, 20
Utley, Robert, xiii, 51, 62
U.S.-Canada border see medicine line
U.S. Geological Survey (USGS), 19

V

Van Horne, William C., 80, 85
VandeVen, George, 1–2, 174, 177–78,
    211, 216–17
violence, 123–26, 129-33, 136–37,
    140

W

Walsh, James, x, 41, 48–50, 53–59,
    62, 65
War of 1812, 6–7
Washinga Sakba, 26
Webb, A.C., 17
Weeks, Mary, 163
Welch, James, 211
whiskey trade/liquor trafficking, 30–40,
    129, 189
Whitaker, Alexander, 195
White Dog, 49–50
"White Father," 65
"White Mother," 65–66
Williamson, Belvina, 149, 154
Wilson, Gary, 129
Winter, Henry, 142, 143
Winters v. United States, 140–46
Wolf Willow, 4, 166, 169, 193, 214
Wood, C.E.S., 72
Wooden Leg, 60

Wooldridge, W.M., 143, 182
World War I, 188, 190–91, 193
Wounded Knee, 113

X Y Z
Zeestraten, Cornelius, 163, 190, 206,
211